THREADS OF CONTACT

ANCIENT TEXTILES 42

THREADS OF CONTACT

TRACING THE RELATIONSHIP BETWEEN EGYPT AND THE SOUTHERN LEVANT THROUGH TEXTILE TOOLS

CHIARA SPINAZZI-LUCCHESI

OXBOW | books
Oxford & Philadelphia

Published in the United Kingdom in 2025 by
OXBOW BOOKS
81 St Clements, Oxford OX4 1AW

and in the United States by
OXBOW BOOKS
1950 Lawrence Road, Havertown, PA 19083

Paperback Edition: 979-8-88857-147-7
Digital Edition: 979-8-88857-148-4 (epub)

A CIP record for this book is available from the British Library

Library of Congress Control Number: 2025937708

Printed in the United Kingdom by Short Run Press
Typeset in India by DiTech Publishing Services

For a complete list of Oxbow titles, please contact:

UNITED KINGDOM
Oxbow Books
Telephone (0)1226 734350
Email: oxbow@oxbowbooks.com
www.oxbowbooks.com

UNITED STATES OF AMERICA
Oxbow Books
Telephone (610) 853-9131, Fax (610) 853-9146
Email: queries@casemateacademic.com
www.casemateacademic.com/oxbow

Oxbow Books is part of the Casemate Group

Front cover: Clockwise from top left: Spindle from Deir el-Medina DeM_2024_M23_1160 © Institut français d'archéologie orientale au Caire; Weavers from the tomb of Khnumhotep, Norman de Garis Davies 33.8.16 © Metropolitan Museum of Art; Loom weight from Beth Shean, 286278/51, courtesy of the Israel Antiquities Authority; Ball of unspun fibres, 500a, courtesy of the Manchester Museum.

The Publisher's authorised representative in the EU for product safety is Authorised Rep Compliance Ltd.,
Ground Floor, 71 Lower Baggot Street, Dublin D02 P593, Ireland.
www.arccompliance.com

Contents

Preface

My interest in textile tools began in 2010 at Tell Afis, where Professor S. Mazzoni invited me to study the spindles recovered at the site. One of the primary challenges was distinguishing objects used as spindles from those functioning as pins. Since most ancient spindles were made of wood – rarely preserved in the Levant – the best comparative evidence came from Egyptian examples, where organic materials have survived in significant quantities. Despite frequent references to Egyptian textiles and tools in comparative studies, detailed analyses of these objects remain surprisingly scarce.

To address this gap, I focused my 2014–2015 dissertation at the Scuola Interateneo di Specializzazione in Beni Archeologici on the textile tools housed at the Museo Egizio in Turin. Initially centred on spindles, the research soon expanded to include other textile-related implements to provide a broader perspective. However, the limited publication of comparable tools from other collections and ambiguities in some Levantine excavation reports constrained the scope of that early work.

Threads of Contact emerged from the need to overcome those limitations. By selecting key sites from both the Southern Levant and Egypt, I sought to analyse the artefacts in greater detail and clarify issues encountered in previous research. Practical considerations, such as the availability of objects in European museum collections, sometimes influenced site and artefact selection. Nevertheless, the simultaneous study of both regions offers several advantages. First, applying a consistent methodology ensures reliable cross-regional comparisons. Second, it highlights differences and similarities in production techniques and material choices that might otherwise remain obscure. Finally, this approach contributes to a more holistic understanding of textile production in these interconnected ancient societies.

Despite the extensive number of artefacts analysed and the thorough search for published parallels, this work should be viewed as a starting point. Further site-specific and regional studies will be necessary to deepen and refine the findings presented here.

The aim of this book is to investigate the development of textile tools throughout Egypt and the Southern Levant to determine whether these regions evolved independently or shared technological and cultural connections at various points. The study focuses on Egypt (including select fortresses in Nubia) and the Southern Levant, covering areas within the modern states of Jordan, Israel, the West Bank, and Palestine.

Chronologically, the research spans from the Neolithic period up to the beginning of the 6th century BC, with particular emphasis on the Bronze and Iron Ages – periods marked by significant technological and socio-political changes that likely influenced textile production.

The tools investigated include objects clearly linked to textile production – such as spindles, spindle whorls, spinning bowls, loom weights, loom components, and needles – as well as more ambiguous artefacts like basalt rings and perforated sherds.

The first phase of research involved collecting relevant materials from key sites, compiled in a catalogue (accessible online at 10.5281/zenodo.15611432). This catalogue forms the foundation of the study, integrating published data with direct examination of objects in museums and archaeological collections. Each artefact was analysed using a consistent methodology, ensuring comparability across sites. By providing comprehensive measurements and detailed descriptions, this research encourages future studies to reuse the raw data, reflecting my commitment to open-access archaeological research.

Subsequently, I gathered additional information from excavation reports, although only a portion of this data could be included in the book. The goal was not to produce an exhaustive catalogue but rather to highlight significant patterns and trends. The interpretative sections explore the evolution of textile tools within geographical, chronological, and socio-political contexts, with particular attention to how these objects may reflect the identities and cultural affiliations of their users.

Threads of Contact is primarily intended for scholars in archaeology and related disciplines, including those not specialising in textile studies. It aims to assist researchers in identifying and interpreting textile tools within a broader cultural and technological context. By providing a comprehensive comparative analysis, the work hopes to encourage more detailed publications of textile-related finds and foster further discussions about textile production in the ancient Eastern Mediterranean.

Beyond its immediate focus on textile tools, this research contributes to broader archaeological discussions on technology, cultural interaction, and identity in the ancient Eastern Mediterranean. Textile production, often considered a domestic and utilitarian activity, can also reflect deeper aspects of social identity, cultural traditions, and community affiliation. By comparing tools from Egypt and the Southern Levant, this study explores how technological choices – such as raw material selection, tool design, and production techniques – may have been shaped by cultural preferences and group identities. Certain objects reveal localised traditions, while others suggest cross-cultural influences, reflecting the complex interplay between continuity and change in material culture. These patterns, in turn, offer insights into how communities expressed identity through everyday practices and how textile production was embedded in broader socio-political and economic networks. This work thus not only deepens our understanding of textile technology but also highlights how everyday objects can reveal broader socio-political dynamics, contributing to the ongoing dialogue about interconnectedness in the ancient world.

The book is organised into six chapters, and is completed by a reference section and by the online catalogue. The **Introduction** outlines the research questions, case studies, and the geographical and chronological framework. **Chapter 2** introduces the categories of textile tools analysed and clarifies terminology, addressing discrepancies in naming conventions across different archaeological contexts. **Chapter 3** examines primary textile fibres and reconstructs the operational sequence of textile production, connecting tools to their practical functions. **Chapter 4** presents site-specific analyses in the first section, followed by an exploration of regional trends. **Chapter 5** mirrors the structure of Chapter 4, with a focus on Egyptian sites and broader regional patterns. Finally, the **Conclusion** synthesises the data from both regions, highlighting comparative insights and suggesting directions for future research.

Acknowledgements

This book originates from my doctoral thesis, 'Textile Tools from Egypt and the Southern Levant', which I defended with honours at Ca' Foscari University of Venice in 2019. A significant part of the research was carried out in 2016–2017, with some additional work on Deir el-Medina conducted in recent years. At the time, the study of textile production in archaeology was still a relatively marginal field, but in the years since, many more publications have emerged, and excavation reports have further enriched the picture. I have made every effort to incorporate these new findings and perspectives into the core of my research. New methodologies, particularly in the study of wear marks on textile tools, were not yet available when I had access to the artefacts.

Transforming this research into a book has been a long and challenging process, and I am deeply grateful to Professor Lise Bender Jørgensen for her thorough revision and insightful comments. I would also like to thank my supervisor, Professor Lucio Milano, for supporting this research in its early stages and for his generous feedback and observations.

Conducting this study required access to numerous collections, and I had the privilege of visiting several institutions and universities that kindly granted me access to their materials. Many of the Egyptian tools examined are housed in museums across England. The largest number is in the Petrie Museum, and I am especially grateful to Anna Garnett and Alice Willems for facilitating my access and for allowing me to concentrate my study sessions into just a few days with special permissions. A second significant collection is in the Manchester Museum, where Campbell Price and Susan Martin made my visit both smooth and productive. In Liverpool, I was warmly welcomed at the World Museum by Ashley Cooke, as well as by the dedicated team of volunteers at the Garstang Museum. Finally, I owe my sincere thanks to Liam McNamara for granting me access to the Egyptian collection at the Ashmolean Museum and to the staff of the British Museum.

I would like to thank the Fondazione Museo Egizio for granting me access to the textile tools in its collection. I am especially grateful to my colleagues Matilde Borla and Valentina Turina for their invaluable assistance, insightful discussions, and enduring friendship over the years.

During my Marie Skłodowska-Curie project, I had the opportunity to expand my research on the textile tools of Deir el-Medina. Some of these are stored at the Louvre Museum, and I would like to express my deep gratitude to Vincent Rondot and Roberta Cortopassi for granting me access and assisting in the selection of objects. A small number of items are also housed in the Neues Museum in Berlin, and I would like to thank Caris-Beatrice Arnst and Franck Marohn for their support.

A substantial number of Deir el-Medina textile tools are located at the Institut Français d'Archéologie Orientale (IFAO) and on the archaeological site itself. I am sincerely grateful to the Deir el-Medina archaeological mission (IFAO) for granting me access to these invaluable materials. I am particularly grateful to Cédric Larcher and Gersande Eschenbrenner-Diemer for sharing their expertise with me and for their help in locating the materials, for sharing their expertise with me and for granting me access to these invaluable materials. I would also like to thank Gillian Vogelsang-Eastwood for welcoming me at TRC in Leiden, sharing her knowledge and passion for Ancient Egyptian textiles and tools and for her support during the study of the material.

I was also fortunate to have full access to unpublished materials from the Megiddo excavations, and I am deeply thankful to Professor Israel Finkelstein for allowing me to study them. My thanks also go to Sivan Einhorn for her invaluable assistance during my stay.

I am grateful to Michael Sebbane, Galit Litani, and Deborah Ben-Ami of the Israel Antiquities Authority for their help in locating materials and granting me access to the collections. I am particularly indebted to Alegre Savariego, Curator of the Rockefeller Museum Collection, for her assistance in finding the objects and providing all the available documentation. A special and heartfelt thank you goes to Orit Shamir for her help in facilitating my access to the collections and, above all, for the invaluable advice and discussions we had in Beit Shemesh. I would also like to thank Naama Sukenik for kindly showing me the textile collection of the Israel Antiquities Authority.

My sincere thanks go to Professor Amnon Ben-Tor and his team for granting me access to the textile tools from Hazor. I am especially grateful to his assistant, Shlomit Bechar, who not only helped me locate the objects and organise my study sessions but also offered her friendship, guidance, and support throughout my research.

I had the opportunity to study artefacts from the École Biblique excavations at Tell el-Farʿah. I am very grateful to Father Jean-Baptiste Humbert for his generous assistance in granting me access to these remarkable materials and to the École Biblique for giving me the opportunity to publish these materials.

Over the years of research, many people have encouraged and supported me in countless ways, and I extend my deepest gratitude to all of them. A special thank you goes to my PhD colleagues – Vanni, Silvia, Enrico, Agata, Clara, Eugenio, Alessandro, and Tiziano – whose friendship and support made the research process far more enjoyable. I am also profoundly grateful to my friends and colleagues, particularly Ilaria, Sara, Maria, Ilaria, Viviana, Martina, and Rachele, who shared with me both moments of joy and frustration along the way.

This book is the result of the generosity, kindness, and expertise of many individuals and institutions, and I am truly grateful to everyone who has contributed to its completion.

I would like to express my heartfelt gratitude to the institutions that have supported this work at different stages. The Danish Institute in Damascus and Marie Skłodowska-Curie grant (EGYarn Grant agreement ID: 890144) provided essential funding that enabled me to carry out my research on Deir el-Medina textile tools.

Dansk Ægyptologisk Selskab and Palæstinafondet generously financed the preparation of this volume and contributed to covering the publication costs. Their support has been invaluable in bringing this project to completion, and I am truly grateful for their trust in my work.

Dedico questo lavoro alla mia famiglia, grande e piccola, senza la quale nessuno di questi risultati sarebbe stato possibile, e a mio marito, che mi ha accompagnata in ogni passo di questa straordinaria ma faticosa ricerca, condividendo con me molti viaggi e incoraggiandomi sempre.

List of figures

List of plates

List of tables

1

Introduction

From the earliest threads spun by ancient civilisations to the sophisticated fabrics woven by modern machinery, textiles have been integral to our daily lives, shaping cultures, economies, and societies. At the heart of this key sphere lie the tools of textile manufacture – implements both humble and ingenious, which have evolved alongside human ingenuity and creativity.

This book explores the world of textile tools by examining the technological developments in textile production across the Southern Levant and Ancient Egypt. By comparing these two regions, it examines whether they followed a common tradition or developed along separate paths, identifying key moments of continuity and divergence. Through the analysis of available data, it explores the evolution of textile industries, the extent of local variations, and the factors driving change over time. Particular attention is given to the types of tools used for spinning and weaving, the materials and techniques employed, and the pace at which innovations emerged in each region. Additionally, the study considers whether one region influenced the other at specific points in history or if they evolved independently, shaped by their own cultural and technological dynamics. Through this analysis, this book seeks to uncover the connections and distinctions that shaped the textile traditions of these ancient civilisations.

Over the years, significant progress has been made in the study of textile tools, offering valuable insights into ancient textile production. This book builds on these advancements by adopting an innovative perspective, integrating archaeological, technological, and cultural approaches to better understand the textile industries of the Southern Levant and Egypt. Expanding our knowledge of spinning and weaving tools is essential for developing a more accurate understanding of ancient textile production. This book contributes to this effort by directly examining materials from selected sites in both regions and integrating data from published excavation reports. By offering a comprehensive overview of textile developments, it sheds new light on the innovations and techniques that emerged in these historically significant areas. As centres of early technological advancements, Egypt and the Levant provide a compelling framework for a comparative study of their textile industries, revealing both shared traditions and unique regional adaptations.

The decision to study two seemingly different areas is based on multiple factors. First, textile tools allow for a transversal approach, as their use remains almost unchanged since the industrial revolution, and sometimes even until the present day. Second, the two areas present an only apparent discontinuity, as political boundaries gave way – bringing the two areas into close contact – at various historical moments, including during the Second Intermediate Period of Egypt or the Egyptian domination of the Late Bronze Age (LBA).

The geographical area of the research is very broad, since it includes Egypt, from the Delta to the Nubian border (although several sites in the south will be considered due to the importance of their findings) and the Southern Levant, *i.e.* Israel, Palestine, and the western Jordan area. The chronology is also extremely wide, considering tools from the Neolithic period to the beginning of the Persian period. Following this period, a decrease in loom weights dimensions in the Levant has been reported (Peyronel 2004), which may hint at the introduction of new fibres, as suggested by textual sources (Gaspa 2017). Therefore, it seems necessary to investigate the second half of the 1st millennium with a much more focused study, which, at the present state of archaeological documentation, was not possible in this work. During the entire period under investigation, few fibres were used for textiles production, mainly flax and wool and will be discussed in Chapter 3.

This study encompasses all objects that could potentially be associated with textile production, ranging from traditional spindle whorls and loom weights to artefacts of more uncertain function, such as perforated sherds, basalt rings, and pin beaters. The primary objective is to determine when these objects first appear in both regions and whether their distribution varies across different periods.

Moreover, incorporating more controversial or ambiguous objects into the analysis allows for a more in-depth examination of their manufacture and use. By considering their find contexts, particularly in relation to other textile-related artefacts, this approach provides valuable insights into their possible functions and their role within ancient textile production systems.

1.1 State of the art

The study of textile production has a long history, with researchers investigating spinning and weaving techniques as early as the early 20th century. Pioneering works (Crowfoot 1921; 1931; 1937; Johl 1924) provided foundational insights into ancient textile traditions, laying the groundwork for further research. In recent decades, growing interest in craft production and technological development has brought new attention to these implements, revealing their central role in shaping textile industries. Over the past 30 years in particular, there has been a marked increase in studies focusing on tools related to textile production, approached from both typological and technical perspectives. A turning point in this field can be attributed to Barber's seminal work, *Prehistoric Textiles* (Barber 1991), which brought weaving tools into focus through a comprehensive, interdisciplinary, and modern analysis. Since then, numerous studies have emerged, particularly in the contexts of prehistoric and medieval Europe, encompassing both Northern and Southern regions (Bender Jørgensen 1992; Andersson 1999; 2003; Nosch and Gillis 2007). Textiles have received much more attention, and the bibliography is extensive, including textiles from Egypt and the Levant, in particular of the Roman and Late Antique period (Scheffer and Granger-Taylor 1994; Walton Rogers *et al.* 2001; Fluck *et al.* 2015).

Today, the Centre for Textile Research in Copenhagen (CTR) stands at the forefront of this field, promoting research on textile tools from philological, archaeological, and experimental perspectives. This institution has introduced new study models and identification criteria for artefacts associated with spinning and weaving (Mårtensson *et al.* 2006; Andersson Strand 2010; 2015; Nosch and Michel 2010; Harlow *et al.* 2014).

In contrast, research in the pre-Roman Near East remains less extensive. While some studies have focused on specific sites, more comprehensive works are limited and often rely on outdated documentation. Key contributions to the study of Mesopotamian and Near Eastern textile tools have been made by Breniquet (2008; 2010; Breniquet and Michel 2014), Völling (2008), and Gleser (2016).

Anatolia has attracted significant scholarly attention in recent years, particularly regarding the early development and use of textile production tools. Research has focused on the emergence of loom weights, the primary fibres employed in textile manufacturing, and the evolution of the tools associated with textile production. This area of study has become especially important as new investigations challenge previous assumptions about the origins and technical advancements in ancient textile production.

Among the most significant archaeological sites for understanding the Neolithic and Chalcolithic periods in Anatolia is Çatalhöyük. This settlement has long been considered a key location for studying the early development of textile-related technologies (Helbaek 1963; Burnham 1965; Vogelsang-Eastwood 1988). In recent years, the evidence from Çatalhöyük has been subject to thorough re-evaluations, shedding new light on its role in the history of textile production (Rast-Eicher *et al.* 2021; Bender Jørgensen *et al.* 2023). In addition to the work at Çatalhöyük, numerous scholars have made substantial contributions to our understanding of the appearance and evolution of the first recognisable textile tools. Researchers such as Çilingirŏglu (2009), Laurito (2013; Laurito *et al.* 2014), and Schoop (2014) have provided valuable insights into the ways in which textile tools first emerged and transformed over time, helping to construct a clearer picture of early textile production techniques in the region.

The most comprehensive book for gaining insight into textile production in the Levant is undoubtedly Peyronel's work (2004). Beginning with an examination of materials from Ebla, the author extends the analysis through comparative studies across both the Northern and Southern Levant. Additionally, several other publications on Syria are worth mentioning, including those by Cecchini (1992; 2000; 2011), Rooijakers (2012), Sauvage (2013; 2014) and Venturi (2020).

The Southern Levant has greatly benefited from extensive publications on textile tool assemblages from specific sites, as well as from studies that synthesise broader trends. Notably, works such as Levy (2019; 2020), along with numerous contributions by Schick (1988; 1995), and Shamir (1996; 2003; 2004; 2007a; 2007b; 2013; 2014; 2015), form the foundational basis of this research.

It must be acknowledged that while extensive archaeological investigations have been carried out in the Southern Levant, research has predominantly focused on Iron Age levels, with comparatively less attention given to the Early Bronze Age (EBA) and Middle Bronze Age (MBA). As a result, the availability of evidence is disproportionately weighted in favour of the Iron Age, leading to an imbalance in the dataset. Consequently, the sheer quantity of textile tools recovered from each phase cannot be regarded as a reliable indicator of the industry's development over time. A more accurate evaluation requires a site-by-site analysis, taking into account the extent of excavated areas corresponding to each period. This approach is feasible only for the selected case studies examined in the present work.

Unfortunately, a significant number of sites lack a comprehensive reassessment of all equipment associated with textile production, particularly in light of recent research methodologies and discoveries. Moreover, many excavation reports include objects of uncertain function, such as spindle whorls fashioned from reused ceramic fragments and perforated stone discs – some of which may indeed be spindle whorls or loom weights. However, even when these tools are identified as such, crucial data – most notably their weight – is often omitted. As demonstrated by experimental archaeology (Mårtensson *et al.* 2009), weight is a fundamental parameter for reconstructing both the type of yarn produced and the overall quality of the resulting fabric. The absence of such data significantly hinders our ability to fully understand ancient textile production techniques and their evolution over time.

There remains a significant gap in scholarship specifically dedicated to the analysis of Pharaonic Egyptian documentation related to textile production. One notable exception is the comprehensive study of Tell el-Amarna (Kemp and Vogelsang-Eastwood 2001), which has provided valuable insights. Excavation reports typically publish only a limited selection of textile-related artefacts, often omitting crucial details such as quantities, find contexts, and morphometric data. This lack of comprehensive documentation presents considerable challenges for reconstructing the broader picture of textile production.

Furthermore, many key archaeological contexts – such as workers' villages – were excavated during the late 19th and early 20th centuries (Petrie 1890; 1891; Bruyère 1939), a period when recording methodologies were less rigorous by modern standards. As a result, much of the essential contextual information is missing, highlighting the urgent need for a broader reassessment of the available evidence.

While studies on textiles themselves have received increasingly more attention – thanks to the work of scholars such as Hald (1946), Hall and Janssen (Hall 1982; 1986; Janssen 1996; 2020; Janssen and Janssen 1990), Tata (1995), Vogelsang-Eastwood (1993; 1999; van 't Hooft, Raven, van Rooij and Vogelsang-Eastwood 1994), Jones (2002; 2008; 2014), Borla (Borla and Oliva 2014; Oliva and Borla 2017; Demichelis, Fiore Marocchetti, and Borla 2024), Hallmann (2016; 2017a; 2017b; 2018; 2023) and Rodríguez Frade (2022; 2024) – these investigations fall outside the scope of the present study. Instead, this research focuses on textile tools and balls of yarn as primary evidence for textile production, referencing textiles only where necessary to illustrate significant technological developments, such as the introduction of tapestry weaving.

The first half of the 1st millennium BC, though well documented in the Levant, remains an elusive period for the study of textile tools in Ancient Egypt. Excavation reports indicate a scarcity of evidence, which can be attributed to two main factors. Firstly, no known workers' villages from this period have been identified in association with Pharaohs' tomb-building activities. Secondly, the publication of excavation data often does not prioritise textile-related artefacts, resulting in a limited number of sites where such tools are systematically recorded.

An initial attempt to synthesise the available data from Egypt and the Levant was undertaken by the author in 2018 with the publication of *The Unwound Yarn* (Spinazzi-Lucchesi 2018). This work provided a detailed analysis of the textile tools housed in the Museo Egizio in Turin, contextualising them within a broader archaeological framework. However, this research also underscored the need for a more in-depth examination of finds from other key sites in Egypt, as well as in the Southern Levant. Such an analysis is crucial for establishing a solid comparative framework that will enable a more cohesive discussion of new discoveries within the field.

1.2 Methodology and sites selection

Given the broad chronological and geographical scope of this study, it does not aim to provide an exhaustive inventory of all textile tools from Egypt and the Southern Levant. Instead, it focuses on a selection of case studies, comparing them with relevant material from both regions. The sites chosen for the Southern Levant – Megiddo, Hazor, Beth Shean, and Tell el-Far'ah (N) – are all large mounds with long and complex stratigraphic sequences, spanning most of the period under discussion. Their extensive occupational history makes them particularly valuable for examining the development of textile production within an urban context and for assembling a substantial dataset to identify regional trends (Fig. 1.1). Initially, Jericho and Tell el-Far'ah (S) were also considered for inclusion. However, due to the limited number of artefacts available for direct study, these sites do not feature as primary case studies.

Each textile tool is examined in detail within the catalogue section of this work (10.5281/zenodo.15611432). However, given that excavations at these sites began in the early 20th century – or even earlier – it has not been possible to trace every single artefact. The catalogue therefore compiles all available information from published sources. For items that were previously unpublished or accessible for direct study, it includes precise measurements and first-hand observations. Every object that could be located has been photographed, measured, and described. While the catalogue

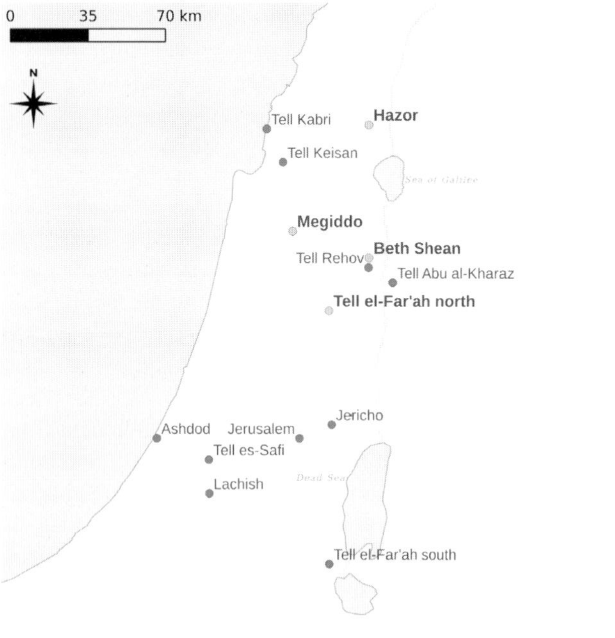

Figure 1.1. Map of the Southern Levant with main case studies and relevant sites

provides this detailed documentation, the site-specific chapters aim to present an overarching analysis of the textile tools recovered, explore diachronic changes, and, where possible, offer insights into the nature of textile production associated with these artefacts.

For the Egyptian context, three sites – Kahun, Gurob, and Deir el-Medina – have been selected as primary case studies (Fig. 1.2). These settlements, known as workers' villages, house the most extensive collections of textile tools of the entire Pharaonic period. The tools are spread in several collections, which include the Museo Egizio in Turin, the Louvre Museum, the British Museum, the Manchester Museum, the Ashmolean Museum, the Liverpool World Museum, and the Garstang Museum. Furthermore, several textile tools from Deir el-Medina were studied on site.

A major challenge in studying these sites is the lack of reliable stratigraphic data, a significant limitation given the large quantity of tools they have preserved. While they are often considered single-phase sites, it is important to acknowledge that some chronological attributions of the tools may not be entirely precise. Despite this, the overall picture that emerges remains clear and broadly reliable.

In addition, this study includes a selection of Pre- and Proto-Dynastic materials, many of which remain poorly published, to provide a more comprehensive understanding of the early development of the Egyptian textile industry. These artefacts, originating from various sites, are catalogued under the entry *Other Sites*. Unlike in the Southern

Figure 1.2. Map of Egypt with main case studies and relevant sites

Levant, where more material is available in published sources, many of these Egyptian finds remain unpublished. Consequently, the catalogue only includes objects that have been directly examined. Tell el-Amarna, previously studied in depth by Kemp and Vogelsang-Eastwood (2001), serves as a point of comparison but is not directly analysed in this work.

1.3 Chronological overview of the main historical phases

The objects investigated here do not permit to create a specific, intrinsic chronology and the study has therefore had to rely on information provided by excavators and the updating of sites' stratification. Furthermore, given the broad chronology and geographic area under study, this work is not focused on micro-chronological changes, but rather on understanding the general picture of textile production. For this reason, there will be no discussion on chronological reassessments between the two areas (especially difficult for EB II – Early Dynastic and for the passage from LBA period to Iron Age), although keeping in mind the objective problems currently under debate (van den Brink and Levy 2002; Mączyńska 2008; Stevenson 2016; Finkelstein *et al.* 2017). Different terminologies used by various authors have also complicated the picture. A simplified chronology was therefore adopted and it is provided in Table 1.1, along with some of the main alternative names. For each case study from Southern Levant, a more in-depth chronological chart is provided, in order to be able to connect the objects in the catalogue with the different phases and areas of excavation. These data have been crucial for dating the individual tools and are therefore necessary to show the chronological distribution at the present state of research. If future studies will change the chronological attribution of these tools, it will be easily possible to update the data in the catalogue. A general overview of the main phases and historical events is here provided, highlighting the relationship between Egypt and the Southern Levant in the different phases.

The Southern Levant: the prehistory

The Southern Levant has been inhabited since the Palaeolithic, with the earliest sedentary settlements traced to the Natufian culture (12500–9500 cal BC). Textile tools are securely identified from the Neolithic period, though they likely predate this era. A key Neolithic site is Jericho, where evidence of a defensive wall and round houses dates to 8500–7500 cal BC (Pre-Pottery Neolithic A, PPNA). By the Pre-Pottery Neolithic B (PPNB), different house types emerged alongside a gradual shift to sedentary life (Banning 2012, 402).

Around 7000 BC, the Pre-Pottery Neolithic period ended, not abruptly but with notable changes in technology, settlement patterns, and possibly social structures (Banning 2012, 406). Sites from the two millennia following the PPNB have received significantly less attention than earlier periods. While the Chalcolithic period of the Southern Levant (*c.* 5000–3800 cal BC) has been studied more extensively than the Late Neolithic, it remains surprisingly under-researched (Banning 2012, 410). Few Late Chalcolithic sites, and no earlier ones, have yielded evidence of metalworking.

Despite continuity from the Late Neolithic and regional variation, the Chalcolithic period is marked by distinct stone tools, stone maceheads, economy, and architecture, suggesting the development of a unique culture during the 4th millennium BC. Pear-shaped maceheads, often made of polished hematite or other hard stones, were common and may have symbolised rank. Some rarer examples, cast in copper using the lost-wax method, were found in the Nahal Mishmar hoard (Bar-Adon 1980). Late Chalcolithic elites appear not to have achieved the levels of economic inequality, ideological systems, or political power seen in contemporary Egypt and Mesopotamia.

Egypt: the prehistory

While in the 10th millennium BC small Middle Eastern communities established the first villages, the Nile Valley followed a different trajectory. Late Pleistocene hunter-gatherer strategies persisted until the 6th millennium BC, when domestic species such as goats, sheep, pigs, barley, and wheat – introduced from Asia – appeared in southern Sinai and the Red Sea coast. By the 5th millennium, these domesticates spread throughout the Nile Valley, the desert edges, and into what is now Sudan (Midant Reynes 2014).

During the 6th millennium BC, increasing desertification altered the landscape, culminating in a shift toward aridity in the 5th millennium that forced migrations to areas with permanent water sources. This climate-driven adaptation shaped the development of Predynastic regional cultures by the late 5th millennium BC. In Lower Egypt, Neolithic sites like el-Omari, Merimde Beni-Salame, and the Fayum reflect this transition. In the Delta, the Maadi/Buto (or 'Lower Egyptian') culture emerged in the early 4th millennium BC, contemporaneous with the Naqada culture of Upper Egypt (Midant Reynes 2014). These groups differed in material culture and funerary practices, reflecting the Nile Valley's dual influences – one from the East, the other from the Sahara. Over time, cultural interaction gave rise to a mixed culture dominated by southern elements (Midant Reynes 2014).

Maadi, near Cairo, exemplifies Egypt's role in 4th-millennium BC trade networks. Imports included asphalt, resin, cedar wood, ceramics, copper objects, and tools like Canaanean blades (Rizkana and Seeher 1987; 1988; Rizkana *et al.* 1989). Maadi also shows evidence of underground dwellings linked to immigrants from the Southern Levant, a pattern mirrored at Buto in the western Delta (Midant Reynes 2014).

The Early Bronze Age in the Southern Levant

In the Southern Levant, the Bronze Age (*c.* 3700–2000 BC) saw significant cultural transformations. Small village communities of the Late Chalcolithic and Early Bronze Age I (EB I, *c.* 3700–3100 BC) evolved into walled urban settlements during EB II–III (*c.* 3100–2300 BC).

Trade intensified during EB Ia, with Levantine merchants residing temporarily at Maadi and Levantine pottery appearing at sites such as Tell el-Farkha (Mączyńska 2008). Egyptian interest in copper, turquoise, and lapis lazuli further strengthened these ties, while Egyptian artefacts found at Levantine sites suggest the establishment of Egyptian waystations. Some sites had significant Egyptian presence, while others showed little to no contact, particularly in the hill country, which lay beyond Egypt's sphere of interest (Hikade 2012).

Table 1.1. Chronological chart of Ancient Egypt (after Shaw 2003b, 479–83; Midant Reynes et al. *2003; Hornung* et al. *2006; Sharon 2014; Stevenson 2016)*

Egypt		*Southern Levant*			*Absolute date*
Upper Egypt	*Lower Egypt*	*Period*	*Alternative names*		
		PPNA			c. 9750–8500
		PPNB			c. 8500–7750
		[PPNC]			c. 7750–6500
		Ln1	PNA, Early pottery Neolithic		c. 6500–6000
		Ln2	PNB, Late PN, Early Chalcolithic		c. 6000–5500
	Fayyum A (5400–4300)		[Middle Chalcolithic]?		c. 5500–4500
	El–Omari (4700–4300)				
Badarian (4400–3800) Tasian?	Merimde (4700–4200)	Chalcolithic	Late Chalcolithic, Ghassulian		4500–3900/3700
Naqada IA–IIB (3800–3450) Predynastic	Buto I/Maadi (4000/3900–3500/3400)				
Naqada IIC–D (3450–3325) Predynastic		EB I	Proto-Urban		3900/3700–3200/3000
Naqada IIIA–IIIB (3325–3085) Predynastic					
Naqada IIIC–D/ First dynasty	3085–2867				
Early Dynastic period/ Protodynastic (Dyn. 1–2)	3000–2686	EB II			3200/3000–2850/2600
Old Kingdom (Dyn. 3–6)	2686–2160	EB III			2850/2600–2500/2300
First Intermediate Period (Dyn. 7–10)	2160–2055	IB	MB I (Albright)	EB IV (Syria)	2500/2300–2200/1900
Middle Kingdom (Dyn. 11–12)	2055–1650	MB I	MB IIA	MB I	2200/1900–1750
		MB II (early)	MB IIB	MB II	
Second Intermediate Period (Dyn. 13–17)	1650–1550	MB II (late)	MB IIC	MB III	1750–1640/1540
New Kingdom (Dyn. 18–20)	1550–1069	LB I	LB I	LB I	1640/1540–1400
		LB IIA	LB II		1400–1330/1300
		LB IIB	LB III (Amiran)	LB II	1330/1300–1200/1150
		LB/IR	IA IA	LB III (Panitz–Cohen/ Ussishkin)	1200–1150/1000
Third Intermediate Period (Dyn. 21–24)	1069–664	Iron I	IA IB	Early IA IIA	1150–1000/900
		[Iron I/II] (Mazar)			
		Iron IIA	IA II		1000/900–925/800
		Iron IIB	IA III	IA IIB–C	925/800–730/700
		Iron IIC			730/700–608–586
Late Period (Dyn. 25–30)	664–332	Iron III/ Persian		IA III	608–586–330

The transition to EB II–III marked a fundamental shift. Settlements coalesced into larger, walled urban centres, with fewer but significantly larger sites (Harrison 2012).

During EB IV (2300–2000 BC), settlement density drastically declined. Most medium and large settlements of EB II–III were abandoned or greatly reduced, with a significant decrease in the number of occupied sites. This collapse led to the emergence of a rural settlement pattern, with populations reverting to basic subsistence (Harrison 2012).

Egypt Early Dynastic and the Old Kingdom

The formation of the Egyptian state took place during the late Predynastic Period, particularly in the Naqada III phase (*c*. 3200–3000 BC). During this time, Egypt transitioned from regional chiefdoms to a unified territorial state, laying the foundation for the Early Dynastic Period. Evidence from Abydos suggests the presence of pre-1st Dynasty rulers – often referred to as 'Dynasty 0' – who played a crucial role in consolidating power (Bard 2003, 61). By the end of this phase, their influence extended northward, even reaching the Levant.

With the emergence of the 1st Dynasty around 3000 BC, Egypt became a centralised polity ruled by a divine king from the Memphis region (Stevenson 2016). This period saw a significant shift in settlement patterns, with a marked increase in burials and urban activity in Lower Egypt, particularly around Memphis. The early Egyptian state controlled a vast stretch of the Nile Valley, from the Delta to Aswan, fostering economic and political integration (Bard 2003, 67). The presence of Egypt in the Southern Levant and the presence of Levantine communities seems, however, to cease during the Early Dynastic period (Stevenson 2016).

The 2nd Dynasty remains less well documented, but it was instrumental in strengthening the state's administrative and economic structures. By the 3rd Dynasty, these foundations supported the rise of the Old Kingdom (*c*. 2686–2181 BC), a period characterised by centralised rule, economic prosperity, and monumental achievements, most notably the construction of pyramids at Saqqara and Giza (Bard 2003, 85). This era also saw increased trade with the Levant, particularly in luxury goods such as cedar from Byblos. Unfortunately, very little is known of Old Kingdom settlements (Malek 2003, 101).

Egypt's political stability endured throughout the Old Kingdom until its decline at the end of the 6th Dynasty, leading to the fragmentation of the state and the onset of the First Intermediate Period (*c*. 2160–2055 BC).

The Southern Levant: Middle and Late Bronze Ages (2000–1200 BC)

The MBA (2000–1550 BC) saw a re-urbanisation process in the Southern Levant, likely influenced by Amorite elements from the north. Egypt's Middle Kingdom also played a crucial role, driving economic demand for Levantine products like wine and olive oil. The MBA marked a peak in Levantine culture, economy, and political power, with strong connections to Egypt, including the settlement of Levantine communities in the Nile Delta (Harrison 2012, 644). These communities later gained control of Lower Egypt, leading to the Hyksos Period (Second Intermediate Period), centred at Avaris (Tell el-Dab'a).

In the mid-16th century BC, the Hyksos were expelled by the Egyptians, marking the transition to the LBA (1550–1200 BC). In the Southern Levant, the expulsion of the Hyksos is often used to mark the transition from the MBA to the LBA, with destruction layers at key sites widely attributed to Egyptian military campaigns during this period (Harrison 2012, 644). Fortified cities like Hazor and Megiddo remained centres of power, accumulating wealth through long-distance trade.

The LBA (1550–1200 BC) was shaped by the rivalry between Egypt, Mitanni, and the Hittites. By LB II (1400–1200 BC), Egyptian imperial influence in the Levant had grown significantly. Thutmose III (1479–1425 BC) extended Egyptian influence into Syria, defeating a coalition at Megiddo (1457 BC) and crossing the Euphrates (1447 BC) (Pfälzner 2012, 771). Later, the Egyptian-Hittite struggle culminated in the Battle of Qadesh (1275 BC) between Ramesses II and Muwattalli II, leading to a peace treaty in 1259 BC. The Levantine kingdoms – including Ugarit, Qadesh, Damascus, Sidon, Tyre, and rulers or officials from Hazor, Akko, Megiddo, Gezer, Jerusalem, Ashkelon, and Lachish in Palestine – maintained diplomatic ties with Egyptian pharaohs, as recorded in the Amarna Letters (Liverani 2008).

Around 1200 BC, the 'Sea Peoples' invasion led to major upheavals. Their origins and role remain debated – some suggest violent incursions, while others argue for gradual settlement, particularly in the Jordan Valley. Archaeological evidence shows widespread destruction at sites like Hazor, Megiddo, Gezer, Lachish, and Beth Shean. By the early 12th century BC, the existing political order had collapsed, ushering in a new era of social and political transformation (Pfälzner 2012, 772 with further bibliography).

Egypt: from the Middle Kingdom to the New Kingdom (c. 2055–1069 BC)

Around 2055 BC, Mentuhotep II of Thebes unified Egypt (2055–1985 BC) marking the beginning of the Middle Kingdom (2055–1650 BC). His successors, particularly the 12th Dynasty (1985–1795 BC), established a stable government and expanded Egypt's influence beyond its borders. Egyptian texts, wall paintings, and archaeological finds indicate active trade and contact with the Levant, though the details remain uncertain (Hikade 2012, 837). Asiatics were also employed as normal workers by the Egyptians, given Egyptian names and apparently assimilated into Egyptian society during the Middle Kingdom (Schneider 2003).

In the early 2nd millennium BC, the rulers of Egypt's 12th Dynasty pursued an assertive expansionist policy beyond the country's borders. To the north, they constructed fortifications along the Way of Horus, a strategic route linking the eastern Nile Delta to the Levant, an area primarily inhabited by semi-nomadic pastoralists (Hikade 2012, 838). Egyptian artefacts such as scarabs, initially used as administrative seals, became popular in the Southern Levant, often serving as funerary amulets (Ben-Tor 2007).

The 13th Dynasty (1795–1650 BC) initially continued the policies of its predecessors, but internal divisions weakened central authority. Increasing numbers of Levantine migrants settled in the Nile Delta, particularly at Avaris (Tell el-Dab'a), which grew into a major cosmopolitan trading centre (Hikade 2012, 840). The short-lived 14th Dynasty was followed by the Hyksos rulers (15th Dynasty), who were not foreign invaders but emerged from the established Asiatic elite at Avaris. They adopted Egyptian royal titles and regalia, though their rule was limited to the northern Delta. Meanwhile, the 17th Dynasty ruled in Thebes, culminating in Ahmose I's military campaign that expelled the Hyksos, marking the start of the New Kingdom (1550–1069 BC) (Hikade 2012, 842).

The 18th Dynasty (1550–1295 BC) saw Egypt assert dominance over the Levant through military campaigns. Thutmose III (1479–1425 BC) expanded Egyptian rule deep into southern Syria, with victories at Megiddo (1457 BC) (Shaw 2003a). In the following years, Egypt maintained control through diplomatic alliances, as recorded in the above-mentioned Amarna Letters (Hikade 2012, 844).

During the 19th Dynasty (1295–1186 BC), Egypt faced rising Hittite power in the Levant, culminating in the Battle of Qadesh in Syria (Van Dijk 2003). A peace treaty in 1259 BC established a fragile balance of power. However, in the late 13th–12th centuries BC, the eastern Mediterranean faced waves of destruction attributed to the 'Sea Peoples', leading to the decline of many urban centres (Hikade 2012, 845). Egyptian sources describe a decisive victory over the Sea Peoples, but one group, the Peleset (Philistines), settled in the southern Levant. Ramesses III maintained some control over Palestine and southern Syria and had some strongholds such as Beth Shean (Mazar 2003).

By the end of the 12th century BC, Egypt's control over the Levant collapsed, leading to a full withdrawal (Hikade 2012, 846). The 20th Dynasty saw internal decline, culminating in the reign of Ramesses XI (1099–1069 BC) and the beginning of the Third Intermediate Period.

The Iron Age in the Southern Levant

The collapse of the LBA world in the 12th and 11th centuries BC marked a profound transformation in the eastern Mediterranean. Previously interconnected states, city-states, and powerful palatial societies disintegrated, giving way to a fragmented landscape of emerging regional powers (Bunimovitz and Lederman 2015, 252).

Around 1200 BC, widespread destruction affected many Canaanite cities, including Hazor, Beth-Shean, Megiddo, Aphek, Gezer, Lachish, Ashdod, and Ekron (Younker 2003, 370). Although some of these sites were rebuilt under Egyptian rule, the reign of Ramesses III (*c*. 1185–1153 BC) marked the final phase of Egyptian hegemony in Canaan (Younker 2003, 373). The withdrawal of Egyptian control left a power vacuum, allowing new cultural groups to emerge.

The Philistines, part of the larger movement of the Sea Peoples, established themselves along the southern coastal plain, occupying long-standing Canaanite cities such as Gaza, Ashkelon, Ashdod, Ekron, and Gath (Yasur-Landau 2012). Archaeological evidence from sites like Ashkelon, Ekron, and Gath supports the idea of Philistine migration, bringing Aegean-inspired material culture, including Mycenaean-style pottery and domestic architectural features (Bunimovitz and Lederman 2015, 254). However, these cities remained culturally mixed, leading to hybridisation between Philistine and Canaanite traditions (Ben-Shlomo 2010; Bunimovitz and Lederman 2015).

Meanwhile, in the highlands of Cisjordan and Transjordan, new tribal and pastoral groups settled, forming small rural villages. These groups, identified as early Israelites, Ammonites, Moabites, and Edomites, occupied previously uninhabited or sparsely populated areas (Younker 2003, 367).

By the early 10th century BC, the highland settlements evolved into emerging polities. The biblical tradition suggests a brief period of political unity under a centralised Israelite monarchy around 1000 BC, though this remains debated (Liverani 1988, 573). The kingdom soon split into two separate entities: Israel in the north, with its capital in Samaria, and Judah in the south, centred in Jerusalem. Meanwhile, the Philistine Pentapolis remained dominant along the coast, while Ammon, Moab, and Edom consolidated their control over the Transjordan (Bunimovitz and Lederman 2015, 256).

Egypt, though no longer an imperial power in Canaan, launched military campaigns to reassert its influence. Pharaoh Shishak (Sheshonq I) invaded the region around 925 BC, targeting Israelite and Philistine cities (Younker 2003, 374). This campaign marked the beginning of renewed foreign interest in the Levant.

Throughout the 9th and 8th centuries BC, Israel emerged as the dominant power in the Levant. However, the region remained politically fragmented, with Israel, Judah, Ammon, Moab, Edom, Aram-Damascus, and Philistia often engaging in shifting alliances and conflicts (Younker 2003, 378).

During this period, the Assyrian Empire began expanding westward. In 734 BC, Tiglath-Pileser III led a campaign that brought much of the region under Assyrian control, including Megiddo. In 722 BC, his successor, Sargon II, captured Samaria, marking the fall of the northern kingdom of Israel and the beginning of direct Assyrian rule (Younker 2003, 374, 380).

With Israel destroyed, Judah and the remaining Levantine states became vassals of the Assyrian Empire. However, Assyrian control weakened in the late 7th century BC, allowing Egypt to reassert its military presence in the region as an ally of Assyria against the rising Babylonian power (Liverani 1988, 760).

By the early 6th century BC, the Babylonian king Nebuchadnezzar II launched a series of campaigns that led to the final collapse of independent Levantine states. In 586 BC, Jerusalem fell, bringing an end to the kingdom of Judah and completing the Babylonian conquest of the region (Younker 2003, 380).

The Third Intermediate Period and the Late Period (1069–332 BC)

The period between 1069 and 664 BC, spanning the 21st to 25th Dynasties, marked a transformative phase in Egyptian history. Centralised rule gave way to political fragmentation, with regional centres of power re-emerging. Egyptian society also underwent demographic shifts due to significant migrations of Libyans and Nubians, which permanently altered the population's composition. Egypt's foreign influence, particularly in the Levant, diminished considerably (Taylor 2003, 330). Although Egypt appeared politically unified under the 21st Dynasty, real power was divided between the pharaohs ruling from Tanis in the north and the High Priests of Amun in Thebes, who also commanded the military. The northern rulers left few records, with Psusennes I (1039–991 BC) and Siamun (978–959 BC) known mainly for their construction projects in Tanis and Memphis. Egyptian activity in the Levant during this period was minimal (Taylor 2003, 330). The 22nd Dynasty (945–715 BC), founded by Sheshonq I, saw Egypt briefly reassert its presence in the Levant. Around 925 BC, following the division of the united monarchy of Israel, the Egyptian pharaoh Sheshonq I (Shishak in biblical tradition) launched a military campaign against the Kingdom of Judah. His campaign is recorded in an inscription at Karnak, listing 154 towns in the Levant that were reportedly conquered and destroyed (Hikade 2012, 847).

By the second half of the 8th century BC, Assyria emerged as the dominant power in the region. Tiglath-Pileser III (744–727 BC) subdued Syria and the Levant, crushing all resistance (Hikade 2012, 847). At the same time, Egypt faced internal turmoil, allowing its southern neighbour, Kush, to rise. In 747 BC, the Kushites established the 25th Dynasty (747–656 BC), ultimately taking control of Egypt (Taylor 2003).

Pharaoh Taharqa of Kush attempted to reassert Egyptian influence in the Levant, forming alliances with city-states such as Tyre and Sidon. This growing Egyptian-Assyrian rivalry led Esarhaddon of Assyria (680–669 BC) to launch a campaign against Egypt's allies, culminating in the complete Assyrian conquest of the Levant (Hikade 2012, 847).

In 674 BC, Esarhaddon attempted to invade Egypt but failed. However, by 671 BC, his forces successfully entered Egypt, and in 663 BC, his successor Ashurbanipal sacked Thebes, defeating the last Kushite ruler, Tanwetamani. The Assyrians then installed Psametik I (664–610 BC), a Libyan prince of Sais, as Egypt's new ruler (Lloyd 2000, 364–74). With the help of Carian and Ionian mercenaries, Psametik I consolidated his power, eventually securing Egypt's independence around 650 BC as Assyria struggled with the rising Babylonian and Median threats.

Taking advantage of Assyria's decline, Psametik I expanded Egyptian influence further into the Levant than previous 18th Dynasty rulers (Lloyd 2000, 374–77). Psametik I's successor, Nekau II (610–595 BC), continued Egyptian expansion into the Near East. However, in 604 BC, he suffered a decisive defeat at Karkemish against Babylon's Nebuchadnezzar II (Lloyd 2000, 374–7). Despite continued hostilities, Egyptian influence in the Levant declined.

In 547 BC, Pharaoh Amasis (570–526 BC) allied with Nabonidus of Babylon and Croesus of Lydia in a failed attempt to counter the growing Persian Empire. Finally, in 525 BC, Psametik III was defeated at the Battle of Pelusium by Persian king Cambyses II (529–522 BC). Egypt was incorporated into the Persian Empire as a satrapy for the next 120 years (Lloyd 2000, 374–7).

1.4 Book structure

This book is structured to provide a comprehensive analysis of textile production tools and techniques in the Southern Levant and Ancient Egypt. It begins with an overview of fundamental spinning and weaving techniques, introducing the main categories of tools used in these processes. The second chapter explores the raw materials available for textile production, offering an introduction to fibres and the earliest textile remains discovered in both regions. This provides essential context for understanding the technological possibilities of the period under study.

The core of the book consists of two dedicated chapters – one focusing on the Southern Levant and the other on Egypt. Each of these chapters examines different categories of textile-related artefacts, such as spindles, spindle whorls, loom weights, and other weaving tools. Within each chapter, case study sites are discussed in detail, with analyses of the materials found at these locations. At the end of each regional chapter, conclusions are drawn regarding the development and characteristics of textile production in that area.

The final chapter brings together the findings from both regions, offering a comparative analysis that highlights similarities, differences, and possible influences between the two textile traditions. This is followed by a comprehensive online catalogue of all studied materials, ensuring that the data is accessible for further research and reference (10.5281/zenodo.15611432).

2

Tools for textile production

Much has been written about spinning and weaving techniques in Egypt and the Ancient Near East. This chapter aims to summarise the principal phases of these processes in order to better understand the archaeological materials and their function that will be presented in the following chapters. For this reason, only a brief presentation of the general topic will be given.

2.1 Spinning

Spinning is the process that transforms fibres in a single, continuous yarn. The operation can be performed by using different methods and tools, and the result can differ considerably. The thread can be more or less even depending on the quality of the fibres' preparation, the technique employed, and the ability of the spinner.

The first threads and cordage were probably produced in the Palaeolithic (Barber 1991, 39) and the first form of spinning was probably hand-spinning. In this method, fibres are simply drawn out from a mass and twisted between hand-palms or palms and thigh; more fibres are then added and rolled again until the required thread is obtained (Carington Smith 1976, 69; Wendrich 1999, 298–300; Levy 2020, 223–4). However, this method is time-consuming and requires winding the yarn around some objects in a separate step otherwise it tends to untwist.

The following step probably consisted of the use of a spindle instead of the palms. A spindle could be a simple stick to help in the twisting of fibres, but simultaneously enables winding up the yarn being produced (Andersson Strand 2015, 45). If a small weight – the spindle whorl – is then added to the rod, the spindle will be able to freely rotate for much longer. With this simple tool spinning becomes much faster, and the thread is much more even than that produced by hand. Furthermore, one hand is now free to control the provision of fibres and keep the spindle rotating. Spinning with a spindle has been performed until the spinning wheel was invented in the Middle Ages (Levy 2020, 142).

Several methods of spinning with a spindle have been used, with Crowfoot classification (Crowfoot 1931, 9–20) distinguishing six methods.[1] For this work, it seems useful to explain the last three methods:

- Grasped spindle spinning: a rove already prepared is passed through a ring or a fork and rotated with both hands. Crowfoot states that this is more suitable for plying (Crowfoot 1931, 14)
- Supported hand spindle: drafting of fibres is a separate action. Spindle rests lengthwise on the thigh. It rotates on the floor or in a cup. Very similar to suspended spindle.
- Suspended spindle spinning/drop spinning: the spindle rotates freely in the air and it can be either rotated by fingers or along the thigh to add momentum.

During the spinning process, the thread must be wound around the shaft. With the drop spindle techniques, it happens when the yarn produced is so long the spindle reaches the ground. After the yarn has been wound up, the process can start again until the shaft is full (Fig. 2.1).

A spindle whorl can be placed either on the top of the spindle or at the bottom (or even in the middle of the shaft). It is generally believed that the position of the spindle whorl on the shaft is culturally determined (Barber 1991, 53; Crewe 1998, 7; Sauvage 2013, 206). However, some technical issues might influence this position. If the spindle is to be rolled along the thigh, a high-whorl spindle is preferred; if it has to be twirled between thumb and fingers,

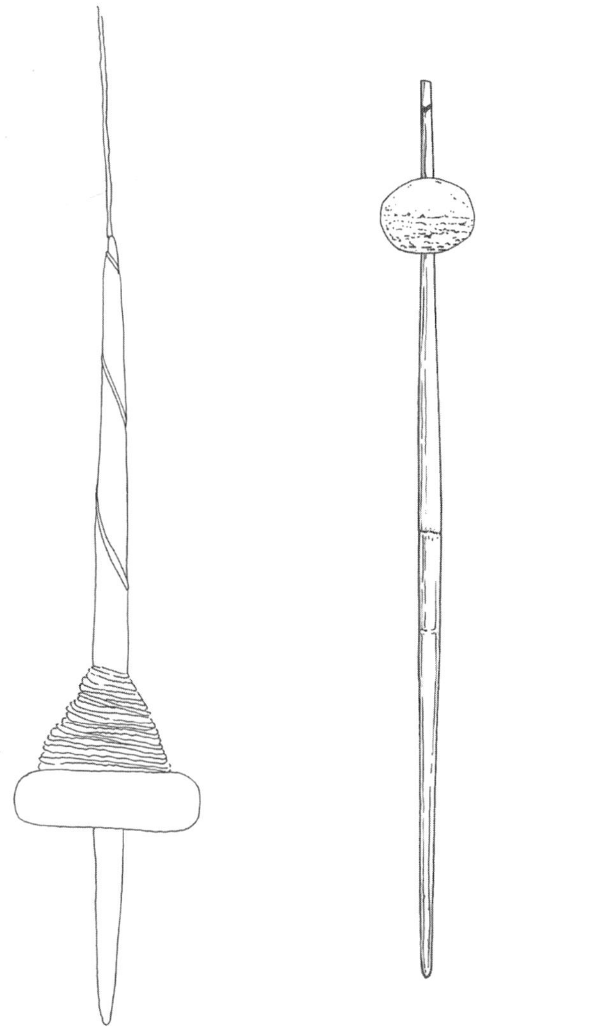

Figure 2.1. Position of the spindle whorl on a spindle, top and bottom (courtesy of the Centre for Textile Research)

Figure 2.2. Spinning direction (courtesy of the Centre for Textile Research)

a low-whorl spindle might be preferred (Carington Smith 1976, 76).

It is generally believed, thanks to iconographic sources, that Ancient Egypt used a high-whorl spindle, while the Aegean-Anatolian area, as well as Europe, a low-whorl spindle (Cecchini 2011, 198; Sauvage 2013, 213). Mesopotamian and Levantine areas have fewer iconographic sources that can help in recognising the spindle whorl position and they will be discussed in the following chapters.

Wet fibres have a natural twisting orientation, which is s for flax and nettle, and z for hemp, while cotton can rotate in both directions but gives best results when it is Z-spun (Forbes 1956, 151). Animal fibres, like wool, do not show an orientation when moistened and can be spun in both directions. The natural orientation, however, might help in the process of spinning but it is not binding; all fibres can be spun in both directions. To prevent the yarn from untwisting and to add strength, the thread is generally doubled or plied, which means that an extra yarn with the same twist of the first is added, and the two are then spun together, generally in the opposite direction to that of the individual yarns. The directions are called S (counterclockwise) and Z (clockwise), from the central part of the letter, which resembles the twist lines visible on a yarn (Fig. 2.2). It means that if two threads are S-spun, they will be plied in a z direction (Z, 2s).[2] When plied threads are twisted together, it is called cabling. Analyses of ancient textiles, however, show very different adaptations to thread directions. Thread quality is determined by its thickness and whether it is tightly or loosely spun. The angle of the twist determines the tightness and can be defined as loose if it is less than 25°, medium if it is between 25 and 45°, or tight if it is more than 45° (Jones 2002, 324).

New and compelling evidence has largely demonstrated that the yarns from bast fibres from Egypt and the Southern Levant were not produced using draft-spinning techniques, as previously described (Shamir 2015; Gleba and Harris 2019). Instead, they were made by splicing and plying (see Chapter 3).

2.2 Spinning tools

As previously discussed, a spindle is a simple rod to which a weight can be attached to prolong its rotational movement. However, identifying a spindle or spindle whorl in an archaeological context can be challenging. Spindles may be mistaken for pins – whether for hair or clothing – or even for kohl sticks. Similarly, spindle whorls can easily be confused with beads, and in many cases, it is impossible to distinguish between the two (Mårtensson *et al.* 2006). For this study, objects have generally been classified according to the assessments of the excavators, as they had the opportunity to handle them and analyse them in context with other site findings. However, in some instances, the original classification appeared inaccurate, and certain objects have been re-evaluated.

2.2.1 Spindles

Spindles can be made from a variety of materials, primarily wood, though more luxurious examples were also crafted from metal, ivory, and bone. Due to the organic nature of these everyday tools, most ancient spindles have not survived, except in specific conditions that allowed for their preservation. As a result, the majority of known spindles worldwide are rare and often represent exceptional specimens. Although spindles could vary in shape and length (a comparison with modern spindles can be a useful exercise in this regard), it is helpful to establish certain characteristics that may aid in their identification.

Length is a crucial factor, as it influences both usability and efficiency. A spindle should be long enough to allow for easy handling and to accommodate the spun yarn, preventing it from unspinning. However, if it is too long, it becomes difficult to twist and will reach the ground more quickly during drop-spinning, producing only a small amount of yarn before needing to be wound up again. In her study of pre-Roman Italian spindles, Gleba (2008, 103) notes that local spindles were generally around 30 cm in length. During the Roman period, this length was reduced to between 12 and 27 cm, although some exceptional examples reached 40 cm. Spindle length is likely related to the weight of the spindle whorl, as well as to the type of fibre used and the desired final product.

The shape of spindles also varies considerably. Some are simple cylindrical rods, while others feature a thicker central section with thinner ends. Generally, spindles taper towards one or both extremities, with the thickest section positioned around one-third of the way along the shaft. The remaining two-thirds gradually narrow towards the tip, which may be either rounded or pointed.

Other features can assist in identifying spindles. The most obvious and easiest to recognise is a notch or groove in the upper part of the shaft, designed to secure the yarn and facilitate the spinning process (Fig. 2.3). This feature can be present regardless of whether the spindle whorl is positioned at the upper, middle, or lower part of the shaft. A similar function can also be performed by a hook attached to the upper end of the spindle (Barber 1991, 68–9).

The spindle whorl is generally not placed at the very top or bottom of the spindle, as some space is needed to secure the fibres at the beginning of the spinning process. However, this does not require a particularly large area – just a couple of centimetres is usually sufficient.

Figure 2.3. Spiral notch on an Egyptian spindle from Deir el-Medina (courtesy of the Museo Egizio in Turin)

2.2.2 Spindle whorls

Spindle whorls might, at first sight, appear a more easily recognisable item, and their use of several materials, often non-perishable, enables us to find a greater number of these tools. However, it is not always possible to be certain of their usage. Spindle whorls can frequently be confused with beads (especially if small and made of good materials), as well as buttons and mace heads, or models of mace heads. Furthermore, some items made of reworked pottery sherds and stone rings may also have been used as spindle whorls. In this chapter, the general parameters to distinguish a spindle whorl are given along with the typology used in this book, while the next chapters deal with specific issues regarding Levantine and Egyptian materials.

A spindle whorl is an object with a central hole that allows it to be attached to the spindle shaft, adding weight and enabling the rotational movement to continue for longer. However, this does not mean it must always be a rounded object; spindle whorls can also be domed, conical, or even cross-shaped. They were produced from a variety of materials. In antiquity, the most common was likely wood, as remains the case today. Unfortunately, due to the perishable nature of wood, it has rarely been preserved in archaeological contexts, resulting in the loss of the vast majority of ancient spindle whorls. Other materials, such as pottery, stone, bone, ivory, glass, and possibly faience, are more commonly found in excavations.

Pottery was a cheap and easily workable material, so it is unsurprising that pottery spindle whorls are frequently discovered in archaeological contexts. Wood, on the other hand, could provide a durable spindle whorl at a low cost, though if the wood was too soft, it would wear quickly, and the hole could deform over time. Stone spindle whorls required a higher initial investment but were more resistant to breakage and deformation, often lasting longer than those made from other materials. Given the same diameter and height, a stone spindle whorl would be significantly heavier than a wooden or bone one, making it suitable only for specific types of spinning.

Bone spindle whorls were an affordable and relatively easy-to-produce alternative. They were resistant to warping and breakage from falls, but – similar to stone – their light weight made them suitable for spinning only certain types of thread. However, experimental archaeology aimed at replicating spindle whorls from Arslantepe has demonstrated that bone and perforated pottery sherd whorls were among the most effective for spinning both wool and hemp (Laurito *et al.* 2014, 164).

Beyond their diverse shapes and materials, spindle whorls also vary significantly in size and weight, depending on the type of fibre being spun and whether they are used for spinning or plying. Tests conducted by the CTR have shown that lighter, smaller whorls are suited to spinning fine threads, while heavier, larger ones produce thicker yarns (Andersson Strand 2015, 47–8). This is because a lighter whorl incorporates fewer fibres into the yarn than a heavier one. Although spinning with a light whorl is more time-consuming, it ultimately yields a greater yarn length from the same amount of raw fibre (Andersson Strand 2010, 13–14). The quality and preparation of raw materials are also crucial. Coarser fibres produce coarser threads and textiles. Additionally, wool takes longer to spin than flax or hemp due to its shorter fibres (Andersson Strand 2015, 46).

A spindle whorl of medium weight (15–30 g) allows for greater versatility in production compared to very light (<15 g) or very heavy (>40 g) ones (Andersson Strand 2015, 48). As a result, medium-weight whorls are more commonly found in domestic contexts. The lightest whorl tested by CTR weighed 4 g, but Liu (1978, 90) identified an example as light as 1 g, with a diameter of just 8 mm – making it difficult to distinguish from a bead. Conversely, large and heavy whorls may be mistaken for loom or net weights. The heaviest known spindle whorls weigh around 140–150 g (Gleba 2008, 106) (Table 2.1).

Table 2.1. Some of the results of the Centre for Textile Research tests on spinning wool (not considering time necessary to prepare the raw material) (Andersson Strand 2010, 13)

Average output of thread/h	
4 g	35 m
8 g	40 m
18 g	50 m
Time for spinning 2 km of yarn (1 m² of cloth)	
4 g	57 h
8 g	50 h
18 g	40 h

The hole size in a whorl can aid identification, as it must accommodate a spindle shaft, whereas beads typically have smaller holes and weights may have large, irregular ones. The expected diameter range for spindle whorl holes is 0.3–1 cm, though larger examples exist (Gleba 2008, 107; see Chapter 5 for complete Egyptian spindles).

Another key factor is the relationship between spindle shaft length and whorl weight. CTR tests indicate that very light whorls (*e.g.*, 5 g) can only function with short shafts (<12 cm) (Andersson Strand 2015, 48). However, this may also depend on fibre type and whorl position (low vs. high), as demonstrated by findings from the Egyptian site of Gurob. Further testing is needed to clarify how spindle rotation was affected in previous experiments and to refine the weight and size parameters for ancient Egyptian tools.

The terminology used in this study for spindle whorls follows the CTR typology, as this system facilitates direct comparison with other Mediterranean regions and ensures consistency in classification. However, where relevant, traditional Levantine and Egyptian terms have also been retained to acknowledge regional naming conventions and historical scholarship. It is important to note that not all spindle whorl types identified in Mediterranean contexts are present in the Near East. For this reason, the classification applied here has been adapted and simplified to better reflect the specific characteristics of the tools found in the southern Levant and Egypt. This approach ensures both compatibility with broader textile studies and a more accurate representation of the material culture of the regions under investigation (Fig. 2.4).

2.2.3 Perforated sherds

Perforated or reused pottery sherds are created by modifying a broken piece of pottery, shaping it into a roughly circular form by trimming its edges. A hole is then drilled in the centre, usually from both sides. While some examples have smoothed contours, a perfectly rounded shape is not essential.

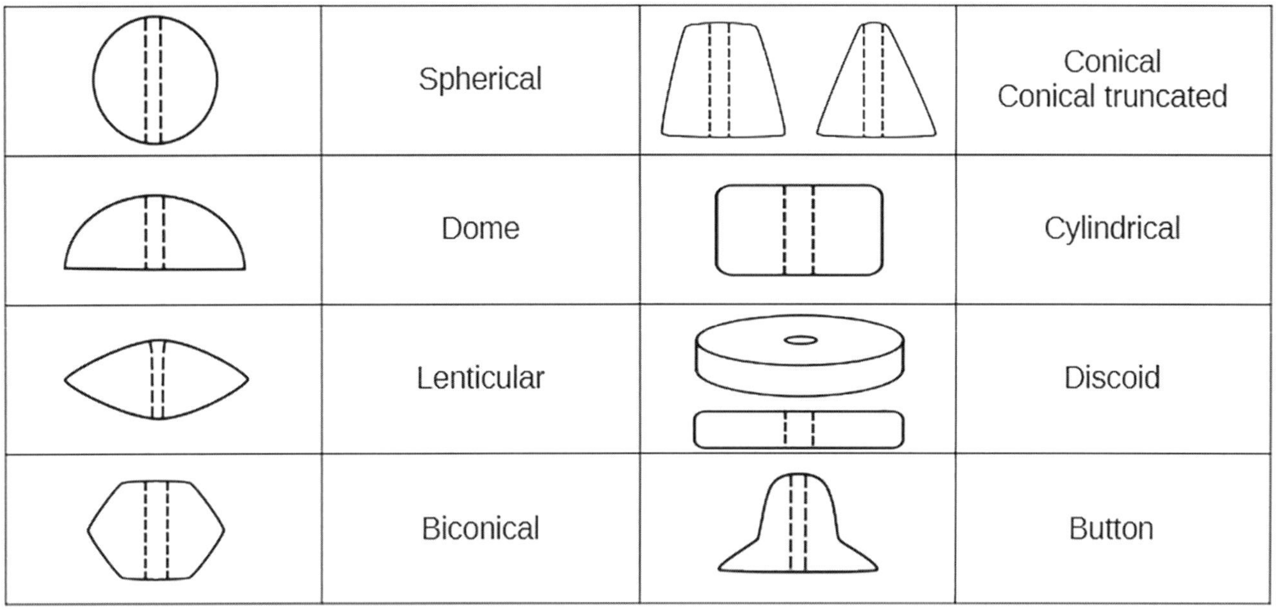

Figure 2.4. Spindle whorls typology (adapted from Andersson Strand and Nosch 2015, fig. 5.1.5)

Various interpretations have been proposed for these objects, including gaming pieces, accounting tokens, pendants, ornaments, and children's spinning tops (Gibbs 2008, 90). However, experimental archaeology has demonstrated that they can be used to spin fibres such as wool and flax (Shamir 1996, 150; Gibbs 2008, 91). Due to their irregular perforations, they tend to cause spindle wobbling, making them a less-than-ideal choice for spinning (Rahmstorf *et al.* 2015, 271). Nonetheless, experiments show that these whorls are quick and easy to produce, requiring only a few minutes to shape and drill using basic tools. While they may not always be the best option, they provide a cheap and effective alternative – sometimes even preferable to traditional pottery whorls (Laurito *et al.* 2014, 164).

The majority of these modified sherds feature hourglass-shaped perforations, a result of drilling from both sides. While this is not the most effective design, it does not necessarily prevent their use as spinning tools. In some cases, perforations appear slanted rather than vertical, and some attempts at drilling from both sides failed to meet in the centre. These unsuccessful examples are catalogued as failed attempts, as they would be ineffective for spinning. Despite their significance, perforated sherds are rarely documented in publications and are often classified alongside ordinary pottery fragments, even when clear signs of reuse are evident. This inconsistency largely depends on scholarly traditions and varies across regions and time periods. In Egyptian contexts, in particular, information on these tools is scarce, complicating efforts to analyse their distribution.

Other objects associated with thread preparation include spinning bowls and basalt rings. Spinning bowls, made of pottery or stone, feature one or more loops inside through which the rove (a spliced but unspun yarn) or yarn is passed during the spinning or twisting process. Basalt rings, typically small and made of basalt or occasionally limestone, are easily identifiable and may have been used for spinning or weaving. As both object types are predominantly found in the regions under study, they will be examined in the next chapter with a focus on Levantine evidence.

2.3 Weaving

Weaving is the process of creating textiles by interlacing two perpendicular thread systems: the warp and weft (Fig. 2.5). The warp forms the textile's structural foundation and must be kept under tension. Its threads run parallel and evenly spaced, typically prepared separately on wall pegs or between two pairs of vertical poles (a warper) before being transferred to the loom. The weft is inserted at right angles to the warp, allowing for various weave patterns.

Weaving techniques fall into three main categories: tabby, twill, and satin weaves. The simplest, tabby weave, is created by passing the weft alternately over and under each warp thread. In a balanced tabby, warp and weft threads are equal in number, while warp-faced and weft-faced fabrics have a dominance of one thread type.

Tabby weave can also vary. In a basket weave, pairs (or more) of warp and weft threads are interlaced together. If only one thread system is doubled, it is called a half-basket weave. A tapestry weave uses a single warp and weft system, but the weft does not span the entire fabric width, instead filling selected areas to create patterns, often requiring

Figure 2.5. Tabby weave with indication of warp and weft

multiple coloured threads. Twill weave, which creates a diagonal pattern by shifting weft interlacements across multiple warp sets, and satin weave have not been identified in the periods and regions examined here and will not be discussed further. This study also excludes classifications related to mats, baskets, cords, nets, leatherworking, or decorative elements like sequins and metal inserts. However, some of these crafts share tools with textile production, such as spindles for net-making and stronger needles for netting, looping, and knotting (Desrosiers 2010, 34–5). Recognising these overlaps is essential when studying textile tools.

Textiles can also be produced using non-woven techniques, which involve a single continuous element rather than the traditional warp and weft systems (Desrosiers 2010, 34–9). These fabrics, found at sites like Naḥal Ḥemar (Shamir 2014, 243), do not require the interlacing of threads, but instead rely on other methods, such as knotting or looping.

Weaving requires basic tools to maintain tension on the warp threads. This tension can be achieved by using readily available elements in the environment, such as trees or poles, which would not be identifiable in an archaeological excavation. However, additional tools are needed to separate the warp threads and ensure smooth weaving.

Weft threads are inserted between the warp threads, which can be done manually or with the aid of tools to speed up the process. In a tabby weave, the warp is divided into two groups (odd and even threads), and each group is raised separately to create a space, or shed, between them. This space is where the weft is passed through. In more advanced looms, the shed naturally forms as the threads are raised and lowered. For a simpler loom, a shed-stick or shed-rod can be used to open the shed by temporarily lifting one group of warp threads, keeping the space open for the weft to pass through. The shed-stick can also function as a beater, an object used to press the weft into place after each pass (Kemp and Vogelsang-Eastwood 2001, 312). Alternatively, a heddle can be used, which is a bar to which the warp threads are attached, allowing for the systematic raising of one group of threads to create the shed.

A loom can vary from basic frames to large, sophisticated wooden structures. The most simple loom structures are the back-strap loom, the horizontal ground loom, the vertical two-beam loom and the warp-weighted loom.

The back-strap loom consists of two rods that hold the warp under tension and remains in use today in regions such as South America and Southeast Asia. One end is fastened to a fixed support (such as a pole or tree), while the other is attached to a belt worn around the weaver's waist. By shifting their body or reclining, the weaver can easily adjust the tension of the warp. To create the shed and counter-shed, the weaver uses shed sticks and heddle-rods, as previously described. Despite its simplicity, this loom enables the production of intricate patterns at a reasonable speed. However, it is best suited for weaving narrow strips of fabric, typically 50–60 cm wide – roughly the maximum width a weaver can reach with their arms (Fig. 2.6).

The horizontal ground loom served a similar function to other weaving devices. It consisted of two beams fixed to the ground with poles and could be operated by one or two weavers simultaneously, allowing for the production of large textiles (Fig. 2.7).

This loom was certainly in use in Egypt from at least the Naqada period, as evidenced by its depiction on a bowl from a female tomb in Badari (Middle Egypt), dated to late Naqada I–early Naqada II (Cortes 2011, 94–5). The bowl's interior rim features a series of vertical lines connected at the top by a long horizontal line, with human figures working at the structure. This is generally interpreted as a rope holding the warp threads (Cortes 2011, 94–5).

Figure 2.6. Peruvian weaver with a backstrap loom

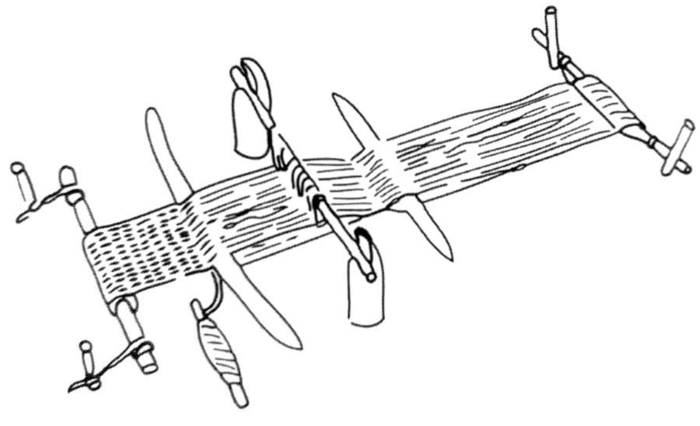

Figure 2.7. Drawing of a horizontal ground loom (courtesy of the Centre for Textile Research, drawing A. Jeppson)

Further evidence comes from the Middle Kingdom, where the loom appears in tomb paintings and wooden funerary models, such as those of Meketra and Usernekhbet (see Table 3.2). However, no representations of this loom are known after this period.

In Mesopotamia, textual and iconographic sources indicate that the horizontal ground loom was in use by at least the 3rd millennium BC (Waetzoldt 1972, 130–2) and possibly as early as the 4th millennium BC (Barber 1991, 84; Breniquet 2008, 304).

There are no examples of fully preserved looms in the Levant, except for some rods from the Cave of Treasures (Bar-Adon 1980; Bender Jørgensen *et al.* 2023), which have been interpreted either as beams for a horizontal ground loom (Shamir 2015, 18), or as beams for a back-strap loom (Barber 1991, 86; Breniquet 2010, 53). No traces for the use of a back-strap loom have been found so far in the Near East, and for this reason Shamir (2015, 18) and Levy (2020, 134) interprets the beams as belonging to a horizontal ground loom.

The vertical two-beam loom is made up of a frame which is set vertically and has to support the upper beam, the heddles, and other tools (Kemp and Vogelsang-Eastwood 2001, 335). The warp is tensioned by a second beam placed on the lower portion of the frame. This seems to appear later in the iconographic documentation from Egypt, while it is unclear when and where it could have been used in the Near East. In fact, it leaves no clear archaeological evidence, and its existence in the Levant has only been speculated upon due to the absence of evidence for the use of other looms. Several tomb paintings show the use of this loom in New Kingdom Egypt, with one or two weavers per loom, both men and women (see Table 3.2). On this type of loom, textiles are woven from bottom to top (Fig. 2.8).

The warp-weighted loom is one of the few loom types that leave clear archaeological traces, making it possible to identify its use with certainty. Structurally, it resembles a vertical two-beam loom, but instead of a lower beam, it relies on a series of weights to keep the warp threads under tension. These weights, usually made of stone or clay, are highly durable and frequently survive in archaeological contexts.

Typically, the loom was positioned against a wall, functioning much like other looms, but with key differences in warping and weaving techniques (Andersson Strand 2018, 23). Before weaving could begin, the warp had to

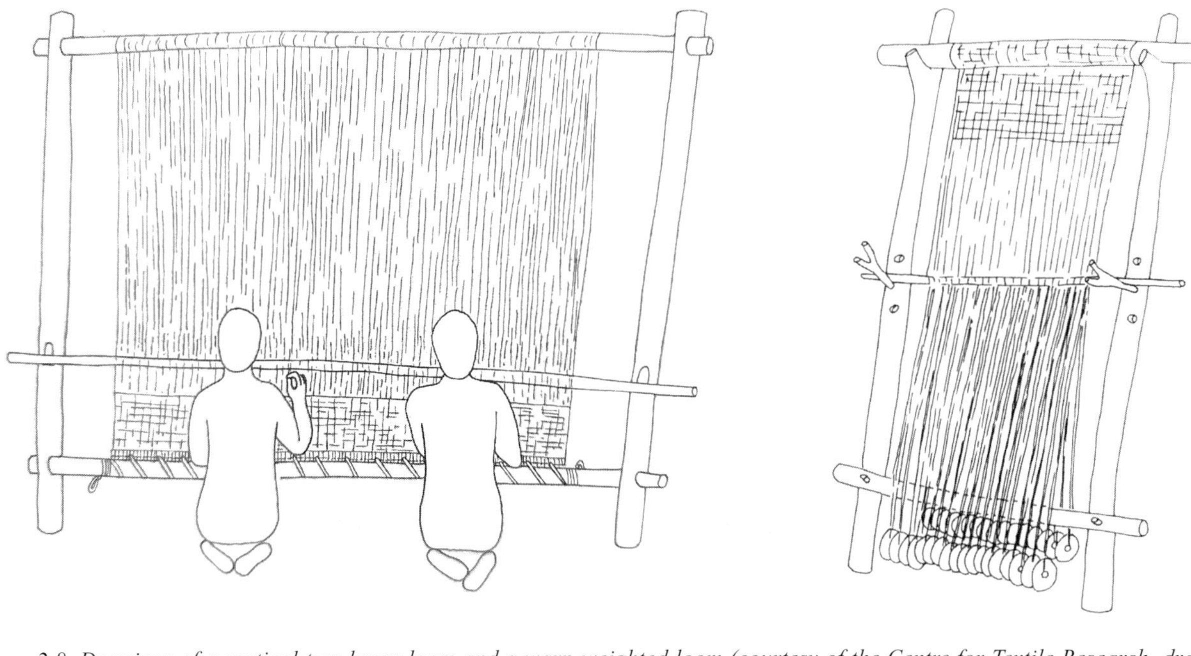

Figure 2.8. Drawings of a vertical two-beam loom and a warp-weighted loom (courtesy of the Centre for Textile Research, drawing A. Jeppson)

be prepared separately and then transferred to the loom, often in the form of a starting border or heading band, whose weft would then become the warp (Gleba 2008, 123). Unlike the vertical two-beam loom, where weaving progresses upwards, the warp-weighted loom is worked from top to bottom.

The length of fabric produced was generally restricted by the height of the loom, but weavers could extend it in several ways, such as standing on a stool, positioning the loom higher, or even using a roller beam as the upper beam. In some cases, a trench was dug beneath the loom to provide extra space, a solution that could leave distinctive traces in the ground, offering archaeologists valuable clues about the loom's exact placement (Gleba 2008, 123–4).

2.4 Weaving tools

Looms have rarely been preserved in archaeological contexts, both due to their perishable nature and their potential reuse as construction materials or fuel. No complete looms are known from the Near East, and our knowledge is based mainly on iconographical sources and scant archaeological traces, including holes in the ground and charred beams, as well as objects directly pertaining to looms. These include heddles, warp spacers, as well as swords, beaters, spatulae, and loom weights.

2.4.1 Loom weights

Loom weights are objects that are normally made of clay or stone, which were attached to the warping threads to give it tension. Given their non-perishable nature, these objects are the most likely part of the warp-weighted loom to survive in archaeological contexts. They can have very different shapes, dimensions, and weights, even in the same context, and are at times difficult to recognise. In fact, weights can be used for several purposes, the most common being counterweights, for example for matting or tensioning straw roofs. They can also be attached to nets for fishing, and this usage tends to be underestimated in archaeological studies. Clay or roughly baked clay weights can certainly be excluded from fishing activities, but stones, pebbles and well baked weights can be used for both activities (weaving and fishing). Weights can even be used in looms to add tension to the warp or beams without being actual loom weights (Johl 1924, 7; Andersson Strand 2018, 24). Context can help distinguish a loom weight from a counterweight, as loom weights are often found in large quantities and, in some fortunate cases, arranged in distinct rows between charred beams or post-holes (Barber 1991, 93, 101–2). However, weights attached to nets can also fall in rows, leaving archaeological traces similar to those of loom weights. Therefore, considering the material of fabrication is crucial in making an accurate identification (see for example Ulucak (Çilingirõglu 2009, 24).

Shapes can vary a great deal and depend on both cultural traditions and practical necessities. Some types of loom weights are found only in certain regions, such as the typical Minoan discoid weights, while others appear to be ubiquitous. Their shape and dimensions can deeply influence the fabric that can be woven on a loom, so there are limits to their variability in this respect. For loom weights, similarly to spindle whorls, the typology and terminology adopted for this work largely depends on CTR typology, but has been adapted to cover the specificity of the Levantine production, as well as traditional scholarly terminology (*e.g.* torus=doughnut shape). Discoid weights are very seldom found in the Levant but they have been kept; other shapes are simpler, such as the cylinder. Finally, a biconical shape with vertical perforation was added. Egyptian weights, which are entirely different from all other known typology and very rare in the catalogue, have not been added but will be discussed separately in Chapter 5 (Fig. 2.9).

Weight plays a crucial role in selecting loom weights during warping, as the required tension varies depending on the thickness of the warp threads and the number of fibres. Thicker yarns demand greater tension and therefore heavier loom weights, whereas thinner threads require lighter weights to prevent breakage. However, loom weights do not correspond to individual threads; rather, they are attached to groups of threads that collectively require a specific amount of tension. For example, a 100 g weight could support 10 threads needing 10 g of tension each or five threads requiring 20 g each (Olofsson *et al.* 2015, 88).

Experimental research from the Tools and Textiles – Texts and Contexts programme (Mårtensson *et al.* 2009, 390, 393) has demonstrated that while it is technically possible to weave with fewer than four or more than 30 threads per weight, such setups are highly unlikely. The number of threads per weight, along with the loom weight's thickness, directly influences the thread count of the fabric. Additionally, experiments have shown that the total width of the loom weight row dictates the final width of the cloth, regardless of the initial border width (Olofsson *et al.* 2015, 91–2). These findings highlight the importance of weight and width in determining the type of fabric that could be produced with a given set of loom weights.

Weave structures further illustrate these relationships. The simplest weave on a warp-weighted loom is tabby, which requires two rows of weights. More complex structures, such as twill (2/2), need four rows. However, in the period and contexts under examination, twill is unknown in textiles, with tabby being the predominant weave. The only attested twill in this timeframe appears in basketry (Bender Jørgensen *et al.* 2023). Meanwhile, tapestries can be woven on any loom type and do not require specialised tools (Smith 2013, 165).

Despite these technical considerations, archaeological finds rarely consist of loom weights of uniform size

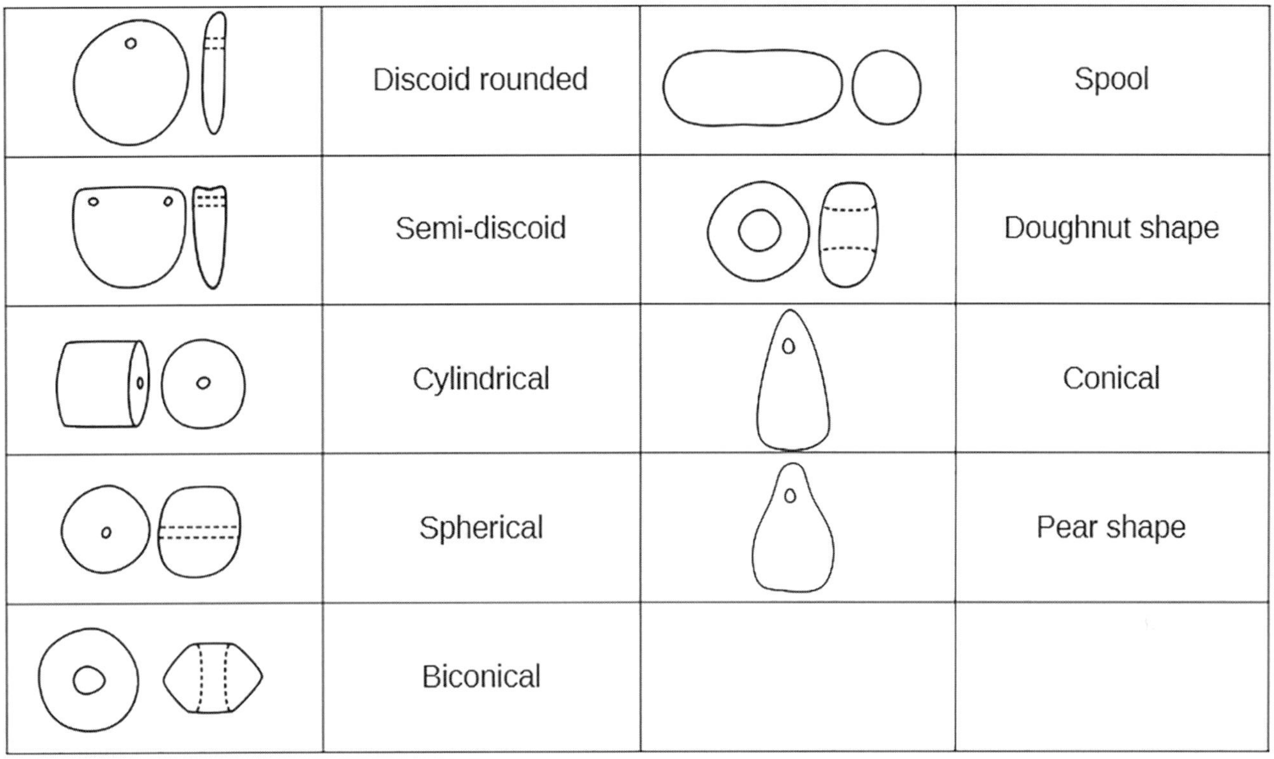

Figure 2.9. Loom weights typology (adapted from Andersson Strand and Nosch 2015, fig. 5.1.4)

and mass, raising questions about their practical use. Ethnographic studies provide valuable insights into this apparent inconsistency. Hoffmann (1964, 65) observed that weavers sometimes used weights of varying masses within the same loom setup, adjusting the number of attached threads accordingly – heavier weights supporting more threads, and lighter ones supporting fewer. In other cases, even when loom weights were relatively homogeneous, slightly heavier weights were deliberately placed at the edges, likely to reinforce the lateral selvedges. These observations suggest a level of flexibility in weight distribution, challenging the assumption that uniformity was always a priority in weaving practices.

2.4.2 Spatulae and pin beaters

Spatulae and pin beaters are a broad category that has not found a precise definition. Although they are known from all over the world and in many prehistoric studies (Cheval and Radi 2013) are definitively considered as tools linked to textile production, in the area under examination they have been considered in many different ways (tools for eating, writing, cutting, piercing, etc.; Ariel 1990, 129).

I propose here a distinction between spatulae and pin beaters. The first is a flat object, generally obtained from the ribs of cows or, more rarely, other mammals. The second are metapodial bones, mainly of sheep and goats, left unworked on one side and cut to obtain a point on the other side (Doyen 1986, 33–9). This distinction is dictated by their potential different usage due to their shape and thickness. While the first type is very thin and can be inserted between the warp threads and parallel to the weft, the second must be manipulated following the warp threads, and was certainly not inserted in the shed.

Doyen proposes several usages for spatulae during weaving, including beating the weft thread, disentangling yarns, or fixing small errors and knots (Doyen 1986, 51). He connects them with the appearance of a specific typology of loom weights; however, this hypothesis has been contested (Cecchini 1992, 16) on the basis of the archaeological evidence, which does not match the chronology of those specific loom weights. She does agree with their interpretation as textile tools, especially for beating the threads (Cecchini 2000, 229). In the work on Tell el-Amarna's textile production (Kemp and Vogelsang-Eastwood 2001, 358–73), the objects defined here as bone spatulae are called pin beaters (Fig. 2.10).

The pin beaters included in this study are very simple tools, made from metapodial bones with a point on one end. This category may include a very large and undefined set of tools, which could be used for very different purposes (Levy 2020, 30). However, direct ethnographic evidence in Peru has suggested the need to consider these tools more carefully, and to at least insert those that are clearly recognisable into the research. The Peruvian weavers use

Figure 2.10. Ancient Egyptian bone spatula (courtesy of Manchester Museum, n. 555)

Figure 2.11. Modern pin beater used in Peru

this tool to keep the warp in order while weaving, meaning they pass the beater over the warp parallel to the direction of weft. They did this very quickly, several times, and with a degree of strength that would have destroyed the thin and fragile spatulae (Fig. 2.11).

2.4.3 Sewing needles

Needles have been used since the Late Palaeolithic period (Barber 1991, 39; Gilligan *et al.* 2024) although only a small quantity are known for the periods under consideration here. Several types of needles exist today, and it is highly probable that needles for different purposes started to develop quite early in history, not only for sewing textiles. Sewing needles were probably the first to be developed, and have different dimensions according to the different tasks they are/were used for. Sewing a coarser textile is obviously easier and quicker with a large needle, but would ruin a fine, dense fabric, for which a smaller and thinner needle is required. Needles served a variety of functions beyond textile production, playing a crucial role in crafting sails, cushions, mattresses, and nets, as well as in tapestry weaving, basketry, and sewing skins or leather. Due to these diverse applications, needles were made in different sizes to accommodate various materials and techniques. However, given the current state of documentation, it is not possible to determine the specific purpose of each needle with certainty. In this study, a distinction is made between needles and bodkins – the latter being thicker tools designed for threading cords or ribbons through pre-made holes in garments. This differentiation helps clarify their respective functions within ancient textile and craft production. Levy (2020, 70, 72, 175, 244) considers them as tools for netting and looping, but in the case of the Egyptian ones it is impossible to know. However, a very large number of objects fall into this category, and since measurements are the only parameter used to distinguish bodkins from needles, the methodology used is far from accurate. Therefore, all the objects are examined together within the vast category of needles and bodkins, being aware of the multiple functions for which they could have been used.

2.4.4 Combs

Combs are essential in the preparation of raw fibres for spinning. Wool, in fact, after being plucked/cut from the sheep, needs to be sorted into different qualities of fibre. The final thread and cloth largely depend on the accuracy of this operation. Several criteria can be employed for sorting, including colour, fineness, or length, and separating long hair from short underwool can be easily done with a long-toothed comb. Moreover, combing helps to remove dirt and tangles, making the process of spinning easier, and the thread spun more even (Andersson Strand 2015, 44).

Nowadays, flax requires three different combs for separating the fibres, after rippling, retting, breaking, and scutching. The combs have different distances between the long iron teeth enabling workers to separate tows from long fibres and to separate short and thick fibres (used for cords and strings) from long and thin fibres (used for weaving).[3] Such tools do not exist in the archaeological record, as combs with iron teeth used for wool preparation appear to be absent until at least the Roman period (Wild 1970, figs 9–10; Rast-Eischer 2008, 161–2; Breniquet 2010).

Wooden, ivory, and bone combs, instead, are frequently found in archaeological records; sometimes excavators sort them in relation to fibre processing, rather than combing hair. When studying the Egyptian and Levantine artefacts, however, actual tools for combing fibres cannot be recognised, with the possible exception of the comb from Wadi Murabba'at (Schick 1995). On the contrary, many objects come from funerary contexts and were certainly linked to hair combing.

Egyptian tombs frequently show the presence of wooden combs in both female and male graves since the Predynastic period (Capel *et al.* 1996, 75), with a very large variety of typologies according to the period (Ashton 2011; de Marco and Marini 2023; de Marco and Eschenbrenner-Diemer forthcoming). Egyptian tombs, however, rarely contain textile tools – except for a few examples from the entire Pharaonic period. This suggests that all of these combs were likely intended as toiletry items.

A similar situation might be suggested for the tombs of Jericho, where combs are frequently found, especially wooden combs dated to the MBA. Jericho is one of the very few sites in the Levant where organic artefacts have been partially preserved. Most of these combs were found near the head or chest of the deceased, and the discovery of hairs plaited in the same points enables us to determine their use as hair combs (Kenyon 1960, 250, 341, 391, fig. 221; Kenyon and Holland 1965, 462). Furthermore, many combs were found in baskets, together with wigs and other toilet implements, but very seldom with possible textile tools. Since the combs from Jericho present a very large typology (single or double, and with short or long teeth), it seems that all the combs known from the archaeological record in the Levant are likely connected with hair combing and not fibre processing. While some of these findings may have been related to textile activities, the available documentation does not allow for a definitive conclusion. Additionally, all ancient Egyptian depictions of spinning and weaving show flax fibre preparation being done by hand or possibly with two sticks, but never with combs. For these reasons, combs have been excluded from this study, except for certain objects that were clearly not used for personal care.

Notes

1 Hand spinning, spinning by twisting a hooked stick, rotation of spindle in hand, grasped spindle, supported hand spindle, suspended hand spindle. Most of the later texts on this subject use this classification as a starting point (Crowfoot 1921; 1931; Barber 1991, 39–50; Kemp and Vogelsang-Eastwood 2001, 74–81).

2 The notation of the yarn composition can vary among scholars. Given the large predominance of Egyptian yarns in this work, it has been decided to follow the one proposed for Amarna, following Kemp and Vogelsang-Eastwood (2001, 58–9)

3 I would like to thank the staff at the Museo Unico Arte Tessile Sarda, Samugheo in Sardinia, for showing me the implements and for kindly answering all my questions.

3

From fibres to textiles

This chapter explores the evidence of fibre exploitation and textile findings in the Near East and Egypt, specifically the first discovery of each fibre and technique. The chapter provides a framework to insert textile tools and connect them to textile remains. It will not only focus on Levantine and Egyptian finds but also a wider geographical area in order to understand which types of fibres were available in Egypt and the Southern Levant during the long period under study. Evidence from the Mediterranean area, Mesopotamia, Iran, and India will therefore be included, although the focus will remain on the geographical area under examination.

3.1 Flax, hemp, and other bast fibres

3.1.1 Flax

There are around 230 species of *Linum* around the world, but the most common wild flax is *Linum angustifolium*: it is widespread in the Mediterranean and throughout most of Europe and produces blue flowers, while other sub-species are characterised by pink, yellow, and white flowers (Baines 1989, 13). *Linum angustifolium* is probably the wild ancestor of the domestic *Linum usitatissimum*, from which the fibre used for textile production is extracted. According to Zohary (Zohary *et al.* 2012), the wild variety grows in the Mediterranean and Atlantic coastal areas as well as in Iran and Iraq, where it was first domesticated, and subsequently it reached the Nile Delta (Larsson 2013). Flax is the term used to denote the plant and its products, seeds, and fibres, while linen is the final product of the process, meaning the yarn and the fabric (Baines 1989, 13). The stem of flax is composed of a central void, called lumen, and a woody core, around which the fibres, known as bast, protect and support the central part where nutrients are carried, enclosed by a cortex and an epidermis. Fibres occur in bundles, which extend from the roots of the plant to the tip, and are glued into a substance composed of pectineus gums, waxes, and non-cellulosic materials, which must be removed in order to prepare the fibres for spinning. The number of bundles in a stem can vary, but is generally between 15 and 35, with each bundle containing between 10 and 40 individual fibres or ultimate bundles; the ultimate bundles generally remain together during the transformation into linen (Kemp and Vogelsang-Eastwood 2001), but the finest Ancient Egyptian textiles can reach 1–2 ultimate bundles (Cooke *et al.* 1991, 71). They are three times thicker at the root end than at the top. The main component of fibres is cellulose, with small cells, which overlap at regular intervals. A single fibre can measure between 45 and 100 cm and its appearance is smooth, cylindrical, with joints along its length where the cells overlap.

3.1.2 Hemp

Hemp (*Cannabis sativa*) is another bast fibre, which has a longer stem than flax (up to 5 m tall) and from which coarser fibres and textile can be produced. Thanks to its strength, it is well-suited to producing ropes, cords, and sails due to its resistance to seawater (Peyronel 2004, 31). If the association of Fiber A with hemp in Midgley's report (Brunton 1937, 145) is correct, then it is highly probable that it was used in Badarian, Predynastic, and pan-graves cloths.[1]

Other ancient findings from Europe date its first usage to 5500–4500 BC, although these consist only of seeds, not actual fabrics (Peyronel 2004, 32). Since it has a very similar structure to flax, it is very difficult to correctly recognise it. They differ in that flax has a natural s-twist, while hemp has a natural Z-twist; this means that the fibre, once wet and stuck at one end, will start to twist at the other, following its natural inclination. More recent studies have claimed that hemp was in use in the Levant in the Chalcolithic phase. DNA analysis showed that not only was it used to produce textiles, but also that a mixture of hemp and flax was employed, making identification of the two fibres extremely difficult without sophisticated analysis (Murphy *et al.* 2011). More recently, an article by Rodriguez Frade (2022) argued that several items from at least the New Kingdom were made of hemp. The process of preparing hemp fibres is very similar to that of flax.

3.1.3 Nettle and ramie

Nettle (*Urtica dioica*) might be employed in textile manufacture; nettle stems contain bast fibres and they are extracted with a similar process as flax (Bergfjord *et al.* 2012). It might be used to produce cloth as well as sacks and ropes. It has been suggested that the use of this plant as a textile and basketry fibre could be very ancient. However, this interpretation remains uncertain, as it relies only on imprints found at Dolní Věstonice in the Czech Republic, dated to 32,000–29,000 years ago, which may or may not belong to *Urtica* sp. (Adovasio *et al.* 2001).

Another member of the *Urtica* family is *Boehmeria nivea*, from which the more widely used ramie is obtained. Nettle fibres have been positively recognised in a textile from Kastelli Chania in Greece that is dated to the Minoan period (Moulhérat and Spantidaki 2009). The fragment of fabric is a dense tabby weave, weft-faced, decorated with an additional thread. The warp is made of S-plied thread, probably flax fibres, while the weft consists of un-plied threads of animal origin, probably goat hair. The additional thread has been identified as being S-plied, of plant origin, and its characteristics make an identification with nettle fibres highly probable, more specifically ramie (Moulhérat and Spantidaki 2009). The use of goat hair and ramie in the Minoan period is very interesting, because it proves the continuity of usage of a larger number of fibres, besides the more common flax and sheep's wool known by textual sources.

3.1.4 Other bast fibres

Other bast fibres, such as those derived from tree bast (including lime, willow, and oak), are described as challenging to process and require multiple steps to produce fine fibres. Tree bark is traditionally harvested in spring, when it can be easily removed along with all bast layers and then left to rot in water to facilitate fibre extraction (Reichert 2020, 166). Evidence suggests that these fibres were likely already in use during the Palaeolithic and Mesolithic periods (Reichert 2020, 166). By the Neolithic, techniques had advanced sufficiently to allow for the production of fine threads (Rast-Eicher 2018, 117). Tree bast fibres are well documented in European archaeological contexts (Rast-Eicher 2005, 117–19). However, their presence in the Near East has only been recognised in recent years (Shamir and Rast-Eicher 2020; Rast-Eicher *et al.* 2021; Bender Jørgensen *et al.* 2023). This discovery raises questions about whether some past identifications of bast fibres as flax may have been incorrect. Given these uncertainties, it has been deemed necessary to discuss flax and other bast fibres together to ensure a more accurate understanding of their historical use.

3.1.5 Fibre preparation

Linen is a fibre that is well suited to clothing, but also for curtains, bedsheets, and towels. It is comfortable, fresh and doesn't itch; it can be washed several times without wearing out, and tends to become softer after lots of use (Harris 2010, 106). It is easy to clean and remove dirt, and its breathability makes it a perfect choice for warm and dusty countries (Barber 1991, 15). All these qualities help to explain its popularity in ancient times, in spite of the difficult and time-consuming process to make it. Egyptian representations show only part of this process – the moment of harvesting and the preparation of yarn for spinning – leaving some doubt as to how exactly fibres were extracted from bundles. Generally, the process includes plucking the plant, beating or rippling it to eliminate the seed heads, retting, drying and beating or scutching it, and finally hackling the stems (Baines 1989, 13–14; Kemp and Vogelsang-Eastwood 2001, 25–34). In antiquity, the system was briefly but exhaustively described by Pliny (Forbes 1956, 29, for description and comment). Stems are dried for a few days, and the seed heads are separated by beating them with a wooden mallet, or with the aid of a wooden comb. To separate stems from fibres, retting is the method that was usually practised in ancient times (although there is no evidence of this available for Ancient Egypt) (Kemp and Vogelsang-Eastwood 2001, 70). The stems can then either be submerged in a flowing stream or low pools, or left in the field and exposed to the effects of dew and rain. The aim is to dissolve the pectinous layer that surrounds the fibres by fermentation. The first method is certainly faster, and produces a golden fibre, while the second yields fibres of a darker and greyish colour. At the end of retting, the fibres must be dried again and cleaned of their bark and woody core, which can be done with sticks (willowing), mallets, or by using a wooden knife to scrape the fibres (scutching). Finally, fibres must be combed (hackling) to separate the long fibres needed for spinning from the shorter (tow), which can either be used to produce a coarser yarn or as padding for cushions and mattresses (Baines 1989, 172–80).

An alternative method requires stripping the fibres from the stem, as described in the volume of Amarna (Kemp and Vogelsang-Eastwood 2001, 25–34) and spliced together. In the *chaîne opératoire*, splicing refers to the manual joining of individual fibres, which are then formed into roves of spliced fibres before being twisted or plied together using a spindle.

Splicing has been identified in Egyptian material over a long period (Bellinger 1959; Barber 1991; Cooke *et al.* 1991; Cartwright *et al.* 1998; Kemp and Vogelsang-Eastwood 2001; Gleba and Harris 2019). It has been observed as early as the Neolithic in the Fayum textiles (Gleba and Harris 2019) and appears to have fallen out of use only around 600 BC (Cartwright *et al.* 1998). In the Southern Levant, splicing has been discussed in relation to the Chalcolithic period and it has been argued to have ceased by the end of the MBA (Shamir 2015).

This suggests that all Egyptian textiles and yarns referenced in this study, along with the vast majority of those from the Southern Levant, were most likely produced through splicing and twisting rather than spinning and plying. As the author has not had direct access to every piece of material, the analyses cited in this text rely on previous scholarly studies, where splicing may or may not have been noted. While the final twist of the yarn can therefore be considered reliable, the data regarding spun yarn may not be, and should be reconsidered in light of the evidence presented by Gleba and Harris (2019).

Flax can be cultivated both for oil seeds and fibres, but it is not possible to obtain both seeds and good quality fibres. To produce seeds, the plants need more space between them in order to have a shorter plant but with more branches. For textile production, the longer the fibre the better it is (Karg 2020). To obtain long stalks, seeds must be sown close to each other so the plant will grow taller with branches on the top. The moment of harvesting also influences the final result of the fibre, as young, green plants give finer and better quality fibres than ripe, yellow plants. To preserve the entire length of the plant, it should not be cut but plucked.

3.1.6 First flax/bast textiles

Flax produces both fibres for textiles and seeds that are useful to eat and produce oil, and its stems may also have been used in early times to produce basketry or cordage, because of its great strength. It is not known which of these products first encouraged man to domesticate it (Karg 2020; Karg *et al.* 2023), but this certainly happened in very early times. The claim that the use of wild flax fibres in Georgia date to at least 30,000 years ago (Kvavadze *et al.* 2009) was later refuted (Bergfjord *et al.* 2010). A similar fate befell the findings from Wadi Murabbaʿat in the Judean Desert. In this case, the thread was not discovered during a formal excavation but was instead purchased from the Bedouin, who had looted the caves. However, analysis using Accelerator Mass Spectrometry confirmed that it dates to 10,220±45 BP. The thread is wound around wooden pegs to fasten them together, forming a sort of wooden comb, and is also coated with bitumen. The yarn is described as Z-spun and S-plied, creating a twine structure that likely originally covered most of the comb (Schick 1995, 201). In a recent article, the thread is described as made with two fine bands of a bast fibre, probably tree bast and using the splicing technique (Shamir and Rast-Eicher 2020).

The first known thread comes from Ohalo II in Israel and is dated to 21,000 cal BC (Nadel *et al.* 1994). It was not possible to determine the fibre, but it was a plant fibre, probably the stem or leaf of a monocotyledonous plant (grass) (Nadel *et al.* 1994, 452).

The earliest examples of linen fabrics come from the well renowned Naḥal Ḥemar cave in the Southern Judean Desert, and are dated to the Pre-Pottery Neolithic B (6900–6300 BC) (Schick 1988). Within this cave, hundreds of artefacts made of vegetable fibres (including *Linum* sp.) were preserved, including cordage, baskets, mats, yarn and fabrics (produced with different techniques like looping, knotting, twining but NOT weaving) (Shamir 2014, 143). The fabrics are not actual textiles since they are not woven; other techniques such as knotted netting and knotted looping are employed, but the most frequent technique is weft twining (Schick 1988). Both warps and wefts are plied S2, *i (Shamir and Rast-Eicher 2020, 28) (i=unspun roves of spliced fibres; Gleba and Harris 2019). Several needle-shuttles and awls were also present, but no other tools directly connected with textile production (*i.e.* whorls or parts of looms) (Shamir and Rast-Eicher 2020, 30).

Woven textiles were found in the Neolithic levels of Çatal Höyük (6700–6500 BC) (Rast-Eicher *et al.* 2021; 2023). These textiles have been preserved due to the extreme temperatures generated by the great fire that destroyed the buildings of Level VI. Beneath the houses and shrines, layers of clay sealed several tombs, which contained textile fragments wrapped around bodies. Both twined fabrics and tabby weave textiles were found, displaying variations in weave density and thread thickness.

The identification of these fibres has been the subject of considerable debate in recent years, which will be briefly summarised here to illustrate the complexity of the issue. Due to their brittle and charred condition, observing the characteristic features of the fibres under a polarising microscope is challenging. Helbæk (1963, 44) was the first to study these fibres, though without advanced analytical techniques, and concluded that most were made of wool, while some strips consisted of plant fibres. A subsequent microscopic analysis by Burnham (1965, 170) identified the presence of surface scales, but the absence of kemp and guard hairs in the textiles led the author to question this identification. Ryder (1965, 175; Ryder and Gabra-Sanders 1987, 91; Vogelsang-Eastwood 1988), ruled out the presence of wool after conducting multiple fibre tests, including SEM analysis. More recently, newly discovered textile fragments from further excavations at the site were subjected to SEM analysis, confirming that they were bast fibres (Fuller *et al.* 2014, 121–2), more specifically tree bast fibres (Rast-Eicher *et al.* 2021). As with the case of Naḥal Ḥemar, the new analysis show that yarns were constructed through splicing (S, *2z), and not as spun and plied (S, 2z).

Flax has been suggested in PPN levels at the Anatolian site of Çayönü, but the organic materials preserved are only carbonised or mineralised. A pseudomorph fragment of twined cloth has been found wrapped around a tool made from an antler and dated to the 8th millennium BC (Vogelsang-Eastwood 1993). Fibres were not spun but rather twisted together (as in twine) and set on a frame made of four sticks, but not produced on an actual loom. Also, linseeds were found in Çayönü that were recognised as wild flax, probably *Linum bienne*, but certainly not *Linum usitatissimum*, which is instead attested in Tell Ramad (Syria) around 7190–6700 cal BC (van Zeist and Roller 1991, 82).

Jarmo, in northern Iraq, provided information about weaving skills but unfortunately not on the raw materials. Impressions of woven textiles and basketry at this site have been found preserved in clay and bitumen, and among the textiles, tabby and basket weaves are present. All these impressions are dated to 7000–6000 BC (Adovasio 1975, 224).[2]

The Late Chalcolithic period (4500–3700 cal BC) has preserved a larger number of linen textiles, especially from caves in the Judean desert. These caves were used as refuges, burial places, and sometimes for living in during the Chalcolithic period, for a short time in EBI (Davidovich 2013), and again in the Roman Period. Textiles from the earlier period are quite different from those of the Roman period, both in terms of fibres and techniques. Wool, for instance, seems not to be used yet, and thread production is characterised by splicing. Several caves have yielded linen textiles, but the most famous are the Cave of the Treasure, Nahal Mishmar (a burial site rich with textiles, basketry, and cordage) and the Cave of the Warrior.[3] Chalcolithic threads are generally described as S-spun and S-plied (S, 2s) but with clear evidence of the use of splicing; the weave is generally a simple tabby, sometimes warp-faced, with very few decorations made by hollows and soumak. No dyes have thus far been recognised, but black stripes made of paint or asphalt are visible. Flax has been suggested to have been cultivated in the Jordan Valley at sites like ʿEn Gedi, Jericho, or the Beth Sheʿan Valley, rather than being imported from elsewhere like Egypt (Shamir 2015, 21; Levy 2020, 114), but no specific studies on fibre provenance have been conducted. This is inferred by the very different quality of contemporary Egyptian textiles, but due to the paucity of evidence for Egyptian production in this period, it seems difficult to make such a strong statement.

Egypt has preserved a very limited number of archaeological sites dating to the period between *c.* 7000 and 5400 BC (Shaw 2003b, 35), and so far, no traces of textiles from this timeframe have been found. The earliest known Egyptian textile dates to the Neolithic Fayum A culture (*c.* 5000 BC) and was discovered alongside evidence of basketry. This textile was found in Upper K Pits, a large series of Neolithic granaries in the Fayum, northeast of Kom W. Specifically, the linen fragment was located inside a disintegrated cooking pot and was also found loose in the gravel outside the annex granary to silo 16 (Caton-Thompson and Gardner 1934, 46) accompanied by two oval polishing pebbles and a fish vertebra. Initial analysis failed to confirm whether the fabric was made of *Linum usitatissimum* (flax); however, in silo 59, a flax seed of *L. usitatissimum* was identified. A more recent examination of the textile has now confirmed its original identification as linen (Jones and Oldfield 2007, 34). The fabric is a tabby-woven textile, composed of loosely spun yarn with a Z-twist and S-ply, exhibiting an uneven weave (Jones 2008, 107). However, in light of more recent studies (Gleba and Harris 2019), it should probably be considered as Z-spliced and S-ply (S, *2z).

Several textiles have been found in the Badarian tombs (*c.* 4400–4000), but these occur less frequently than skin garments (Brunton and Caton-Thompson 1928, 40). This is an interesting detail, since the subsequent tradition would tend to exclude the use of animal skins and fibres from funerary rituals. These skin garments were more frequently worn by men than women and there is hair inside, in contact with the bodies. Generally, they are goat and antelope skins, but in at least two cases, black fur has been recognised. Linen garments, shrouds, and bandages are present, but less frequently and in poor condition. They can occur in the same burial as skins, and can also cover the head of the deceased, while skins seem not to go higher than the shoulders. Unfortunately, these textiles are in such poor condition that it is difficult to recognise the fibre from which they are made. In his reports, T. Midgley states that they are probably not made of linen but of a vegetable fibre like grass (Brunton and Caton-Thompson 1928, 67). Flax was known in these sites, since one flax seed has been recognised (Badari tomb 3000, object 3, identified as *Linum bienne*; Brunton and Caton-Thompson 1928, 63). Recent analysis conducted by J. Jones (2002, 326), however, is questioning the identification of fibres in the early analysis and it is likely that most of the Egyptian fibres were actually flax. One peculiarity of Badarian textiles is that the warp and weft are not at right angles, but rather weft yarns are placed diagonally (with an angle that varies between 20–40°) to prevent the textile from fraying. The same characteristic is present in certain Predynastic textiles, but seem to disappear from Naqada III onwards (Jones 2008, 113). It has also been suggested that a change in the weaving equipment occurred in the Predynastic period, but this has not yet been confirmed.

Table 3.1. Spinning directions in first textiles

Date	*Site*	*Description*
Neolithic	Wadi Murabba'at	Z-spliced, S-plied (Schick 1995, 201; Shamir and Rast-Eicher 2020)
	Naḥal Ḥemar	cordage Z-plied nets Z-spliced, S-plied; fewer S-spliced, Z-plied examples of cabled threads (Shamir 2014, 143)
	Çatal Höyük	spliced, S-plied (S2*i) (Burnham 1965, 171; Bender Jørgensen and Rast-Eicher 2022)
	Fayum fragment	Z-spun, S-plied (Jones 2008, 107)
Chalcolithic	Badarian textiles	Z-spun, S-plied (Brunton and Caton-Thompson 1928, fig. lix)
	Nahal Mishmar and other Chalcolithic caves	S-spun, S-plied (Schick 2002, 231)
	Cave of the Warriors	Z-spliced, S-plied (S2*z) (Gleba and Harris 2019)
	Predynastic textiles	Transition from Z to S (Jones 2008, 111) Naqada IIB S-spun (or spliced?), S-plied

A significantly greater number of linen textiles have survived in Egypt from the Predynastic period onwards (Jones 2008, 101), providing a more comprehensive understanding of Egyptian textile production than that of any other ancient culture. However, it is important to remember that the vast majority of these textiles come from tombs, which inherently restricts the range of cloth types that have been preserved. As a result, our knowledge of the garments and fabrics used in everyday life remains limited.

It has been observed that the earliest flax threads were spun in the Z-direction, while the plying followed the opposite S-direction. Notably, this pattern is consistent in textiles from both the Near East and Egypt, as shown in Table 3.1. During the Chalcolithic period, a shift in spinning direction has been identified, with S-spun and S-plied threads becoming more prevalent, at least in the Levant (Schick 2002, 223–4). However, this claim needs to be reconsidered in light of the widespread use of splicing in Ancient Egyptian and Levantine textiles (Gleba and Harris 2019; Shamir and Rast-Eicher 2020). While the plying direction remains accurate, the so-called spinning direction may actually reflect the splicing direction instead. Therefore, this data should be approached with greater caution.

According to Jones (2008, 109, 111) flax textiles in Egypt began to be characterised by the combination of S-spun and S-plied threads (or better S-spliced, S-plied?) in the Egyptian Predynastic period. This possibly begins at the end of the Naqada I phase but continues during the Naqada IIA phase; by the beginning of the IIB phase, textiles show a complete adoption of the S-spun, S-plied method. This structure would remain prevalent for all the subsequent Pharaonic phases, with Z-twisting only found to a lesser extent. Textiles generally show an S, 2s structure of threads, both for warp and weft, although Z-twist can occasionally be observed on nets and sewing threads (Kemp and Vogelsang-Eastwood 2001, 60). In Amarna textiles, for example, the S direction for splicing and plying covers 99% of the entire set of samples (Kemp and Vogelsang-Eastwood 2001, 59).

Splicing has been identified in Egyptian textiles as late as 600 BC (Cartwright *et al.* 1998), while Shamir argues that it is no longer found in the Southern Levant after the MBA (Shamir 2015), and Levy states that it fell out of use after the middle of the 1st millennium BC (Levy 2020, 117; Table 3.2).

3.2 Cotton

Cotton is native to India, Senegal, and Sudan, where first evidence of the plant was found (Fuller *et al.* 2024). It does not belong to the bast family, but rather is derived from many trees and herbs of the *Gossypium* family. Its fibres are very short and grow on branches as padding for seeds. It is generally thought that cotton arrived in the Mediterranean area from the Indus Valley, where it was used to produce textiles in Mohenjo Daro and Harappa from at least 2500 BC onwards (Peyronel 2004, 33). After these first examples, cotton disappears from Mesopotamia and the Levant, only to reappear in the 1st millennium BC; garments made of cotton fibres have been found in the Assyrian Queen's Tomb in the 8th century BC (Gaspa 2017, 50). Also, texts appear to indicate the exploitation of cotton during the 1st millennium. The Akkadian word *kitinnû* and the Neo-Babylonian term *karpassu* have been proposed to be identified as cotton, as well as *biršu* in Assyrian texts. The first mention of cotton trees appears in the royal text of King Sennacherib (704–681 BC), which quotes a 'tree bearing wool'. However, the origin of these trees is indicated as Babylonia, so this fibre may have been known in that region before it arrived in Assyria (Gaspa 2017, 157–8).

Table 3.2. Occurrences of spinning and weaving scenes in the Egyptian iconography

Object/site/period	*Description*
Representations of spinning and weaving scenes	
Bowl from el-Badari	Bowl with representation of a horizontal loom. On the side, two figures beside vertical poles might have been engaged in warping (Cortes 2011, 94).
Saqqara, VI Dynasty (Old Kingdom)	Relief of a man with a spindle on one hand (note the conical spindle whorl!) and a ball of yarn under left leg (Firth and Gunn 1926, 36; Barber 1991, 76).
Tomb of Baqt, Beni Hasan (Middle Kingdom)	Upper register: three men spinning, one with grasped spindle, two drop spindle. One man preparing a net, two men preparing balls of yarn. Lower register: four women couching on the floor preparing roves; three spinners, each with two spindles (drop spindle) and two spinning bowls; seven women attending two looms (Newberry and Griffith 1893, fig. iv).
Tomb of Khety, Beni Hasan (Middle Kingdom)	Upper register: three men spinning, one with grasped spindle, two drop spindle. Two men preparing a net, one man matting. Lower register: four women couching on the floor preparing roves; three spinners, each with two spindles (drop spindle) and two spinning bowls, five in total because they share the same bowls; seven women attending two looms (Newberry and Griffith 1893, fig. xiii).
Tomb of Khnumhotep, Beni Hasan (Middle Kingdom)	A spinner with one drop spindle and two yarns, two bowls and a crouching woman preparing fibres. A horizontal ground loom with two female weavers and a male supervisor (Newberry and Griffith 1893, fig. xix)
Tomb of Daga, Thebes (Middle Kingdom)	Upper register: a woman warping, two women crouching and attending to a horizontal loom. Lower register: three women preparing fibres, one attending to a spinning bowl and another spinning with two drop spindles (de Garis Davies 1913, fig. xxxvii).
Tomb of Djehutyhotep, el Bersheh (Middle Kingdom)	Upper register: five women couching on the floor preparing fibres/roves. Three spinners with one spinning bowl each. One woman attending warping on three pegs. Lower register: Two women pulling threads from boxes of balls of yarn (?). Three women warping a loom (Newberry and Griffith 1893, fig. xxiv).
Tomb of Sarenput I, Elephantine, (Middle Kingdom)	Upper register: one person couching on the floor preparing fibres/roves. Two spinners with two spinning bowls each (Müller 1940, 41).
Neferhotep, Thebes, 18th dynasty (New Kingdom)	Representation of temple estate: a vertical two-beam loom with one operator and probably a second one on the right, with a second weaver (de Garis Davies and de Garis Davies 1933, 38, pl. xlix).
Tomb of Djehutynefer, Thebes, 18th Dynasty (New Kingdom)	Two people preparing fibres, two preparing coils of yarn. Grasped spinning scene, one spinner, two spindles fixed to a ring each and both rotating in a bowl. Two vertical two-beam looms with a total of three weavers (de Garis Davies 1929, fig. 1a).
Talatat, Tell el-Amarna, 18th Dynasty (New Kingdom)	Talatat representing a possible two-beam loom (Kemp and Vogelsang-Eastwood 2001, 338, fig. 9.22).
Tomb of Neferrenpet, Sheikh Abd el-Qurna Chief of the weavers in the Ramesseum (Ramesses II)	Two people couching on the floor preparing roves. Two warping frames with an attending person each. Four vertical two-beam looms with a total of five weavers (men and a woman). Upper register in a very bad state, a man, four women and one or two children are employed. Scale with coils of thread and raw material (white and yellow) (de Garis Davies 1948, fig. xxxv).
Tomb of Ramose, Sheikh Abd el-Qurna, 19th Dynasty (New Kingdom)	Two groups of workers: each group has one person preparing skeins, one warping on vertical poles in U-shape, and finally two people working on a vertical two-beam loom. Note the presence of a warp spacer on the loom (Rodríguez Frade 2019).
Ostracon from Deir el-Medina (New Kingdom)	Grasped spinning scene: two spindles hanging from a ring (Vandier d'Abbadie 1937, fig. lxiv).
Funerary papyrus of Dirpu, 21st dynasty, Deir el-Bahari (Third Intermediate Period)	The deceased is taken by hand by a cat-headed goddess and in the other hand carries a high-whorl spindle with dome shaped spindle whorl and thread wound around the shaft. (Piankoff 1957, fol. 7).

(Continued)

Table 3.2. (Continued)

Object/site/period	Description
Funerary models	
Weaving model, tomb of Meketra, Thebes, 11th Dynasty (Middle Kingdom)	Three couched women preparing fibres; three spinners with two spindles and a spinning bowl each; two women warping on the wall with a spindle each; two horizontal ground looms, with three weavers in total (Winlock 1955, 29–33, pls 26–7, 66–7).
Weaving model tomb of Anpuemhat and Usernekhbet, Saqqara (Middle Kingdom)	Two people couching on the floor preparing fibres/roves. A spinner with two spindles and a spinning bowl. A horizontal ground loom with two weavers (Tata 1995, 133–6, fig. 16; Kemp and Vogelsang-Eastwood 2001, 325).
Weaving model of Gemniemhet, Saqqara (Middle Kingdom)	Two people couching on the floor preparing fibres/roves. A spinner with two spindles and a spinning bowl. A horizontal ground loom with two weavers on their left. On the other side less clear part with a standing spinner, two people preparing fibres and three people working on a loom (Firth and Gunn 1926, 52–4, pls 22b, 31c).
Model from Girgeh (Middle Kingdom)	A woman preparing fibres, one spinner, one woman warping on a warper fixed to the ground, two weavers (Hayes 1953, fig. 172; Tata 1995, 129–30).
Model from tomb of Khetya, Beni Hasan, Tomb 575 (now Liverpool) (Middle Kingdom)	No walls represented. A spinner with two spindles, one with high whorl and the other with low whorl, but originally both were high whorl. Spinning bowl is now lost. Two weavers work on a horizontal ground loom (only poorly preserved) (Garstang 1907, 133; Tata 1995, 136–8).
Sedment tomb 1525 (Middle Kingdom)	No walls represented. Standing spinner (yellow skin) and crouching figure (red skin) (Petrie and Brunton 1924, fig. 17; Allen 1997, 31).
Deir el-Bahari, Montuhotep (Middle Kingdom)	Possible model of textile workers: two men with raised leg (spinners?), rods which might have belonged to the model (Arnold 1981, 33, pl. 50a, 58d; Allen 1997, 31).
Model from tomb of Djehutynakht, el-Bersheh 10A (Middle Kingdom)	No walls represented. A spinner with one spindle, a crouching person attending the spinner. Two weavers work on a horizontal ground loom (only poorly preserved) (Allen 1997, 31; Boston MFA 21.891).
Unknown, Munich	Model of a man with raised leg, possibly a spinner (Breasted 1976, 53, pl. 47c; Allen 1997, 31).
Unknown, Berlin	Model of a weaving room, with remains of a standing figure and four squatting figures (Johl 1924, 9–10, abb. 41–3; Allen 1997, 31).
Karenen and Nefersemdet, Saqqara (Middle Kingdom)	Model of a room with arched beams which possibly represented a weaving workshop. No figures or implements preserved (Breasted 1976, 53; Allen 1997, 32).
Karenen and Nefersemdet (Middle Kingdom)	Model of a room with arched beams which possibly represented a weaving workshop. Five figures preserved, one with right leg raised (Breasted 1976, 54; Allen 1997, 32).
Djehuty, el-Lisht	Workshop with granary, bakery and weaver's shop. One woman preparing fibres, one probable spinner with spinning bowl and two weavers (Allen 1997, 31; Indiana Univ. Art Museum, 58.34).
Iti, Lahun, tomb N17	Small model of a spinning bowl with a hole in the bottom, where a peg to attached to the model should be inserted (Petrie Museum UC 6665i; Petrie *et al.* 1923, 33–4).
Unknown Lisht, tomb 428	Model of limestone spinning bowl (Allen 1997, 31; MMA 15.3.99).

Herodotus writes that a corselet made of cotton was sent from Pharaoh Amasis as a gift to Athena (Barber 1991, 33), but no findings of cotton are known from Egypt in this period.

The site of Dhuweila in eastern Jordan has provided some textile impressions on plaster, but also small tufts of fibres, which have been radiocarbon dated to 4500–3000 cal BC, *i.e.* Levantine Chalcolithic or EBA phase (Betts *et al.* 1994). There can be little doubt about the correct identification since it was observed under a Scanning Electron Microscope, which clearly shows the typical convolutions of cotton fibres (Betts *et al.* 1994). However, no other cotton findings are known in Egypt and the Levant in the Bronze Age.

3.3 Wool

Wool is an animal fibre that forms the protective fleece of several animals, especially sheep, goats, and camels. It is composed of a protein, keratin, and a small percentage of lipids, while plant fibres, such as cotton or flax, are mainly composed of cellulose. Wool fibres are covered with small scales, which facilitate the adhesion of the fibres during the spinning and felting process, without needing the addition of other substances. Wool fibres have a good compatibility with dyestuffs, which means they are easier to dye than vegetable fibres. Furthermore, wool occurs in nature in several hues, from black to white, giving the chance to create multicoloured textiles. By the 4th millennium BC, selective breeding had led to significant genetic changes, resulting in the emergence of woolly sheep in the Near East. Among the various morphological transformations in early domesticated sheep, the most relevant here is the development of a woolly fleece, which appeared in different colours, including white (Breniquet 2008; 2020; Bergfjord *et al.* 2010). Both archaeological findings and textual sources from the Near East provide evidence for this development (Barber 1991, 23–5).

The quality of wool is generally stated by referencing various factors, including colour, crimps, yield, and fibre diameter, which is the most important element. Generally, a sheep's fleece is made up of three elements: kemp, hair, and underwool (Ryder 1983; Bender Jørgensen and Rast-Eicher 2018). Kemp is the coarser outer part, with long, thick fibres that break easily. It is not possible, therefore, to spin them on their own. The hair (and especially the underwool) are thinner, and can be spun either separately or together, depending on the type of yarn desired (Andersson Strand 2015, 42). The quality of the fibres can depend on several factors, such as the origin of the fibres on the animal's body (thighs, shoulder, or side), as well as the animal itself – ram, ewe, or wether (wethers are the best choice for wool).

3.3.1 First woollen textiles

Originally, sheep fleece was quite different from that of modern sheep. It was probably more similar to that of modern mouflon, and it was only through domestication and selection that it became woollier. Herding probably began around 8500 BC in Taurus, and spread to the Levant and Mesopotamia gradually (Vila and Helmer 2014, 22). Neolithic communities utilised sheep for breeding and selected animals for meat, milk, and fleece. Zooarchaeological data, however, show that sheep only began to be kept for their fleeces from 6500 BC (Vila and Helmer 2014, 23). The selection for quality wool and the presence of sheep with a uniform fleece – *i.e.* with little or no kemp fibres – took place in different periods in the Mediterranean area. Samples from Tell el-Amarna (14th century BC) and Akrotiri (1645–1600 BC) show that this was already achieved in the Middle–Late Bronze Age in the Eastern Mediterranean (Gleba 2012, 3648).

In the Near East, the first findings of woollen textiles are dated to the end of the 4th millennium BC and come from the site of Šahr-i-Soḫta in eastern Iran (period I) (Good 1999, 110) and from Novosvobodnaya in the northern Caucasus (Maikop culture 3700–3200 cal BC) (Shishlina *et al.* 2003). The Iranian textile is made from fibres of the Urial sheep (*Ovis vignei*) in two colours, yellow and brown, and likely represents a starting border. The textile of the Caucasic Maikop culture (3700–3200 cal BC) is even more interesting. Most of it is composed of wool, but it also contains plant-fibre. The warp yarns are brown and beige in colour, while the weft is only beige, and neither are plied. This forms a pattern of dark stripes on a light background (Shishlina *et al.* 2003, 333).

A fragment of a woollen textile comes from the Anatolian site of Arslantepe and was found in level VIB2 (Early Bronze Age I (EB I)) in a royal tomb. It is of fine quality; the fibres are of goat hair and not sheep hair (Laurito *et al.* 2014, 160).

Wool was certainly the predominant fibre in Mesopotamia, but our knowledge is based on textual sources rather than on actual archaeological finding. Zooarchaeological findings in southern Mesopotamia testify a gradual decrease of usage of cattle and pigs and an increase of presence of sheep and goats for meat, dairy products, and probably wool. Texts show a large-scale exploitation of wool from the second half of the 3rd millennium onwards, but it starts to occur from the Late Uruk documentation. It was manufactured at all levels of society, from the domestic production to temple and palace workshops, from everyday usage to goods for gods and exports as a currency of exchange (Breniquet and Michel 2014, 2).

The first discoveries of wool in the Southern Levant come from the tombs of Jericho (Crowfoot 1960, 521; Shamir 2015, 22), which do not predate the MBA, and are thus certainly later than other regions. Future excavations might predate the beginning of the wool exploiting to the EBA, but certainly not to the Chalcolithic period, since cave findings have shown that only plant fibres were in use (Shamir 2015).

There is little evidence for the use of wool before the Roman Era in Egypt, and what there is comes scattered from all periods of Egyptian history. Unfortunately, no ^{14}C test has been conducted on these specimens, so their chronology, deduced by their archaeological contexts, can be challenged. The first findings come from the Neolithic site of el-Omari and have been labelled as wool (Bender Jørgensen and Rast-Eicher 2018, 26). Hairs of wool have been reported to come from A 16 room C, but were not directly studied by Greiss (1957, 228); no. 15 from A 91 is a piece of sheep skin with wool of different colours directly studied by Greiss (1957, 229).

Another finding dates to the 1st Dynasty and was found at Helwan (Saad 1951, 44). It is an actual cloth, which was wrapped around a body in tomb 36H5, but no other indications are given. Greiss (1957, 231) does not confirm the identification (if he even identified the correct textile) and writes 'fibrous material associated with a coffin remains. Light and dark golden colour; human hair'. Several findings have been dated or redated to the post-Pharaonic period: an Old Kingdom specimen from the Pyramid of Menkaure at Giza, where a skeleton is recorded as being 'enveloped in coarse woollen cloth of a yellow colour' but is generally considered as intrusive (Lucas and Harris 1962, 147). Several examples of wool are known from Middle Kingdom Kahun, but these have been radiocarbon dated and were proved to be Roman (Vogelsang-Eastwood 2000, 269).

Forty-eight fragments of sheep wool come from the workmen's village of Amarna, 36 of which are definitively identified as wool, some of them from intact deposits. Other woollen objects come from the Main City, but were excavated at the beginning of the 20th century (Kemp and Vogelsang-Eastwood 2001, 35–8).

Ovine bones are commonly found in Egyptian excavations from all periods and are frequently mentioned in textual sources. Sheep and goats also appear in numerous artworks, including rock art from at least Predynastic times in Southern Egypt and Lower Nubia, as well as in tomb paintings from the Pharaonic era. Two distinct species of sheep are typically depicted: one with long, spiralled horns (*Ovis longipes palaeoaegyptiacus*), which appears in the earliest representations, and another with curled horns (*Ovis platyura aegyptiaca*), which is believed to have produced higher-quality wool (Kemp and Vogelsang-Eastwood 2001, 34).

Besides sheep and goat wool, Egypt has possibly provided evidence of camel wool from the Fayum Neolithic culture, where a rope was identified as being made of this fibre (Caton-Thompson and Gardner 1934, 88). Camel wool is not frequently used in Egypt, but there are a few hints, which prove their knowledge from the Egyptians. A figurine of a camel is known from Maadi, and camel bones were recognised at the site of Helwan (Saad 1951, 38). Camel hair has not been recognised in the Near East prior to the 5th century BC, except for an uncertain identification from Šahr-i-Soḫta (Völling 2008, 73, tab. 1).

Although wool was certainly present in Egypt, very few specimens have been discovered so far. Tata (1995, 184–6) suggests that wool may have been exported to regions where it was more widely used. However, the most plausible explanation remains that of Herodotus, who stated that the Ancient Egyptians considered wool impure (Hdt.1.79.81). As a result, it was excluded from funerary contexts, which form our primary source of evidence for Egyptian textiles. This exclusion significantly reduces the likelihood of finding woollen textiles in archaeological records. Nevertheless, it is remarkable how strictly this prohibition appears to have been followed, as no wool has been found in any tomb, from any period of Pharaonic Egypt, regardless of the social status of the deceased.

3.3.2 Wool processing

Primitive sheep breeds naturally shed their fleece once a year, usually in early summer, as new wool begins to grow. This allows wool to be harvested by plucking or rooing, though it often comes off in pieces rather than as a whole fleece (Rast-Eicher and Bender Jørgensen 2013). To obtain finer fibres, coarser ones must be removed by hand or with a comb. Shearing, which enables farmers to control when wool is collected, improved flock management over time (Rast-Eicher and Bender Jørgensen 2013). During the Bronze Age, wool was probably obtained by plucking or cutting with knives (Breniquet 2020). Shears and the term for 'cutting' appear in Near Eastern sources at the end of the 2nd millennium BC (Wisti Lassen 2010).

After the wool is obtained, it can be sorted according to several criteria, such as colour, fineness, crimp, and length (Gleba 2008, 98). Wool can be washed before cutting or plucking, but in this case it is necessary to add a little fat to help the spinning process; this is not necessary if it is washed after spinning, because lanolin is still present. However, washing the sheep before the wool is extracted makes the wool easier to comb (Forbes 1956, 21). Washing the fibres is also necessary before the dying process, otherwise the dyestuffs will not be able to penetrate inside the fibres; generally, fibres are dyed before the spinning process (MacCorriston 1997). It is not clear which tools were in use during the period under examination, since combs were generally linked to personal care (Barber 1991, 20).

This brief overview of fibres and textiles in the Near East and Egypt highlights the ongoing debate in the field and how recent discoveries and fibre re-examinations are significantly reshaping our understanding. Although much research remains to be done, it is likely that more evidence of bast fibre use in the Near East will emerge in the coming years. Additionally, early bast yarns and textiles were probably produced through splicing and twisting.

Wool, on the other hand, can only be confidently identified in the Southern Levant during the MBA, while its introduction and frequency of use in Egypt remain unclear. Cotton and silk do not appear to have been widely used in the regions and periods under study.

These findings have important implications for the analysis of textile tools. If bast fibre production techniques remained unchanged over time, then spinning tools would not necessarily evolve due to technical requirements but rather due to refinements and cultural influences. Only with the introduction of wool should we expect to see significant changes, such as those observed in Anatolia (Laurito *et al.* 2014).

Notes

1 See Barber (1991, 15) for another proposal of identification as *Hibiscus cannabinus*.
2 For a reassessment of the first textiles and basketry see Bender Jørgensen *et al.* (2023).
3 For a complete list of caves and textiles see Schick (2002) and Shamir (2015).

4

Textile tools from the Southern Levant

This chapter examines the evidence for textile tools in the Southern Levant. The chapter is structured in two main sections: the first presents the textile tool assemblages from four major sites, while the second integrates these findings into a wider analysis of textile production across the region.

The key sites selected for this study are Megiddo, Hazor, Beth Shean, and Tell el-Farʿah (North). These sites were chosen due to the richness of their textile tool assemblages, as well as their long and well-documented occupational histories. Their stratigraphic sequences encompass multiple historical phases, allowing for an examination of the development and continuity of textile production over time. The analysis of textile tools is based both on previously published material and on the direct study of artefacts held in various institutions, as outlined in the catalogue. While an effort was made to include sites spanning all chronological periods, the key sites do not provide substantial evidence for the Neolithic and Chalcolithic periods. As noted in the introduction, initial attempts to incorporate sites from these early periods were hindered by the very limited number of textile tools available for study.

The textile tools discussed in this chapter include spindles, spindle whorls, perforated sherds, loom weights, basalt rings, bone spatulae, beaters, and needles. Spinning tools include bone shafts, which may have functioned as spindles, and spindle whorls, including those fashioned from reworked and perforated sherds. Loom weights are examined as well, while ring-shaped basalt weights are considered separately due to their distinctive form and their likely, though not yet fully understood, role in textile production. Needles are included in the study as a potential indicator of textile processing, even though they are not directly associated with textile manufacture. Additionally, bone spatulae and pin beaters are analysed to assess signs of wear that may suggest their use with soft materials, as well as to explore possible functional connections with other textile tools. The analysis considers not only the typology and function of these tools but also the archaeological contexts of clusters, providing insights into the spatial and chronological distribution of textile production activities. Finally, a discussion of the development of textile tool assemblages at each site, considering changes over time and potential influences from broader technological and economic developments.

The second part of the chapter expands the discussion beyond the key sites to offer a more comprehensive overview of textile tools in the Southern Levant. This includes comparative analysis with data from additional sites across the region and a meta-analysis of specific tool types, such as basalt rings and spools, to identify broader patterns and trends in textile production.

4.1 Megiddo

4.1.1 Introduction

Tell es-Mutesellim is a large mound situated in a strategic position, at the foot of the northeast flank of the hills of the Carmel Ridge, through which the nearby Wadi Ara acts as a pass. It also overlooks the alluvial plain of the Jezreel Valley, which connects the Jordan Valley with the coastal plain of Palestine. An abundant spring, Ain el-Kubbi, is situated below the northern slopes of the terrace; another, Ain er-Ruzz, is not far to the northwest. Another spring is located in a cave on the southwest slope of the mound (Davies 1986, 7). The Jezreel Valley is crossed by various tributaries of the river Naḥal Kishon, which runs to the northwest into the Mediterranean, and by Naḥal Ḥarod, which flows into the Jordan River in the southeast.

Both rivers are quite near to the site, at a distance of only a few kilometres, and could provide it with a source of freshwater fish (Lernau 2006, 492).

Several excavations have been conducted during the 20th century, which have exposed large areas of the mound and provide an initial chronological frame. Between 1903 and 1905, a German Expedition directed by G. Schumacher dug several trenches at the top and on the slope. Between 1925 and 1939 the Oriental Institute of Chicago led an extensive new campaign of excavations under the direction of C. Fischer, P.L.O. Guy, R.S. Lamon and G. Loud. The Hebrew University of Jerusalem carried out three seasons of excavations and several soundings under the directorship of Y. Yadin between 1960 and 1972 (Davies 1986, 12–24).

From 1992, a new excavation project explored Megiddo on behalf of the Institute of Archaeology at Tel Aviv University, directed by Israel Finkelstein and David Ussishkin. The 1992–1996 seasons excavated five areas, both on the edge of the mound and in the lower part:[1] F on the lower mound; G in the LBA gate; H on the northwestern edge of the mound; J in the EBA temples compound; and K on the southeastern edge of the mound. The 1998–2002 seasons saw the continuation of work in four areas, F, H, J, and K, and two new fields were opened: L in the northeastern sector of the mound and M in and around the Schumacher trench in the centre. The 2004–2008 seasons continued the work in areas H, J, K, L, and M, and two new areas were investigated: P in the Lower Terrace, and Q in the southeastern sector of the mound (Finkelstein, Ussishkin, and Cline 2013, 3; Table 4.1).

Megiddo has yielded a substantial number of textile tools, spanning from the EBA to the Iron Age. The archaeological finds from the site are housed in two main institutions: Tel Aviv University, which holds the materials from the most recent excavations directed by I. Finkelstein, and the Israel Antiquities Authority (IAA) in Beth Shemesh, which stores the already published artefacts. Both institutions were visited for this research to allow direct examination of the available materials.

A small number of artefacts from the older excavations are located at the Rockefeller Museum. However, the majority of these finds are now held in collections abroad and were therefore not accessible for this study. Regarding the artefacts from the renewed excavations, only some of the objects published in previous reports were available for analysis, along with approximately 100 unpublished items.

To gain a more comprehensive understanding of the textile tool assemblages at Megiddo, it was also necessary to review artefacts published in earlier excavation reports. These publications do not always provide detailed morphological descriptions, making it important to consider as many sources as possible. Whenever feasible, data from older excavations have been incorporated to offer the broadest possible perspective on textile production at the site. As a result, the catalogue includes not only the objects I have personally examined but also those published but unavailable for direct study. This approach enables access to a wider variety of shapes and materials, which strengthens the statistical analysis of textile tools from Megiddo.

4.1.2 Spindles

As with many other Levantine sites, Megiddo has preserved several bone and ivory shafts which might be spindles, or parts of them. This production seems to begin in Megiddo in the very end of the MBA or the beginning of Late Bronze Age I (LB I), and reaches its peak during the Late Bronze Age II (LB II), with a decrease in production during the Iron Age. Only two specimens of complete spindles (meaning with the spindle whorl inserted on the shaft) have been recovered, and both are dated to the LB I period. None of these objects is a 'traditional' spindle, as they are quite peculiar items. The first, M 3530, is formed by three elements joined together, forming a shaft with one flat end and the other tapered (Lamon and Shipton 1939, fig. 95.38). One of the joining points is used to insert two spindle whorls, both dome-shaped, with the base in contact between them. They are therefore not properly mounted on the shaft, but on the peg that connects the two elements of the rod, with a hole diameter much smaller than that of the shaft. A similar reconstruction has also been suggested for M 3568 (Loud 1948, fig. 197.2), although the two spindle whorls were not found on the shaft (Fig. 4.1).

An entirely different example is b 433a, which was found in a funerary context together with whorl b 433b (Guy and Engberg 1938, 172, pl. 142). It is cylindrical and made of several bone rings, most of them decorated. The core has disintegrated, but it is stated that it was reassembled as found in burial. The spindle whorls are shown as they were mounted on the core, as in the previous case. Petrie probably recovered a similarly composed shaft in Tell el-Ajjul (Petrie *et al.* 1931, fig. XXIII.6), but the elements are drawn separately.

Other shafts have been found complete but without spindle whorls, even if in many cases spindle whorls were present in the same context. These were made from a single element or by several elements joining together, as was the case for M 5368, as well as other examples from the Levantine region. Their production is particularly numerous between LB II–III, with very few examples from Iron Age I–II. It is interesting to note that a large number come from LB II tombs (*e.g.* 1122, 877B1, 989C1), where

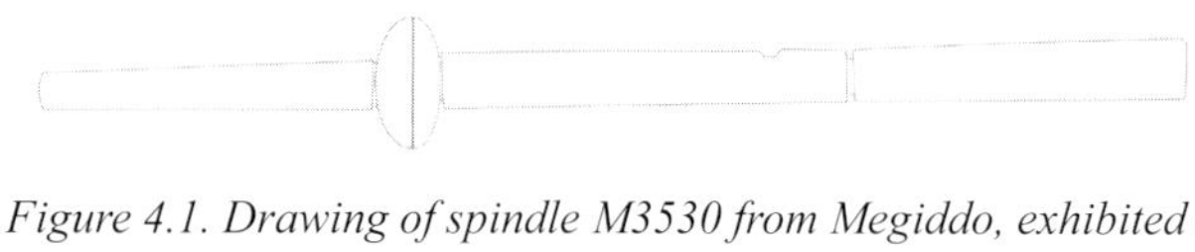

Figure 4.1. Drawing of spindle M3530 from Megiddo, exhibited at the Rockefeller Museum

Table 4.1. Chronological chart of Megiddo (Finkelstein et al. *2013 tab. 1.1)*

Area Q	*Area F*	*Area H*	*Area J**	*Area K*	*Area L*	*Area M***	*Area N*	*University of Chicago strata*	*Period*
			J-1					XX	EB I
			J-2					Phase in XIX: not identified as a separate level	EB Ib
			J-3					XIX	EB Ib
			J-4					XVIII	EB Ib
			J-4n					Not detected	EB Ib
			J-5, J-6b					XVII	EB III
			J-6a					XVI	EB III
			J-7					XV	EB III–IBA***
			J-8					XIV	MB I
			J-9					XIV	MB I
			J-10					XIII	MB I
	F-12		J-11			M-11		XII	MB II
			J-12			M-10, 9		XI	MB II
	F-11		J-13	K-10		M-8	N-2, 3, 4	X (X–IX)	MB III–LB I
	F-10		J-14, 15, 16	K-10		M-7	N-1	IX	LB I
	F-9		J-17?	K-9?				VIII	LB IIA
	F-8			K-8, 7				VIIB	LB IIB
Q-9	F-7	H-12 (LBIII–IAI)		K-6		M-6		VIIA?	LB III
Q-8	F-6	H-10, 11		K-5		M-5		VIB	Early Iron I
Q-7	F-5	H-9		K-4	L-5	M-4		VIA	Late Iron I
Q-5, 6		H-8, 7, 6		K-3	L-4	M-3, 2, 1		VB	Early Iron IIA
Q-4		H-5		K-2	L-3			VA-IVB	Late Iron IIA
Q-3	F-4b	H-4, 3		K-1	L-2			IVA	Iron IIB
		H-2						Not detected	Iron IIB
	F-4a	H-1			L-1			III	Iron IIB
	F-3							II	Iron IIC
	F-2								Late Roman
	F-1								20th century AD

several bone spindle whorls are also present. Among these objects there is also a pomegranate element to be mounted on a shaft, with several parallels to other sites, like Ugarit (Gachet-Bizollon 2007, 16, 119).

4.1.3 Spindle whorls

The first spindle whorls are known in Megiddo from the EBA I, though their numbers remain very small throughout the EBA, probably due also to a smaller extension of the excavated strata of this period. They share the same material of production, *i.e.* pottery, while just two examples are produced in stone: one a perforated pebble, the other a dome-shaped basalt whorl. The shapes are very different, including discoid examples, which constitute the largest group, but also biconical, lenticular, cylindrical, and dome-shaped spindle whorls. The measurements are only available for some of them, and their weight appears to span between 27 and 50 g, indicating a medium quality yarn production (Plate 1).

The MBA shows a more significant number of spindle whorls, but extremely few when compared with later periods. Spindle whorls made of baked clay continued to be produced during the MBA, and although several other materials are now employed, clay still represents one of the largest groups. During the MB I, bone starts to be used as a material, specifically the epiphysis of cow or sheep/goats bones, which will always influence the shape of the spindle whorls extracted from them. Almost all the bone spindle whorls are, in fact, dome shaped. To these two materials should be added a small sample of stone spindle whorls. Their morphologies are quite varied, with biconical, cylindrical, spherical, discoid, and dome shapes. Pottery spindle whorls seem to prefer rounded and spherical shapes; stone spindle whorls, meanwhile, tend to have flat shapes, such as the discoid (Plate 1). For the former period, few measurements are available, and seem very different between each other, with the largest diameter for a limestone spindle whorl (08/K/119/AR4). Excluding bone items, most weights span between 20 and 40 g, indicating a medium quality yarn production. Some bone spindle whorls are extremely small and light, and therefore may not be spindle whorls after all (Fig. 4.2). They might have been, in fact, beads, buttons or decorative elements for textiles. However, two elements should be considered. First, spindles may have had more than one spindle whorl at the same time, as seen in M 3530, so the two weights and the overall height may be more satisfactory than they first seem. Second, Egypt has preserved some very small and light wooden spindle whorls (see Chapter 5), which might have a similar effect on threads to the items under consideration. These two elements together are the reason for considering these kinds of objects as possible spindle whorls.

From the LBA phase, a huge number of spindle whorls has been recovered, especially for the LB II period (Plate 1). For the entire period under consideration, bone spindle whorls greatly outnumber those of other materials, while pottery spindle whorls are a small fraction of those recovered. It is interesting to note that most of the pottery

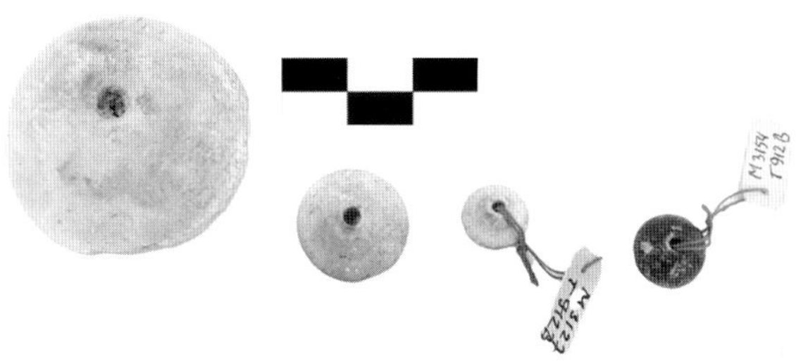

Figure 4.2. Spindle whorls and buttons from Megiddo (© Rockefeller Museum, courtesy of the Israel Antiquities Authority)

spindle whorls, as in the preceding period, have a rounded shape or a form quite close to a sphere. A small number of stone examples is also represented, generally made of limestone or steatite. Since the majority of the spindle whorls are made of bone, most of them are also dome shaped. However, some dome-shaped stone whorls are known (Plate 2). From LB II the button shape is also present, which is a conical shape with convex sides. These spindle whorls are also generally made of bone or ivory. Several other shapes are in use, but always in small quantities: conical, biconical, discoid, and lenticular (Fig. 4.3).

For the other periods, the measurements and weights are only available for a limited group of objects. However, it seems reasonable to state that the majority of the spindle whorls for which a weight is available can be divided into two groups: the first with a small weight around 3–5 g, and the other between 15–20 g. Heavier spindle whorls are also represented, with weights up to 60 g (Plate 1). Some of the bone spindle whorls can weigh 1 g or less, and therefore it seems quite unlikely that they were used for spinning. However, they are listed in the catalogue to better represent the complexity of tracing a clear line between what is a textile tool and what is not. A few examples of stone spindle whorls have the same problems, like 98/F/94/AR1 with a diameter of 1.6 cm, height 0.6 cm and a weight of 1.7 g. In this case, the hole is just 0.2 cm – very small, but not too small if it was mounted on a peg rather than a shaft (as for M 3530).

For the Iron Age period, it seems more reasonable to separate Iron Age I from Iron Age II, since some differences can be noted. In Iron Age I, a huge number of spindle whorls were produced (117, similar to the quantity known for the entire LBA). Unfortunately, most of them are published by Paice in Harrison's report of Stratum IV (Paice 2004, 59–109 pl. 30), and lack all basic information, such as their shapes or measurements. For the small group for which data are available, the material most commonly employed is bone/ivory, with 42 examples, not just for dome-shaped examples but also for other morphologies. A large number is also represented by spindle whorls made of stone, of which 37 examples are recognisable, although the choice of material can vary a great deal between limestone and steatite, which are the most common, and fewer examples made of hematite, gypsum, and serpentinite. Similar to the LB period, pottery whorls are quite rare, with only 18 examples reported (Plate 1).

An extensive set of morphologies is employed, and the most common shape is the dome, made from bone as well as stone. Other common shapes are conical, with whorls made of bone and serpentinite, and discoid, with stone and bone as the only materials used (Plate 2). Very few examples are known for biconical, cylindrical and lenticular. It is worth noting that the button shape is represented by only two specimens in this phase. A new shape appears, *i.e.* the conical truncated, which was unknown in previous

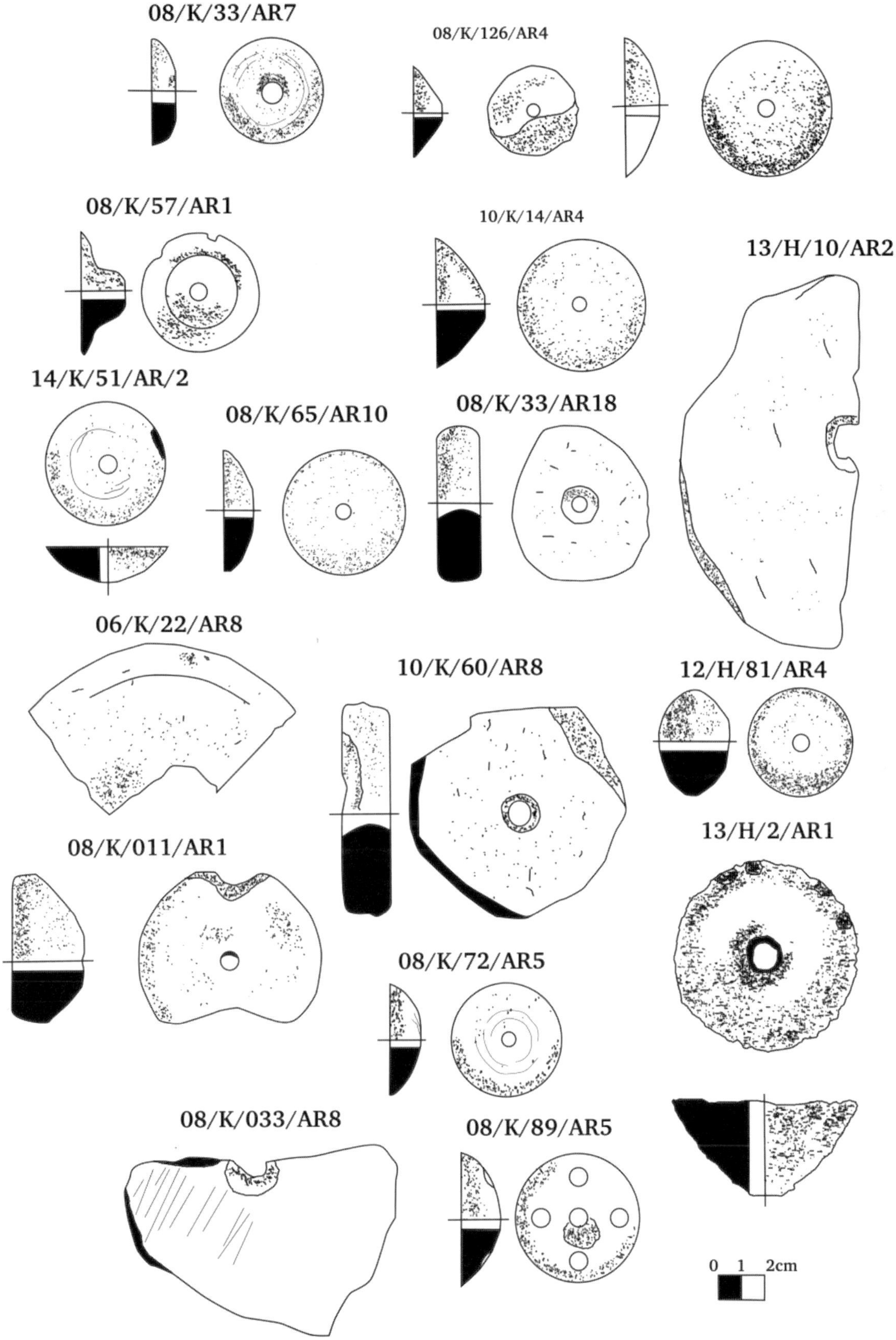

Figure 4.3. Selection of spindle whorls and perforated sherds from Megiddo

periods, but would continue to be produced in the following periods, albeit in minimal quantities. As in the preceding periods, pottery spindle whorls have a spherical shape. For the items for which measurements are available, diameters span from 0.9 to 6.4 cm, also with many variations in height and weight. It is worth noting that a large group of stone spindle whorls have large diameters and heavier weights. Two groups of weights can be identified: the first with very light weights, under 10 g, which includes almost only bone and serpentinite spindle whorls; the second group is between 25–35 g, and includes a wider range of materials. The heaviest whorl weight is 82 g and is the same whorl with a 6.4 cm diameter.

The Iron Age II period has returned the largest number of spindle whorls (225), but it is also the period for which the fewest measurements are available. It is marked by a completely different choice of materials, while the morphologies are almost the same as Iron Age I. 164 stone spindle whorls have been recovered, definitively overtaking the use of bone (Plate 1). For this period, only 41 bone spindle whorls and three in ivory are known. To these, 18 pottery spindle whorls must be added. Stones typologies are quite varied, but the most common are limestone and steatite. Other types of stone, such as slate, hematite, basalt, gypsum, and serpentinite, are represented by very few, if not single examples. The morphologies do not change in this period, with more than half of the shapes divided between conical (67) and dome-shaped whorls (86). In both categories, as we might imagine, stone spindle whorls are the majority. It is not possible to link a certain material to a shape (or vice versa) for Iron Age II, except for pottery spindle whorls, which continue to be produced in rounded shapes, including spherical, biconical, and cylindrical (Plate 1). It is interesting to note that the button shape is represented by only four specimens, witnessing the scarce consideration that was paid to this category in the Iron Age. Given the minimal number of measurements available, it is not possible to identify trends or specific characteristics. Diameters, as usual, span a broad range (1.4–5.5 cm), and weights are between 2.1 g and 99 g, without clustering around specific measurements.

4.1.4 Perforated sherds

Perforated sherds are known in Megiddo for all the periods under consideration. However, they were quite rare during the EBA and MBA, though much more common in later periods. The peak of use is undoubtedly the Iron Age I, when their number was almost double that of the LBA and Iron Age II periods. If we consider all of these as possible spindle whorls, it is interesting to note that they represent almost one-third of all spindle whorls dated to Iron Age I, but only 13% of the LBA or the Iron Age II spindle whorls. They are characterised by a fairly large diameter, 5 cm on average, and a rather small thickness, 0.86 cm on average. The biggest object (00/K/31/AR2) measures 1.4 cm in height and 13 cm in diameter, and is not to be considered to be a spindle whorl. In fact, its weight probably exceeded 200 g (as 98/K/33/AR7). Perforated sherds in Megiddo weigh between 7.1 and 107 g, with an average weight of 32.8 g. Most of the specimens weigh between 20–30 g.

The catalogue includes all the perforated sherds with a single hole, whether the hole is hourglass or not perpendicularly perforated, which makes fastening it to the spindle more difficult, but not impossible (Plate 2). Since the most significant of the perforated sherds is that of Hazor, these will be discussed in much more detail in its chapter.

The context of finding of reworked sherds is generally domestic, and very seldom funerary. It seems, therefore, that their mundane aspect makes them suitable only for a functional purpose – they are not 'precious' or symbolic enough to be found inside tombs, as spindle whorls and loom weights sometimes are. Some of these perforated sherds have been found in contexts with other tools, especially grinding tools, but only rarely with other perforated sherds, and in very few instances in association with other textile tools, including spatulae and needles.

4.1.5 Spinning bowls

Only a single fragment of a spinning bowl has been found in Megiddo for all periods under consideration. It is dated to LB III, and has the characteristic feature of two loops inside. Textile production in Megiddo is very well documented by large quantities of textile tools, and the finding of just a single bowl provides evidence that such an implement was very rarely employed at the site, and unknown for most of its history.

4.1.6 Loom weights

As seen in the previous chapters, loom weights are objects with a specific weight to keep the warp of the loom in tension. It is not clear when the warp-weighted loom was first used in the Levant, nor in which sites, and for this reason all the objects that can be used for this purpose are included and discussed in the catalogue, allowing us to reject some of these specimens. Basalt rings will be discussed in the next chapter, given the difficulty in distinguishing between a spindle whorl and a loom weight (or something else).

During the EBA, very few objects that could have been weights have been recognised in Megiddo. Most of these are pebbles with a through hole, which can be used as loom weights as well as counterweights, but given their small quantity and their significant difference in shape and size, it is difficult to recognise them as a uniform category.

The MBA saw the appearance of a new category of objects: conical clay loom weights (Fig. 4.4). In Megiddo, these are present in small quantities from Stratum XIII to Stratum X, which means from the very beginning of the MBA to the transition to the LBA. Conical clay objects are probably the most recognisable type of loom weight from

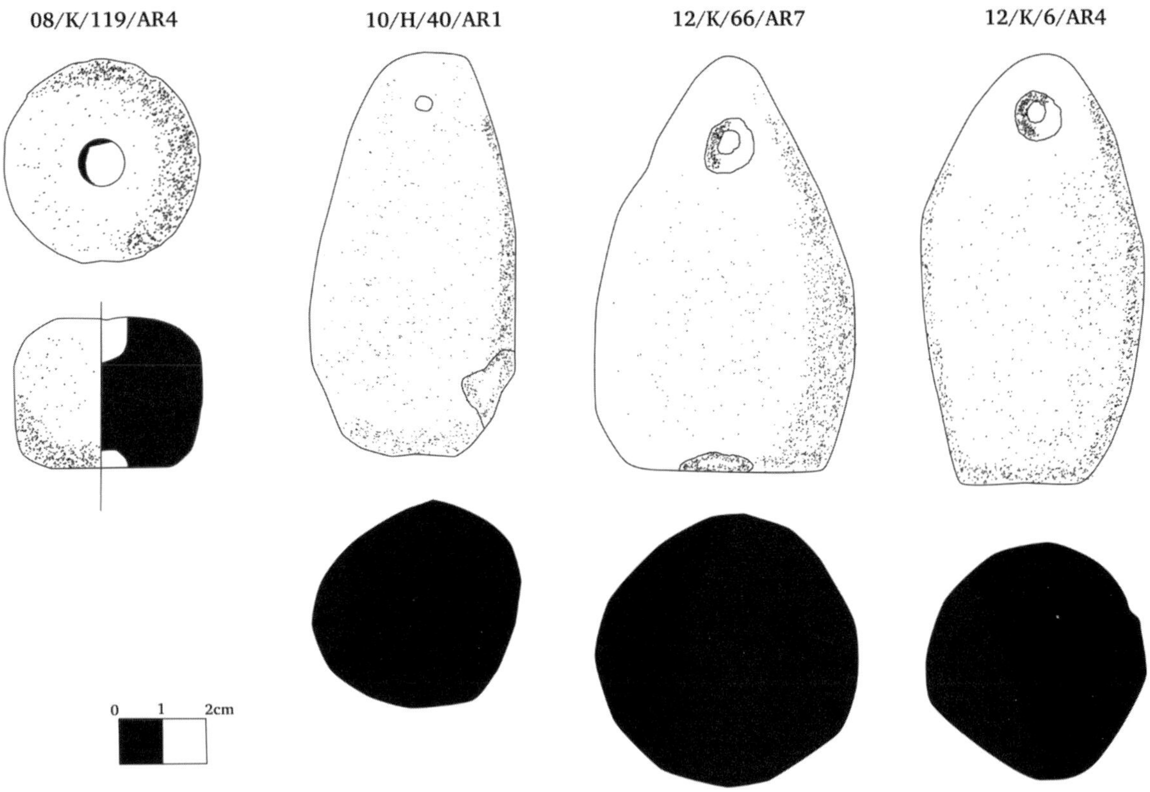

Figure 4.4. Loom weights from Megiddo

the Levant; however, these can vary a great deal in their aspect, morphology, and weight. One of the most striking features of Megiddo loom weights is the presence of vertically perforated conical examples, meaning from top to bottom, while the perforation is usually made parallel to the base, near the top of the object (Fig. 4.5). In MBA Megiddo, both types are present. Another unusual characteristic is the presence of a surface treatment on some objects (Fig. 4.6). These are carefully shaped, baked, covered by a red slip, and burnished. Some examples do not show such a surface treatment but are nonetheless well-fired, while most of the examples are made of simple, unfired clay. The reason for such a different finishing is not clear. Furthermore, some loom weights show the imprint of a sealing, usually made by a scarab, and in some cases Egyptian motifs are clearly recognisable (Fig. 4.7). Conical loom weights generally measure between 9 and 12 cm in height and 6 to 7.7 cm in diameter. Very few weights are available, but it seems clear that they are quite heavy, with the smallest weighing 337 g and the largest 628 g.

The LBA period in the Levant is generally characterised by the absence of loom weights. However, Megiddo sees the production peak of conical clay loom weights in the transitional phase between MB and LB, and some specimens are also known for the LB I period. The following LB phases (II–III) see a situation similar to that of the EBA, where no specific objects can be positively identified as loom weights, although a few perforated pebbles might have been used in textile production.

New types of loom weights appear in the Iron Age, and Megiddo is no exception. However, the number of published items is meagre, so very little can be said about them (Fig. 4.8).

Unfortunately, most of the Iron Age I loom weights have been published with little data (Paice 2004). Most of them are made of clay, probably fired, and a few are made of stone with a perforation, and for this reason have been listed as loom weights. For most of the weights, the shape is not given. However, at least from the very end of the Iron Age I the doughnut shape – typical of the Iron Age – has been recognised. From Megiddo, a spool or bobbin made of unbaked clay has also been recovered, and this typology seems to continue in the following period. The available measurements of their weight seem to indicate quite heavy weights, with an average of 500 g. A cylindrical type, with vertical perforation, is also present.

During the Iron Age II, most of the weights are produced in unfired clay with rounded shapes, which are divided between spherical, biconical, and doughnut. Only one item made of stone is listed, but its purpose is not certain.

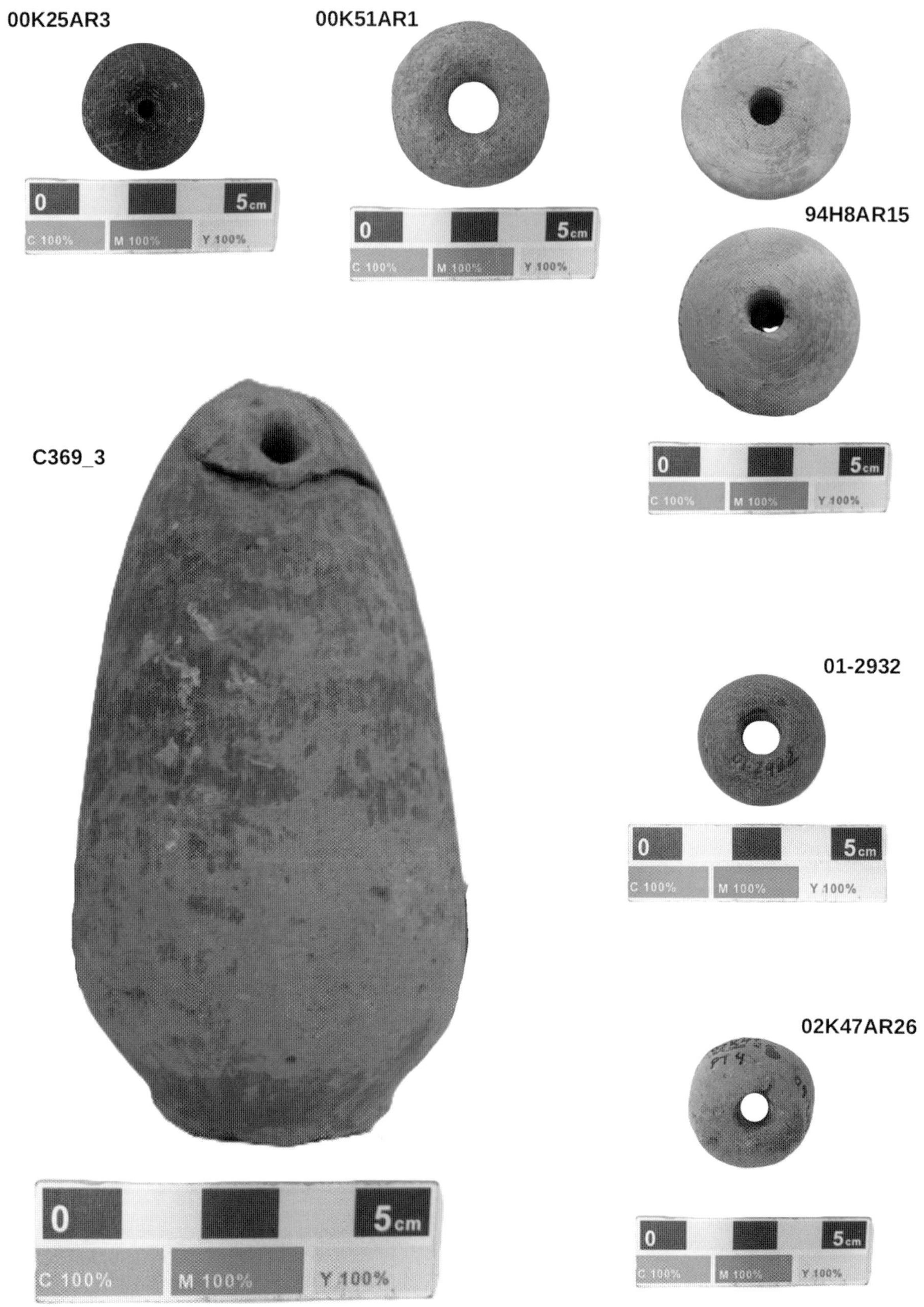

Figure 4.5. Selection of Megiddo textile tools 00K25AR3, 00K51AR1, 94H8AR15, C369_3, 01-2932, 0247AR26 (courtesy of the Israel Antiquity Authorities)

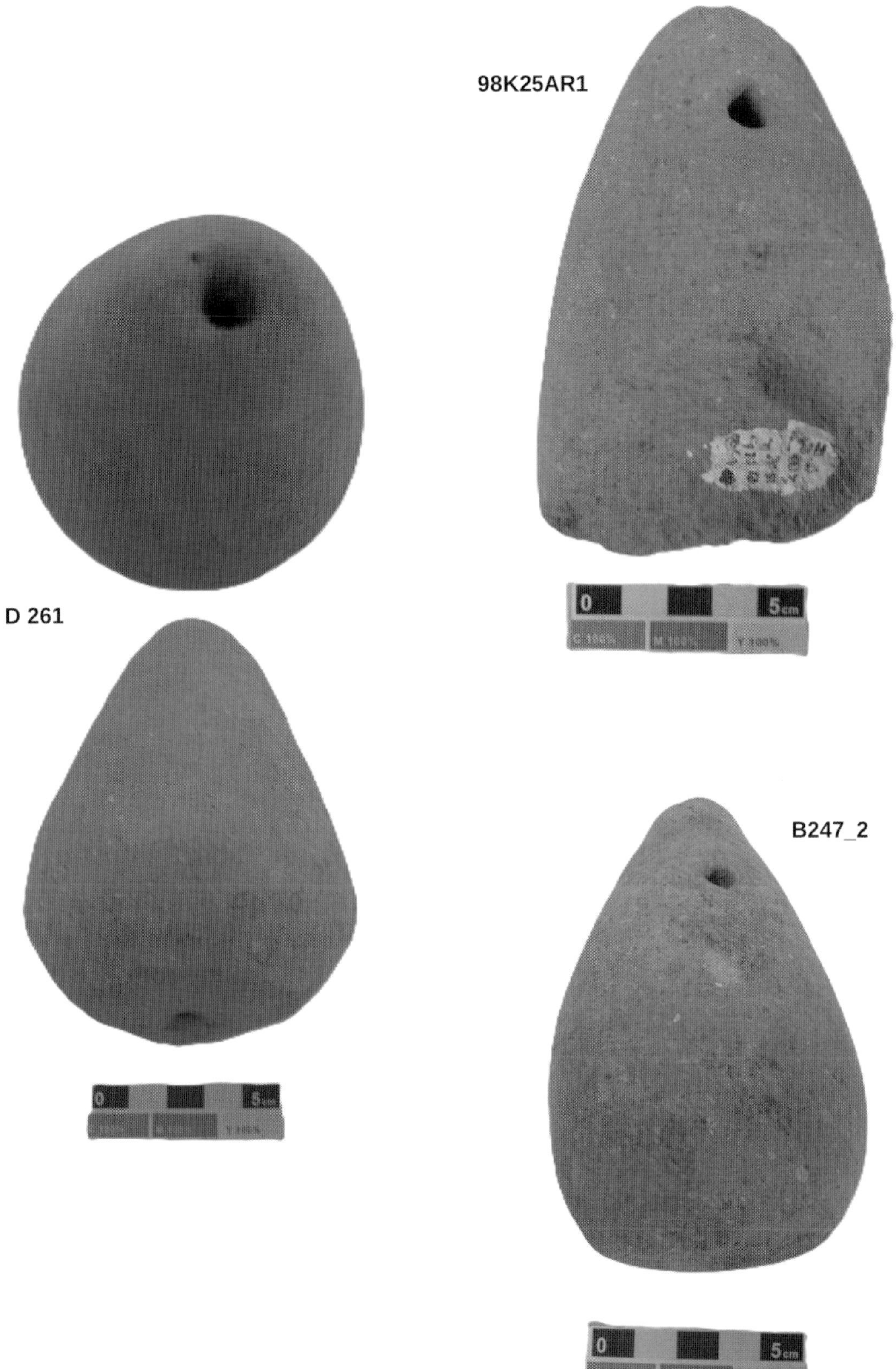

Figure 4.6. Selection of Megiddo textile tools 98K25AR1, D261, B247_2 (courtesy of the Israel Antiquity Authorities)

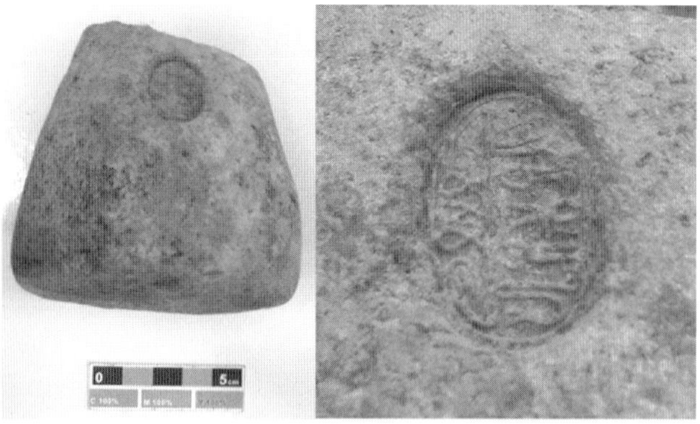

Figure 4.7. Sealing on C637 (© Rockefeller Museum, courtesy of the Israel Antiquities Authority)

Since only a few measurements of weight are given, it seems difficult to draw a conclusion (Plate 2).

Among loom weights, it is possible that a category of objects made from the reworked bases of vases should be recognised. Few items of this typology are known from Megiddo, while a large collection comes from Hazor. For this reason, it seems more useful to discuss them in the chapter related to Hazor.

Loom weights are generally found in domestic contexts, though in Megiddo, a few items have been recovered from burials, as well as spindle whorls. Two are conical loom weights made of fired clay that come from burial sites at MB (one from MB I, the other from MB III/LB I), while for the other two, it is unfortunately not possible to assign a precise chronology. One is conical and made of basalt, the other is spherical and made of unbaked clay. It is therefore interesting to note that the most mundane objects, even those made of unbaked clay, can also be placed inside tombs.

Only a few loom weights have been found together in context, while the vast majority come from scattered loci across the whole town. Twenty-six conical loom weights made of unbaked clay were found in Locus E 3036 (Loud 1948, pl. 170); unfortunately, they were published with no other information about their context of finding, nor if and how they were grouped together.

Room 2069 has yielded more than 20 cylindrical loom weights, found together inside a broken vessel. Their shape is not standard, since they seem perfectly cylindrical, although they are usually produced quite crudely (Harrison 2004, 105, fig. 33; Paice 2004, 59).

Non-perforated cylindrical weights also come from Buildings 2072 and 350 (Harrison 2004, 18). Another cluster of loom weights comes from an open area with trees in sq. R9, L.1750, although with no description of the loom weights (Harrison 2004, 20).

From the renewed excavations at Megiddo, no numerous clusters have been recovered. Furthermore, only sporadically textile related tools appear in the same locus. Only L. 96/H/44 has returned 10 loom weights and a bone spatula (Sass 2000, 372, 12.16). This context is dated to the Iron Age II, and is mainly composed of domestic buildings. These loom weights are doughnut shaped.

4.1.7 Basalt rings

Stone objects with the shape of a torus are widespread in the Levant, especially for the EBA and MBA periods. As discussed in Chapter 2, they form a uniform category of objects, probably connected with textile production, although their specific function remains unknown (Plate 2). Even if they are easy to distinguish from other ring-shaped objects, publications often lack essential details such as their diameter and weight, making their identification from schematic drawings (when present) very difficult. This problem is particularly evident in Megiddo, given the long history of excavations and the different sensibilities towards these objects. In the catalogue, pivots for drilling and other tools that have nothing to do with our basalt rings are also listed, and where possible, it is clearly stated that they were not textile tools. In many cases, however, it is possible only to imagine that these tools had other functions, but it has not been possible to exclude them for sure. As in other Levantine sites, basalt rings are quite common in the EBA. In Megiddo, they appear as early as the EB I and continue to be produced during the EB III. For those for which the weight is given, they are light objects, ranging from 22 to about 68 g. If they were considered as spindle whorls, they would be medium weight, while if they were considered loom weights their weight would be considered extremely light. They come both from tombs and domestic contexts.

During the MBA and LBA, the production of basalt rings seems to disappear, and they should thus not be present in layers dating to the Iron Age. However, several specimens, personally seen and measured, come from Iron Age levels, apparently contradicting what is generally known from other Levantine sites. For Iron Age I, only five items can be considered as basalt rings, while all the others are larger, very heavy objects with other purposes. Most of the objects that are called basalt rings for Iron Age II strata were undoubtedly not basalt rings, since their diameters and weights enable us to exclude their use in textile related activities. However, even for this period, a small number of actual basalt rings can be identified, thus confirming that their use during the Iron Age was not common, but still present.

The only cache of basalt rings was recognised by Braun for the EB I at the East Slope (Braun *et al.* 2013, 101–2). Unfortunately, he did not publish any description of the objects, nor even their total numbers. He hypothesises that they may have been connected to a loom.

4.1.8 Bone spatulae and beaters

Several examples of what can be called spatulae and beaters have been found from all periods of Megiddo history

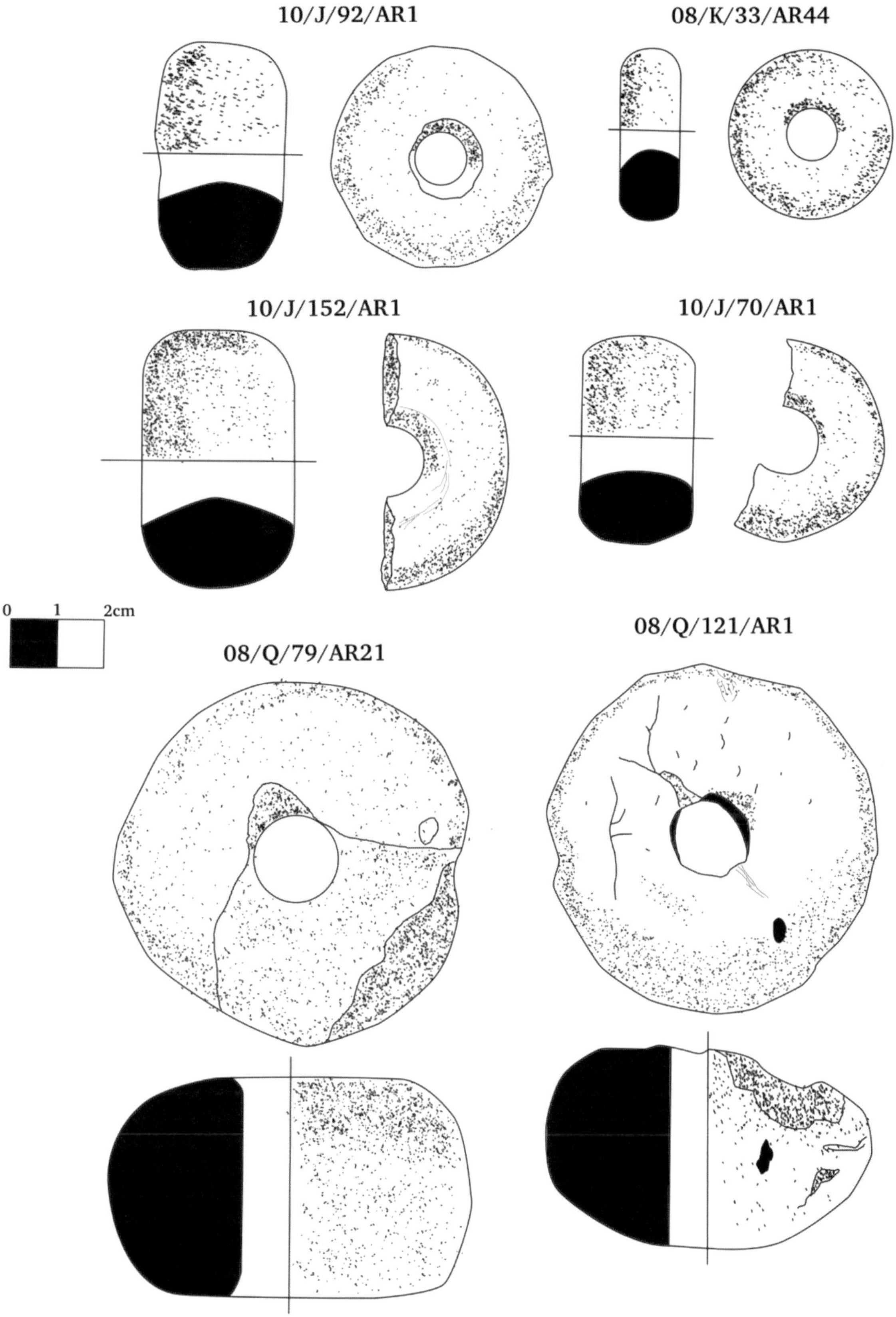

Figure 4.8. Loom weights and basalt rings from Megiddo

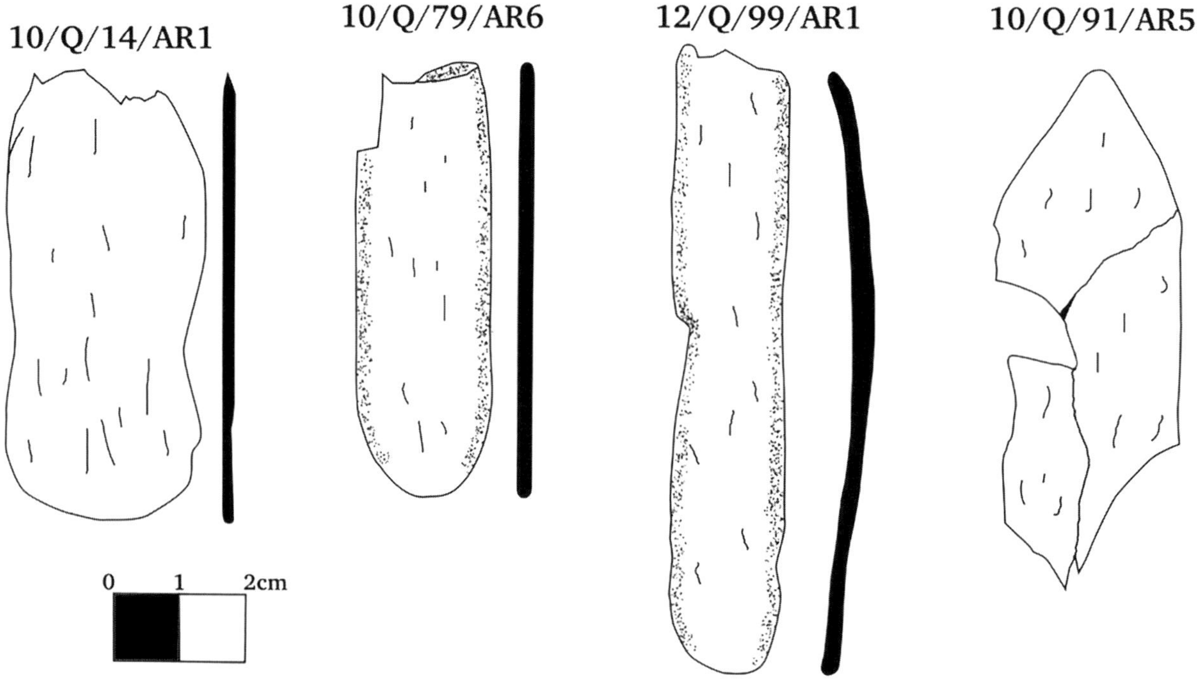

Figure 4.9. Bone spatulae from Megiddo

(Plate 2). As discussed in Chapter 3, it has been decided to study the two categories together, since they would have shared a similar function, meaning fixing small errors during the weaving process and keeping the warp threads in order to avoid overlapping (Fig. 4.9).

Some items might have come from layers preceding the EBA; however, their chronology is far from accurate. Several bone spatulae are known from the EB layers, with triangular and pen-nib points. Their production decreases during the MBA, when most of the findings are pin beaters, with long, thin points. The LBA and the Iron Age I have preserved only a minimal quantity of both categories, suggesting that other tools or other materials, such as wood, might have been employed during these periods. The manufacturing of bone spatulae reaches its peak during the Iron Age II, to which most of the items belong. They include long and triangular points, while the other end is generally simply rounded to adapt their shape. A few objects with pen-nib points are also known.

4.1.9 Needles

The category of needles includes actual needles as well as bodkins as it is impossible at the present state of the research to distinguish their function. They may in fact have been employed to sew actual textiles, even if coarse, or to produce nets, mattresses, and cushions. They have been included in this study above all for their clear link with textiles in the broader sense, as well as to check if the context of findings might be the same as other textile tools.

Eighty needles and bodkins have been published from Megiddo, which is a very small number. However, we must consider that wooden bodkins would have certainly existed, as well as very thin bronze needles which might have been lost, broken (and therefore be unrecognisable), or recast.

Only a few objects from the EBA, very different from each other, have been found. A group of five bodkins are made of bone, though they are fragmentary, and only one has the eye preserved. A bone needle with a large triangular head was certainly not employed for sewing. Finally, a bronze needle has a central thickening and the eye missing, which makes its place in this needle category far from certain. A few more needles have been preserved from the MBA, most made of bronze with an eye made by bending the upper part of the shaft, like those at Beth Shean and several other Levantine sites. Two bone needles are also present, one from a tomb. The LBA shows a similar situation, with bronze needles both from tombs and domestic units, all made of bronze. Their dimensions are widely different, with small thin needles as well as long thick items. The most significant number of needles come from the Iron Age I levels, with very different dimensions and materials. One needle case has also been found, with needles still present. As in previous periods, most of the needles have an eye made by bending the upper part of the shaft. Ivory, bone, and iron specimens are also present. Fewer needles are known from Iron Age II, almost all are made of bronze and one of bone. Measurements and morphologies are the same as the previous period.

Needles are present both in tombs and domestic contexts, proving the continuity of their presence in funerary assemblages. In recent excavations at Megiddo, they are seldom found in the same loci with other textile tools. However, Chicago expeditions found several contexts where needles are associated with spindle whorls and loom weights, albeit always in small quantities.

4.1.10 Contexts of findings

Textile tools are found in all areas of Megiddo excavations and for all periods under consideration. Very few are known for EBA levels, but this is understandable given the small size of the areas where the most ancient layers have been exposed. Textile tools are generally found individually, and large batches are quite rare. This is particularly true for recent excavation objects, although the Chicago excavations have seen more frequent connections between the various textile tools. Generally, spindle whorls are found in groups of two or three items. It is interesting to note that they are generally made of different materials, mixing bone with stone whorls and (more rarely, given their lower number), with pottery and perforated sherds. Other textile tools, such as bone spatulae, needles, and loom weights can appear in the same contexts with whorls. However, it should be noted that the vast majority of textile tools come from scattered contexts, without objects clearly connected to the textile industry. The two batches of loom weights, 96/H/44 and E=3036, were found with other textile tools, one bone spatula for the first batch and a possible needle or toggle pin for the second. It is therefore clear that no textile workshop or large, industrial production area can be identified in Megiddo. Textile manufacture was probably carried out at a domestic level, with the different phases of production located in different buildings. However, the materials employed and the careful polishing of bone and stone spindle whorls suggest that it involved quality production. Furthermore, the presence of trends in the choice of materials, shapes, and dimensions indicate that a certain level of centralisation or uniformity of the materials and final products was required.

Textile tools are frequently found inside tombs, especially spindle whorls, which start to appear among grave goods in the MBA. During the LBA, this tradition intensifies, as can be seen especially by bone spindle whorls and buttons, while during the Iron Age it is less frequent. Whorls found in tombs can be made of bone, stone, or even pottery; sometimes even perforated sherds can be found. Loom weights are rarely attested, especially for the MB III/LB I, even those made of unbaked clay. Most of the EB/MB basalt rings included in the catalogue come from tombs, which make their contextualisation even more difficult. Bone spatulae and needles are rarely found in tombs, generally dated to MB or LB periods, and probably had no significant meaning for the afterlife.

4.1.11 Conclusions: development of textile tools at Megiddo

Textile tools from Megiddo are very numerous and constitute a highly interesting case study. Bone spindles and shafts are fairly abundant, and at least one actual spindle has been recognised. The fact that spindle whorls were mounted on a peg and not on the shaft has important implications for the minimum hole diameter of the spindle whorls. A second item, with several rings and a possible spindle whorl, may have been a completely different object. However, even in this case, the possible 'whorl' was mounted on a core, not on a true shaft. Bone spindles appear in Megiddo at the very end of the MBA or the beginning of the LB I, and their production reaches its peak during the LB II–III, before decreasing during the Iron Age. This is a trend common throughout all the Southern Levant.

Spindle whorls are indeed the most numerous textile tools at the site. The EBA and MBA spindle whorls were mainly made of pottery, and it is only from the Middle Bronze Age I (MB I) that bone whorls begin to be produced, even if in small quantities. Stone spindle whorls were also present, but were not numerous. During the LBA, bone becomes the most exploited material for whorls, substituting pottery. Pottery and stone whorls are quite rare in this phase. The dome shape becomes prevalent, influenced by the shape of the natural source. During the Iron Age, stone becomes more widely used. During the Iron Age I, bone is still the most prevalent material, but shapes are more varied than in the preceding period. Stone whorls are mostly made of limestone and steatite, and shapes are generally conical or dome. A new shape appears in this period, namely the conical truncated, but this would never become widespread in Megiddo. In Iron Age II, stone whorls are twice as numerous as bone whorls. Shapes are generally conical and dome, except for pottery spindle whorls, which continue to tend towards rounded shapes such as spherical and biconical. To spindle whorls, perforated sherds must be added. These are quite rare during the EB–BM periods, and they reach their production peak during the Iron Age I. Loom weights are introduced during the MB I, while the EB examples may simply have been counterweights. MB loom weights are conical and made of both baked and unbaked clay. Three elements are remarkable: some are vertically perforated, which implies a very different system of binding; some of them are also covered by a slip and highly refined and polished; and many of them present scarab stamps. They are produced throughout the entire MBA but also during the LB I, lasting longer than in other Levantine contexts. During the Iron Age period, the production of clay loom weights flourishes again, with cylindrical, doughnut, and spherical shapes. There is only a single example of a spool loom weight from an Iron Age I context.

Basalt rings can be considered either loom weights or spindle whorls. Their very light weight, however, is in contrast with the heavy weight of clay loom weights. The wide hole and its hourglass shape also make their use as spindle whorls difficult. The evidence from Tell Abu al-Kharaz, however, points to their use both as loom weights and spindle whorls. They are common during the EB phases, as in many other Levantine sites, and very rare in the following phases. A few examples were recognised for Iron Age I–II.

Bone spatulae and beaters are not very common in Megiddo. Spatulae appear during the EB phases, if not earlier, giving way to beaters during the MBA. They are not present for LB and Iron Age I phases, and reach the peak of production in Iron Age II.

Few needles are known for the EBA phase, with very different shapes and materials. During the MBA a new type of needle is introduced, with an eye obtained by bending the upper part of the shaft back on itself; this typology would become the most common in the following period, as in many other Levantine sites.

4.2 Beth Shean

The large mound of Beth Shean (Tel el-Ḥuṣn in Arabic) is situated in a strategic position at the junction of the Jezreel Valley and the Jordan River Valley. It is a steep mound that dominates the fertile Beth Shean Valley, and the site was built on a natural hill. It is located near two streams, ʻAsi and Ḥarod Rivers, which join together to the east of the mound. The presence of several water sources enabled the sustenance of many communities, which now form clusters of small mounds and are a typical feature of this region (Mazar and Mullins 2006, 3). The mound is more than 4 ha in area, however, only a part of it was occupied during the Bronze and Iron Age periods. Furthermore, the whole summit of the mound was occupied only during the EBA and Byzantine periods or later, while during the 2nd millennium BC the settled area was limited to 1.5–2 ha, which can accommodate around 500 people (Mazar 2010, 241–2). During this period, the largest and most important site of the Valley was Tel Reḥov, 5 km south of Beth Shean.

The Egyptian centre during the LBA appears quite small and without defensive walls; most of its buildings were administrative and cultic, but a residential area has also been excavated.

The first excavations were carried out between 1921 and 1933 by the University Museum of the University of Pennsylvania (henceforth UME), led by C.S. Fisher, A. Rowe, and G.M. Fitzgerald. Several layers of occupation were exposed and divided into 18 different phases, from the Neolithic period to the medieval period. The most important findings belong to the Egyptian occupation during the LBA and Early Iron Age periods, with the identification of temples, a 'Governor's residency' and the households of the Egyptian garrison (Mazar and Mullins 2006, 8).

The final excavation reports only appeared decades after the excavations, and especially thanks to the commitment of Frances James; unfortunately, not all the layers that were excavated have been published. A second excavation project was conducted by Y. Yadin and S. Geva in 1983, which focused on layers from the Iron Age I period, although the project was not continued afterwards.

Nine excavation seasons were conducted by the Hebrew University of Jerusalem from 1989 to 1996 under the directorship of A. Mazar. These new excavations were able to fully document the areas exposed by the UME and to investigate almost the entire stratigraphic sequence. The levels uncovered by Mazar's team span from the EBA period to the Islamic period, and are divided into 10 areas: L, P, G, Q, S, R, N, M, T (a small probe), and H (Byzantine). Area L is located on the slope of the mound where UME excavations only exposed Byzantine periods, while the new excavations also brought to light burials from the Middle Age and part of the EBA. In area P, levels from the medieval to the Hellenistic phase have been uncovered, as well as an occupation from the Iron Age II period. Area G is a small trench that has demonstrated the presence of MBA layers immediately under the Byzantine layers, thus indicating a lack of occupation of this part of the mound for most of 2nd and 1st millennium BC. Area Q is a key area, situated at the top of the mound, where UME excavations uncovered the so-called Building 1500 and the Governor's Residency. The periods exposed in this area are the LB II and the Early Iron I. Area S covers a similar chronological frame, but also exposed important buildings from Iron II. It is a large area on the southeastern corner of the mound and is published in volumes I and III (Mazar and Panitz-Cohen 2006; Panitz-Cohen and Mazar 2009). Area R was first excavated by UME and exposed a series of temples. Evidence from the EBA to the LBA has been published in volumes II and IV (Mazar 2007; 2012). Area N is located where UME identified building 1700, along with some houses north of it. The chronology of this area spans between the LB II and Iron Age B and is mainly focused on the period of the Egyptian occupation. Area M is located on the southeastern terrace of the mound where the UME excavations partially exposed EB levels, which are the focus of this trench. The last two areas, T and H, did not reach levels that are of interest within this work (Table 4.2).

The textile tools from the excavations by the Hebrew University are well studied and published (Yahalom-Mack and Mazar 2006; Yahalom-Mack 2007; Panitz-Cohen and Yahalom-Mack 2009). Nonetheless, the site was chosen as one of the key sites for this research for three main reasons: the first is that the materials, already studied, have provided a reliable starting point to understand the different terminological issues and labels given to textile tools in the region.

Table 4.2. Chronological chart (Braun 2004, fig. 5.1; Mazar 2010, tab. 1)

Period	*Century BC*	*UME level*	*HU local strata in Area R, S*	*HU local strata in other areas*
Medieval		Ia		P-1
Early Islamic		Ib		P-2; L-1; H-1
Byzantine		II		P-3; H-2; L-2
Roman		III		P-4
Hellenistic		III		P-5
Iron IIB	Late 8th			P-6 (squatters)
Iron IIB	8th until 732	IV and parts of V		P-7
Iron IIB	9th–early 8th	Parts of V?		P-8a-b
	Mid-9th	Parts of V		P-9 (surface in probe)
Iron IIA	10th	Parts of V	S-1 (massive buildings)	P-10 (surface in probe)
Iron IB	11th	Temples od V and structures of Late VI	S-2 (revival of town)	N-2?
Iron IA	12th, Egyptian 20th Dynasty	VI Late VII	S-3 S-4 S-5?	Q-1; N-3a-b
LB IIB	13th, Egyptian 19th Dynasty	VII VIII		Q-2; N-4 Q-3
LB IIA	14th	IX1	R-1a	
LB IB	Late 15th	IX2	R-1b	
LB IA–B	15th	–	R-2	
Late MB IIB	16th	XA	R-3	
Late MB IIB	Late 17th	XB	R-4	
MB IIB	Late 18th/17th	XB/XI	R-5	
GAP				
Intermediate Bronze Age (EB IV/MB I)	23rd–21st	XI (mixed)	R-6	
EB III	27th–24th	Parts of XI & XII	R-7-R-12	M-1
EB II	29th–28th	Meager remains	GAP	Scattered sherds
Late EB IB	32nd–30th	XIII XIV		M-2 M-3; L-4
EB IB	33rd–32nd	XV		
Early EB IB	34th–33rd	XVI		
Early EB IB	35th–34th	XVII south		
Late Neolithic–Early Chalcolithic	6th–5th millennia	XVII north		
Late Neolithic–Early Chalcolithic	6th–5th millennia	XVIII		
Late Neolithic–Early Chalcolithic	6th–5th millennia	XIX = below lev. XVIII		

Second, the renewed excavation gives a trustworthy chronology, within which the items from the UME excavations can also be examined. Finally, the site was under direct control and administration of the Egyptians during the LBA/Iron Age I and is evidently relevant to the aims of this research (Mazar 2010). It is clearly stated that the items used for the textile production were of Levantine production and were not influenced by the Egyptian domination (Mazar 2009, 20–21). However, given the paucity of Egyptian textile tools thus far published, it seemed an obvious choice to test this statement in light of the objects studied during the research.

Beth Shean has returned an abundant quantity of textile tools, spanning from the very beginning of the EBA to the Iron Age. Priority has been given to the findings of the renewed excavations directed by A. Mazar. A very small number of objects from the UME excavations are at the Rockefeller Museum, while most of the findings are in the University of Pennsylvania Museum of Archaeology and Anthropology (henceforth Penn Museum). All the items available in these publications (Fitzgerald 1930; FitzGerald and Bache 1935; James and McGovern 1993) and in the Penn Museum's online catalogue have been added to the objects I have been able to study directly, in order to provide the largest quantity of textile tools possible. Those in the Penn Museum are recorded in the catalogue with their inventory number preceded by a 'P.' in the field 'notes'. Unfortunately, the notes indicate that a large number of these tools were discarded (Braun 2004, 56).

4.2.1 Spindles

Complete spindles have not been preserved at Beth Shean for the periods under consideration. Even the bone and ivory rods, which constitute a general feature of Levantine sites during the LBA and Iron Age, are not present at this site. Only one ivory shaft might be recognised in the broader category of spindles/shafts, which is dated to the Iron Age II.

4.2.3 Spindle whorls

The first spindle whorls are known in Beth Shean from the Neolithic/Chalcolithic period. There are very few examples for all the earliest periods, including the EBA, probably due to the small areas that reach these layers. Neolithic and Chalcolithic layers have been published by Braun (2004) as revising the UME excavations and spindle whorls first appear in UME level XVIII. However, the stratigraphic sequence is somewhat compromised, and the tools do not provide their own chronological sequence. Furthermore, it is clear that only a small number of the objects were retained by Fitzgerald, while the others were discarded (Braun 2004, 56). Evidence of textile tools within these earlier layers are therefore limited and only partially reliable. The available data show that all the spindle whorls are made of stone, mostly limestone, and that the most common shape is discoid. A similar pattern is also clear for level XVII, but in this period the dome shape also begins to appear. In total, seven spindle whorls are published for level XVIII and six for level XVII.

The EBA period shows a small number of spindle whorls with only 10 recorded. Most of these are made of stone, with limestone the most common, but in this period, pottery spindle whorls are also produced. Their shapes are more varied than in the earliest periods, but the discoid shape is still prevalent. However, cylindrical and biconical shaped objects are also used (Plate 3).

A larger number of spindle whorls is published for the MBA, but the numbers are still quite low, with 27 objects for the whole period. Stone spindle whorls (limestone, gypsum, and a few made of basalt) continue to be produced, but to a lesser extent than in the previous periods, and they are matched in numbers by bone spindle whorls which now appear for the first time. For the other sites, the shape of the source material influences the object made from it, with most of the bone spindle whorls cut as a dome. It is worth noting that not a single example of a pottery spindle whorl is known for the MBA. When compared to Megiddo, where pottery is the only material used for the EBA and continued to be prevalent during the MBA, while stone is rarely employed, the difference between the two sites is remarkable. During the MBA in Beth Shean, the most common shape is the dome, especially used for producing bone spindle whorls but also one of gypsum; the discoid spindle whorls, all made of stone, are also well represented. A very few examples of cylindrical, conical and lenticular forms are also known, and one button-shaped item appears for the first time. Very few weights are available for this period, and it seems that light spindle whorls under 10 g were preferred, while a couple of examples are between 10 to 20 g, and another couple over 20 g (Plate 3).

The largest group of spindle whorls comes from LBA levels and numbers 77 objects. Compared to Megiddo, the entire assemblage of objects at Beth Shean is small, but it has to be remembered that the settlement was somewhat reduced for the whole 2nd millennium BC, and that Tel Rehov was the most important site in the region during that period. Another point to be kept in mind is the difference in the chronological division that is adopted for Megiddo and Beth Shean. In fact, for Megiddo the LB III phase is used to indicate most of the 12th century BC, while for Beth Shean this century belongs to the Iron Age IA phase. This work, as indicated in the general discussion, does not provide a new chronological frame for each site, and follows the indications of the site excavators. This choice may generate some confusion, and for this reason macro-differences such as those seen for the LBA–Iron Age transition will be noted (Fig. 4.10).

During the LBA in Beth Shean, spindle whorls were produced in bone/ivory or stone (Plate 4). Forty-five bone spindle whorls have been excavated, most of them dome-shaped and only a few conical, discoid, or button-shaped. Thirty spindle whorls are made of stone, mostly of gypsum, but also of limestone and steatite. Only a very limited

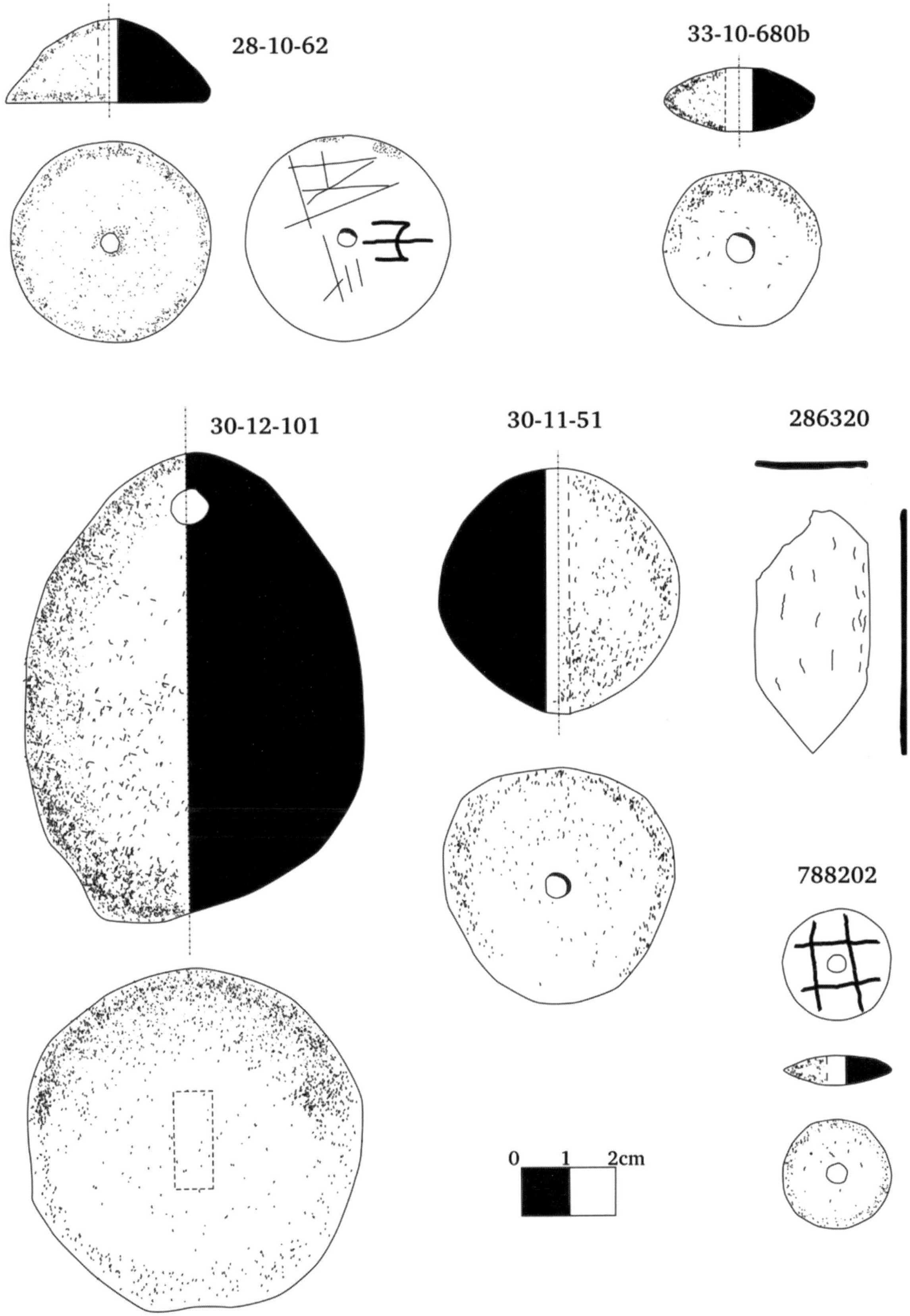

Figure 4.10. Textile tools from Beth Shean

number is made of serpentine, slate, and sandstone. The dome shape is the most common, also among the stone whorls, and constitutes the overall preferred shape (52 out of 77). Two pottery spindle whorls have also been recorded. Besides the dome shape, conical spindle whorls are quite numerous (12 in total) as well as discoid (seven), while only four spindle whorls have different forms, *i.e.* button, lenticular, and biconical. A very few spindle whorls have their weight recorded, 9 out of 77, and the minimum is 2.34 g, while the maximum is 30.49 g, with no clear, recognisable pattern of distribution (Plate 3).

Similarly to the other sites, Iron Age I and Iron Age II have been divided to better understand the development during this crucial period. As stated before, Iron Age I coincides with the 12th century BC, and includes the Egyptian domination under the 20th Dynasty. Spindle whorls from Iron Age I levels are quite numerous, but less so than in the LBA, with 53 examples recorded. There are a large variety of materials, especially regarding the stone whorls, which are the largest group. More than half, in fact, are made of stone (29), with gypsum dominant, some limestone, and a few examples of chalk, basalt, marl, serpentine, and steatite. Bone and ivory spindle whorls are still numerous (19) but less than those made of stone, contrary to Megiddo. Five spindle whorls are also made of pottery, which continues to be a rarely used material for this kind of tool. Finally, one bronze spindle whorl is recorded and it is, thus far, the only known example in the Levant for the period under consideration.

Their shapes are extremely varied. The most common shape is the dome, but numerous examples are conical and cylindrical. A few are lenticular, discoid, button (all made of bone), biconical (made of pottery), one spherical (pottery), and one conical truncated (bronze). The weights are available for a large number of items (35 out of 55) and clearly point to a preference for light and very light spindle whorls. Most of these, in fact, are under 10 g, with some extremely light and probably not spindle whorls (see the discussion for Megiddo). A very few are between 10 and 20 g, seven between 20 and 30 g, and just five are over 30 g (Plate 3).

For Iron Age II levels, only 44 spindle whorls have been identified, with a large variety of materials employed. As already seen for Megiddo, in this period stone spindle whorls are the predominant group, with just one example made of bone, and two of pottery. However, in contrast to Megiddo, the stone spindle whorls are mostly made of steatite, with a smaller number of limestone, although there is more variety. In fact, gypsum whorls are the most common (18), followed by those made of limestone; small groups of steatite, sandstone, and serpentine have also been recorded. Shapes, on the contrary, are very homogeneous, with most of the spindle whorls dome-shaped (32), only two conical, four cylindrical, and a single example of discoid, biconical, and conical truncated. This is clearly a different pattern than that of Megiddo, where in this phase conical whorls are the most frequent group, together with dome-shaped, while in Beth Shean only two conical examples occur. Unfortunately, no weights are provided for this period (Plate 3).

Some spindle whorls appear in funerary contexts; however, the same tombs also contain intrusive Roman materials (*e.g.* tomb 42 (Oren 1973, fig. 34)), which make the attribution of these objects to the periods under consideration uncertain.

4.2.4 Perforated sherds

Perforated sherds are known from Beth Shean for all the periods under consideration. They begin to appear in Level XVIII (Neolithic/Chalcolithic phase), where they are not very numerous (although it is likely that only part of these were retained (Braun 2004, 56)); this is true for the early phases as well as the later periods. The highest numbers are reached in Iron Age II (nine objects), although a similarly small number also appear for the EBA. However, if summed with the spindle whorls, their percentage over the entire corpus of spinning tools is much more relevant. In fact, they represent 22% of the Neolithic/Chalcolithic spindle whorls, and reach their peak during the EBA, where they form 44% of the entire spinning assemblage. In later phases, their percentage is certainly less relevant, with 17–18% during MBA and Iron Age II, and under 5% for LBA and Iron Age I. They are characterised by a fairly large diameter, 4.9 cm on average, and a rather small thickness, 0.89 cm on average. The largest sherd measures 7.4 cm in diameter, the smallest 3 cm. Weights can measure between 8.5 and 59.4 g, with an average weight of 22.9 g. However, it should be noted that the few available weights do not show a regular distribution, but are divided between light weights (around 10 g) and heavier weights (slightly over 50 g). The heaviest examples all belong to Iron Age II, but in the same period, lighter weights are also present.

Similarly to Megiddo, the catalogue includes all the perforated sherds with a single hole, even if the hole is hourglass or not perpendicularly perforated, making the fastening to the spindle more difficult (but not impossible). Since the largest corpus of perforated sherds is that of Hazor, they will be discussed in much more detail in the corresponding chapter.

They appear in domestic contexts as well as in large public buildings, and in many cases (for example 281338 and 380553 in the catalogue) they are found in the same context with basalt rings for the EBA, and with loom weights for the Iron Age, as well as with spindle whorls.

4.2.5 Spinning bowls

As seen in Chapter 4.4, spinning bowls are bowls with loops inside, which can vary from a single loop to four, which can be attached either to the base or the interior rim. Beth Shean has returned a very large collection of these items, spanning from the LBA to the beginning of the Iron Age (Fig. 4.11). The base is generally flat, but disc and ring bases are also known (Martin 2009, 445), there are generally two loops (but examples with a single loop are also known) (Dothan 1963, figs 1.10–11), attached to the base (Plate 4). They were locally made but are considered as products of the Egyptian domination of the Southern Levant, and for this reason are labelled as Egyptian-style pottery. A large quantity of Egyptian-style pottery was found in Beth Shean for levels corresponding to the 19th and 20th Egyptian Dynasties, while a very small quantity of this pottery is known for levels corresponding to the 18th Dynasty. This was generally locally produced, with only a very low percentage imported from Egypt. Egyptian-style pottery includes mostly household vessels, most of which are coarse products, and certainly not copies of luxury items (Martin 2016, 70). However, cooking pots were made following local typologies. It seems that an Egyptian population, with Egyptian workers, lived alongside a local population. It has been noted that three commonly considered female activities – food processing by grinding cereals, cooking, and textile production – were characterised in Beth Shean by the use of local objects, like those found in other Canaanite sites. This fact may indicate that these activities were carried out by local women married to Egyptian people or working for the garrison. Among the textile tools, only the spinning bowls did not belong to the local tradition (Mazar 2009, 19), as using a spinning bowl meant adopting the splicing technique that was no longer used in the Levant. However, changing the technique of textile production is not so simple as the excavator appears to suggest. Spinning and weaving is a very traditional craft, with few changes over long periods. It seems more probable that Egyptian spinners and/or weavers were present at Beth Shean alongside the local population. If the spinning bowls were not used for plying fibres after splicing but only for plying any kind of threads, then their adoption by the local population might be more easily explained, as this does not imply a complete change in the fibre preparation technique. Furthermore, the only textile fragments preserved from Beth Shean, are not described as showing splicing (Shamir 2009, 608).

The first example of a spinning bowl comes from level IX of the UME excavations, and should therefore be placed at the end of the 18th Dynasty or at the very beginning of the 19th Dynasty. A few other examples are known for the LB II period, corresponding to the 19th Dynasty, while the large majority belongs to the Iron Age, which should be placed during the Egyptian 20th Dynasty. After this phase, spinning bowls disappear, with a single example dating to Iron Age IB, and not a single example dating to later phases. The sudden disappearance of this tool from the site might indicate a resistance in adopting it by the local population, and to a use that was confined to Egyptian spinners, or at least closely linked to the Egyptian garrison. When the garrison left at the beginning of the Iron Age, the spinners who used the tool seem to leave too. This is highly significant data. Unlike other sites in the Levant (see Table 4.6), which do not exhibit a comparable number of spinning bowls, the concentration of these artefacts strongly suggests they served as a cultural marker associated with the Egyptians. If Orit Shamir is correct (Shamir 2015) in asserting that the splicing technique ceased in the Southern Levant before the LBA, the presence of these bowls may point to several factors:

- The presence of Egyptian spinners;
- The spinning of linen, as further supported by palaeobotanical evidence;
- A fundamentally different *chaîne opératoire* for linen processing.

Given that the Southern Levant was already producing yarn through draft spinning without the use of spinning bowls, it is reasonable to conclude that these bowls were introduced to accommodate spinners accustomed to a different flax-processing tradition. This necessity likely led to local potters being commissioned to produce them, as evidenced by the local origin of the pottery.

4.2.6 Loom weights

All the objects that can be used as loom weights are included and discussed in the catalogue. Basalt rings will be discussed in the next chapter, given the difficulty of distinguishing a spindle whorl from a loom weight.

During the EBA, no possible loom weights have been recognised, while in the late MBA conical loom weights begin to appear. They are known for level XB of the UME excavations and from area R of the Mazar excavations, spanning from stratum R-3 to R-5, with just one item that could be slightly earlier (R-5-7). MBA loom weights at Beth Shean are very homogeneous: all are made of clay, baked or unbaked, and are carefully shaped and pierced, except in one case, where the holes made from the two sides do not join. None of the examples shows a surface treatment or a vertical hole as in Megiddo, and they are quite simple objects. The only feature typical of these examples is a slight convexity on the sides at the height of the hole. Furthermore, none of them exhibits a scarab imprint, as is the case at Megiddo and Farʿah (S) (Fig. 4.12).

They can measure from 7.9 cm to 11 cm in height, with a maximum diameter from 5.1 cm to 8.2 cm. They are generally lighter than those of Megiddo, with a maximum weight of 596 g, and a minimum weight of 267 g.

From the LBA, loom weights have generally not been recovered in the Levant. However, in Beth Shean some objects from the UME excavations belong to levels IX–VII, which correspond to the LB II. The most striking feature is that all the possible typologies of loom weights seem to be

288120

288053

188297/6

Figure 4.11. Selection of Beth Shean textile tools 288120, 288053, 188297/6 (courtesy of the Israel Antiquity Authorities)

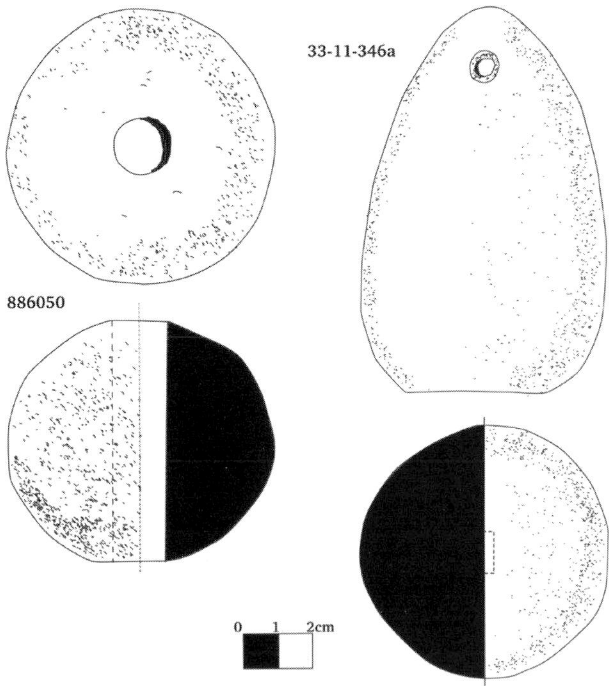

Figure 4.12. Loom weights from Beth Shean

represented. In fact, a couple of the typical MBA conical clay loom weights are recorded, which might be a relic from the previous period. The other types are doughnut and spherical loom weights made of clay, a pear-shaped gypsum and a clay spool loom weight. While the other typologies are all represented in later periods and do not represent a problem, spool shaped loom weights are more puzzling. They appear in LB II levels (15 for level VIII and 8 for level VII) and in Iron Age I levels; some were found in clusters, one for level VIII with 15 spools grouped together in a semicircular stone niche, and one for level VII, where three objects were found together with a total of eight objects (James and McGovern 1993, 188). The publications refer to them as bread models (James 1966, figs 105.8–12; James and McGovern 1993, 188), but from the beginning of the Iron Age, a spool was a common shape for loom weights, and measurements of these objects are similar to those of the other sites (Rahmstorf 2005). One item has five scarab impression on the surface, which were interpreted by James (1966, fig. 105.9) as imnyt 'daily offerings'. However, it seems quite strange that several imprints of the same type were made on a single object and there seems to be no reference of a similar tradition of offering clay models of food in Egypt for contexts that are not related to tombs. An alternative explanation was offered by Brandl (2009, 662–3), who views clay balls with several seal impressions objects as being connected with the faience industry, with parallels from Tell el-Amarna. In his hypothesis, only the spool with hieroglyph impressions should be considered as pertaining to bead production, while the other similar objects were actual spools. This explanation seems more plausible, even if the early chronology of the other spools constitutes a problem. However, this must be taken with added caution given the presence of other loom weight typologies, which seem quite misplaced in LBA levels. Finally, we must also remember that spool clay loom weights are not a very common find in the Southern Levant, compared to the impressive numbers of the Northern Levant and Anatolia (Laurito 2013; Lumb 2014; Venturi 2020). Finally, it must be considered that their appearance partially overlaps with the presence of the Egyptian garrison and the spinning bowls. If their interpretation as loom weights is correct, then textile production in LBA Beth Shean must have been extremely composite, utilising a unique and unprecedented milieu of different traditions, combining spinning bowls and warp weighted looms.

Iron Age IA levels show a few examples of clay spools, as well as some examples of clay spherical loom weights and one made of gypsum.

All these objects thus far considered do not appear in great quantities until the Iron Age IB–II, when Beth Shean finally shows features similar to the other Levantine sites. A huge number of loom weights were recovered, especially from building 28636, from which 109 examples are known, all made of unbaked clay and doughnut-shaped (Yahalom-Mack and Mazar 2006, 476, tab. 13.1). They were found in two main clusters in the central hall, while some others are scattered through the hall. A wooden beam found nearby might have been part of the loom. In the report, two or three looms have been postulated near the eastern wall. In one of the two clusters, the weights spanned an extension of 1.5 m and may have been divided in two rows (Yahalom-Mack and Mazar 2006, 481). Together with these loom weights, three unfired conical objects were found. They could not have been used as loom weights since each object weighs more than 1 kg, and thus would have broken the warp threads. Their usage is not known – a function as jar stopper has been proposed (Yahalom-Mack and Mazar 2006, 474), although this is not satisfactory since it does not explain the presence of a hole in each of them. Another possible explanation could be that they might have been used in the loom as counterweights, as can be seen in several ancient and modern looms.

To this large batch, we must add another 185 loom weights found in the Mazar and UME excavations. They are varied and different in terms of their shape and materials employed. The largest group (85) is again represented by spherical and doughnut-shaped loom weights, almost all made of clay (baked or not), except one example which is made of basalt. Another very large group (75) is represented by pear-shaped objects, to which we should probably add the conical specimens (18). In this case the material is not homogeneous, but stone is the prevalent choice. In fact, only one pear-shaped and eight conical weights are made of clay. All the others are made of stone, with a strong prevalence of gypsum, which is very common in this valley. Forty-seven pear-shaped and 10 conical loom weights are made of gypsum, 16 of basalt, and 9 of limestone (Plate 4). The use of stone loom weights is typical of this region as the excavations in Tell 'Amal (Shamir 2013, 1–2) and Rehov prove (Mazar 2019).

4.2.7 Basalt rings

Mazar's excavations of Beth Shean have provided a well-documented and chronologically reliable corpus of basalt rings, as defined in Chapter 4.6 (Plate 4). They are divided between polished and unpolished objects, although this distinction seemed unnecessary for this research (Mazar and Rotem 2012, 368). A few items excavated by the UME were also available in the Rockefeller Museum and therefore appear in the catalogue. Unfortunately, in most cases it has not been possible to clearly link these objects to specific objects in publications. Twenty-seven basalt rings have been identified in Mazar excavations from area M-3 and M-2. Thirty-six objects are listed in the catalogue. To these, many others should probably be added from the Fitzgerald excavations in the 'Deep cut', but only a small part was retained. In fact, a few are drawn in his publications, but in level XIV it is clearly stated that 'smaller rings of basalt [...] were numerous enough to form a characteristic feature of this stratum' (Fitzgerald and Bache 1935, 13). Both Mazar and UME basalt rings are dated to the EB IB, no basalt rings are known for EB III, in contrast to sites such as Megiddo. Only three possible basalt rings are known for the MBA, which then disappear in later periods. The height of the rings spans from 0.7 to 3.8 cm with an average value of 2.07 cm; the diameter from 1.8 to 5.3 cm with an average value of 3.9 cm; the hole from 0.5 to 1.5 cm, with an average value of 1.08 cm. The weight is given for the vast majority of these tools and ranges between 19.78 and 67.78 g, with an average value of 41.03 g. Similar measures are also known for other sites, such as Megiddo and Tell el-Far'ah (N).

4.2.8 Bone spatulae and beaters

Some examples of what can be called spatulae have been found in small numbers in Beth Shean, though not for all the periods under consideration. It is probable that other examples should be included, but many items lack a drawing or picture that could allow their identification as pertaining to the textile industry. For this reason, it has been decided not to include these items in the catalogue.

The first examples of bone spatulae are recorded for the EBA, from EB I strata as well as from EB III. They generally have a triangular point, when preserved, and none has the other end preserved. No MBA spatulae have been recorded, and only two from the LBA levels. These examples have a large rounded point, and are therefore different from all the other specimens. Only one bone spatula comes from the Iron Age I levels, while 10 examples are known from Iron Age II periods. These can have both a triangular or pen-nib point, and the other end, when preserved, is rounded. Only a single bone spatula comes from building 28636 (and just three spindle whorls, proving that spinning activities were performed elsewhere), where the large batch of loom weights was found.

4.2.9 Needles

As seen for Megiddo, the category of needles includes actual needles as well as bodkins, since it is impossible to clearly distinguish between the two typologies. While the needles from Megiddo were small in number, those of Beth Shean appear to be even less. Certainly, as has been noted for Megiddo, wooden needles and especially bodkins certainly existed. Furthermore, many needles without their eye preserved might not have been recognised. However, the quantity is definitely very small. Both bodkins and needles seem to be used in the site and the eye can be produced by perforating the shaft or bending the upper part of the shaft back on itself. This technique was in use from the MBA in Israel, but known in Beth Shean only from the LBA (Bonn *et al.* 1993, 205).

4.2.10 Contexts of findings

Textile tools are found in all areas of the Beth Shean excavations and for all periods under consideration. Very few are known for the EBA levels, but this is understandable given the small areas of the most ancient layers that have been exposed, and the selection they have been subjected to. Textile tools are generally found individually and large batches are quite rare. As for Megiddo, spindle whorls can be found in groups of two or three items. It is interesting to note that these are generally made of different materials, mixing bone with stone whorls, and more rarely with pottery whorls. Other textile tools, such as bone spatulae and loom weights, can appear in the same contexts with whorls. However, it should be noted that the majority of textile tools come from scattered contexts, without objects clearly connected with the textile industry. The largest batch of textile tools found grouped together are those exposed in building 28636 and studied by O. Shamir in the first volume of Mazar's publications (Yahalom-Mack and Mazar 2006, 477–81). The building is a large dwelling (14 × 14 m), the largest found in this area for the Iron Age, one of the largest excavated in Israel, and was destroyed by a violent conflagration. It includes a central hall with six rooms on its three sides and was probably the residency of a high-ranking family (Mazar 2006, 33). Two batches of loom weights come from the central hall of this building, but, in my opinion, they were not found in rows. The first batch, near the grinding installation, comprised *c.* 70 weights, with two wooden beams that could belong to the loom (Mazar and Sumaka'i Fink 2006, 202–68). They did not appear aligned, but rather piled in the corner, as if partially fallen. A second batch of 30 loom weights was found slightly to the north with a few others scattered around the hall. It is interesting to note that this hall was used both for food processing and weaving activities. However, cooking was not performed in the building since no ovens have been excavated, and therefore was probably carried out outside the building (Mazar and Sumaka'i Fink 2006, 219). As noted before, spinning was probably carried out in other spaces and not near the looms, since just three spindle whorls were found in the building. The only other textile implement is a single example of a bone spatula.

Only a very small quantity of textile tools is known from funerary contexts, and it seems that their presence in tombs was not a common feature.

4.2.11 Conclusions: development of textile tools at Beth Shean

Spindles are not present in Beth Shean and bone and ivory shafts are also extremely rare, in contrast to the other Levantine sites where at least some specimens are generally attested.

Spindle whorls are quite numerous and are known at the site since the Neolithic/Chalcolithic period. All the recorded items are made of stone, while pottery begins to be used only later, during the EB I. Stone spindle whorls continue to be produced during the MBA, but they are exceeded in number by bone spindle whorls, which are introduced to the site in this period. During the LBA period, bone spindle whorls are the most numerous, but those made of stone are also numerous. During the Iron Age I and II, stone spindle whorls prevail again over those made of bone, even if they continued to be used frequently in the Iron Age I, while they became extremely rare in Iron Age II. Pottery spindle whorls are extremely rare at this site, while in other cases, such as Megiddo, clay is the prevalent material for the EBA. Among the stone spindle whorls, gypsum appears to be a common material, especially from the LBA, which would also be exploited for loom weights. Gypsum items are a typical feature of the Beth Shean Valley and other sites in the region that share the same materials for textile tools, such as Tel ʻAmal, Tell el-Hammah and Tel Rehov (Yahalom-Mack and Mazar 2006, 482; Mazar 2019). The local source was probably the gypsum layer near Gesher, not far from Beth Shean. Steatite, instead, seems to be quite rare at this site.

Along with spindle whorls, we must include perforated sherds. Only a few specimens are recorded, but they appear in all the layers from the Neolithic/Chalcolithic level XVIII onwards.

Spinning bowls are certainly numerous in Beth Shean and are known from layers dating to the LBA and Iron Age I. The first examples belong to layers that should be considered related to the 18th Egyptian Dynasty; more examples occur in layers connected with the 19th Dynasty, but the majority can be dated to the Iron Age IA, under the 20th Dynasty. Only a single example can be placed in Iron Age IB, meaning after the withdrawal of the Egyptian garrison.

In Beth Shean, conical loom weights do not predate the MBA II, while in Megiddo they seem to appear earlier. The LBA appears to be a critical period for loom weight history in Beth Shean. In fact, the Mazar excavations did not find any loom weights for this period, although the UME excavations brought to light some specimens, which should be typical of Iron Age II. Their chronology thus seems highly problematic, and probably not very reliable. Spool objects might, in my opinion, be loom weights, as in all the other Levantine, Anatolian, Cypriot, or Aegean sites (Rahmstorf 2005), but their chronology is, again, quite problematic. Warp-weighted looms were not in use in the Southern Levant before Iron Age I, a period in which Beth Shean appears strictly connected to Egypt, a country in which this type of loom was not in use. Their chronology at the site covers exactly the LBA and Iron Age I periods, and is one of the earliest sites to introduce this kind of loom weight.

Iron Age II loom weights do not present any problem. They are quite numerous, and varied in shape and materials. Beside the spherical and doughnut-shaped loom weights, which are typical of the Southern Levant in this period, pear-shaped and conical examples are also known, most made of stone, which appears to be a typical feature of the region.

Bone spatulae, beaters, and needles are very rare at this site, a feature that clashes with evidence from other Canaanite sites but also with Egypt, where these tools were also in use – never in great numbers, but more numerous than in Beth Shean. Their absence from Building 28636 is especially problematic, given the large evidence of textile production found in this context.

Textile tools found at Beth Shean seem to show that textile production on the site was not performed at an industrial scale, but rather points to domestic production. Even the largest batch of loom weights was found in connection with other household activities, such as food processing, and with a very low number of other spinning or weaving implements.[2] Therefore, no evidence of textile workshops (*i.e.* a specific place where textile production was performed) were found in Beth Shean.

4.3 Hazor

4.3.1 Introduction

Hazor (Tel el-Qedah) lies in the Hula Valley, at the eastern ridge of the Upper Galilee mountains, 25 km north of the Sea of Galilee and 5 km southwest of Lake Hula. To the south it is bounded by the Wadi el-Waqqas (Yadin *et al.* 1958, 1). The site thus has access to abundant fresh water, and Lake Hula offered a wide range of fish. It stands in key position to control the route connecting Southern Canaan with Syria, and from there Mesopotamia. It is worth noting that the material culture of the site shows stronger connections with its northern neighbours than with the south (Ben-Tor 2016, 11).

The site is divided into two main parts, an acropolis or Upper City measuring about 6 ha and a Lower City, a large rectangular plateau to the north of the Tel, measuring about 50 ha. At its widest point, the site was only inhabited during the MBA and LBA, while during the EBA and the Iron Age only the acropolis was occupied. According to Ben-Tor (2016, 9), the estimated population for the 2nd millennium BC is around 15,000 people, and only 1200–1500 people for the Iron Age.

The site was identified by a traveller (J. L. Porter) in 1875, but the first excavations were conducted by John Garstang in 1928 and never fully published (Yadin *et al.* 1958, 3; Ben-Tor 2016, 11). He conducted soundings both in the Upper and Lower Town, giving a first assessment of the period of occupation. Larger excavations were conducted by Y. Yadin on behalf of the Hebrew University of Jerusalem. Yadin conducted five seasons of excavations from 1955 to 1958 and in 1968 with an impressive quantity of workers, opening up 15 areas, six in the Upper City and nine in the Lower City.

Since 1990 new excavations have been carried out by A. Ben-Tor on behalf of the Hebrew University of Jerusalem, co-directed by S. Zuckerman from 2006 to 2014, thanks to the Selz Foundation Hazor Excavations in Memory of Yigael Yadin. The renewed excavations mainly focused on two areas, namely A and M in the Upper City, in order to verify the chronology of the site and answer some remaining questions after Yadin's work. Area A is the central part of the acropolis, while area M is northern, at the junction of the Upper and Lower cities (Ben-Tor 2016, 14–16).

In order to better understand the differences in the quantity of textile tools, it seems necessary to briefly sum up the history of the site. In fact, not all periods show the same pattern of occupation, and some periods show moments of crisis and abandonment of the town.

The first occupation of the site occurred during the Neolithic and Chalcolithic periods, when it shows traces of human activities, especially pottery sherds and flint tools. A Mesopotamian cylinder seal with female figures producing pottery or weaving is dated to the 4th millennium (Ben-Tor 2016, 29, fig. 8). A first settlement seems to only appear from the EBA II, although this period was only exposed in very limited trenches during the excavation. The town already shows traces of massive construction and public building in the EBA III. It is clear, however, that the settlement was restricted to the Upper City, while the Lower City, as stated, was occupied only during the 2nd millennium BC. The Intermediate Bronze Age (Yadin MB I) was a period of general decline in the region, and Hazor was probably reduced to a rural village.

Between IBA and MB II a phase of abandonment might have occurred, with isolated burials and poor structures found on the acropolis. MB IIB sees the flourishing of Hazor, with the beginning of the occupation of the Lower City, which would continue during the LBA. The transition from the MBA to the LBA seems to be gradual, even if the acropolis was entirely reorganised (Ben-Tor 2016, 79). Hazor was probably not destroyed during the military campaign of Thutmosis III (1457 BC) and continued to be wealthy during most of the LBA. Material culture continues to be local, with few pottery examples showing evidence of Egyptian influence, although some luxury items and at least 18 statues were brought from Egypt. In the 13th century BC Hazor shows signs of decline, and is then destroyed by a violent conflagration after the middle of the 13th century BC. The renewed excavations exposed only public and cultic buildings of the LBA, as no residential or domestic units were excavated.[3]

The site remained abandoned until the middle of the 11th century BC, when the Upper City was partially, and only sparsely, reoccupied. Towards the middle of the 10th century BC the settlement is enlarged and fortifications are constructed. In the following century, the town is enlarged outside the gate, with public buildings in the western part and residential units in the eastern part (A5 and M). The 8th century BC marks another period of decline for Hazor, even if the general urban planning is maintained. Stratum V is the last stratum before the Assyrian destruction in 732 BC by Tiglath-Pileser III. After that, the city never recovered its previous greatness (Ben-Tor 2016, 166–7) (Table 4.3).

Hazor has returned a rather large collection of textile tools, very few for the EBA, and many more for later periods. Both published and unpublished items were examined, and bibliography is provided for each tool in the catalogue. Published objects were included because they were only cursorily published, and much more information was needed for this study. Where possible, all the available data from the previous publication has been considered, in order to have the largest corpus possible.

4.3.2 Spindles

Hazor has preserved several bone shafts that might have been used as spindles, as well as pins and cosmetic sticks. This production seems to appear very late at Hazor, especially when compared to Megiddo, with only one shaft datable to LB II. A second item, made of bronze, is listed because of its dimensions, but it is very similar to kohl sticks of the Persian period from the same site. No traces of bronze spindles have so far been recovered in the Southern Levant, but some examples do exist for Anatolia. Furthermore, a spindle whorl from Beth Shean, during the Roman period, preserves traces of a metal shaft. Although improbable,

Table 4.3. Chronological table of Hazor (Zuckerman 2013, 69)

Stratum: Upper Tell	*Stratum: Lower City*	*Archaeological period*	*Absolute date (centuries BC)*	*Archaeological remains*	*Historical references*
XXI		EB II–III	28th	Residential units	
XX–XIX		EB III	27th–24th	Residential units & monumental structures on acropolis (?)	
XVIII		Intermediate Bronze Age	22nd–21st	Residential units on acropolis	
Pre-XVII		MB IIA–B	18th	Burials & structures on the upper tell	Egyptian Execration Texts
XVII	4	MB IIB	18th–17th	Erection of the earthen rampart of the Lower City (?)	Mari Archive
XVI	3	MB IIB	17th–16th	Both Upper and Lower Cities are inhabited, public structures.	
XV	2	LB I	15th		Annals of New Kingdom pharaohs
XIV	1B	LB II	14th		Amarna Archive
XIII	1A	LB II	13th		Papyrus Anastasi I
XII–XI		Iron Age I	11th	Pits & meager architecture	
Xb–Xa Ixb–IXa		Iron Age IIA	Mid-10th–early 9th	6-chambered gate, casemate wall, domestic structures	United monarchy (Solomon?)
VIIIb–VIIIa VIIb–VIIa		Iron Age IIA–B	9th	Casemate wall still used, administrative structures & domestic units	Kingdom of Israel (Omride dynasty)
VIc–VIa Vc–Va		Iron Age IIC	8th	Casemate wall still used, administrative structures & domestic units	Kingdom of Israel: Jeroboam II – Pekah Assyrian destruction by Tiglath-pileser III
IV		Iron Age IIC	8th	Sporadic settlements	Post-Assyrian destruction; Israelite (?) settlement
III		'Assyrian'	7th	Governmental structures on & around the tell	
II		Persian period	5th–4th	Citadel, tombs	
I		Hellenistic period	3rd–1st	Citadel	

metal spindles should be considered as one of the many possible materials with which these tools were produced.

All the other specimens belong to the Iron Age II, mostly to Iron Age IIC. Most of them are broken or small fragments, so they may have belonged to other objects, such as pendants. The surface is left undecorated, and sometimes is not perfectly polished.

In general, these objects are difficult to define with certainty and seem quite different from the other shafts spread throughout the Levant that could have been used as spindles.

4.3.3 Spindle whorls

The first spindle whorls are known from Hazor from the MB II. Early and Intermediate Bronze Age layers show no evidence of spindle whorls but, as stated before, the layers from these early periods were only uncovered to a limited extent. MBA spindle whorls are almost entirely homogenous; all are made of bone, and almost all share a dome shape, which is normal given the source of material (Plate 5). Two spindle whorls, conical truncated and discoid, have very small holes. All these spindle whorls have been published by Yadin but were not available for this study; the dimensions and weights are thus not given in the catalogue (Fig. 4.13).

Spindle whorls belonging to LBA strata are much more numerous, although not if compared to Megiddo. Thirty-seven items are listed in the catalogue, most of them datable to LB II, while only a very limited number are datable to LB I. Shapes and materials are much more varied than during the earlier period. The large majority are still made of bone, with 22 items made of bone or ivory. Stone

Figure 4.13. Selection of Hazor spindle whorls

spindle whorls are also quite widespread, with 10 objects made of stone, most of them likely of serpentinite. Finally, two pottery spindle whorls are also present. These two have a spherical shape, a feature that is common to other sites, such as Megiddo. Stone spindle whorls are mostly dome-shaped, but conical truncated, button and cylindrical examples are also present. All the bone spindle whorls are dome-shaped, except one which is lenticular. Few measurements are available, and some objects are broken. However, it is possible to infer that these objects appear quite small and light, suggesting a textile production oriented towards fine yarns. In fact, the minimum weight is 1.24 g (for the bone button) and the maximum 37.42 g, with an average value of 11.6 g (Plate 5).

Sixty-one spindle whorls were recovered in the Iron Age levels, spanning from Iron Age I to Iron Age IIC, almost twice as many as the LBA. Again, as for LBA levels, it is impressive to see how few examples there are when compared with Megiddo, which shows 120 spindle whorls for Iron Age I and 171 for Iron Age II. There could be many reasons for this difference, not least the failure to trace most of Yadin's materials. Hazor was almost deserted during Iron Age I, and in fact only one spindle whorl belongs to this phase. Nine spindle whorls are dated to Iron Age IIA, 17 to Iron Age IIA–B, and 34 to Iron Age IIC, a total of 60 spindle whorls for the entire Iron Age II. Only nine spindle whorls are made of bone, a fact that appears opposed to the trend of the 2nd millennium BC. Ten spindle whorls are made of pottery, which constitutes a rather large assemblage (Plate 6). The largest set of spindle whorls for Iron Age II are made of stone, with 41 examples preserved (Plate 5). This fact appears consistent with what we have seen for Megiddo, where stone overtakes bone during the Iron Age II period. Several kinds of stone are present, limestone being the most common, but hematite, alabaster, chalk, and probably serpentinite are also present.

The shapes are quite varied in this period, the most common being the dome, with 26 whorls, and the conical, with 17 examples. Conical truncated (7), discoid (4), cylindrical (2), biconical (2), and button (1) are represented to a lesser extent (Plate 5). It is interesting to note that different materials are associated with all the shapes, so there is no evident specialisation (Plate 6). Only the biconical forms are made exclusively of one material, in this case clay. In all other cases, stone is predominant, as is obvious since it is the most common material used in the period. However, conical spindle whorls are all made of stone, except for a single example made of pottery. For Megiddo, buttons are extremely rare and appear not to have had great popularity at both sites.

A fairly large sample of measurements is available, enabling some considerations. The minimum weight is 4.48 g, the maximum 81.04 g, and the average value is 29.86 g. When compared with the LBA, spindle whorls have become much heavier, pointing towards a textile production of medium quality. On closer inspection, however, it appears that they are not homogenously diffused. Almost all the items weigh less than 35 g, and only seven whorls weigh between 54 and 81 g. Between 4 and 35 g they appear more evenly distributed.

4.3.4 Perforated sherds

Perforated sherds have been found at Hazor for all the periods under consideration. However, they were quite rare during the EBA and MBA, while much more common in later periods. They reach their peak during Iron Age II, when their number is almost double than of the LBA. If we consider them as possible spindle whorls, it is interesting to note that they represent almost a third of the entire assemblage of the LBA, and that a similar percentage is also present in the Iron Age II.

Only one perforated sherd is known for the EBA, three from the MBA, and 17 for the LBA. As seen for spindle whorls, Iron Age I was a period of abandonment for the site and only one sherd is known. In Iron Age II, there are 27 perforated sherds. These are characterised by a large diameter, spanning from 3 to 7.7 cm and an average value of 4.9 cm. Their height is generally small, with 0.6 cm as a minimum, 2.8 cm as maximum, and 1.13 cm as the average. Their weights very between 6.4 and 65 g with an average weight of 30 g, comparable to that of the spindle whorls. Half of the specimens weigh between 10 and 20 g.

The catalogue lists all the perforated sherds with a single hole, even if the hole is not perpendicular or is an hourglass shape (Plate 6). Furthermore, rounded and smooth objects are inserted together with irregular objects, which may have had a different purpose.

Since Hazor has preserved a rather large typology of these objects, it seems interesting to discuss them in more detail. Perforated sherds are the perfect candidate for a spinning implement, since they are cheap, widely available, light, and with a large diameter. However, not all the objects that are included within this very broad definition can be considered equally suitable for spinning. The ideal sherd should be similar to A 56432, which is perfectly rounded, with a smooth edge and an almost cylindrical hole. However, the variations can be infinite. A 46615, for example, is a well-rounded and smoothed sherd but has a small, hourglass hole. Another object, A 3804, is rounded but the edge has not been smoothed and the hole is cylindrical. A 5062 is similar, but in this case the hole has an hourglass shape. A 44890 is partially rounded, not smoothed, and has a tiny hole. A 13410 does not have a rounded shape, but the edge has been smoothed and it has a nice cylindrical hole. A 27060 is not rounded and not smoothed, but has a cylindrical hole. Finally, A 41698 has an oblique hole and is not rounded or smoothed at all. This short list highlights how different perforated sherds can be from each other. A 56432 is perfect and A 41698 is its total opposite (Fig. 4.14). They can be rounded or irregular, smoothed or untreated – the most important thing is the hole. The hole should be suitable to insert a shaft. The more hourglass, oblique, or irregular it is, the less probable it is that the sherd was used as a spindle whorl. As is evident from the list, a cylindrical hole can appear in both well worked sherds and in irregular ones. There is no direct correlation between shape or smoothness and cylindrical holes. Could a quadrangular or irregular sherd work as a spindle whorl? Perhaps it would not be the best choice, but it could work.[4] On the contrary, oblique or overly small holes can compromise the usage of the object. To conclude, the most important parameters for a perforated sherd are the shape, diameter, and position of the hole.

4.3.5 Spinning bowls

Traditional spinning bowls were not found at Hazor by Yadin, nor by the Ben-Tor Excavations. Some bowls with a hole on the bottom have at times been considered as spinning bowls; however, they are quite the opposite to spinning bowls, since the latter were (possibly) used with liquid inside and a hole in the bottom would have compromised this function.

A curious sherd with an internal loop was found in a public building in area A1 (Bechar 2017, 334, fig. 7.72). It is interesting to note the peculiar form of the loop, which closely resembles that of a handle. If the loop/handle had been found without the clear profile of the bowl, it would have been classified as an external handle. Its position on the inner side of the bowl enables us to speculate its use as a spinning bowl. However, no traces of thread rubbing inside the loop are present, while most spinning bowls, including those from Beth Shean, clearly show them. Its use as spinning bowl is thus far from conclusive.

4.3.6 Loom weights

Besides the (easy to recognise) perforated pottery sherds and clay loom weights, perforated ring bases are also present. These are much thicker than traditional perforated sherds and were therefore not included in this category. It has been suggested that they might have been loom weights and for

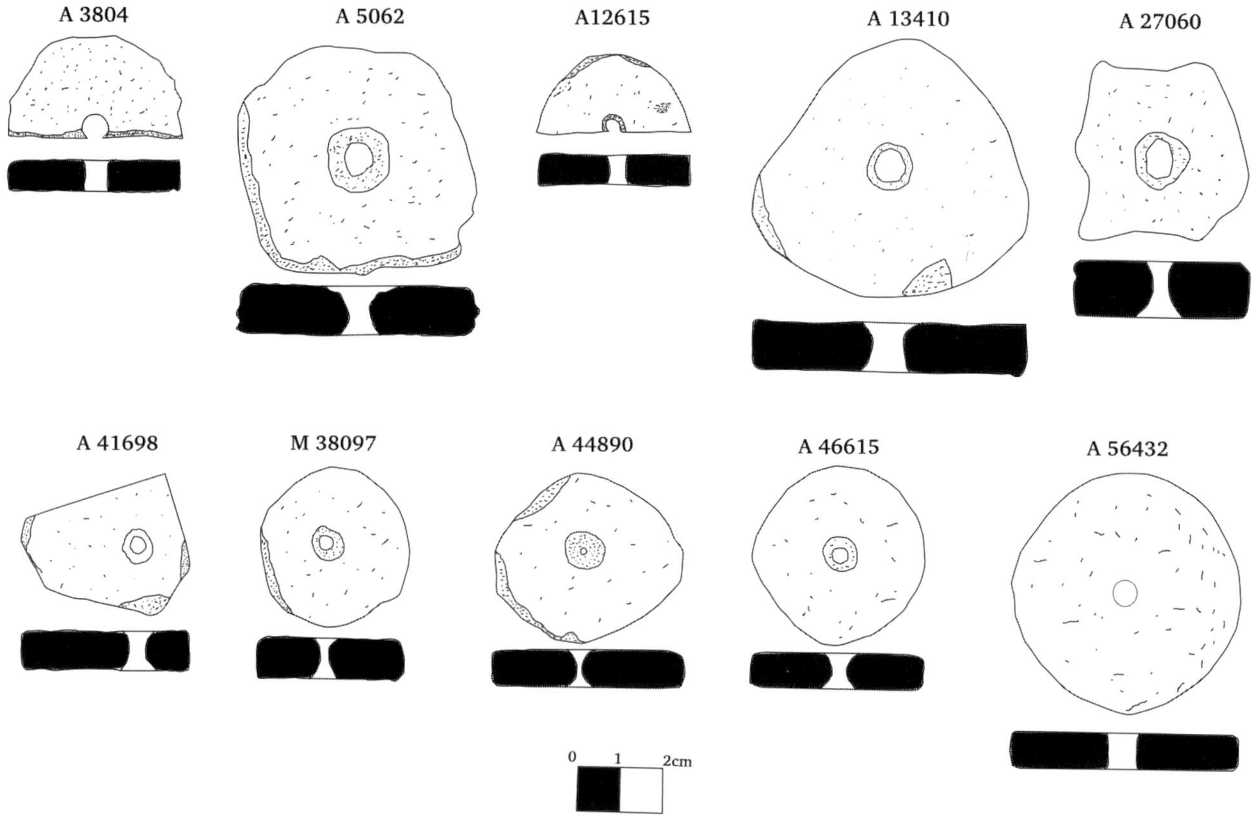

Figure 4.14. Selection of Hazor perforated sherds

this reason they will be discussed in this paragraph, after the 'traditional' loom weights, and they are listed in the catalogue as loom weights (Fig. 4.15).

During the EBA and MBA, no loom weights were produced at Hazor, and the only object listed in the catalogue was probably a counterweight. The conical loom weight, typical of the MBA period, is not present in this phase, but does appear in the LBA. Two of these objects have been excavated by Yadin in area BA (Yadin *et al.* 1989, fig. CCXXXVI: 24–5) and are dated to local phase 11, str. XV, meaning LB I. These are the only two objects of this type known at Hazor, as they have not been found from earlier nor later periods; this is a very intriguing fact, and entirely different from other Levantine sites. Other possible loom weights are known for the LBA, such as a flat trapezoidal weight, which is only partially preserved, and two (or more) spherical clay loom weights, one of which is preserved in small fragments. A spherical stone weight might have been an unfinished spindle whorl, but its conical hole makes it unsuitable to use with a shaft. Finally, several perforated ring bases belong to this phase, although these will be discussed later.

Only one loom weight was identified in the levels corresponding to Iron Age I, which is doughnut-shaped and made of baked clay. The only other materials classified as weights are the perforated ring bases.

Iron Age II is the first period in Hazor in which the use of the warp-weighted loom can be recognised with certainty. Excluding the perforated ring bases, 103 loom weights are listed for the entire period of Iron Age II, 29 for Iron Age IIA–B, and 74 for Iron Age IIC (Fig. 4.16). They are mostly made from clay or baked clay, with several examples only poorly fired (Fig. 4.17). A few objects are made of stone, but in these cases, they are not among the common types of loom weight, even if they could have worked perfectly as such. The large majority, 86 objects, have a rounded, spherical or doughnut shape. In some cases, it is difficult to separate between the two shapes, since most of the objects are broken, fragmented, or partially squashed. Five objects have a biconical shape, but in many cases their place in the category of loom weights – rather than that of spindle whorls – is far from certain (Cimadevilla 2012, 559). Only one object (M 75352) made of stone has a conical shape, but this is a very peculiar tool and might not have been a loom weight. Three objects have a cylindrical shape, two of which are made of stone, and one of which has a discoidal shape. Unfortunately, most of the loom weights were only

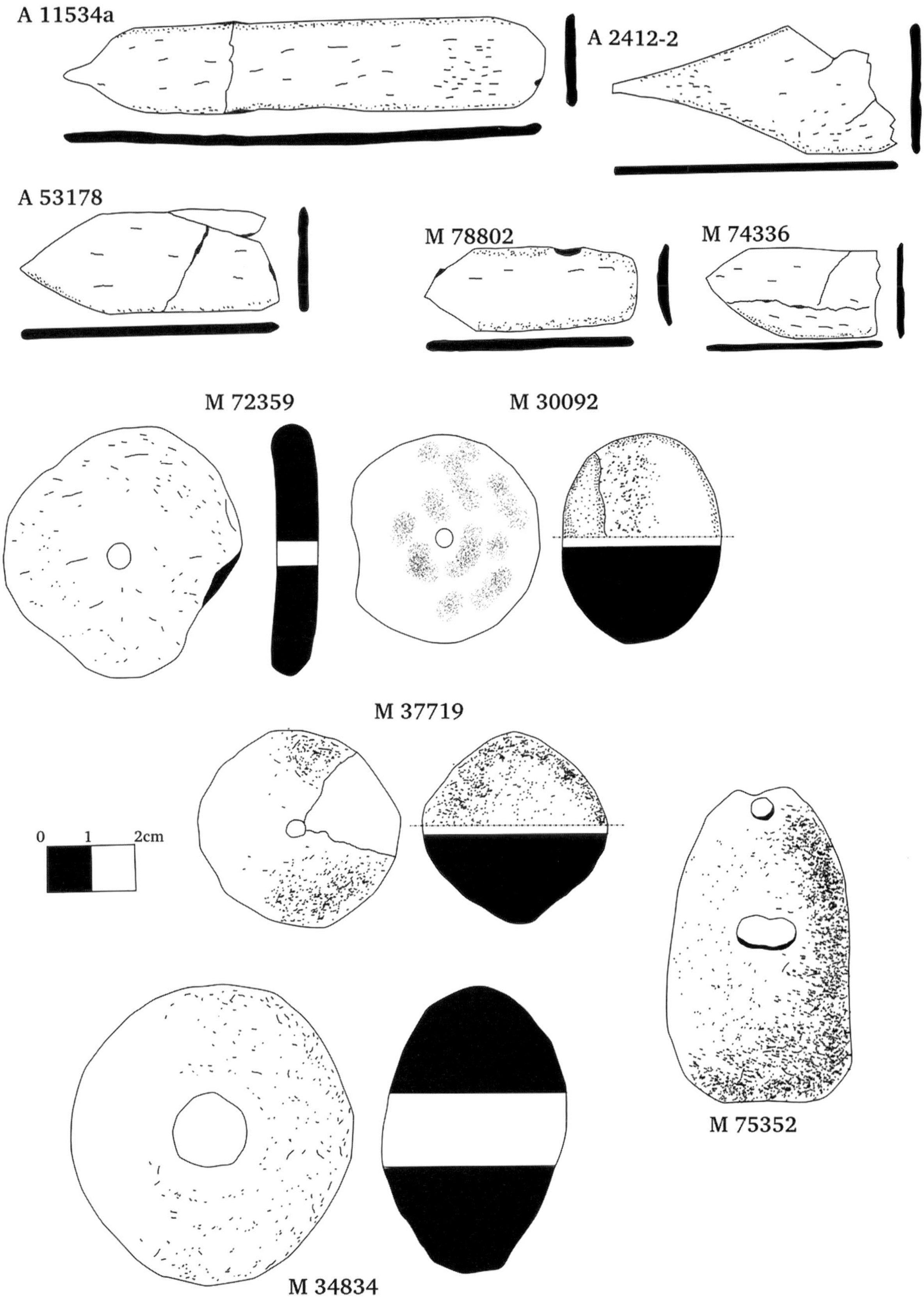

Figure 4.15. Selection of Hazor loom weights and spatulae

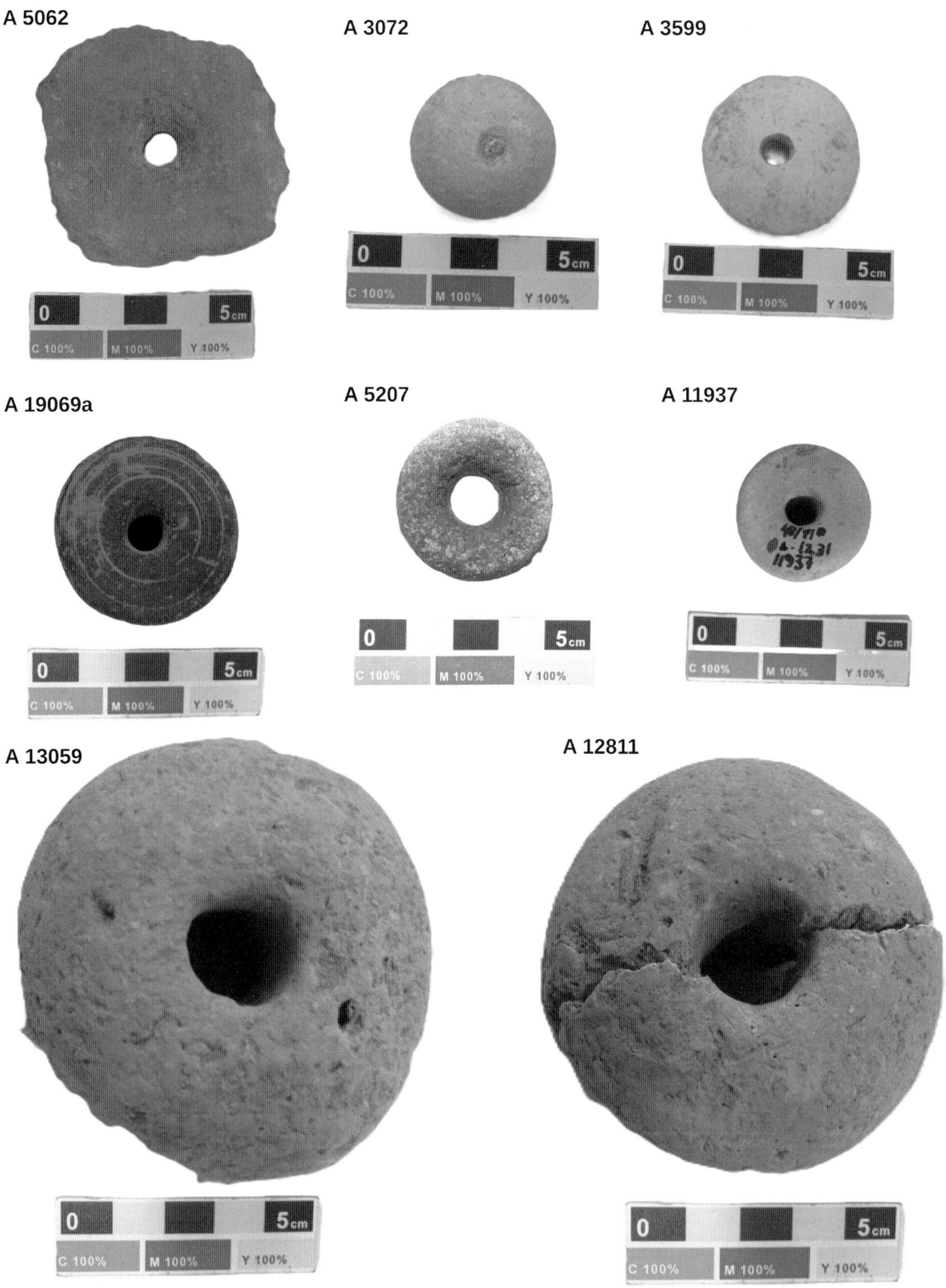

Figure 4.16. Selection of Hazor textile tools A 5062, A 3072, A 3599, A 5207, A 19069a, A 11937, A12811 (courtesy of the Selz Foundation Hazor Excavations in Memory of Yigael Yadin)

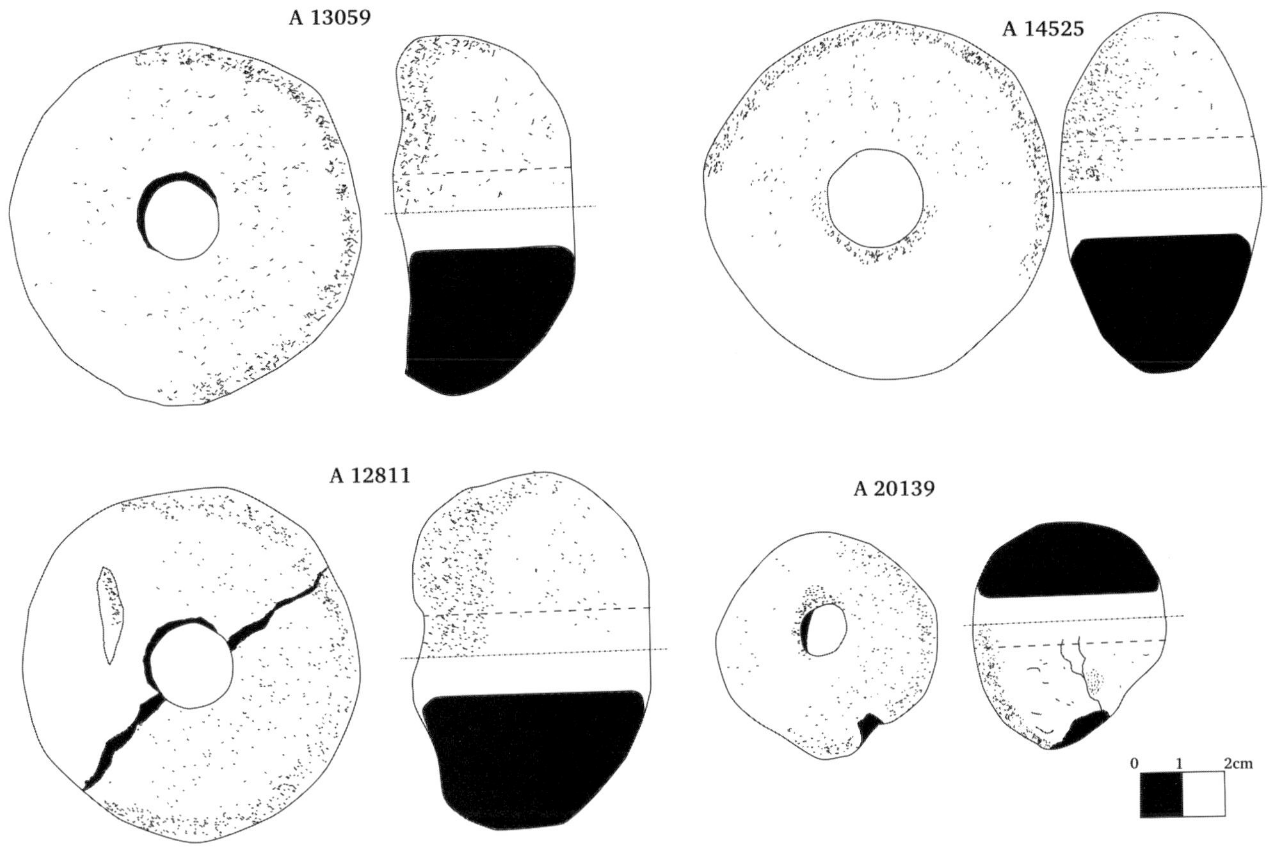

Figure 4.17. Selection of Hazor loom weights

partially preserved if not entirely disintegrated, so very few weights are available. The lightest weight measures 27 g, but this could have been a spindle whorl with a failed perforation. The maximum weight is 571 g, but one incomplete weight reaches 977 g. Most of the weights are around 200 g, and the average value is 206 g, which indicates a medium fine production.

It is interesting to note that not a single spool was present at the site, contrary to the large diffusion they have in Syria (Cecchini 2011).

Only a few loom weights have been found together in context, while the large majority were found scattered throughout the town, or in pairs. In L. 3066 of area B, four loom weights are published but there were certainly more, at least nine (Yadin *et al.* 1958, 31, 44). L. 1045 preserved four loom weights and a spindle whorl, while L. 9390 has five loom weights but no other objects used in connection with textile production. In area M, L. 10-306 two loom weights were excavated as well as two bone spatulae. L. 10-326, meanwhile, preserved at least 17 clay loom weights, which crumbled when they were studied. No other textile tools were present in the locus, but spindle whorls were uncovered in other loci of the area.

Perforated ring bases are present in Hazor since the LB I, become more common in LB II, and reach their peak in Iron Age II. The perforated sherds, meanwhile, are characterised by a great difference between each piece; they largely have smoothed and regular edges, but there are examples with irregular breaking points. Generally, they have hourglass or badly shaped holes, which prevent their use as spindle whorls. They have a height that can vary between 0.8 and 2.7 cm, with an average value of 1.8 cm. The diameter can range between 4.6 and 8.2 cm, with an average value of 0.75 cm, with a hole between 0.3 and 2 cm, and an average value of 0.75 cm. Many of the objects under study were not complete, so only a small number of weights are available. Their weight seems to fall within 32 and 138 g, but most of the objects would have had a weight greater than 50 g, which is much higher than perforated sherds. All considered, they appear in a different category from perforated sherds, but show also many differences with loom weights. First, their weight is (in general) lighter than that of loom weights, although this does not constitute an obstacle, since they might have been employed to weave finer textiles. Second, their appearance in the LBA in such larger numbers is in contrast with loom weights, which are extremely rare in this phase.

There is no proof that perforated ring bases were used in connection with textile production, but whatever their function was, a use as loom weights cannot be excluded *a priori*. Unfortunately, the Hazor contexts do not provide more information, since they generally appear isolated or in pairs and are not associated with other textile tools.

4.3.7 Basalt rings

Basalt rings are not present in the EBA layers, which is a remarkable fact, and those of the MBA (47 according to Ebeling 2012, 554, fig. 11.8) lack any detail about their dimensions, so they could not be recognised with certainty. However, Hazor has preserved some actual basalt rings, even though they are dated to Iron Age levels. In fact, these tools are typical of the EBA and MBA periods in the Levant, but they are uncommon after the end of the MBA. It would be convenient to say that those found in Iron Age contexts are intrusive and originated from earlier strata, but since it is not possible to say with certainty whether basalt rings have been found in earlier strata, this seems contradictory. Whether or not they share the same function as the older examples, and whatever the reason was for their late appearance in Hazor, it seems clear that they share the same characteristics as the other Levantine basalt rings. Besides shape and material, their dimensions are perfectly comparable. They have a height ranging from 1.2 and 2.2 cm, with 1.6 cm as an average. Their diameter falls between 3.2 and 4.6 cm, with an average value of 3.7 cm, and their weight seems quite light, between 20 and (probably) 30 g. Furthermore, they are attested in Iron Age levels in Megiddo and Tell el-Farʿah (S) (Fig. 4.18).

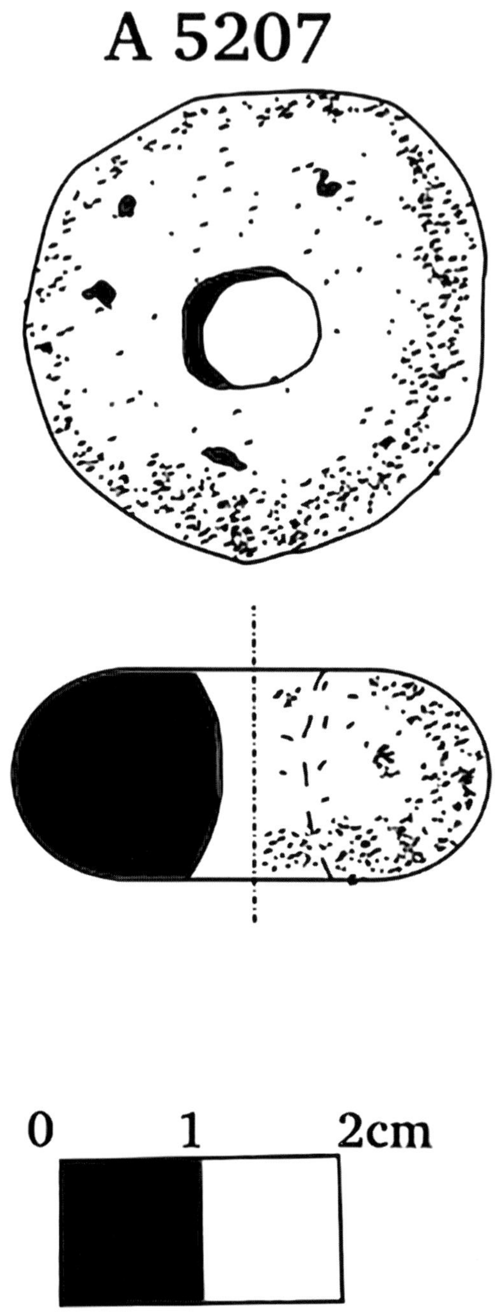

Figure 4.18. Basalt ring

4.3.8 Bone spatulae and beaters

Bone spatulae are quite numerous at Hazor, although they are not equally spread across all periods, as for the other textile tools. The largest number come from the Iron Age II levels (Plate 6). As for the other sites, bone spatulae and points or beaters are listed together, since they probably shared a similar function in textile production, as discussed in Chapter 2.

The earliest objects are two points (not actual spatulae), one from the Intermediate Bronze Age period and the other from the Middle Bronze Age II (MB II) period. The LBA sees the appearance of pointed objects besides actual spatulae. One of the spatulae preserves a triangular point, is very well shaped, and is perfectly smoothed on both sides without showing traces of cancellous bone (Fig. 4.12).

Iron Age I preserves only one point of bone, broken at one end. As previously stated, the largest quantity of bone spatulae come from the Iron Age II levels. Specifically, 29 objects dated to Iron Age IIA–B, and 24 for Iron Age IIC, a total of 53 items.

Generally, these have one end in the shape of a point and the other rounded, with varying degrees of care. Most of the items are manufactured from cattle ribs and follow the original shape and convexity of the bone. The points, when preserved, are generally short and triangular, but examples of long points and pen-nib points are also present. Most of the items appear smoothed on both sides, but cancellous bone is also present. It is evident that the spatulae were manufactured by cutting the bone in half longitudinally. Many of the objects under study were completely smooth on the upper surface, as well as on the concave side, until all traces of cancellous bone are removed.[5] However, several objects (A 1533, M 75009, M 78802) show that wear is mostly responsible for the disappearance of the bone matrix. In fact, they show both sides smoothed near the pointed end, while the cancellous bone starts to appear towards the other tip, similar to the examples from Gurob (see Chapter 5). It thus seems that the flat end was the area where the objects were handled, while the point was used in contact with (probably) textiles or leather.

One spatula, A 57619, is left unfinished. It has a triangular point and it is not smoothed at all. It was cut to expose the cancellous bone and shows no traces of wear, either in the matrix or on the edges, which are crudely cut.

4.3.9 Needles

The category of needles, as for other sites, includes objects that are very similar to our modern concept of needles, albeit longer, as well as bodkins and some shafts, whose use is uncertain. Forty-nine needles are listed in the catalogue, most belonging to Yadin's excavations. Unfortunately, I was not able to see Yadin's materials, except for a small part. Some were lacking an identification number, so I was unable to relate them to the needles published by Yadin.

Before starting to describe the needles from Hazor, it seems important to make a terminological disclaimer. Three types of objects are present at Hazor under the category of needle and loop-headed pin. Ben-Tor (2012, 534) considers the objects with a drilled eye as needles, and bent or loop-headed objects as pins, but this distinction was not always followed in previous publications. The problem is that what is here considered as a bent or loop-headed object is not a needle, but an actual pin, and the bent part remains open (or folded), rather than welded to close the eye (see for example Yadin *et al.* 1989, CCV: 12–13). Generally, when I refer to an object with the upper part bent back on itself, it is always welded to close the eye (see for example Yadin *et al.* 1989, CCXXI: 12–13).

Only one object is dated to the MBA, and this comes from a grave. Twenty-two objects belong to the LBA layers, and both types of needles are represented: the eye obtained by perforating the shaft, and by bending the upper part back on itself. One very interesting object is a needle case made from a hollow bone, which contains five long, thin needles, all of them with the eye formed by bending the upper part.

As usual, Iron Age I has preserved a small quantity of objects, which can barely be defined as needles. Some, in fact, are complete but do not show any trace of an eye.

Iron Age II has preserved a limited number of needles (12) and even in this case some objects probably had a different function than sewing. Those that can be recognised as needles preserve the eye bent back on itself.

At Hazor, the limited number of excavated tombs explains why the vast majority of textile tools have been recovered from settlement contexts. Nevertheless, the discovery of a needle in a grave aligns with burial traditions observed at other Levantine sites.

4.3.10 Conclusions: development of textile tools at Hazor

Textile tools from Hazor constitute a fairly large corpus and a very interesting case study. Bone shafts are not very numerous in Hazor, and are mostly dated to Iron Age II, while the production of the Southern Levant is particularly developed during the LBA.

Spindle whorls are quite numerous at the site and are known since the MBA. In this period, production is characterised by a great homogeneity of materials and shapes, and the dome-shaped bone spindle whorl is almost the only type present at the site. Objects dated to the LBA are more numerous, and show greater differentiation. Besides bone spindle whorls, stone and pottery whorls also appear, and while the dome shape is still prevalent, spherical, conical truncated, cylindrical, and lenticular objects are also present.

Several texts enable us to infer that MBA and LBA Hazor would have been an important centre of textile production and redistribution. One of the most famous texts is a letter in which a huge number of textiles and other goods must be sent to Mari and then brought to Ekallatum, probably for the marriage between Yasmakh-Addu and Beltum (Ben-Tor 2016, 72–3). Furthermore, two LBA administrative documents that deal with textile production and linen were also retrieved (Ben-Tor 2016, 113, 195). A document from the Amarna archive mentions a Hazor-style garment, which would have been well renowned. However, archaeological traces found so far point to a very modest textile industry. The impossibility of viewing the materials excavated by Yadin, as well as the excavations' focus on public buildings rather than domestic structures, may serve to explain this difference with the textual sources. Other factors might also have reduced our chances of comprehension, the most important being the loss of organic materials, which were certainly employed to produce textile tools, as Jericho proves. Furthermore, it might also be possible that part of the textile production was not performed at the site, but rather in small villages nearby. Hazor, therefore, would have functioned as a centre for finishing and/or distributing the textiles produced in the region.

In Iron Age I, the site was almost abandoned, and only one spindle whorl was identified for this period. The largest number of whorls come from the Iron Age II layers, and it is possible to see a very different trend from the Bronze Age onwards. Bone spindle whorls are still present but are far from the dominant type, since the most common material is now stone, as can be seen from other Levantine sites, such as Megiddo. The shapes appear to be quite varied, with dome and conical shapes the most common. The change in materials probably reflects a change in quality, since bone spindle whorls are lighter than those made of stone. Iron

Age II textile production was very likely of a lower quality than that of the Bronze Age.

Perforated sherds must be considered together with spindle whorls; in Hazor they are quite rare in EB–MB, but more common in later periods, reaching their peak in Iron Age II.

Spinning bowls were certainly not employed in spinning activities in Hazor, since only one possible fragment has been recognised so far.

Loom weights are the most numerous items in Hazor, but these present certain differences when compared to other sites. They were not in use during the EB–MB, while at other sites the MB sees a diffusion of conical loom weights. However, this typology is not unknown at the site, since a couple of conical loom weights appear in the LBA levels. A few other loom weights are known for this phase, including some spherical weights. With Iron Age II, loom weight production increases; this is the only period in which the presence and use of the warp-weighted loom can be established with certainty. The vast majority are made of clay, baked or poorly baked, and have a spherical or doughnut shape. No spools were recovered from the site. Batches are extremely rare, and loom weights generally appear scattered across the site, individually or in pairs. It is possible that perforated ring bases must be added to this corpus and counted as loom weights, even if there is no clear proof from the site under study.

Basalt rings are not very common in Hazor and there are no examples for EBA, although some basalt rings may have been present during the MBA. Some basalt rings belong to the Iron Age II levels, similar to other sites, although it should be more common to find them in the EBA levels.

A fairly large corpus of bone spatulae was found at Hazor. These were found in the levels of the LBA, although some beaters/pointed objects might have been similarly employed in earlier periods. As usual, the largest quantity comes from the Iron Age II levels. These show a quite large variety of shapes, with triangular, pen-nib, and long points. The other end is generally rounded. Surfaces are generally smoothed, but in some cases it is evident that the polishing is a result of its use rather than an intentional process.

Needles are known at Hazor since the MBA, but the largest number come from LBA contexts. For this period, both types of needles – the eye obtained by perforating the shaft and by bending the upper part of the shaft back on itself – are present. Most of the objects listed as needles that derive from the Iron Age levels probably had other purposes. The few objects that were certainly needles, all feature the eye formed by bending the upper part back on itself.

4.4 Tell el-Farʿah (N)

4.4.1 Introduction

Tell el-Far'ah (N) (identified with the biblical Tirzah) is situated in the central part of the Samaria hills, on a limestone plateau 11 km northeast of Shechem. Two perennial springs, the Ain Duleib and Ain Far'ah (one of the richest sources of the country) made it attractive to ancient populations, who began to visit it during the Neolithic period. Furthermore, the conformation of the site provides natural defences on its south and northeast sides. It is well connected to the east, through the Wadi Far'ah, which joins the Jordan River and the Middle Jordan Valley towards the Transjordan. To the north and south, it is situated on the route from Beth Shean to the plain of Schechem. To the west, communications are more difficult, due to the Samaria hills (Chambon 1984, 9).

The tell has a quadrangular shape of 600 × 300 m, with a surface of 10 ha, but it was not fully occupied in all periods. The first traces of occupation can be dated to the Pre-pottery Neolithic B, but the settlement was probably quite small, with pit dwellings. In terms of materials, bone spatulae and awls are quite frequent (de Miroschedji 1993, 34). The site was subsequently abandoned for a very long time, until a reoccupation during the Chalcolithic period. It is followed by a thin sterile layer, and similar architecture is detectable for the beginning of the EBA period. The architecture and material culture shows a radical change with the beginning of the EB II, which attest to a continuous occupation until the end of the EB II, and an abandonment in EB III, since no pottery from this period could be identified. The site was resettled only in the MB II, with two major phases of occupation, VA and VB.

The transition to the LBA sees no major break, although the LB remains are quite poor and scarce, as well as deeply damaged by later constructions. Iron Age phases I and II are well preserved and documented throughout the site and are divided into five successive periods (VIIa–e) (Chambon 1984, 11). This phase is marked by several layers of destruction: the destruction of the VIIb layer, which is generally attributed to the biblical Omri conquest, is followed by a period of abandonment. Layer VIId is characterised by public buildings and large houses which end with a violent fire, probably linked to the conquering of Samaria by the Assyrian king Sargon II in 721 BC. The town was partially reoccupied and gradually abandoned between the 7th and 6th century BC (Chambon 1993, 440). No sherds from the Persian period have been detected, while some findings from the Roman and Byzantine Periods can be identified. A medieval cemetery was excavated by R. de Vaux.

A first survey was conducted in 1930 by W.F. Albright, who was looking for the ancient biblical town of Tirzah. Excavations were launched by the École Française de Jerusalem, which were directed by R. de Vaux between 1946 and 1960, for a total of nine seasons. He published the preliminary results in the Revue Biblique (de Vaux 1947a; 1947b; 1948; 1951; 1952; 1955; 1957; 1961; 1962), but unfortunately never published the final report, due to major works in Khirbet Qumran. From the 1980s, some publications have contributed to shedding light on the materials excavated by de Vaux, but unfortunately some important works remain unpublished.[6] The subsequent publications have substantially revised the chronological scheme created by de Vaux and the terminology has been adapted to follow the new results of the international research. This creates some problems in recognising how different periods are considered in different publications, and since the terminology used by da Vaux is needed to understand the preliminary reports, it cannot be abandoned. Therefore, a small chart that compares different periods was needed. Nonetheless, LB layers cause problems. It is clear that part of the structures originally ascribed by de Vaux to the LBA should be dated to the Iron Age period (Chambon 1993, 439; Finkelstein 2012, 335, tab. 1), but part of them should probably be kept in the frame of the LBA period (Table 4.4).

A rather small quantity of textile tools was found in Tell el-Far'ah, partly due to the small extent of the excavated areas. Much of the site, such as the eastern area and the centre, was not investigated. However, these represent a very interesting corpus for comparison with the other chosen sites. The material culture is generally local, with some items imported from other areas but in general locally produced, and therefore constitutes an interesting case study for the production of the inland central Palestine.

To study the materials, of which only a small part has been published, I was allowed to use the catalogue of objects (1946–1960) excavated by de Vaux and compiled by several scholars of the École Biblique. Plans and notes stored at the École Biblique, and partially still available, were also of great help. Nonetheless, some items are not dated since I was unable to trace the chronology of all the loci. I hope that new studies, especially of the periods still lacking full publication, might help to shed light on the precise chronology of these tools.

When possible, all the available data from publications are used to provide the broadest possible picture of textile production in Far'ah. This means that the catalogue includes not only the objects I have personally measured, but also those published but not available to my research. In this way, a larger number of shapes and materials are available on which to carry out the statistical analysis.

4.4.2 Spindles

Tell el-Far'ah did not preserve any examples of bone rods that could be related to spinning activities, like those from Megiddo. The items listed and discussed in the catalogue are very different from the bone rods known from other Levantine sites, and were probably used for different purpose,

Table 4.4. Chronology of Tell el-Far'ah

de Vaux (1955)	*Chambon (1984)*	*Mallet (1988)*	*de Miroschedji (1993)*	*Charloux (2006)*	*Finkelstein (2012)*
Néolithique	I		I PPNB		
Chalcolithique Moyen–Enéolithique Moyen	II		II Chalcolithique	Chalcolithique Récent	
Chalcolithique Supérieur– Enéolithique Supérieur	III		III EB I	Bronze Ancien Ia	
Chalcolithique Supérieur–Ancien Bronze I	IV		IV EBII	Bronze Ancien Ib	
Ancien Bronze I (périodes 1 et 2)				Bronze Ancien II	
Ancien Bronze II (périodes 3–5)					
Niveau 5 Moyen Bronze	V	V Phase A et B	V MB IIA MB IIB MB IIC		
Niveau 4 Récent Bronze (?)	VI		VI		
Niveau 4 Récent Bronze	VIIa (XII–XI siécle)				Late Iron Age I–early Iron Age IIA
Niveau 3 Fer I (XI–IX siècle)	VII b–c (IX–debùt IX)				Late Iron Age IIA – Gap – Iron Age IIB
Niveau 2 (IX siècle à 723)	VII d (IX–VIII)				
Niveau 1 (723 à 600)	VII e–e1 (VII–V siécle)				

such as handles. It is interesting to note, however, that the surface decoration, such as the lattice pattern, is similar to the bone rods and therefore not linked to a function, but rather to the material.

4.4.3 Spindle whorls

Unfortunately, only a small number of whorls was available for this study, to which those published by A. Chambon (1984, figs 75, 77) have been added to the catalogue (Fig. 4.19).

The first example of a spindle whorl comes from the Chalcolithic layers and is the only specimen found for this period. It is made of pottery and has a biconical shape.

A small number of spindle whorls are known from the EB I and EB II layers, all of them made of stone. It is interesting to note the difference with Megiddo, which in this period has almost entirely pottery spindle whorls, and a similar trend can be seen in Beth Shean. Their shapes are quite varied, since spherical, conical, cylindrical, and discoid types are all present (Plate 7). The diameters are quite wide, the smallest at 4 cm and the largest 5.5 cm; their heights are extremely different, from 0.7 to 3.4 cm. Unfortunately, most of the objects are broken so the weight can only be inferred from the surviving parts. Two objects, the lightest, were around 20 g, while another two are between 50 and 80 g. Only one object weighs more than 100 g (and another very likely one), but the choice of a very fine stone and accurate polishing made it possible to identify these as mace-heads rather than spindle whorls. The quality of yarn that could be produced with these objects seems to be medium-coarse.

The MBA shows a similarly small quantity of spindle whorls, while bone spindle whorls also start to be produced at the other Levantine sites. However, stone is still dominant (for the samples available), although a specimen made of pottery has been also found (Plate 7). The shapes appear less varied than the EBA, with almost all the objects cylindrical, while the dome shape is still relegated to bone. The measurements are greatly varied, even between the same class of material. Diameters vary between 2 and 4.8 cm, while heights are between 0.6 and 2.8 cm. Weights range between 2 (?)g and 87 g, with no clear pattern of distribution. However, since a majority of the spindle whorls are between 15 and 40 g, it is highly probable that the production was oriented to a medium quality yarn.

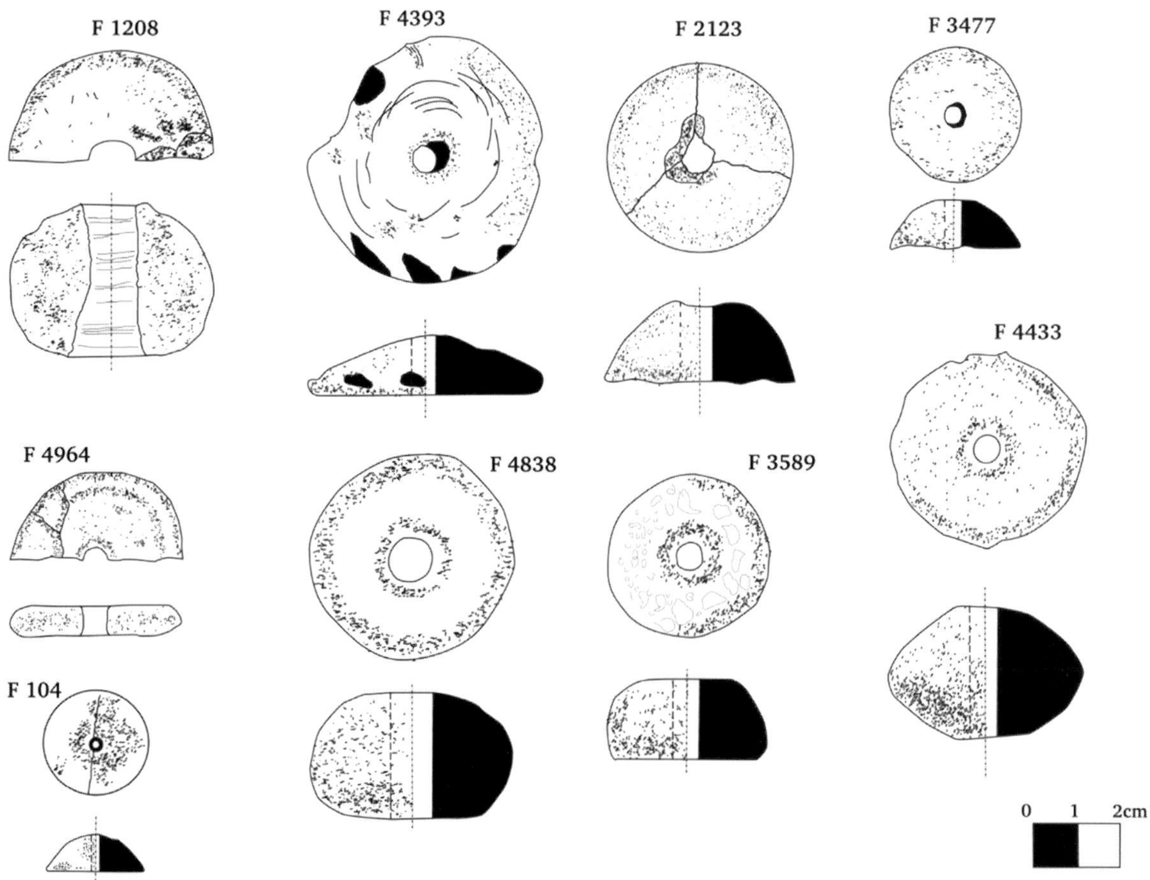

Figure 4.19. Selection of Tell el-Far'ah (N) spindle whorls

A small number of spindle whorls have been found from the LBA at Far'ah, though this phase remains complex. Stone remains the predominant material, while bone spindle whorls appear in smaller quantities. This contrasts sharply with Megiddo, Beth Shean, and Hazor, where bone was the most common material throughout the LBA. The whorls exhibit a variety of shapes, with the dome form being the most prevalent in both bone and stone examples. Cylindrical, conical truncated, lenticular, biconical, and conical examples are also present, similar to the other sites. Their dimensions are quite varied, but less than in the earlier periods. Heights range between 0.5 and 2.1 cm, but most of the objects have values around 1.1 cm. Diameters vary between 2 and 3.8 cm, and most of them are over 3 cm. Similarly, weights are varied but less than in other periods. The lightest whorl weighs 2.39 g, and the heaviest 33 g. Five spindle whorls, three made of bone and two made of stone, are extremely light, from 2.39 g to 9.91 g. These objects are very similar to the very small items already discussed for the LBA spindle whorls from Megiddo. As in that case, perforations are very small, ranging from 0.2 to 0.4 mm. The other whorls are much more varied in weight, ranging between 15 and 33 g. If the very light objects should be considered as spindle whorls, they indicate a very fine quality production, while the other whorls suggest a medium or medium-fine quality.

Iron Age I was identified by de Vaux as *Niveau* 3 and by Chambon as period VIIa. However, Finkelstein (2012, 335) argues that no layer at Tell el-Far'ah can be confidently attributed to Iron Age I. Given that Finkelstein's study is among the most recent works on the Iron Age I–II sequence at the site, his chronology is considered the most reliable and up-to-date. Consequently, Chambon's period VIIa will be treated as spanning the late Iron Age I and early Iron Age IIA, following Finkelstein's proposal. The associated artefacts will be analysed alongside those from other Iron Age II layers.

Spindle whorls from the Iron Age II layers appear in greater numbers than in earlier periods, a pattern consistent with all the settlements examined in this study. Nevertheless, even when combining the specimens currently available at the École Biblique with those published by Chambon (1984, fig. 75), only 39 examples are documented. Stone spindle whorls are the most common, as is the typical trend for Iron Age II in the region. Bone spindle whorls are relatively rare, with only a few examples recorded. In contrast, pottery spindle whorls are more common, nearly matching the number of stone specimens (Plate 7). The cylindrical shape predominates in both stone and pottery whorls, a pattern that diverges from the broader regional trend. Only five conical and five dome-shaped whorls are documented, made from both stone and bone. Other shapes – such as truncated conical, lenticular, button, biconical, and discoid – are present but represented by very few specimens. Due to incomplete data, reliable statistics are available only for diameters and heights. The heights vary between 0.5 and 2.7 cm, with an average value of 1 cm. Diameters range from 1.2 to 4.2 cm, with an average value of 2.5 cm. Very few weights are unfortunately available, though most are between 2.2 and 5.2 g, so extremely light. One item weighs 32.26 g.

4.4.4 Perforated sherds

Perforated sherds are relatively rare at Far'ah, with only a few recovered across all the periods examined. As at other sites, they are uncommon in earlier periods but become more frequent during the Iron Age. If all are considered potential spindle whorls, it is noteworthy that they account for nearly 40% of the EBA assemblage, 50% of the MBA, 44% of the LBA, and 28% of the Iron Age II group.

They are characterised by a relatively large average diameter of 4 cm and a thin profile, averaging 1 cm in thickness. The largest specimen measures 6.6 cm in diameter, while the smallest, at 1.9 cm, likely falls outside this category. Weights range from 2.9 to 48.9 g, with an average of 16 g – significantly lighter than comparable examples from Megiddo.

The catalogue includes all perforated sherds with a single hole, regardless of whether the perforation is hourglass-shaped or angled, which may make attachment to a spindle more difficult but not impossible.

The contexts in which reworked sherds were found are consistently settlement-related and never funerary, reflecting patterns observed at other sites. While some of these sherds were discovered alongside various tools, they were rarely found with other perforated sherds and only occasionally associated with textile tools such as spatulae and needles.

4.4.5 Spinning bowls

Not a single fragment of a spinning bowl has been recovered in Far'ah for all the periods under consideration.

4.4.6 Loom weights

In the EBA, very few objects could be considered as weights. All of these are made of stone, with very varied weights. Two of them have an hourglass perforation, which in one case is unfinished. Because of their small number and the great difference in shape and size, it is difficult to recognise them as a uniform category and they probably had different purposes (Fig. 4.20).

A new type of object emerges in the MBA: conical clay loom weights (Plates 8 and 9). Seven examples are listed in the catalogue, all pierced horizontally – unlike those from Megiddo, where vertically perforated specimens are also found. Although none show evidence of surface treatment, they have been carefully modelled. One weight features a groove at the top, possibly intended for attachment to an additional element before fastening to the warp. Another bears a scarab impression, similar to examples from Megiddo. Only one object has a spherical shape, resembling those of the Iron Age. Three conical weights

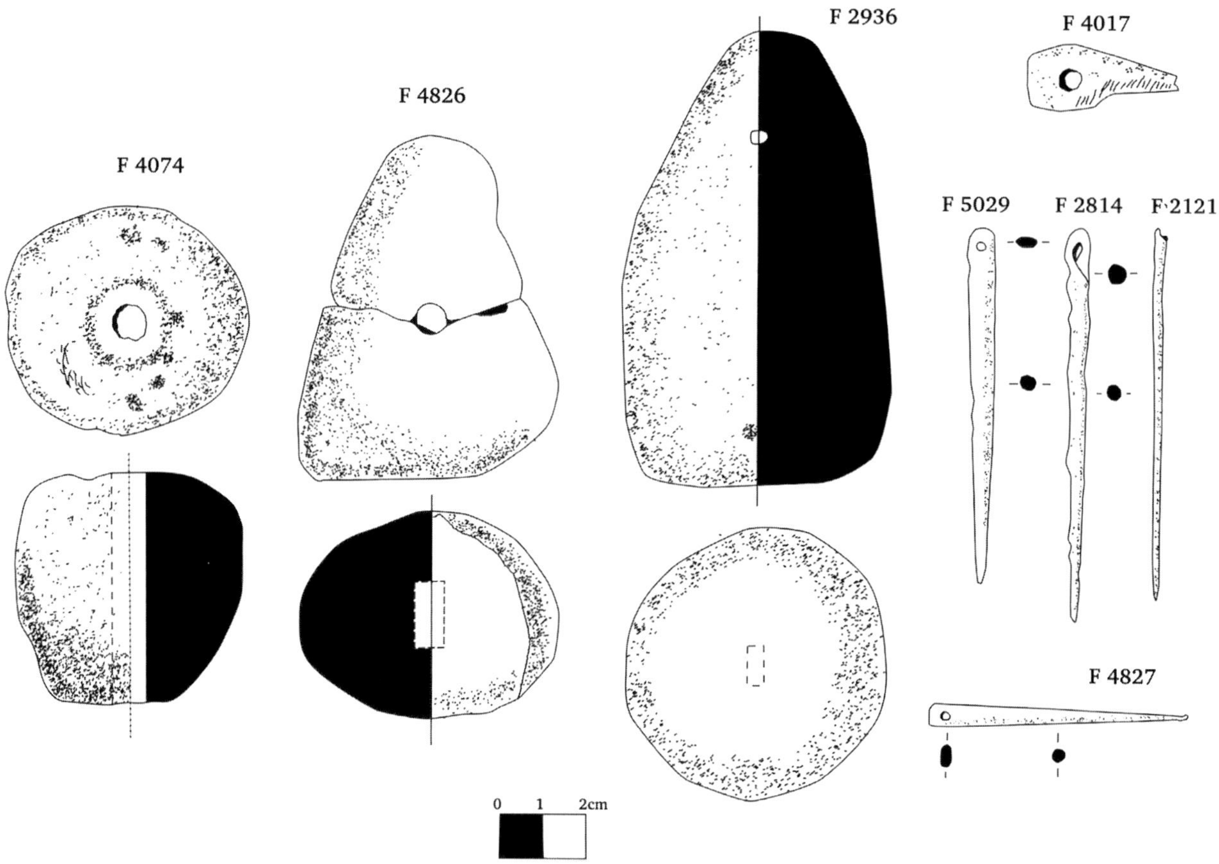

Figure 4.20. Selection of Tell el-Far'ah (N) loom weights and needle

were recovered from the same locus (L. 571), with a fourth found beneath it.

During the LBA, conical clay loom weights disappear, accompanied by a general scarcity of objects identifiable as weights. In the EBA, such objects cannot be confidently classified as loom weights due to significant variation in material, size, and shape.

The vast majority of Far'ah loom weights come from the Iron Age II layers, with 97 objects recorded, although many more were identified during the excavations. Due to their fragile nature, it is likely that many crumbled and were not stored. Most of the loom weights are made of clay, which can be unfired, poorly fired, or well-fired (Plate 8). Seven weights are made of stone. They generally have a rounded shape, which can range from spherical to more flattened or irregular doughnut-like forms, though the differences are not always distinct. Some cylindrical examples are also present. Stone weights vary significantly in shape and size, with cylindrical, spherical, and discoid forms recorded. Their weights range from 68 to 252 g.

Clay loom weights are often incomplete, but a significant number are well preserved, providing reliable data. Their measurements and weights are highly variable. Heights range from 2.4 to 7.6 cm, with an average of 4.5 cm. Diameters range from 2.5 to 10 cm, with an average of 6.3 cm. Weights range from 81 to 576 g, with an average of 167 g, which is relatively light for a loom weight.

Unlike the other sites under study, most of the loom weights from Far'ah were found in two large batches, with only a few scattered across various loci. These two batches were recovered from Loci 150 and 430. Locus 150, dated to level VIId, is associated with palace 148. Around 100 clay loom weights were found against wall W, along with a stone weight. The stratum in which these loom weights were found appeared to be a mixture of burnt earth and wood (Chambon 1984, 108), and the pottery was also burnt (Chambon 1984, 80). Of the original 100 loom weights, only 56 were stored at the École Biblique, along with some small fragments. Only a few objects are complete, but it is clear that these weights are slightly lighter than the average. The minimum weight is 81 g, the maximum is 391 g, and the average weight is 141 g.

The second batch comes from Locus 430, where 34 loom weights were found in a pile near one corner of the room (Chambon 1984, 134). These weights belong to layer VIIb. Thirty-two of the 34 loom weights are still stored at the École Biblique and are in good condition. They are much more uniform than the first group, with weights ranging from 116 to 127 g, and an average of 158 g, which is slightly heavier than the previous batch.

4.4.7 Basalt rings

As discussed in previous chapters, stone rings were primarily found in the Levant during the EBA and MBA. After this period, they seem to disappear and are not used again. However, Hazor, Megiddo, and Far'ah have yielded objects that, in terms of shape, materials, and dimensions, fit perfectly within this category, and they are also dated to the Iron Age. This suggests a similar pattern of use across periods (Fig. 4.21).

The first basalt rings appear in Far'ah during the EBA, and 10 objects are recorded for this period. They appear quite different from each other in terms of dimensions and weights. Their height ranges between 1.3 and 3.1 cm, with an average of 2 cm; diameters between 3.3 and 5.5 cm, with an average of 4.1 cm. The holes appear quite large, varying between 0.9 and 1.7 cm, 1.2 cm on average. The weights are extremely different, varying between 28 and 116 g, with an average value of 48 g. However, most of them are lighter than 50 g, and only one object is greater than this. All the other examples perfectly fit into the category of basalt rings. If they should be considered as spindle whorls, they would have a medium weight, while if they were considered loom weights they would be considered very light.

Only one specimen is known from the MBA, while six examples are listed for the LBA. Unless their chronology is reassessed in the future, this represents a very unusual occurrence. The measurements and weights are similar to those from the EBA, with heights ranging from 1.5 to 2.6 cm, diameters from 3.6 to 4.7 cm, hole sizes from 1.1 to 1.5 cm, and weights ranging from 31.53 to 73 g. All are made of basalt, as in the EBA.

Six basalt rings are also recorded for the Iron Age II. These appear very similar to the earlier examples, though they are slightly smaller and lighter. Their heights range from 1.5 to 2.3 cm, diameters from 2.6 to 4.6 cm, holes from 0.8 to 1.2 cm, and weights from 13.6 to 49.9 g, with an average weight of 34.5 g.

As in previous periods, all these rings are made of basalt, and the holes are typically hourglass-shaped, though some specimens feature more regular, cylindrical holes. The surface treatment varies from highly polished to roughly smoothed surfaces.

4.4.8 Bone spatulae and beaters

Several bone spatulae come from EBA layers, 17 in total. Depending on the shape of the bone from which they are cut – mostly cattle and sheep/goat ribs – they vary in terms of width and thickness. The points are elongated or triangular, while the pen-nib type seems to be absent. The other end, when preserved, is simply rounded or smoothed (Fig. 4.22).

Ten beaters or points have been selected (Plate 9). It must be said that several other pointed objects were rejected during the study phase, as their shape or surface treatment seemed not to be suitable for weaving activity, or they were simply points that could have been used in many other ways (Fig. 4.23). Beaters are a very difficult category and, as seen in general discussion, their function is not clear and many potential uses have been indicated. Since their shape is suitable for weaving activity, their polishing seems to have been caused by rubbing with soft materials, as an ethnographic parallel of their usage in weaving was found, they are included in the catalogue. Each of them is discussed and described, with attention paid to the shape of the point and to macro wear traces.

For the MBA, only six spatulae were found, and all of the complete examples have an elongated point. There are eight beaters, all of which have a polished surface, and in many cases there are wear traces.

Only one bone spatula was recovered in the LBA layers, which has a triangular point. The beaters are more numerous, since six were found. These show a polished and smooth surface, when preserved, but in one case the point is too thin and sharp to have been used during weaving.

Only one beater is known for Iron Age II, while five spatulae are known for this period. The points appear to be the triangular and elongated types, while the pen-nib point seems not very common in the site – only two examples are known (from undated contexts).

As with the spatulae from Hazor, it is clear that these objects were made by cutting the bone in half longitudinally. Many of the specimens examined were thoroughly smoothed on both the upper and concave surfaces, removing all traces of cancellous bone (Plate 9). Both sides are polished near the pointed end, while the cancellous bone begins to appear towards the opposite tip. This suggests that the flat end was used for handling, while the pointed end was likely employed in contact with soft materials, possibly textiles.

4.4.9 Needles

A total of 37 needles and bodkins have been recorded from Far'ah, which represents a significant number compared to other tool types. It is also important to note that wooden bodkins were likely in use during this period, as well as very thin bronze needles, which may not have survived to be recovered (Fig. 4.16).

For the EBA, eight bone needles or bodkins are recorded, all characterised by a squared, flat head with a pierced hole. Moving into the MBA, both bronze and bone needles are present, though in very limited numbers. Only five specimens are known from this phase, with the bone needles resembling those from the earlier period. The bronze needles, on the other hand, are long and thin, with the eye formed by bending the shaft back on itself.

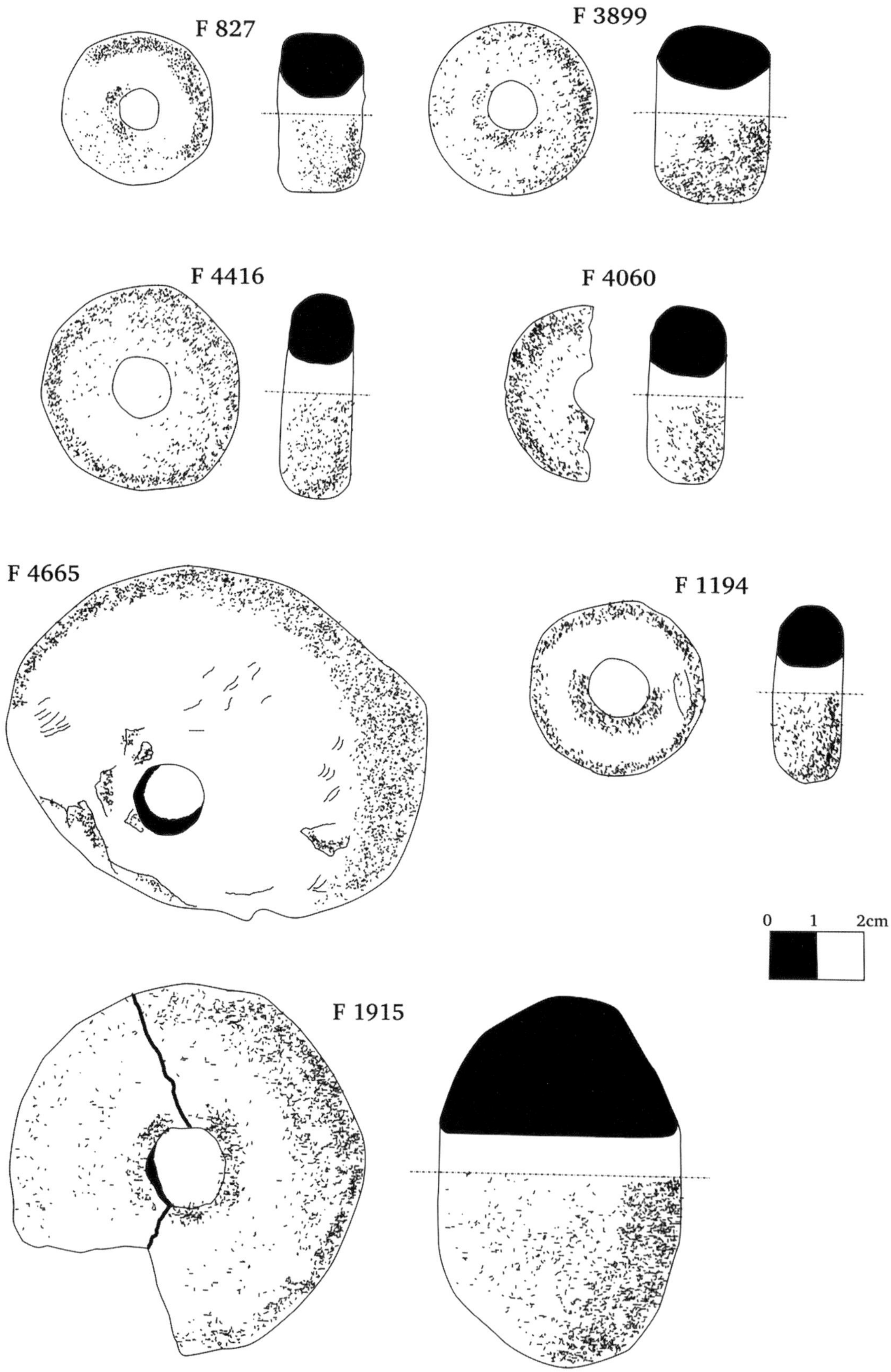

Figure 4.21. Selection of Tell el-Far'ah (N) loom weights and basalt rings

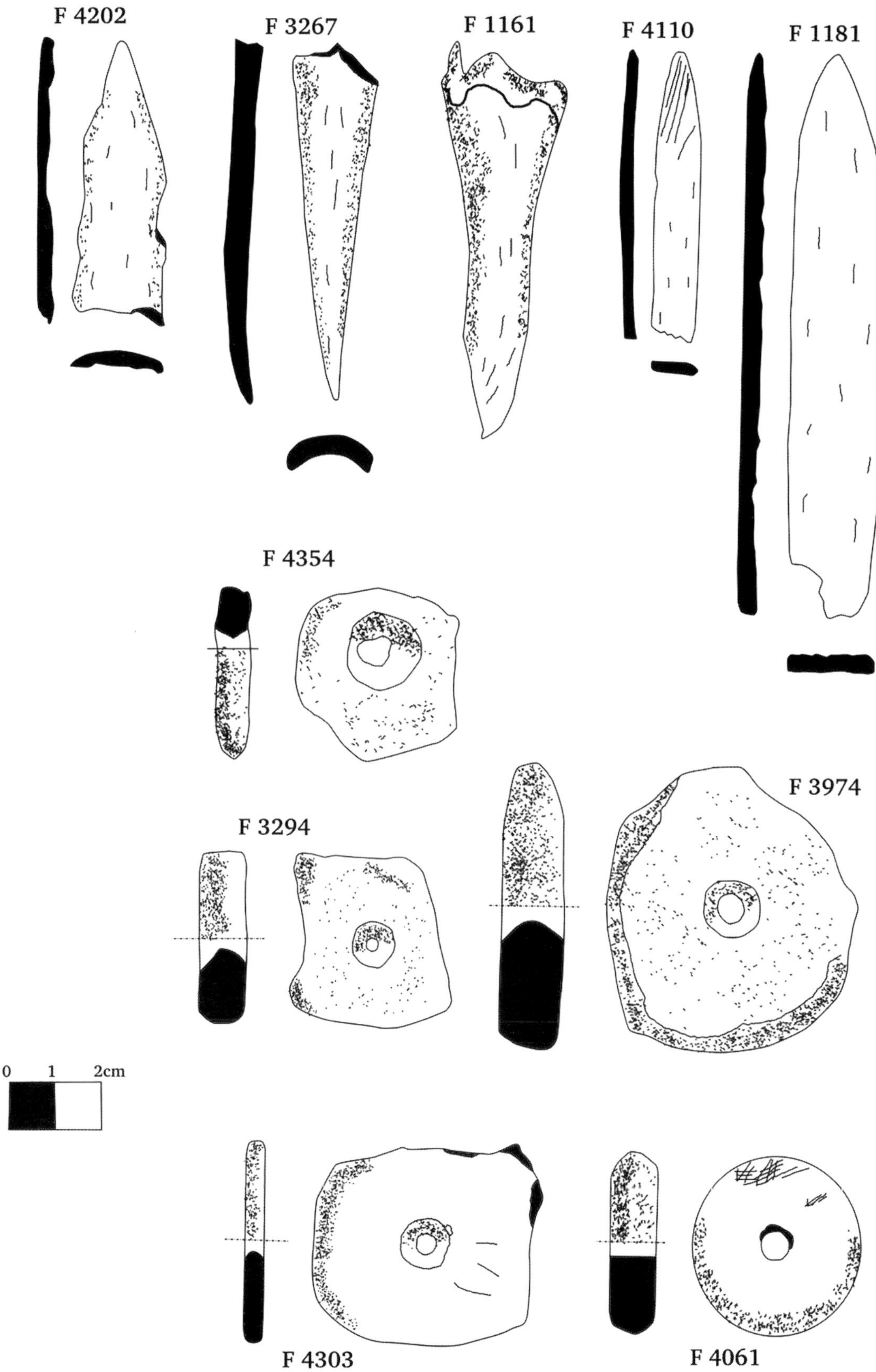

Figure 4.22. Selection of Tell el-Far'ah (N) perforated sherds, pin beaters and bone spatulae

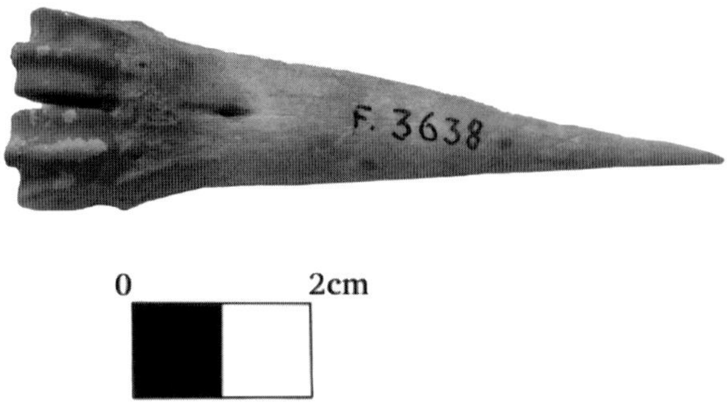

Figure 4.23. Pin beater F. 3699

The LBA sees a slight increase in the number of needles, with 13 objects recorded. Almost all of these are made of bronze, with only one bone needle, which is incomplete. A variety of needle types are represented, including the common form where the upper part of the shaft is bent back to create the eye, and a type that closely resembles toggle pins. These toggle-like needles have the eye formed by enlarging the shaft at the end or slightly more centrally, though unlike toggle pins, the shaft remains thin, making them more needle-like in appearance. Additionally, there is a unique type characterised by a very long, thin eye formed by melting the metal, giving it an irregular shape.

Finally, for Iron Age II, only nine needles are known, including both bone (one bodkin) and bronze examples. The bronze needles follow the familiar design, with the eye created by bending the upper part of the shaft back on itself. Interestingly, the typology where the shaft is perforated through from one side to the other seems to be entirely absent from the Far'ah assemblage.

4.4.10 Conclusions: development of textile tools at Far'ah

Tell el-Far'ah (N) preserved a rather small but very interesting assemblage of textile tools. Bone spindles and shafts are not present for any period under consideration, showing that they were not uniformly distributed in the Levant.

Spindle whorls that are still available to study or are published are not very numerous. Nonetheless, some remarks can be made. The first example of a spindle whorl belongs to the Chalcolithic layers, and is made of pottery, while all the EBA specimens are made of stone. Their shapes and dimensions are quite varied, but the whorls seem to be oriented towards a low quality production. During the MBA, stone is still the preferred material, even if bone begins to be employed, as is the common trend in the Southern Levant. The shapes and dimensions are still very varied, but seem to indicate a medium quality production. In contrast with the other Levantine sites under investigation, bone spindle whorls are not the predominant typology in LBA Far'ah, as stone still prevails. Some examples are very small, and the yarn production seems to have shifted to a fine or medium-fine quality product. Finally, Iron Age II whorls are mostly made of stone, which follows the trend of the region; bone remains rarely employed, while pottery examples are much more numerous, again in contrast with the regional trend. Furthermore, dome and conical shapes are not the dominant type, but the most common shape is cylindrical. Perforated sherds must be added to the spindle whorls. These are quite rare during the EB–BM periods, and reach their production peak during the Iron Age II, as is common in all the other sites investigated.

Spinning bowls are not present at all in Far'ah.

Loom weights are certainly introduced during the MB I, while the EB examples may have been merely counterweights. MB loom weights are conical and made of both baked and unbaked clay. All the specimens are horizontally perforated and do not feature a surface treatment. One example has a scarab impression, as in the case of Megiddo. An example of a spherical loom weight is also known.

Commonly to the other Levantine sites, loom weights appear to be unknown in the LBA, but are very numerous in the Iron Age II, and the most common shape is spherical or doughnut. Most of them are made of clay, baked or unbaked, but a very small number of stone objects is also known. The large majority were found grouped in two large batches, one with all the weights still preserved, while the other with only half of the loom weights available for study.

Basalt rings can be considered as either loom weights or spindle whorls. They are generally common in the EB and MB phases, and tend to disappear in later periods, but Far'ah does not fit the general picture. In fact, the first basalt rings appear in the EBA levels, while only one object is known from the MBA levels. They appear again in the LBA layers, and are common in the Iron Age II levels. They present similar characteristics to those of the earlier periods, such as dimensions, weights, the hourglass hole, and the diversity of their surface polishing.

A fairly large collection of bone spatulae and beaters are known from all levels of the Far'ah excavations. These are made from cattle and sheep/goat ribs, while the beaters are made from the metacarpal or metatarsal bones of sheep/goats. The typical shape of the spatulae from Far'ah is elongated or with a triangular point, but one example of a pen-nib point is also present. Beaters are generally only worked and polished near the point, while the other end is left unworked. These tools are more common in the earlier periods than in the Iron Age, while bone spatulae are generally more frequent in Iron Age layers in the region.

Needles and bodkins are quite numerous at the site and appear as early as the EBA, with bone specimens characterised by a square head. From the MBA onward, bronze needles are also present and show the characteristic Levantine eye obtained by bending the upper part of the shaft back on itself. More examples are known for the LBA, almost all made of bronze, with several types of eye. However, the eye obtained by simply perforating the shaft is not present in the site at any period. The Iron Age II level does not show a change in the typologies of needles nor in the materials employed, since both bronze and bone are still employed.

4.5 Case studies and the regional development of textile tools

4.5.1 Spindles

Very few spindles have been preserved from throughout the Near East, which will all be presented here. These can in fact help in the discussion to understand the position of the spindle whorl, namely at the top or the bottom of the shaft.

Some examples of complete spindles are known from graves of the 3rd millennium BC. At Kish, in Iraq, several examples of spindles were found, four made of copper and three of wood (Völling 2008, 247), which are dated to the Early Dynastic IIIa (2500–2350 BC). One example has a hook on the upper part immediately over the spindle whorl, which is dome-shaped. A second example has a discoid spindle whorl near one end, while the other end is pointed. Two examples have flat heads and could thus not be considered as spindles nor distaffs.[7] Similarly, the example from Abu Salabikh (Postgate and Moon 1982, 131, 134, pl. Vc; Barber 1991, 57) with a flat head is not convincing as a distaff. The three wooden shafts from Kish palace do not have a spindle whorl preserved and are broken at their ends (Völling 2008, 248). Their cigar shape and shortness make them very different from any kind of spindle analysed in the Near East; however, as noted by E. Völling, the presence of a groove that is useful for fastening the fibres might indicate a use in spinning (Völling 2008, 248).

At Abu Salabikh a copper spindle was found in a grave, in context with other metal pins and the flat head 'distaff' already cited. The possible spindle has a large discoid spindle whorl near one end of the shaft, while the other shows a thickening near the point. Two discs, made of silver (probably beads) with a tiny hole, were also present in the grave (Postgate and Moon 1982, 131, 134, pl. Vc).

At Tepe Hissar, in Iran, a copper spindle dated to the 3rd millennium BC (Hissar IIb) has been excavated. The shaft is 22 cm long and has a long, spiral groove on the upper end, while the lower end has a rounded tip. Under the groove, in the upper part of the shaft, two spindle whorls are present: one is conical, and the second appears to be spherical (Schmidt 1937, 120, pl. 29). A second object, made of schist, is considered by E. Völling (2008, 247) to be a spindle, but its huge dimensions make this unlikely (Schmidt 1937, 222, pl. LXIV).

Two precious spindles (or distaffs, Völling 2008, 255) come from the cemetery of Alaca Höyük, in Türkiye, one from tomb L and the other from tomb H. They are made of silver and gold or electrum, both with a discoid spindle whorl on the shaft; in both cases this is placed around the middle of the shaft (Barber 1991, 60–1). They are dated to the EBA, as are the two examples from Horoztepe, which are very similar to those from Alaca, and another two from Merzifon (Barber 1991, 61) (Table 4.5).

Table 4.5. Table summarising the main findings of spindles in the Near East, with position of the spindle whorl

Site	*Material*	*Date*	*Position of spindle whorl*
Kish (Iraq)	4 copper 3 wood	Early Bronze Age	2 top
Abu Salabikh (Iraq)	1 copper	Early Bronze Age	Near one end
Tepe Hissar (Iran)	1 copper	Early Bronze Age	Two whorls, top
Alaca Höyük (Turkey)	2 silver & gold	Early Bronze Age	Middle
Horoztepe (Turkey)	1 bronze 1 electrum	Early Bronze Age	Middle
Merzifon (Turkey)	2 bronze	Early Bronze Age	Middle
Karataş-Semayük (Turkey)	1 silver	Early Bronze Age	2 whorls at 2/3
Troy (Turkey)	2 wood	Early Bronze Age	
Troy (Turkey)	1 ivory	Late Bronze Age (Troy VIIa)	Middle
Ugarit (Syria)	3 bone/ivory	Late Bronze Age II	Middle?
Megiddo (Israel)	3 bone/ivory	Late Bronze Age II	2/3
Marlik (Iran)	1 bronze	Iron Age	top
Deve Höyük (Turkey)	2 metal	Iron Age	Middle 2/3
Kamid el-Loz (Southern Levant)	1 bronze	Iron Age/Persian	middle
Achzib (Southern Levant)	1 bone	Iron Age II	Near one end

An object from Karataş-Semayük is entirely different, and features a thin silver shaft, pointed at both ends. It preserves a biconical spindle whorl upon it, at one third of its length. Not far from the object, a disc was found and the excavator reports that it 'fits neatly against the truncated biconical whorl' (Mellink 1969, 323, pl. 74).

From the second half of the 2nd millennium BC onwards, bone and ivory spindles and distaffs begin to spread throughout the Mediterranean area, including the Southern Levant, which will be discussed later. Syria, Anatolia, Cyprus, and subsequently Greece and Italy show the diffusion of this category of objects (Borgna 2003; Sauvage 2014). Most of the items are missing a spindle whorl, and can thus only tentatively be indicated as spinning tools. Some objects, however, still preserve a spindle whorl and their use can be linked to thread production with more certainty. Since complete spindles and bone shafts have already been extensively discussed (Cecchini 1992; Borgna 2003; Peyronel 2004; Sauvage 2013; 2014; Spinazzi-Lucchesi 2018), this chapter will consider only complete examples from the Northern Levant and Anatolia (not from other Mediterranean areas), while specimens from the Southern Levant will be discussed later.

Several spindles were also found in Troy. Two fragmentary objects made of wood are dated to the EBA, one of which was found charred in a box with traces of yarn and a clay spindle whorl (Götze 1902, 340, 390; Peyronel 2004, 51). A third example is made of ivory with a flat end, while the other seems to be a tenon with a small hole through it. A spindle whorl, slightly dome-shaped, is placed near the middle of the shaft (Balfanz 1995, 107–8; Völling 2008, 257). It is dated to Troy VIIa (*c.* 1250–1180 BC).

Ugarit has preserved three examples of spindles made of bone and ivory. Unfortunately, none of these objects can be considered complete. One has a flat end, and the shaft tapers towards the other end, which is missing; the dome-shaped spindle whorl is placed at ¼ of the length of the spindle, near the flat end. A second example is very similar to this one, but is broken into three pieces; the smallest end is also missing here. A third object, which will be compared with one from Lachish, is complete, but a mortise at the end of the flat tip suggests that a further element would be expected. The other end preserves a large pomegranate-shaped decoration. A discoid spindle whorl is placed at the middle of the shaft. All of these are dated to the LB II (Gachet-Bizollon 2007, 16:115–16, 120, 260–1, pl. 19). Excluding the examples from Megiddo (which will be discussed later), no other shafts with a spindle whorl in place have been recorded.

Other complete spindles are known in the Levant for the 1st millennium BC, but these are made of metal, although bone and ivory shafts continued to be extensively produced.

In Marlik, Iran, a complete spindle made of bronze was found. It shows a groove for attaching the thread near one end of the shaft, while the other has a rounded point. The spindle whorl is a flat bronze disc and is placed immediately under the groove, and is dated to the beginning of the 1st millennium BC. The shaft is 26 cm long and the total weight of this metal spindle is only 50 g, so it could have been used in thread production (Barber 1991, 59; Negahban 1996, 302, pl. 132; Völling 2008, 247).

Two spindles from Deve Höyük, in Anatolia, are made of metal and still preserve their original spindle whorl. Both have one flat end, and taper towards the other end, which is well decorated. In one case the spindle whorl is placed near the flat end (or it was, now it appears to have moved toward the middle of the shaft), while on the other it is near the middle of the shaft. They have generally been interpreted as kohl sticks given the large collection of these found at the site (Moorey 1980, 98, fig. 16). Examples from Kamid el-Loz appear to point in the same direction, albeit slightly later, with one 'spindle' example and several bronze kohl sticks (Poppa 1978, 78, taf. 7; Völling 2008, 255).

If the objects here listed should be considered as spindles (and not distaffs or kohl-sticks) then the position of the spindle whorls appears to be quite variable. Some objects that have a hook or a groove can be oriented with certainty, and in these cases the whorl is placed in the upper part of the shaft, giving a high-whorl spindle. However, many others from Anatolia seem to have the spindle whorl in the middle of the shaft. No examples that could be considered as low-whorl spindles are known so far from the areas under consideration (Syria, Anatolia, Mesopotamia, and Iran). If we compare this scarce, tentative evidence with the few available iconographic sources, however, the picture seems to become clearer.

A mosaic panel of Mari, dated to the early 2nd millennium BC, represents a group of women who are working with some threads. If we view the object held by the standing woman as a spindle, then it is possible to say that the yarn is wound around the top of the spindle with the whorl placed on top of it, as in the case of high-whorl spindles (Barber 1991, 57).

No other iconographic sources are available for the 2nd millennium BC, although many more are known for the 1st millennium BC. A relief from Susa portrays a lady spinning, with the whorl placed at the higher part of the shaft (Porada 1965, 68, fig. 43; Barber 1991, 58). Other examples of spinners are represented on Syro-Hittite reliefs, in which ladies generally hold two objects that could be interpreted as spindle and distaff (Cecchini 1992, 10), and where the thread is always wound on the upper part of the shaft. However, it should be noted that all the examples cited here (except for the Elamite spinner) show the spindle held in the hand of the woman, without a clear representation of the spindle whorl, which may even be absent, and as already noted by E. Barber (1991, 59), no scenes of drop-spinning are known for the Near East.

In any case, Mesopotamia, Northern Syria, and Anatolia seem to have preferred to spin with a central or high-whorl, although other techniques may certainly have been in use at the same time. So far, no archaeological artefacts or iconographical elements are known that prove the Near East and Egypt shared knowledge of the low-whorl spindle spinning in this region – but what about the Southern Levant?

4.5.1.1 Spindles from the Southern Levant

Discoveries of spindles are even more rare in Southern Levant, and the very few items that might have been used as spindles are very different from each other, come from different periods, and do not allow any form of general consideration or typologisation.

A possible spindle was found in the Ashalim Cave, in northern Negev Desert; it is a wooden shaft with a lead perforated object still attached to it. Fibres found on the object might be due to post-depositional animal activities (Langgut *et al.* 2016, 981). The shaft has a length of 22.4 cm and a thickness of 1.5/1.7 cm and is made of *Tamarix* (tamarisk) wood. The weight is 26.6 g. On one of the ends, an incised groove is present and the spindle whorl is placed directly underneath it. The whorl weighs 155.75 g, and is thus too heavy for spinning. However, a use for plying yarns cannot be ruled out. If this item is in fact a spindle, it is certainly a high-whorl spindle. Several lead mace heads are known in the Chalcolithic Levant, and this object could have been a mace (Bar-Adon 1980, 130; Sebbane 2014). However, the lead head is light in comparison with the other mace heads, and the groove does not explain this usage.

Another cave, the Qina Cave in northern Negev Desert, has preserved evidence of four wooden shafts, without whorls. Three perforated basalt objects were found in the same cave, 30 m from the shafts; however, their hole perforation is not suitable for using with the shafts. The shafts are made of *Tamarix* (tamarisk) wood, as with the Ashalim object, and have very different lengths and weights: they are 19 (broken), 40, 48, and 56 cm long, and weigh 9.3, 15.9, 19.9, and 59.8 g. One of the shafts has a groove near one end. Some fibres found on the shafts were identified as bast (Langgut *et al.* 2016, 981). These objects have been interpreted as spindles and/or distaffs. All the objects are dated to the Chalcolithic period and the ^{14}C analysis places them at the very end of the 5th millennium BC (Langgut *et al.* 2016, 980, tab. 1). However, other explanations have been proposed as well, such as cultic objects (Ben-Yosef *et al.* 2017).

No spindles are preserved for the EBA or MBA, and three possible spindles are known from LBA Megiddo. These items are well known and published (Barber 1991, 62; Peyronel 2004, 319), but some considerations are nonetheless necessary.

The first item has been found with the position of the whorls still recognisable, with 'a pin passed through the whorls into holes in the spindles' (Guy and Engberg 1938, pl. 84:1); a second was reconstructed based on the first. All three items are made of several cylindrical parts, attached to one another with different methods. In the first two cases with tenons and mortises, in the third case with a 'core' that originally kept in place the various parts. The last item is very difficult to link to use as a spindle; if it had to be linked to textile production, it would be a distaff, but other uses are possible as well.

The first two items are very likely to have been spindles. However, the way spindle whorls are placed on the shaft is extremely interesting. In fact, two spindle whorls are in use at the same time, so when considering very small and light whorls from Megiddo, we should remember that they may have been used doubled.[8] Furthermore, whorls are not placed on the shaft, but on a peg. This means that the hole of the whorl has to be adapted to fit into the peg, not the shaft, which is much smaller. This creates problems in distinguishing small whorls from beads, since even a hole 2 mm in diameter can be acceptable for whorls. Finally, the position of whorls on the first two shafts is on the opposite side. In the first case, it is near the thinnest part of the shaft (and the mortise on the flat end would lead us to believe that further elements were added), while in the second it is near the large, flat end of the shaft.

A spindle with linen thread wrapped around it from the 1st millennium BC was found in Tell el-Hammeh, but no other indications are given (Cahill 2006, 441). Dozens of wooden whorls were also present. Another fragmentary spindle is known from the Phoenician town of Achzib, which is dated to the Iron Age II. The preserved length is 6.7 cm and it has a very large diameter, 3 cm. At one of the broken ends, a discoid whorl has been placed.

During the LBA several bone shafts, very similar to those interpreted as spindles, were found at Megiddo and other Levantine sites, similar to the case in the Northern Levant. No spindle whorls were found on these items, so their interpretation as spindles, although in many cases probable, remains uncertain. Their production continues throughout the Iron Age, although they are less numerous. In the sites discussed here, the largest quantity was found in Megiddo, but a few were also found in Beth Shean, Hazor (especially for Iron Age II) and Far'ah.

Lachish deserves a special mention, for ivory objects closely resembling complete 'spindles' from Ugarit. Six complete shafts were found in a votive cache of the so-called 'fosse temple' and are dated to the end of the LBA. Three of these have an elaborate top, in two cases resembling a pomegranate (Tufnell *et al.* 1940, 59–62, pl. XX). Another, similar object comes from a grave (Tufnell 1958, 87, pl. XXVIII). Similar objects are known from other sites in Iron Age levels, such as Achzib and Tell Sera.

These objects are very thick, however, and seem very different from actual spindles in everyday use. It is thus possible that they were used as distaffs to hold fibres rather than for spinning.

4.5.2 Spindle whorls

Spindle whorls are quite a common find in the Near East since the Neolithic period. From the end of the 7th millennium BC, several sites in Mesopotamia and Syria provide evidence of spindle whorls, in particular biconical and pottery perforated sherds (Rooijakkers 2012, 101).

In Anatolia, the Late Neolithic phase has provided a very limited number of sites with evidence of spindle whorls and perforated sherds (Schoop 2014).

Spindle whorls are known in the Southern Levant since at least the Neolithic period, as the evidence from Jericho suggests (Wheeler 1982, 626). However, they are quite a rare find for early periods, and it is difficult to draw a trend. Furthermore, the purposely made spindle whorls should be placed in relation to the reworked pottery sherds (Rooijakkers 2012), which are very common in all periods under consideration and will be discussed in the next chapter. Slightly better represented is the EBA, but it is only by the LBA that we can identify large quantities of spindle whorls and draw more representative conclusions of trends in the region.

Neolithic levels, as stated, provide very little evidence of spindle whorls. In Jericho, a couple of stone spindle whorls can be dated to Pre-pottery Neolithic B, one spherical and the other discoid. Pottery spindle whorls appear in levels of Pottery Neolithic and have a discoid shape. With these, another two discoid stone spindle whorls must be noted (Wheeler 1982, 626). The earliest Beth Shean whorls are dated to level XVIII, but whether they belong to the Neolithic or Chalcolithic phase is unclear. All of them are made of stone, mostly limestone, except one perforated pebble of ovoid shape (Braun 2004, fig. 4.9). From Late Neolithic levels of Tel Kabri are known six discoid pottery whorls, but there are no stone specimens (Oren 2002, 368, fig. 10.14). Several are also reported in Sha'ar Hagolan (Garfinkel 1999, 29; Levy 2020, 78–9), including biconical, lenticular, and discoid spindle whorls, as well as perforated pottery sherds. Interestingly, Levy (2020, 80) identified 37 stone spindle whorls, mainly of limestone. Biconical clay spindle whorls and perforated pottery sherds were also found, such as those from Jebel Abu Thawwab (Qadi 2001), Tell Te'o (Gopher and Eisenberg 2001), Munhata (Perrot 1966), and Hagoshrim (Levy 2020, 85–7).

Spindle whorls recorded for the Chalcolithic period are much more numerous. In Beth Shean, some spindle whorls belong to level XVII, dated to the Chalcolithic period (or the beginning or the EB I), and show great continuity (Braun 2004, fig. 4.9). The three basalt discs (or should they be considered as rings?) found in the Qina cave have already been noted. These have a diameter ranging between 4.2 and 4.9 cm, a height between 1.4 and 1.7 cm, and a weight between 50 and 68 g. This data shows that they are very homogeneous (Langgut *et al.* 2016, 981, tab. 3). Limestone and basalt discoid whorls also appear in Nahal Mishmar (Bar-Adon 1980, 183–4).

Besides discoid spindle whorls made of stone and pottery, other sites preserve some examples of well-shaped biconical spindle whorls (Shamir 2014, 147, 166).

Discoid and biconical whorls (including perforated sherds, which will be treated in the next chapter) are known in large numbers from sites in the Beer Sheva valley, where a dramatic increase in their numbers can be detected (Levy and Gilead 2013, 31). Biconical spindle whorls are reported to have an average diameter of 4.5 cm and an average weight of 64 g.

Two discoid basalt whorls with fragments of the wooden shafts still inside the hole have been recently published (Ben-Yosef *et al.* 2017). They were discovered in one of the Nahal Ze'elim caves as part of Aharoni's expedition to the Judean Desert. Their weight is 63.3 and 94.8 g, in line with the evidence from the other sites.

In a recent publication, Levy presents an extensive and thorough assessment of Chalcolithic spindle whorls in the Southern Levant, incorporating previously unpublished material. Her analysis reveals that the largest group consists of perforated sherds (107 examples), with the number of stone whorls (98 examples) only slightly lower. Ceramic whorls also form a substantial group (Levy 2020, 118, tab. 6.1).

The average weight of both stone and ceramic whorls ranges between 50 and 60 g, whereas perforated sherds average 29 g. Levy describes ceramic whorls as predominantly biconical and spheroidal in shape (Levy 2020, 120). Stone whorls – made from limestone, chalk, basalt, and flint – include biconical, lenticular, and discoid forms (Levy 2020, 121). Notably, she also includes basalt whorls in this category, which, in some cases, may be classified as basalt rings.

The EBA saw a continuity in shapes and materials from the Chalcolithic, but also an increase in their variety. Biconical, cylindrical, and discoid shapes are also dominant in the EBA strata at Beth Shean, made of both pottery and stone. A similar production is also known from Megiddo, but almost all the specimens known from this site are made of pottery. Furthermore, beside discoid and biconical whorls, dome-shaped and cylindrical whorls are also present, showing a broader range of typologies. Unfortunately, objects from both sites are broken and cannot allow a comparison of weights. The probable weight of those from Megiddo should range between 27 and 50 g, which means a medium quality yarn. A wide typology of shapes is also known from Tell el-Far'ah (N), where cylindrical, spherical, conical, and discoid whorls are present. However, all the whorls available for study are made of stone, contrary to the production known for Megiddo. Furthermore, they are much heavier than those from Megiddo, showing a lower quality production. A very large batch of spindle whorls comes from the EBA layers of Jericho. Almost all the objects have a discoid shape, showing continuity with the Chalcolithic period, but cylindrical whorls and one dome-shaped whorl are also present. As in Beth Shean and Far'ah N, the majority are made from stone, but several items made of pottery are known as well. A single specimen of a dome-shaped bone whorl was found for these layers (Wheeler 1982, 635, fig. 258:16). Few EB I whorls are known from Ashkelon (Area E), but they are very interesting since they provide useful data for comparison with basalt rings, which will be discussed later. Two of the 12 whorls are disc-shaped and made of limestone. Their measurements are 3.2 and 4.2 cm in diameter, 0.8 and 1 cm in height, and 9.5 and 25.2 g in weight (Shamir 2004, 98). Similar to the objects from Ashkelon are those from Tell Yarmuth, where discoid limestone spindle whorls were found (de Miroschedji 1988, 88, pl. 49). A continuity with Late Neolithic materials is visible in Tel Kabri, where five discoid pottery whorls were found in EBA contexts (Oren 2002, 368, fig. 10.14). Cylindrical spindle whorls are known from several sites, including Azor (Golani *et al.* 1999) and Qiryat Ata (Shamir 2003).

Tell Abu el-Kharaz in the Jordan Valley is a key site for comprehending textile tools, since they are quite well published and organic materials have sometimes been preserved, providing a good understanding of their use. However, spindle whorls are almost absent from EBA layers (excluding basalt and limestone rings, which will be treated separately) – just one single limestone whorl is known (Fischer 2008, 147). Furthermore, not a single perforated sherd has been reported.

Another element to consider when discussing the EBA spindle whorls is the large production of basalt rings. Whether these should be considered spindle whorls is not entirely clear (see Chapter 4.6), but there is a very high chance that many, if not all were used for producing yarn.

MBA layers show a slight increase in spindle whorl findings, as well as the introduction of new typologies and materials. In Megiddo, pottery spindle whorls are still predominant and biconical shapes are still in use together with a conical specimen. MB I sees the introduction of bone spindle whorls, which are generally dome-shaped since they are cut from animal bones epiphyses, but occasional conical examples are known. Stone spindle whorls also begin to be produced, and they show a large variety of typologies: discoid, dome, cylindrical, and spherical. Weights vary a lot but, excluding an object with a weight of 130 g, all the other specimens weigh less than 50 g. Bone spindle whorls tend to be small and extremely light, weighing from 1 to 5 g. Although some were probably not considered as spindle whorls, the presence of two spindles with a double whorl mounted through a peg does not allow us to safely exclude any of the objects at this site.

Similar to Megiddo, Beth Shean includes the introduction of bone and ivory spindle whorls, mostly dome-shaped. Discoid stone whorls continue to be produced, but pottery whorls disappear entirely. Many other typologies of stone whorls are known, such as cylindrical, lenticular, and conical. For the bone/ivory whorls, button and conical examples are also present. Very few weights are available for this period, but as in the case of Megiddo, they seem oriented towards very fine yarn production, with many whorls weighing *c.* 10 g. However, Megiddo preserves a large quantity of objects weighing less than 5 g, which constitutes a remarkable difference.

Hazor has shown little evidence of spindle whorls (only for MBII layers) and, contrary to other sites, they are completely homogeneous in terms of their shape and material. In fact, all the specimens are made of bone, and almost all have a dome shape. One discoid and one conical truncated whorl, still made of bone, are the only exceptions.

Tell el-Far'ah (N)[9] shows a great continuity with the EBA layers. In fact, stone is still the most common material employed and only one pottery whorl is present, as in the earlier period. Like the other sites considered here, bone whorls are introduced during the MBA and have a dome shape. Weights show a remarkable difference and are oriented to medium-low quality production. One of the bone 'whorls', however, is extremely small and would have had a very light weight, similar to the lightest from Megiddo.

Many other sites have provided examples of MBA spindle whorls, and Jericho is certainly one of the most important. Unfortunately, the settlement was badly eroded for this phase and spindle whorls come mainly from graves, continuing a funerary tradition that was already established in the EBA. Most of the whorls are made of stone, but pottery is also widely employed. Bone spindle whorls also appear in this level, but discovery of three wooden whorls (Wheeler 1982, 586) is remarkable. Shapes continue the tradition of earlier periods, being mostly discoidal and partly biconical. Wooden whorls, meanwhile, are conical and dome-shaped.

Another highly interesting MBA context is Tel Kabri, where textile tools have been well published. Many loom weights were found (and will be discussed in Chapter 4.7), but very few whorls are known for this period. Of the 12 found in the palace area, only six come from clear contexts. Furthermore, two more whorls come from graves. Most of the whorls are made of pottery, but bone, faience and hematite whorls have also been found. Shapes vary between discoid, biconical, and dome (Oren 2002, 368–9, fig. 10.15).

Some whorls from Gezer probably belong to MB phases, but Macalister's publication is far from clear (Macalister 1912, 70–3, pl. 132; Peyronel 2004, 191).

The MBA is a highly interesting phase in the development of spindle whorls in the Southern Levant. It is during this period that we see the introduction of bone spindle whorls, which would become so frequent in later phases. It is also a phase where we see a more widespread practice of placing spinning tools in funerary contexts. It is important to note that although widely attested, this practice is not a rule, and discoveries of spinning tools in graves remain limited.

The LBA period is characterised by a very rich production of spindle whorls, which is nonetheless merely a precursor of the impressive quantity of the Iron Age layers. In Megiddo, bone whorls have become the most common type at the site and, obviously, they are largely dome-shaped. However, pottery and stone whorls are still present. Besides the common dome shape (which is not confined to bone, since stone implements are present too), spherical, conical, biconical, discoid, lenticular, and a few button-shaped objects are known from the site. As will be discussed in Chapter 4.9, it is very difficult to clearly understand which of the smallest items should be considered as whorls; some of the objects weigh less than 1 g and have a hole diameter of 0.2 cm, which appear too small to be spindle whorls.[10] Other objects have a weight of 15–20 g and 50–60 g, proving that different types of yarn were produced at the site.

For Megiddo, even in Beth Shean, bone is the most common material used for producing spindle whorls and, as usual, almost all are dome-shaped. Another large group of whorls is made of stone, especially gypsum, which is a typical feature of that region. Only two pottery whorls are known from the site. Unfortunately, very few weights are recorded for this phase and it is not possible to draw many conclusions about the type of yarn production. However, the widespread presence of bone whorls points to a production of very fine quality.

Fewer spindle whorls are available for LBA Hazor, although no domestic buildings have been excavated for this period. However, they show a trend very similar to those of Beth Shean. The large majority of whorls (almost twice as many) are made of bone, while stone is more rarely employed. Pottery whorls are very rare, but still attested. The shapes are quite varied, even if dome, as would be expected, is predominant. However, different shapes are present: conical truncated, button, spherical, cylindrical, and one lenticular item. Yarn production was certainly of a very fine quality, since the heaviest (recorded) object weighs 37 g, and the average weight is only 11 g.

In Tell el-Farʿah, stone is the dominant material, contrary to Hazor, Megiddo, and Beth Shean, even if there are very few objects available. Bone whorls are present, but to a lesser extent. However, similar to the other sites, dome is still the most common shape, both for stone and bone whorls. Whorls can be divided in two groups, one with very light whorls weighing less than 10 g, the other with weights ranging between 15 and 33 g. The possible quality of yarn should therefore be considered as very fine and medium quality.

The practise of placing spindle whorls in graves is well exemplified by Megiddo, but some whorls are also known from tombs in Akko, found in a salvage excavation. All four specimens are made of stone and can be considered dome-shaped (Ben-Arieh and Edelstein 1977, 10, 12, 26, figs 14:16–8).

Several spindle whorls are known from the settlement of Tel Dan, mostly made of black stone, probably serpentine, and conical or button shaped. Dome-shaped bone and ivory whorls are also present (Ben-Dov and Gershuny 2011, 333, fig. 198). Dome and conical whorls have a diameter between 1.5 and 3 cm and a height ranging between 0.4 and 1.5 cm. Another interesting context is a grave, the so-called Mycenean grave, which contained 34 possible dome spindle whorls (although many could have been decorative implements), 100 button whorls, and 18 button/dome whorls, a total of 152 possible whorls (Biran *et al.* 2002, 157). They are mostly made of bone and ivory, but stone objects are also numerous. Button whorls have a diameter between 1.5 and 3 cm and a height of 0.4–0.8 cm. Ten bone shafts were present in the grave, but only a couple of these could have been employed as spindles (or pins), while the others are certainly not (Biran *et al.* 2002, 155, fig. 2.120).

The Iron Age period saw a tremendous increase in the findings of spindle whorls, but we should remember that these phases have mostly been extensively investigated in Israel, due to their connection with the Biblical text. The result is that larger areas of mounds are exposed for these periods than any other period in history, and many sites are known only for their Iron Age levels. Given the large quantity of materials available, and that the change occurred between Iron Age I and II, it has been decided to investigate the two phases separately, where possible.

In Megiddo the most common material is bone, which is used for producing dome whorls as well as other typologies. Stone is also very frequent, almost as much as bone, with a predominance of limestone and steatite. The most common shape is dome, however, conical and discoid are also quite widespread. Other shapes are much rarer. Some pottery whorls are also present, most of which fall into two groups of weights: a very light weight of less than 10 g, and a second group ranging between 15 and 25 g. Very few whorls are heavier. Production seems quite differentiated, and different types of yarn could be produced with these objects. However, most of the production was oriented toward a fine or medium-fine quality yarn.

In Beth Shean, stone is the most common material, and several types of stone were employed to produce whorls. Gypsum is very popular, as in all the Beth Shean Valley, but limestone was also widely used. Several whorls are made of ivory/bone and a small number is made of pottery. For Megiddo, although the dome shape is predominant, conical and cylindrical whorls are numerous as well. Beth Shean's textile production was likely geared towards producing very fine fabrics, as the largest group of whorls weighs less than 10 g. Several weights are present between 10 and 30 g, and very few exceed 30 g.

Hazor and Far'ah materials were not possible to separate between Iron Age I and II, so these will be treated in the next section.

The number of spindle whorls known for Iron Age II levels in Megiddo is impressive (225 listed in the catalogue), and no other Levantine site has given similar evidence of spinning activity. A distinct change, compared to LBA and Iron Age I levels, is seen by the choice of stone as the favourite material for producing whorls. Bone whorls are still present, but to a lesser extent, and a few groups of pottery whorls are also known. Steatite and limestone are the most common stones to have been employed, and very few other materials are known from the site. A large majority of the whorls are conical or dome-shaped, and conical are the most frequent. Other shapes, such as spherical, cylindrical and biconical are also represented. Very few weights are available for this period, but some extremely light objects (buttons) are still present, as in earlier periods. Medium and quite heavy weights are also present, proving that production was quite differentiated.

In Beth Shean, as for all sites under consideration, stone is the most common material employed for whorls, while bone and pottery are almost absent. Most of the whorls are made of the typical gypsum of the region and only other materials – especially limestone and to a lesser extent steatite – have been used secondarily. Almost all the whorls are dome-shaped, with few examples of conical and cylindrical objects.

In Hazor, the largest group of whorls belonging to Iron Age I and II is of those made of stone, while bone whorls appear very rarely, and pottery whorls are quite common. The shapes are quite varied, but dome and conical shapes are the most frequently employed. Only a few conical truncated, discoid, and cylindrical shapes are known. The weight is quite heavy, and lack the extremely light objects typical of the LBA, which have weights of 1 or 2 g. However, light whorls weighing less than 10 g are present, as well as those with a medium weight and a heavy weight. Production appears, therefore, to have been highly differentiated, mostly pointing to a medium quality product.

In Tell el-Far'ah, stone is the most common material used for producing whorls. For the other sites under consideration, a typical feature of Iron Age II levels is the rarity of bone whorls and the appearance of a quite substantial group of pottery whorls. Dome and conical shapes are not very frequently found, contrary to the other sites, while the most common shape is cylindrical. Unfortunately, nothing can be said for the typology of yarn that was produced in this period.

Forty-four whorls are known from Iron Age levels of Tell Keisan, and this site is also very interesting for the coexistence in the same loci of various objects linked to textile production. Several shapes are present, mostly dome, conical, and cylindrical. Conical and conical truncated are the most common type of whorl in Keisan, which are mainly made of stone, with a very few ivory and pottery examples present. The weights are quite light, mostly under 10 g or between 10 and 20 g. The dome shape is also very common and even in this case whorls are made of stone, except for one object made of bone. They are certainly heavier than the conical examples, since only one specimen weighs less than 10 g, and most weigh between 10 and 20 g, with a few exceeding 20 and even 30 g. Some whorls are also biconical and discoid, but their weights are very different. All of them are made of stone (Nodet 1980, 315–17, pl. 96).

The evidence coming from Iron Age layers of Tell Abu al-Kharaz, especially of Iron Age II, is remarkable. Similarly to the other sites considered here, the production of spindle whorls is mainly made from stone, especially limestone, while bone and pottery examples are much more limited. Conical and biconical shapes are very common, while the dome shape is present but to a lesser extent (Fischer 2014). However, weights are very different from those of the sites so far considered, since they are much heavier. Of the objects with a recorded weight, only six have a weight under 10 g, six between 10 and 20 g, 15 between 20 and 30 g, nine between 30 and 40 g, eight between 40 and 50 g, and finally four between 50 and 60 g. This distribution points towards a medium quality production, but fine and low quality yarns were also made, albeit to a lesser extent.

Very few spindle whorls are known from Tall Jawa, but the site is extremely important since the contexts were well preserved and the materials are very well published. Furthermore, it is interesting to note the quantity of perforated sherds in comparison to that of whorls. One hundred and fifteen whorls are recorded, four made of limestone, three of basalt and one of ivory. These have dome, conical, and cylindrical shapes, although the basalt whorls very closely resemble basalt rings. All the other whorls are perforated sherds (Daviau 2002, 184, figs 2.145–9).

Another interesting context, Iron Age Beth Shemesh, has provided a very large quantity of loom weights but only 15 spindle whorls, mostly made of perforated sherds, although some stone implements are also present. Furthermore, these do not belong to layers where textile production is largely testified, but from earlier layers (Bunimovitz and Lederman 2016, 583). Other sites testify to a similar incongruity between spinning and weaving implements, which has been explained by the loss of wooden whorls or the import of finished yarns.[11] Both explanations may be valid, since spinning could happen in rural and domestic contexts and prepared yarns could be brought to the weaving workshop. Many other sites have preserved spindle whorls in Iron Age contexts, as for example: stone dome spindle whorls (and an ivory rod) from the fort area Horbat Rosh Zayit

(Gal *et al.* 2000, 8:134, fig. III.112), stone dome and pottery spherical spindle whorls from Tel ʿIra (Ben-Dov 1999, 448–9).

This brief presentation of certain key sites of the Southern Levant enables a discussion of some problems specific to the region, and others that are common to anyone working with whorls. The first challenge, which involves the corpus presented here, is the distinction between a spindle whorl, a bead, and a decorative element. As seen for Megiddo, light and small objects with small holes could have been used as whorls, since they could have been mounted on tenons rather than shafts and used in pairs. However, the batch of objects from Tel Dan is much more problematic. In fact, an incredible number of whorls have been found in a grave, some of which are quite large, while others are very small and light, and many were found grouped together. Even if most of these objects could have been used as whorls without specific technical problems, this does not seem very likely. The excavators propose an explanation as decorations for dresses or other objects, which seems quite reasonable. However, objects that are very similar to those of Dan – both dome and button shaped – have been found in almost all Southern Levantine sites, and there is currently no means to distinguish them from actual whorls. A similar problem was mentioned by J. Carington Smith, since large groups of steatite whorls appear in Mycenaean contexts, mostly made of conical shapes. They appear to be very similar, in terms of diameter and weight, to the Levantine whorls discussed here and, as in the Levant, they can be found in single specimens as well as in large batches (160 in Tsountas), with no distinction between the sex of the deceased, nor a specific connection to graves, since they also occur in settlements (Carington Smith 1976, 440–2).

Placing whorls in tombs appears to have been quite a common feature in the Levant, especially in the Bronze Age, and many examples can be found, from Megiddo to Jericho, Akko and Gezer. Almost all sites with large cemeteries exposed share this practise, and a very interesting example is Tell el-Farʿah (S). Graves of both MBA and LBA lack evidence of whorls, as well as other textile tools.[12] It is possible that whorls were made of wood and therefore have not been preserved, or that other beliefs and rituals were practised at the site (for example the Egyptian aversion to placing textile tools in graves, except needles, see Chapter 5. There are also very few whorls that come from graves in Tell el-Ajjul, but in this case a small number were found (Petrie *et al.* 1931, 16, pl. XVIII). The symbolic reason for the presence of whorls in graves has been suggested as a connection between the female sphere and textile activity. Such an explanation is certainly possible, but it does not seem to perfectly match the archaeological evidence. Other theories have supported the idea of a specific meaning for the deceased (Maeir and Panitz-Cohen 2004, 44), but again the archaeological evidence – which features large quantities of whorls and spindles, as in Megiddo, or of loom weights, or even perforated sherds – appear not to point in this direction. It seems evident that these simple objects symbolise textile production, but why they were ultimately brought into tombs is still far from clear.

Stone and bone spindle whorls both show similar traces of manufacture. Generally, in conical and dome-shaped objects, the upper part of the whorl has circular concentric signs left by a lathe, while flat bases have evident, perpendicular scratches. Some specimens also instead have circular signs on the base, and sometimes these signs are voluntarily deepened to form decorative motifs. Circular signs indicates that the objects were refined with a wheel, and the scratches are left over from scraping after cutting the object (Fig. 4.24). Similar traces have been identified in other Northern Levantine sites, such as Ugarit and Ebla (Peyronel 2004, 163; Sauvage 2013, 190–1).

One of the big issues regarding Levantine whorls is their position on the shaft of the spindle – whether they are a high or low whorl spindle. As seen in the preceding chapter, Egypt has a high-whorl tradition (but see Chapter 5 for discussion), the Aegean has a low whorl tradition, and the extant examples from Anatolia seem to point to a high or middle whorl tradition. The few iconographic sources available for Mesopotamia and the Northern Levant seem to point to a high-whorl tradition, but nothing has survived from the Southern Levant. Given that most of the surrounding areas seem to prefer high-whorl spindles, it would seem logical that the same tradition would be present in the Southern Levant as well. The few complete surviving spindles do not permit a firm conclusion, since the Chalcolithic spindle from Ashalim Cave (if it is a spindle) points to a high-whorl spindle, while the examples from Megiddo include both the possibilities.

By analysing spindle whorls, it is possible to note that non-symmetrical shapes, such as dome or conical, tend to have a slightly conical hole, which thickens toward the base

Figure 4.24. Two whorls from Megiddo, one made of stone (12/H/40/AR8) and one of ivory (08/K/89/AR6). In both cases, they are decorated by circular incisions, but other criss-cross lines, possibly due to wear and manufacture, are visible (courtesy of the Megiddo expedition)

of the object, with a difference of 0.5–1 mm. This enables a better cohesion of the whorl to the shaft, especially if the shaft is not perfectly cylindrical but tapers towards the point. This would suggest a usage on the lower part of the shaft. However, a study of Egyptian spindles (see Chapter 5) has shown that this conical hole can be perfectly valid even if the whorl is placed at the top of the spindle, especially if the spindle has a sort of thickening in the middle. A second interesting element is constituted by wear traces near the hole and on the edge of non-symmetrical whorls (a similar discussion will be made for Egyptian Predynastic spindle whorls in Chapter 5.2). On stone and sometimes bone whorls, it is possible to see that the inferior hole is neatly cut and does not show any traces of manufacture. However, the upper hole frequently shows small chips, fractures or entirely damaged areas, which seem to indicate an area that was intensively exposed to wear/damage, also present on the external edge of the whorls. Similar wear traces are compatible with a low-whorl spindle, while a high-whorl position would have damaged only the lateral edge. However, the stone spindle whorls from Deir el-Medina (see Chapter 5) again seem to show the same type of damage. As there is very little doubt that they were used in a top position, this means that it is not possible to use this type of macro-wear damage as an indication of spindle whorl position. It is not clear, however, what causes this type of damage, both in the Egyptian and the Levantine corpus. As the area next to the top of the whorl is not particularly stressed during spinning with a top whorl spindle (in the case of the Egyptian spindles it is always the lower part of the hole that is more stressed due to the frequent use of wedges), we must hypothesise a different cause, possibly involving post-depositional and storage factors. As these areas on the top of the whorls are the most prominent, it is reasonable to think that they could also be more exposed to rubbing or bumping. More research on wear traces is thus needed to fully understand the possible causes of this damage.

4.5.3 Perforated sherds

As seen in Chapter 3, perforated sherds are simple pottery sherds reworked to obtain a rounded object with a perforation in the middle. Nodet considered these objects to be the result of using body sherds as a pivot for drills while perforating other objects (Nodet 1980, 320). Once the perforation of these discs was complete, they could have been used as spindle whorls. Some objects, which bare traces of several hollows, of varying depth, could have been used in this way. However, it does not seem likely that all these objects were the result of a single perforation made from both sides by accident; the intention of obtaining a through hole is evident.

Even if the perforation was intentional, it does not mean that they were used as spindle whorls, but simply that this is one of their possible usages. In fact, many of the objects present in the corpus should certainly not be considered as whorls, with Megiddo providing a perfect example. A hole is generally made by drilling the sherd from both sides and, in most cases, the result is an hourglass perforation. In some specimens, the hole has been intentionally regularised and the final result was an almost cylindrical hole (00/K/42/AR1 or 98/K/41/AR14). In other cases, nothing has been done to refine the hole, which keeps its hourglass shape. Furthermore, some holes are slim and oval and could not allow the insertion of a shaft (as 08/K/17/AR3). In some cases, the hole has been made by perforating the sherds not vertically but diagonally, making the objects unlikely to have been whorls (as 13/H/10/AR2). All these elements must be considered when deciding if a perforated sherd could have been used as a whorl, but publications have not always recorded this information.

Perforated sherds are a common element of Near Eastern and Levantine excavations since the Neolithic period, and reach their peak of production during the Iron Age (Shamir 2007b, 267).

Several perforated sherds were found for example in Pre-pottery Neolithic B Mureybet (Stordeur and Lebreton 2008), Tell Maghzaliya (Bader 1993), Abu Hureyra (Moore *et al.* 2000), Aswad and Ghoraifé (de Contenson 1995), Ramad (de Contenson 2000), Kumartepe (Roodenberg *et al.* 1984), and Halula (Molist Montaña *et al.* 1996). A large number is known from the Neolithic site of Naḥal Zehora, of which 112 are perforated sherds (Types B and C) (Orrelle *et al.* 2012, 638–41). The edge can be perfectly round and smooth, or roughly cut. Many other Neolithic sites display similar artefacts, including Jericho (Wheeler 1982, 626), Tabaqat al-Bûma, (Banning *et al.* 1992), Tell Te'o (Gopher and Eisenberg 2001), 'Ein el Jerba (Kaplan 1969), Wadi Raba (Kaplan 1958), and Munhata (Perrot 1966).[13]

They continued to be found in large numbers during the Chalcolithic period, often with a discoid stone counterpart. The analysis by Levy and Gilead (2012, 131) for Ghassulian sites comprised between Beersheba and the Negev show that perforated whorls (after discarding unfinished or unsuitable objects) constitute almost half of the total whorls assemblage. Interestingly, some of these have also been found in the Cave of the Treasures (Bar-Adon 1980, fig. 58).

During the Bronze Age, their production seems to decrease, but they are still present in the sites considered here, as well as in many other sites such as Jericho (16 for the EBA and only 9 for the MBA) (Wheeler 1982, 626), Ashkelon (Shamir 2004, 98), Yarmuth (de Miroschedji 1988, 87, pl. 47), Jerusalem (Shamir 1996, 149), and MBA Tel Kabri (Oren 2002). One example from Kabri was found in a grave, as well as a few examples from Megiddo (5529). Only one perforated sherd has been published for EBA Tell Abu al-Kharaz (Fischer 2009), although they are common in the Iron Age. The LBA sees a new increase in their production, especially in Megiddo and Hazor, but their peak of production is certainly reached in the Iron Age.

In Megiddo, they are very common both in Iron Age I and II, but during the same period we also see an increase in the production of spindle whorls. These represent almost one third of the Iron Age I production of whorls, but are much less used during the LBA and Iron Age II. Very few perforated sherds have been reported for all periods of Beth Shean, but they seem more common in the Iron Age II period. However, compared to spindle whorls they reach their peak of usage in the EBA. In Hazor, they are very rare during the EBA and MBA, quite common in the LBA, but their peak of production is reached in Iron Age II. In Tell el-Far'ah (N), perforated sherds are not very common, especially for the Bronze Age and, as in many other Levantine sites, they are more common in the Iron Age.

For most of the sites under consideration, they represent a small percentage of the corpus of Iron Age whorls, but this is not the same across all Levantine sites. In fact, some sites have attested to a larger presence of perforated sherds than purposely made spindle whorls, showing a preference for these simple, cheap objects. In Tall Jawa, Jordan, 115 spindle whorls are listed for the Iron Age, but only seven are purposely made; the others are all perforated sherds. This number is undoubtedly impressive, but they appear similar in dimensions and features to the other implements known from the Levantine region. The largest sherds measure 8.5–9 cm, while the smallest are 3–3.5 cm. Thickness can range between 0.6 and 2.5 cm, and their holes are between 0.2 and 1 cm. Some holes are slightly off-centre, but show traces that prove that they were not discarded (Daviau 2002, 184–8, fig. 2.144). A similar situation (but with smaller numbers) is found in Kadesh Barnea, where 23 spindle whorls out of 27 are made from reworked pottery sherds. Only one has an incomplete perforation (Shamir 2007b, 265). Similarly, in Beth Shemesh spindle whorls are mostly made from perforated sherds, and only secondarily made on purpose. The peak is reached in Iron Age I, as in Megiddo, while very few whorls were found in Iron Age II (Bunimovitz and Lederman 2016, 583).

4.5.4 Spinning bowls

Spinning bowls are typically identified as Egyptian; however, evidence shows that they were also used in other Mediterranean and European regions (Svilar 2017; Ruiz de Haro 2018). Bowls with loops inside have been known archaeologically since Petrie's excavations in Egypt (Petrie 1890, 25) and were recognised early as the objects represented in funerary paintings and models, in connection with spinners (see Table 3.2). In these scenes, it is evident that threads are pulled through the bowl and spun or plied, and most archaeological findings show traces of rubbing under the loops.

When complete or partially preserved they are quite easy to identify. In fact, they are characterised by the presence of one or multiple loops inside the bowl, attached to the bottom of it. This can vary from a single loop to four, and in one case a double row of loops is present. Several of these bowls are known in LBA contexts in the Southern Levant, and they are generally considered as products related to the Egyptian domination of the region. In fact, in Egypt they appear quite early, at least in the Predynastic, and continued to be in use until the Late Period. However, for some unknown reason, studies on spinning bowls have always ignored the Ghassulian bowls published by Perrot in 1967 (Perrot *et al.* 1967). It is possible that this omission depends on the different shape of these bowls, and it is thanks to the work of Levy that they have been correctly recognised (Levy and Gilead 2013; Levy 2020). In fact, one comes from the Neve Ur in the Beth Shean Valley, the other from Safadi, near Beersheba, and both are dated to the 5th millennium BC. However, they do not feature loops inside, but rather a quadrangular feature attached to the bottom and the side of the bowl, which could have been used in the same way as the loop.

After this early appearance, no other actual spinning bowl is known in the Southern Levant before the LBA. The oldest example comes from Tell el-Ajjul, in a context dated to the 14th–13th century BC and has two loops inside (Petrie 1932, fig. pl. XXVII). Beth Shean has preserved a very large collection of these bowls, dating from the LB II to the beginning of the Iron Age (from the very end of the 18th Dynasty/beginning 19th to the 20th Dynasty). Most of the bowls belong to the Iron Age I period. Many other sites have preserved examples of spinning bowls, with the latest examples coming from Tell Qasile (level VII, 8th century BC) and Tell Jemmeh (level 198, 7th century BC). This last example is very important, since its shape closely resembles Late Period findings from Mendes (Allen 1997, 26) (Table 4.6).

Levantine spinning bowls are spread throughout the Southern Levant and are not typical of a specific region. However, they are not present at each site, but are quite rare finds, except in Beth Shean. It must be said, however, that they are certainly underestimated since they are produced following local pottery traditions, and the broken parts of many spinning bowls may have been found without being recognised.

From the available evidence, it seems that spinning bowls were first used in the Levant and after that dismissed, only appearing again with the Egyptian domination of the region. I agree with this traditional interpretation. Spinning bowls in Egypt appear to be connected to splicing. Splicing is also known in the Levant in the early periods, but it has been argued that it disappeared in the MBA (Shamir 2015) and was probably not used in the LBA and Iron I periods, when spinning bowls are found. This would seem to point against

Table 4.6. Spinning bowls from the Southern Levant

Site		*Period*	*Bibliography*
Bir es-Safadi	1	Ghassulian	Perrot *et al.* 1967
Beersheba	1	Ghassulian	Perrot *et al.* 1967
Ajjul	1	LB II	Petrie 1932
Megiddo	1	LB III	Loud 1948, fig. 70:3
Hazor	1	LB II	Bechar 2017, fig. 7.72
Beth Shean	6 33	LB II Iron Age IA–B	Fitzgerald 1930; James and McGovern 1993; Martin 2009; Panitz-Cohen and Yahalom-Mack 2009; Panitz-Cohen 2012, 437
Tell Jerishe	1 2	LB II Iron Age	Dothan 1963, 99
Keisan	1	Iron Age I	Briend *et al.* 1980, 224, pl. 73:10
Ashdod II-III	1	Iron Age I	Dothan 1971, 105
Tell Qasile	2 3 2 3	Level XII/XI Level X Level VII Unstratified	Dothan 1963
ʿIzbet Ṣarṭah	1	Iron Age I	Finkelstein 1986, 48–9
Beth Shemesh	1	Iron Age I	Grant 1932, 27
Tell Jemmeh	1	Iron Age II	Petrie 1928, 22

a relation between splicing and spinning bowls, and if this is true for the Levant (and all other areas where splicing is used) it might be true also for Egypt. Vogelsang-Eastwood strongly argued against a connection between splicing and spinning bowls, even for the Egyptian area, and interprets spinning bowls as tools for plying and cabling threads (Vogelsang-Eastwood 1987). Both activities (spinning after splicing and plying) can probably be performed with such bowls. If they could be used as tools to keep the balls of yarns in order and avoid tangles, like modern knitting bowls, why are they so rare in the Levant? The most plausible explanation may lie in the period of Egyptian domination in the region. These artefacts make their appearance in the Levant as Egyptian influence strengthens, only to nearly vanish following the withdrawal of Egyptian forces. This pattern suggests that the objects were likely produced specifically for Egyptian families residing in the area, becoming redundant and thus falling out of use after their departure. Even the most recent examples maintain strong ties to Egyptian materials and design, indicating that these items were not adopted by the local population. This could be attributed to a range of factors, including scepticism towards foreign customs or differing local spinning traditions that did not need such tools. Although this is just one of many possible explanations and the evidence remains far from conclusive, it is supported by the materials discovered at Beth Shean, as well as the notable scarcity of similar finds at other sites. The pattern observed suggests a close association with the Egyptian presence, underlining the cultural and practical discontinuities between the Egyptian settlers and the indigenous populations.

4.5.5 Loom weights

Looms have not been preserved in the Southern Levant, with the exception of a few wooden pieces that may have been beams, though this remains uncertain. These fragments, discovered in the Cave of the Treasures, could have been used to produce narrow strips of cloth. Shamir (2015, 18) interprets them as components of a horizontal ground loom, while Breniquet suggests they may belong to a backstrap loom. Both interpretations are plausible; however, there is no evidence to confirm that the backstrap loom was known in the region. Nonetheless, given the lack of definitive information regarding the type of loom in use, this possibility cannot be ruled out.

No other evidence of looms is known so far until the introduction of the warp-weighted loom, which leaves clear proof of its existence: loom weights.

Loom weights are well known from Anatolia and Mesopotamia since at least 6000 BC, with findings at Ulucak Höyük and Mersin (Völling 2008; Çilingirǒglu 2009; Schoop 2014; Gleser 2016; Bender Jørgensen *et al.* 2023).

However, the Southern Levant does not show evidence of such an early usage of loom weights. In the EBA, there is no clear evidence of the usage of the warp-weighted loom, since the objects possibly recognised as loom weights, besides basalt rings, are mostly pebbles or irregular objects that do not constitute a recognisable category – they could have been used for many purposes, from net weights to counterweights. The first objects that can be considered loom weights with a degree of certainty begin to appear in the Southern Levant in the MBA. They have a conical shape with a horizontal perforation, and are generally well fired, but unfired specimens were also produced.

This kind of object appears in Megiddo at the very beginning of the MBA, and were produced until the beginning of the LBA, but a few examples also appear in LBA contexts. Shapes can slightly vary, from conical to slightly pear-shaped, but they clearly belong to the same category of objects. Some exceptions of the examined sample are known, although only from Megiddo. The first exception is the presence of loom weights with a suspension hole pierced vertically through the object, rather than horizontally as in the other implements. This does not constitute an obstacle to their usage as loom weights, since they could have been attached to a ring or another element before being suspended from the warp (similar to what is generally hypothesised for all loom weights). The second peculiar feature is the presence of a surface treatment on some examples, which include a red slip and burnishing, which is generally not known for this category of objects. This proves a certain amount of attention was given to these mundane tools. Another feature, the presence of a scarab sealing on a few examples, is known from Megiddo and other sites, such as Tell el-Farʿah (N and S) and Tel Kabri. This practice is known not only from loom weights but also for other objects, especially pottery vessels. Scarab sealings have generally Egyptian and Egyptianising iconographies on their bases, even if this practice is typical of the Syro-Canaanite region. From the few examples for which weights are available, it seems that the sealing impressions did not denote a specific category of objects or link to a specific production, but they could be considered as property marks placed on a few items from a whole group; otherwise they could indicate their production in a specific workshop (Peyronel 2004, 208–10). Few weights are available for this period in Megiddo, but what there is seems to indicate a preference for heavy tools, spanning from 337 to 628 g.

In Beth Shean, conical loom weights seem to appear slightly later than Megiddo examples, but they are well attested for in MB II. They are carefully produced and made both of clay and unbaked clay. No examples such as those of Megiddo, with a vertical hole or burnishing, are present. Beth Shean loom weights are slightly lighter than those of Megiddo, ranging between 267 and 596 g, but are wholly comparable.

Similar to Beth Shean, conical loom weights from Tell el-Farʿah (N) do not show the striking features of those from Megiddo. They appear well shaped and made both of fired and unfired clay, but it is evident that some attention was paid in producing them. Even if they represent a very small sample, three of them were found in the same context, evidence of their contemporary use. They appear quite light, ranging between 233 and 446 g, but the sample is too small to be statistically valid.

No conical loom weights are known from MB Hazor, but a few are known from LB levels, which is quite problematic. It is possible that they were relics of earlier periods, but their absence from lower levels does not suggest this explanation (see below).

Similar weights are known in many other sites from the Southern Levant, and Jericho has preserved some groups of conical loom weights found together (Wheeler 1982, 623–4). They appear perfectly comparable with those so far examined, and almost all are from contexts datable to MB II–III.

A very interesting context is provided by the excavations from Tel Kabri, where 73 loom weights were found in MB IIB levels, 63 from the palace area. The intact items are all conical shaped with horizontal perforations and are made of fired clay, except for a single stone specimen (Yasur-Landau *et al.* 2015, 348). The largest batch is represented by 26 weights found in Room 690 in the palace, where they were divided in two groups of 13 objects. Another 10 weights were found nearby, and five more in successive excavations. They were found in the debris of the collapse of the second storage, similar to the Minoan palaces (Goshen *et al.* 2013, 47). Weights range between 235 and 600 g, similar to the other Southern Levantine contexts. Six of them show traces of scarab sealings.

Conical loom weights are also known in southern sites, such as Tell Beit Mirsim (Albright 1938, 56, pl. 45) and Tell el-Farʿah (S), even with a scarab imprint (see catalogue). This shows a great diffusion in the Southern Levant of such a type of loom weight, with a great degree of homogeneity. However, they appear not to be known in Syria, excluding isolated examples from Alalakh (Peyronel 2004, 200–1), nor in Egypt.

LBA levels do not show evidence of a large production of loom weights, and it has been hypothesised that the warp-weighted loom was abandoned for the vertical two-beam loom known in contemporary Egypt, or even that the invention of such a loom was made in Syria or the Palestinian area (Cecchini 2000, 213). The disappearance of the conical loom weights was probably not sudden, since some examples can be found in LBA levels, as is the case for Megiddo, Hazor (where they appear for the first time in LBA I contexts), and Beth Shean. In Beth Shean and Rehov they would become the dominant shape during the Iron Age, but would be made from gypsum (Mazar 2019). In Tell Ta'annek, conical loom weights appear in MBII/LB I contexts (Peyronel 2004, 205).

Iron Age I sees the re-introduction of the warp-weighted loom, on an unprecedented scale. The production of loom weights becomes ubiquitous, reaching its peak during the Iron Age II, with thousands of weights excavated, and findings of hundreds of them at single sites.

At Megiddo, a large quantity of loom weights has been documented for the Iron Age I phases; however, they have been published without details regarding their shapes or measurements. These weights appear to be made of both fired and unfired clay. A new type, the doughnut-shaped weight, is attested, although one example was recovered from a LB III context. Additionally, a single conical loom weight is present. Only one spool weight is known from Iron Age I and another from Iron Age IIB.

From Iron Age II levels, a total of 45 loom weights are recorded. Most specimens exhibit the typical Iron Age forms – spherical or doughnut-shaped – though a few biconical weights and reworked vessels are also noted. Finally, there is a group of 20 cylindrical weights.

Few loom weights are known from Iron Age I Beth Shean, and are almost all made of clay. They have a cylindrical shape, but some specimens are of the spool-type,[14] a typology known in the site since the LB IIB. An oval object made of gypsum was found, but no examples of pear-shaped gypsum weights, which instead were present in LB levels. A very large quantity of loom weights is known for the Iron Age IB–IIA phase, mainly made of clay, either fired or unfired. The clay weights generally have a doughnut/spherical shape, although a couple of conical examples were also found. A typical weight from Beth Shean and the surrounding valley, the pear-shaped gypsum loom weight, is also well represented. Most of the Iron Age II weights from Beth Shean are a doughnut shape, are made of clay, and were almost all found grouped in the same room. Some pear-shaped or slightly conical examples, generally made of stone, are also present. Spools, however, disappear after the Iron Age I.

Only a single object can be recognised with certainty as a loom weight for Iron Age I Hazor, while most of the items are dated to Iron Age II. They appear spherical/doughnut-shaped and are made of baked or poorly baked clay. Very few objects have a biconical shape, and these are quite small. No spools were found at the site, a remarkable feature considering the generally strong connections with Northern Levantine sites, where spools are widely used. However, since they are mainly known from Iron Age I levels, their absence in Hazor might be due to the difficult phase of the site in that period.

Several loom weights are known from Iron Age II levels at Tell el-Far'ah (N), and are mostly spherical/doughnut-shaped and made of clay, either fired or unfired. Very few examples of weights made of stone are also present. The most remarkable difference in the weights at Far'ah compared to the other sites is their lightness – only 167 g on average.

Iron Age loom weights are known from almost all sites in the Southern Levant, but are also common in Syria (Peyronel 2004, 250–7, 288–91). Some contexts appear particularly interesting, both for the presence of large quantities of loom weights and because they are well published.

Tell es-Safi/Gath witnessed intense weaving activity, with some 600 loom weights found in different contexts, suggesting both household and industrial production (Cassuto 2018, 56). Three loom weights have been exposed for Iron Age I levels and are defined as the spool type, with a central perforation. However, from the picture (which is not clear), they appear to be of the cylindrical type found in a large batch in Megiddo (Cassuto 2017, 193, fig. 17.5) and not of the spool type. Many loom weights are known from Iron Age II phases. In stratum A, almost 300 spherical loom weights made of clay were found, in association with a domestic context. Other clusters of loom weights were identified in area D, a total of almost 300 objects, in connection with a cultic area (Cassuto 2017, 193–4).

Not far from Safi, another possible textile workshop of Iron IIB was discovered in Ḥorbat Shim'on. Almost 160 loom weights were excavated in clusters inside a large building, which was originally identified as a workshop for pottery production. Most of them are doughnut/spherical shaped, but a large number of spools and a few conical weights are also present. These suggest that weaving was widely practised at the site, and that the production would have been quite differentiated, given the different typologies of loom weights recovered (Dagan and Cassuto 2016, 44, fig. 6). In association with loom weights, some spindle whorls were uncovered at the site, together with basins and stone tools, which could have been used for many purposes, not least for the preparation of dyes and other materials required by textile processing. It is possible, therefore, that an actual textile workshop was present at these small sites, similar to those hypothesised for Tel 'Amal and Tel Burna (Dagan and Cassuto 2016, 45).[15]

Another interesting context in the Tell el-Hammah area A is dated to the 10th century BC. Two adjacent rooms, which were destroyed in a conflagration, were excavated, preserving part of the carbonised wood and organic material. Among the numerous finds, several wooden spindles and spindle whorls were recovered, as well as several gypsum – typical of the Beth Shean Valley – clay loom weights and bone spatulae (Cahill 2006, 441). The context is highly interesting, as it proves not only that wooden implements were used (and therefore should always be considered), but also shows the complete set of textile tools, from spinning objects to loom weights and spatulae. A second, very large batch of spherical clay loom weights is dated to the 9th/8th century BC from the same area (Cahill 2006, 446), proving the continuity of textile production in that part of the site.

Another interesting Iron Age II context is provided by Tel 'Ira (Ben-Dov 1999). In Stratum VI, around 130 doughnut-shaped loom weights have been identified. Some were scattered throughout the site, but most were concentrated in area E, in building 521 and casemate Room 194. Two rooms in particular are interesting, as Room 1582 has preserved 44 loom weights weighing between 100 and 200 g, while Room 1638 has yielded 34 loom weights. Only two loom weights are significantly heavier, weighing 540 g and 600 g, and these have been considered as jar stoppers due to the presence of jars with neck diameters that match the loom weights. A similar interpretation has also been provided for the comparable items in Horbat Rosh Zayit (Gal *et al.* 2000).

Tel Rehov deserves a special mention. The Iron Age IIA strata have yielded a total of 1,032 loom weights, most of which were found inside buildings (Mazar 2019, 124–5). An additional 172 weights were recovered from the less extensively excavated Iron Age IIB strata. The assemblage reveals a clear shift in material use: while the earliest layers predominantly contain clay loom weights, the vast majority of those from the Iron Age IIA are made of gypsum (Mazar 2019, 125). In contrast, the Iron Age IIB weights are mainly composed of clay. The clay weights are primarily doughnut-shaped, whereas the gypsum weights typically exhibit a pear-shaped form (Mazar 2019, 126).

Finally, a few words are necessary to summarise the spools *affaire*. In fact, the Iron Age sees the introduction of completely new typologies of loom weights, such as the doughnut/spherical clay loom weights that would become extremely common, especially during the Iron Age II, and the so-called spools. The sudden reintroduction of loom weights and the warp-weighted loom at the very beginning of the Iron Age has been sometimes connected with the arrival of foreigners and the appearance of a specific loom weight typology – the spool (Dothan 1998, 154–5; Yasur-Landau 2010, 267–70; Cassuto 2012, 469–70, 480; Boertien 2013). Even for the MBA, a similar exogenous explanation was adopted, since other regions of the Near East (especially Anatolia) knew the warp-weighted loom and were considered to be responsible for its introduction in the Southern Levant (Barber 1991, 300). The extreme rarity of loom weights from the Syrian area, however, does not weigh in favour of a similar interpretation.

Spools are notably absent from the dataset available to the author and are not commonly found in the Southern Levant, with a few exceptions. As discussed in the dedicated chapter, the spools from Beth Shean – if indeed identified as such – are dated to the 13th century BC, making them the earliest known examples in the Southern Levant. However, these spools were excavated during the UME excavations, and their stratigraphy has been subject to debate, which raises questions about their precise chronological context.

Recent excavations at the nearby site of Tel Rehov offer a more reliable confirmation of the early presence of spools in the region. The excavator describes the discovery of a cache of 14 spools found in a layer transitional between the 13th and 12th centuries BC (Mazar 2019). This discovery strengthens the case for an early appearance of spools in the Southern Levant.

Spool loom weights have been extensively investigated, mainly by Rahmstorf (2003; 2005; 2011: 320–3) and in relation to their connection with the Philistines. In fact, other sites in the Southern Levant have yielded evidence of spools, particularly from the Iron Age, but these are predominantly associated with the Philistine areas of Ashdod, Ashkelon, Tel Miqne/Ekron, and Tell Qasile (Dothan 1998, 154–5; Rahmstorf 2005, 153–4; Yasur-Landau 2010, 267–70). The sudden emergence of spools in the region has often been linked to the arrival of foreign groups, possibly from the Aegean. However, the connection between these loom weights and the Aegean people remains uncertain. Notably, the early appearance of spools in Beth Shean and Tel Rehov coincides with the earliest examples found in the Aegean (Rahmstorf 2005). This contemporaneity suggests the possibility of parallel developments or direct cultural exchange between these regions. Furthermore, while spools in the Southern Levant are relatively sparse during the 12th century BC, their presence is more prominent in northern Syria and southern Anatolia (Cecchini 2000; Laurito 2013; Lumb 2014; Venturi 2020). This broader distribution further complicates the understanding of their origins and movement.

The phenomenon of spools, and more generally loom weights, in the Southern Levant warrants further investigation. A more extensive body of data is necessary to fully comprehend their presence in the region. Moreover, a broader geographical approach that encompasses the Aegean, Anatolia, and the entire Levant is essential for understanding the cultural and chronological dynamics of these artefacts.

4.5.6 Basalt rings

Basalt rings are distinctive and easily recognisable objects, widely distributed throughout the Levant, particularly during the EBA. Although predominantly made from basalt, specimens crafted from limestone can occasionally be found. These rings typically measure between 3 and 5 cm in diameter, with a central hole of approximately 1 cm. The hole is usually hourglass-shaped, with the upper and lower surfaces slightly convex, contributing to the characteristic ring-like appearance of the objects.

The height of basalt rings can vary significantly, generally ranging from 1 to 3 cm. Some specimens may even appear almost spherical in shape. While some rings are perfectly rounded and smooth, others display a more rudimentary, less refined finish. In terms of weight, these rings are relatively light, typically ranging from 20 to 60 g. Their compact size distinguishes them from the broader category of perforated discs, which includes a variety of other objects such as pivots for drilling, digging sticks, and similar items.

The precise function of basalt rings remains unclear. However, their association with textile production is largely inferred from the findings at Tell Abu al-Kharaz in Jordan (Fischer 2009, 112), where similar objects were discovered in contexts suggesting such use.

At this site, two findings are most important. The first is the discovery of one such basalt ring with part of a wooden shaft still in the hole, which suggests a very probable use as a spindle whorl (Fischer 2009, 112). In this case, the basalt ring appears quite thick, but individual measurements are not given. The recorded weight is 38 g (Fischer 2008, 118, fig. 119:8 N381; 2009, fig. 6). This object certainly has an hourglass hole and shows beyond a doubt that similar objects could be used as spindle whorls. A second important recovery was made in Area 1 (L316 and 328), where the remains of two vertical warp-weighted looms were found. The organic materials of which the looms were made have not been preserved; however, charred traces of beams and poles are still detectable. At the foot of one of the looms, eight rings (seven of basalt and one of limestone) were found packed in a strict row. They probably belong to Fischer's 'group 2' classification, which includes poorly finished basalt rings, and are heavier than 'group 1', reaching up to 90 g (individual weights are not given and are not possible to obtain from Fischer publications).

Other objects associated with textile production were found in the same room, including spindle whorls, bone spatulae, and an awl (Fischer 2009, 111). However, there are several objections to their interpretation as loom weights. Firstly, these objects appear in a single row – if they were indeed used for textile production, at least two rows of weights would have been necessary to weave a basic tabby weave. Secondly, the number of objects is quite limited, meaning they could have produced only a very narrow strip of fabric. Finally, their weight is rather light, even when considering the maximum weight for the group, which is 90 g. Assuming that a fine yarn requires a tension of 10 g, a maximum of nine threads could be attached to a single loom weight, yielding a maximum of 72 threads in the entire warp. This number would be even lower if the weights were lighter or if a thicker yarn were used. Based on the measurements from Figure 4.10, the row of weights is 15 cm long, meaning that the warp threads would be spaced 4.8 per square cm, resulting in a very open weave. Given these considerations, it seems highly unlikely that these objects were used as loom weights in a warp-weighted loom. For comparison, the lightest Iron Age loom weights found at the same site range from 189 to 272 g, more than double the weight of these objects. Therefore, alternative functions for these objects should be explored.

Beyond the findings at Kharaz, basalt rings appear frequently in excavation reports from as early as the Chalcolithic period, with a Neolithic example also recorded at Tel Te'o (Savage 2011, 102). They are particularly common during the EBA and continued to be produced into the early phases of the MBA. These small rings have a widespread geographical distribution, extending as far south as Egypt and north to Syria. However, the centre of production and/or consumption appears to be the Southern Levant, where the largest concentration of finds has been recorded.

For the example at Tell Abu al-Kharaz, Savage proposes their use as spindle whorls (Savage 2011, 101–2). However, this explanation is neither fully convincing nor comprehensive. It fails to account for the second type of evidence from Kharaz – specifically, the weights found in a row. Furthermore, the extensive diffusion of these objects cannot be easily explained by the use of simple spindle whorls, especially in Egypt. Basalt is not as widely sourced as limestone, which could be used to produce similar objects, yet basalt was preferred, likely because of its superior durability. This raises the question: could these basalt rings have been used as net weights, designed to withstand prolonged periods underwater? This seems a reasonable possibility. However, not all of the sites where these objects were found are located close enough to water sources to support this hypothesis.

Another issue relates to their chronology. While basalt rings were indeed produced extensively during the EBA, several examples with identical shapes, features, measurements, and weights are also dated to Iron Age levels. It seems unlikely that all of these examples could be considered out of context.

To sum up, basalt rings may indeed have been used as spindle whorls, or at least part of them, but it is highly probable that they had another purpose, as shown in Kharaz. This purpose does not seem to be connected with the warp-weighted loom, since these weights appear very light for tensioning a warp, and the finding from Kharaz shows only one row present, not the required two. Finally, no other objects that could be interpreted as loom weights have been found in the Southern Levant during the entire EBA. What this other function could be, requiring a hard material such as basalt and allowing a diffusion into regions far from the Southern Levant, is far from clear. Their production decreases in the MBA and LBA but does not disappear, as Megiddo materials clearly show.

4.5.7 Bone spatulae and beaters

As seen in Chapter 2, bone spatulae and beaters are two different objects that may have been used during the process of weaving to keep the warp in order and beat the weft, although in different ways.

Bone spatulae are generally made from ribs that have been cut in half longitudinally and worked to obtain a point, while the other end could be slightly polished or worked to become rounded. The surface with the inner bone part exposed (which will be considered as the lower part) could either be left coarse, or polished to obliterate the cancellous bone and obtain a perfectly smooth object. Both types of treatment appear in the corpus, but those that have not been artificially polished are extremely interesting since they clearly show the smoothing of the object through repeated contact with a soft material, which might be identified with threads. Their points can be divided into different categories, and three of them appear to be more adapted to this work: the short, triangular point; the pen-nib point; and the elongated point (Fig. 4.25). Bone spatulae seem to have been present since the Neolithic period in the Southern Levant (Levy 2020), but according to Peyronel (2004, 363), their usage could have been different from those of later periods, and it is thus more complex to link them to textile production than their Iron Age parallels. Furthermore, he connects these spatulae to the usage of the warp-weighted loom (Peyronel 2004, 371–2), a hypothesis that should probably be rejected in light of the Egyptian documentation, where the same objects with the same patterns of use are known, but without any evidence of using the warp-weighted loom. These simple tools appear not to be connected to a specific loom nor, so far, to a specific type of weaving (*e.g.* tapestry). It is more probable that they were simply used for beating small portions of threads, and we should also remember that similar wooden tools were certainly also known; this is the case for Ancient Egypt, as it is for today.

The corpus used for this book is limited and it was not possible to examine all the bone spatulae from the Southern Levant. For this reason, all the objects from sites that have

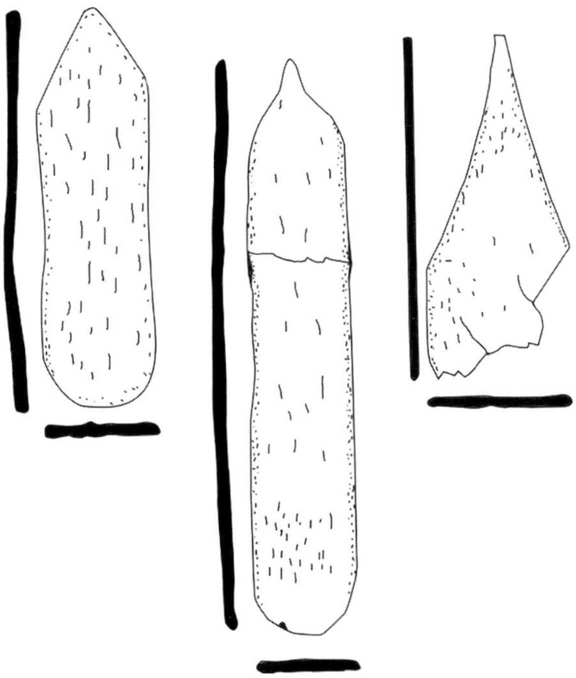

Figure 4.25. Three bone spatulae from Hazor, from left to right, with triangular point (A 63041), pen-nib point (A 11534a), and elongated point (A 2412-2), (courtesy of the Selz Foundation Hazor Excavations in Memory of Yigael Yadin)

not been directly studied are considered based only on their morphology and the description given by the publications. Hopefully, a completed study of bone spatulae, their manufacture and their wear traces will be available and will enable more specific conclusions.

Pin beaters are much more difficult to classify and certainly had a broad range of usage, of which that linked to weaving is only a small percentage. In fact, they were probably more frequently used as borers and in relation to the preparation of leather, but it is not always easy to understand when this is the case.

Bone spatulae appear for the first time in the Southern Levant during the Neolithic period, as attested by findings in the Nahal Hemar Cave (Bar-Yosef and Alon 1988, fig. IV:1) and slightly later at Ard es-Samrra (Getsov and Bazilai 2009). Similarly, pin beaters have also been found in Neolithic and Chalcolithic contexts, such as Nahal Hemar Cave (Bar-Yosef and Alon 1988, 18) and the Cave of the Treasures (Bar-Oz and Yeshurun 2014), two very important contexts for the discovery of textiles.

The production of bone spatulae with triangular and pen-nib points, as well as pin beaters, is well represented in Tell Abu al-Kharaz, where several examples were excavated in EBA layers (Fischer 2008, 118, fig. 119). In this site, some objects were analysed looking for micro-wear, and the results were compatible with contact with fibres (Cristiani 2008). Furthermore, some of these bone spatulae (defined as shuttles in publications) and a pin beater were found in the same context with the two 'looms' at Kharaz (Fischer 2009, 111, fig. 8).

Several objects that could be considered as bone spatulae and beaters are known from Megiddo EBA levels, and three spatulae (one with a triangular point the other with a pen nib point are earlier). The only object of these phases available for study is a very smoothed bone spatula, with convex inferior side and worn off tip. Small traces of wear are detectable on the surface and some parts of the surface appear completely polished probably by rubbing with soft materials.

Several bone spatulae are known from EBA Beth Shean as well, mostly with a triangular point. Only a single pin beater comes from these layers. Tell el-Farʿah (N) has preserved a large sample of points and spatulae belonging to the EBA, but only part of them has been selected for this study. Those with a very sharp point, which could have been used as borers, have been excluded. Differently from Megiddo, the spatulae with a pen-nib point are not present in this phase, while several examples of triangular and elongated point are listed in the catalogue.

A situation similar to the EBA levels is witnessed both in MBA Megiddo and at Tell el-Farʿah, with numerous examples of spatulae and beaters. No examples are known in this period in Beth Shean, while they begin to appear in Hazor, although in very few examples.

The production of both categories seems to enter a deep crisis for the entire LBA and Iron Age I period, which is very interesting. In fact, several bone spatulae are known from New Kingdom Egyptian sites (*e.g.* Gurob and Amarna) and were probably used on the vertical two-beam loom, which is the common loom in Egypt (Kemp and Vogelsang-Eastwood 2001). A similar loom is supposed to have been introduced from the Levant to Egypt or vice versa (Cecchini 2011), but its presence can only be speculated for LBA Southern Levant. It is therefore noteworthy that bone spatulae seem to disappear with the alleged presence of this type of loom. It might be connected with specific types of production or weaving that were no longer in use in the Levant but continued in Egypt, but it is difficult to prove this from the available data.

The Levantine production of bone spatulae and, to a lesser extent, of pin beaters, again flourished during the Iron Age II, with hundreds of excavated examples (Peyronel 2004). The four sites used as a case study do not constitute an exception, and thus larger numbers of implements were available for study.

In Megiddo, the shapes are not much different from earlier periods, with triangular and elongated points as the most common types, while pen-nib points are quite rare. In Beth Shean they continue to be quite rare finds. The common shapes are the triangular and the pen-nib point. The absence of these implements from a context where at least two looms were found is noteworthy, since only a single bone spatula is recorded. Hazor is the most interesting context, since a larger number of objects were available for study. Their point shape is generally triangular, with less occurrences of elongated and pen-nib points. In some cases it has been possible to see that the wear traces were mainly located towards the point and in general the first half of the spatula, while the second half, that with a rounded or flat end, was less exposed to wear. This is clearly visible by a cancellous bone that is almost invisible, or has disappeared near the pointed end. A similar wear pattern is also visible on the spatulae from Far'ah and the Egyptian sites.

4.5.8 Needles

As seen in Chapter 2, sewing needles and bodkins are grouped together under the category of needles. They were selected for this research even if they are not directly connected with the production of a textile, but rather with finishing operations, which can happen immediately after its realisation, or far from the time and place it was made. However, since they are clearly connected with the processing of textiles (and leather), their appearance in the same contexts with other textile tools might be relevant to identify workshops and rooms connected with textile manufacturing. It must be stressed that we know very few of the finishing operations on textiles, since very few hems and fragments of stitching have survived. It seems, however, that embroidery was not known (or very rare) for the regions and periods under consideration, so the needles examined here were used mostly to join pieces of textiles or to refinish hems. From the extant Egyptian textile materials, it appears clear that sewing was not very common, since clothes were frequently worn simply wrapped around the body and closed with knots, fibulae, and pins (Vogelsang-Eastwood 1993). It should therefore not be so surprising if needles do not appear as frequently as we might imagine. No wooden needles or bodkins have been preserved in the Southern Levant, and only bone and metal implements are known. Bone needles appear quite frequently in the Neolithic and Chalcolithic period, but are less common during the Bronze and Iron Ages (Peyronel 2004, 138). They appear generally highly polished and carefully manufactured, but the differences in size are remarkable, highlighting the different usage of the tools.

The corpus from Megiddo is quite small yet comprises a very large typology of different objects and materials. It appears clear that bone needles become less frequent from the EBA to the LBA, but – even if there are very few specimens – they continued to be produced through to the Iron Age. In the MBA period, needle eyes could be produced by bending the upper part of the shaft back on itself and then melting the joining point. This appears to be the most common typology in Megiddo, but a few examples of eyes made by perforating the shaft from one side are still present. Needles appear in Megiddo in all possible contexts, from tombs to domestic unities, and can be sometimes associated with other textile tools.

Very few needles and bodkins were recovered from Beth Shean. Bone is extremely rare, since almost all the specimens were made of bronze. The hole seems to be perforated from one side of the shaft, but at least from LBA strata, the second typology (with the eye produced by bending the upper part of the shaft on itself) is also present.

Some more needles are known from Hazor, whereas there is very little evidence for textile tools made from other materials for early periods. Therefore, it is not possible to verify a decrease in the production of bone tools, since almost all the specimens are made of bronze. For the other sites considered so far, both techniques of producing the eye are known and used at the sites simultaneously. Both Megiddo and Hazor have preserved needle cases, with groups of needles still present inside. This is a very interesting feature, since it proves that some form of specialisation was present in the site that required more than one needle with similar dimensions. One needle comes from a grave, showing that the practice of placing needles in a funerary context was also known at this site.

At the site of Tell el-Far'ah (N), EBA levels clearly show a widespread use of bone needles, which become less common during the MBA with the introduction of bronze implements, and even more rare in later periods. Bone needles are characterised by a very well-polished surface and by the presence of a large, square head where a round hole is cut. Interestingly, the bronze needle shows the first appearance of type 2 during the MBA. During the LBA, typology 1 (made by perforating the shaft from one side of the needle) also becomes common, and both typologies would be present in the Iron Age. Many needles come from contexts where other textile tools were found, but do not show a recurring association and, in general, are found with only one other textile tool, and never in groups.

From this brief presentation, it seems clear that only a small quantity of needles is known, and this is common to many other Levantine sites, such as Tell Abu al-Kharaz (Fischer 2008), Tel Dan (Ben-Dov and Gershuny 2011), and Tel Jawa (Daviau 2002, 201), for example. They did not prove to be useful in identifying the contexts of textile production, since they are generally found scattered throughout sites, and only rarely in association with other textile tools. However, the two types of eye manufacturing are very interesting, especially if compared with the Egyptian materials, where only one tradition would be carried forward from the early periods to the Late period. Finally, needles can be found in graves, as is the case with spindle whorls, loom weights, basalt rings, etc.

4.5.9 Conclusions: Levantine textile tools

Textile tools are a quite common finding in Southern Levant excavations, especially for the Iron Age levels. In fact, although almost all periods have preserved important quantities of objects linked to spinning and weaving, a remarkable change is visible in favour of the Iron Age period. This is mainly due to two reasons, which are entirely different from each other. The first is inherent to the documentation under study, since loom weights, which often constitute the largest evidence of textile production, become common and ubiquitous in Iron Age II. The second reason is due to the choices of the excavators, who for a very long time focused their attention mainly on layers that may have been related to the Biblical text, thus devoting less attention to later or previous periods. This produced an impressive amount of excavations of Iron Age sites and of pottery and other objects from this period, which has no comparison with other Levantine historical phases.

Spindles are a rare find in the Near East, and the Southern Levant is no exception. Very few objects that could be considered as spindles were found, and these are very different from each other. It is not possible, from this very scarce evidence, to draw any conclusion about the shapes of spindles, but two implements from Megiddo are particularly interesting. First, they show that spindle whorls could be used in pairs and could be mounted on pegs, rather than on shafts. Second, similar bone shafts are well known from other Mediterranean contexts (Syria, Anatolia, Cyprus, Greece, and Italy) but these are generally found without spindle whorls. Even if the function of many of these rods can only be supposed, the Levantine tools add some more hints at the general picture.

The appearance of spindle whorls can be dated very early, since some stone spindle whorls were found in Pre-pottery Neolithic B levels. The production appears quite varied, but some trends are recognisable. In fact, stone whorls are quite common in the early levels, especially those made in discoid shapes, but these are soon outnumbered by biconical pottery whorls. The MBA sees the appearance of bone whorls, which are generally dome-shaped, and which would become quite widespread during the LBA, decreasing in the Iron Age. In fact, Iron Age II sees a more frequent use of stone spindle whorls, to the detriment of other materials. Pottery spindle whorls, as always, appear to be rarely used in the Southern Levant. Besides these general trends, we must remember that many local and regional patterns are present in the area, at times due to local resources (such as gypsum in the Beth Shean Valley) or to a specific necessity linked to the production (*e.g.* heavier whorls for the production of thicker yarns).

Many of the whorls under consideration may in fact have been beads or decorative elements, and it appears very difficult to trace a clear line between each category. Furthermore, findings from Levantine sites are often contradictory, with the same objects used as whorls as well as (probably) decorative elements (*e.g.* dome-shaped whorls from Megiddo and Tel Dan).

The evidence for the position of the whorl on the shaft is also far from conclusive. If the findings of spindles from the Levantine area seem (but only seem) to point towards a high-whorl spindle, then wear traces near the holes of spindle whorls seem to testify of dropping to a low-whorl position.

Besides traditional spindle whorls, some perforated sherds were likely used as whorls and in the Chalcolithic period they constitute a very high percentage of all the findings linked to spinning. However, it is important to check if the perforation is suitable for the insertion of a shaft, *i.e.* with a rounded and sufficiently large hole that goes straight through, not diagonally. In fact, many objects in the catalogue cannot be considered as possible whorls, and thus had another usage.

Spinning bowls are quite rare finds in the Southern Levant and appear to be casually distributed. Some sites preserve a large quantity of these bowls, some sites just one specimen, and most sites have not a single specimen. They were known since the Ghassulian period, but ceased to be produced after this. They appear again in the LBA and in a few sites of the Iron Age. Even if produced as local pottery, they often resemble Egyptian artefacts and their rare usage might be linked to the presence of Egyptian families involved in textile production.

Other objects common both to the Levantine area and Egypt (as well as many cultures around the world) are the small bone tools for beating the weft and keeping the warp in order: pin beaters and spatulae. These have appeared frequently in excavations since the Neolithic period and, even if their usage in connection with textile production is often difficult to prove, it seems quite a reasonable explanation for many of them. Interestingly, they are quite rare during the LBA and the Iron Age I, and become more widespread with the Iron Age II. It is possible that they were linked to specific weave, but probably not to a specific loom, as has been commonly stated.

Basalt rings appear as a clear and easy to recognise category, spread throughout the Levant and reaching sites in Lower Egypt. However, defining their function is much more problematic. Some of them, probably the smallest and most refined, could have been used as spindle whorls, but the others were very unlikely to have been used as loom weights. In fact, they appear very light, groups are generally not so numerous as to allow the creation of a textile, and no other objects that could be used as loom weights are known for contemporaneous phases. It is worth noting that they do not disappear after the MBA, but their number is certainly smaller than that of the EBA.

Loom weights represent a well-known category of objects for textile production. Excluding basalt rings, they seem not to appear before the MBA, when a conical typology becomes quite common and widespread throughout the region. LBA findings are much more limited and problematic, since they appear to be mixed with later materials. From the Iron Age I and even more the Iron Age II, clay loom weights, spherical or doughnut-shaped, appear as a common feature of the Levantine region. However, regional differences can be detected, as with the more common usage of the spool type in sites connected with Philistines, while in the Beth Shean Valley pear-shaped gypsum loom weights are quite common. While spools have sometimes been connected with different cultural traditions, gypsum loom weights seem linked to the exploitation of local resources. Shamir (2013, 9), based on the region and the somewhat low weight of the loom weights, sees a possible link with the production of linen textiles. In fact, the few findings of fibres in the region are made of flax, and archaeobotanical studies are proving the production of flax in that area. Therefore, it is probable that the Beth Shean Valley produced linen (although there is no reason to completely exclude wool); however, the connection of linen with specific types of loom weights seems quite problematic given the present state of our knowledge.

Needles and bodkins are quite rare finds in Southern Levantine sites. They do not show any specific connection with other textile tools and appear in all possible contexts. However, even for this type of object some trends can be identified. In fact, bone needles appear to be quite common in early phases, while they become rarer after the MBA. Two types of metal needles can be recognised: the first with a hole perforated through the shaft, and the other with the hole obtained by bending the upper part of the shaft back on itself. This second type is quite specific to the Levant, since the MBA and the two types coexist.

An impressive feature of Southern Levantine contexts is the homogeneity of the region in its adoption of typologies of textile tools. Even if there are differences from site to site and regional specificities, it is evident that the entire Southern Levant adopted the same textile technologies, *i.e.* bone shafts and stone spindle whorls in the Iron Age, conical loom weights in the MBA, doughnut-shaped weights in the Iron Age, etc. This is impressive, especially when compared to nearby regions, where some of these trends would never be adopted.

Notes

1 The areas explored do not use letters A–E, since these were employed by the Chicago team (Finkelstein *et al.* 2000, 5).

2 Following Cassuto (2008, 67) in the distinction of workshop and household production.

3 Bechar, pers. comm.

4 At the TRC of Leiden, a wonderful sheep-shaped spindle whorl was perfectly functional.

5 A similar treatment was identified by Ariel (1990, 129).

6 See for example the work of J. Balensi on the Late Bronze Age period and of P. de Miroschedji on the early periods.

7 For their interpretation as distaffs see Barber (1991, 57).

8 The doubling of the whorls is very different in the case of Hissar, since there the second whorl could be added or removed during spinning according to weight needs. In this case, the two whorls are fixed to the shaft and cannot be removed until the thread has been taken away.

9 As discussed in Chapter 4.12, only part of whorls were available for study and therefore all the consideration here presented has to be considered as partial.

10 It is true that the lightest whorl reported by Liu (see Chapter 3) weighs only 1 g, but this was used to spin short and delicate cotton fibres. There is no proof that cotton was known in the Near East before the Neo-Assyrian period, and this fact makes the use of such small objects as whorls highly unlikely.

11 Such as Tel Miqne/Ekron (Shamir 2007a, 46) and Tel Batash/Timnah (Mazar and Panitz-Cohen 2001, 259).

12 Pappalardo, pers. comm.

13 For other references see Levy and Gilead (2012, 131), Orrelle *et al.* (2012, 639) and Levy (2020).

14 See Chapter 4.10 for the discussion about spools with several scarab impressions.

15 Another workshop was identified in Beth Shean area S-7 (see Chapter 4.10) with two clusters of loom weights and several grinding stones from the same room. Although this interpretation is fascinating, no conclusive evidence has been brought to light and it might also be a case of multi-tasking spaces, meaning food preparation and weaving.

5

Textile tools from Egypt

One of the most remarkable aspects of working with textile tools from Ancient Egypt is the frequent preservation of organic materials. Most of the objects discussed in this chapter are made of wood, and, in many instances, spindles and whorls retain attached fibres and threads. What can only be hypothesised in other contexts can be firmly established for Ancient Egypt. This exceptional preservation enables a far more nuanced analysis than is possible for the Southern Levant and prompts intriguing new questions.

Notably, studies at the sites of Gurob and Deir el-Medina have yielded unexpected findings, raising questions concerning the organisation and scale of production, the processing of fibres, and the identities of key individuals involved in the industry. As these areas of inquiry fall outside the scope of this book, they are outlined here only briefly and will be explored in greater detail in future research.

Apart from funerary contexts and the workers' settlements or towns such as Amarna, Lahun, Gurob, and Deir el-Medina, the preservation of organic materials is rare. Consequently, the primary sites selected for this study are Lahun, Gurob, and Deir el-Medina. Amarna, already extensively examined (Kemp and Vogelsang-Eastwood 2001), provides valuable comparative data. These sites were chosen for the exceptional richness of their textile tool assemblages, which are unparalleled in Egyptian history. However, they represent a relatively brief span of the Pharaonic period, namely the Middle and New Kingdoms. To address this chronological limitation, additional materials from other sites – held in European collections and marked in the catalogue as 'other sites' – have been analysed, alongside published tools from excavation reports.

The textile tools discussed in this chapter include spindles, spindle whorls, perforated sherds, spinning bowls, loom weights/net weights, basalt rings, bone spatulae, beaters, and needles. Parts of looms are also highlighted. Both spindles, and spindle whorls, including those fashioned from reworked and perforated sherds are examined. Loom weights are listed as well, while ring-shaped basalt weights are considered separately due to their distinctive form and their likely, though not yet fully understood, role in textile production. Needles are included in the study as a potential indicator of textile processing, even though they are not directly associated with textile manufacture. Additionally, bone spatulae and pin beaters are analysed to assess signs of wear that may suggest their use with soft materials, as well as to explore possible functional connections with other textile tools.

The second part of the chapter expands the discussion beyond the key sites to offer a more comprehensive overview of textile tools in Ancient Egypt. This includes comparative analysis with data from additional sites across the region and a meta-analysis of specific tool types, to identify broader patterns and trends in textile production.

5.1 Lahun

5.1.1 Introduction

The site of Lahun is located at the entrance of the Fayum Oasis, near to a modern town called el-Lahun. The name is a misunderstanding of its excavator, W.M.F. Petrie, who asked a local person the name of the place and he understood Kahun and always uses this name. Modern studies continue to use this name as well as the correct name, Lahun. Petrie led two seasons of excavation at the site, in 1889 and 1890, and less extensive excavations on selected areas in 1911, 1914, and 1920. Recently, a mission led by Nicholas Millet on behalf of the Royal Ontario Museum cleared some already excavated areas and provided new documentation.

Unfortunately, the early death of the excavator prevented the publication of the results of his work, which were inherited by the Museum of Fine Arts of Budapest and which also started a survey project of the region.

The Fayum Oasis lies on the western side of the Nile and is the largest oasis in Egypt. The fertility of this area is due both to natural springs and to a canal, the Bahr Yusef, which flows from the Nile to the lake of Birket el-Qarun.

The area was used as a burial site in the Early Dynastic period; only scattered evidence remains concerning the Old Kingdom, when the site seems to be rarely used. The Middle Kingdom shows a rise of interest in the Fayum by several pharaohs, beginning with Amenemhat I and Senusret I, who chose Lisht as the new royal residence. Lisht is not in the Fayum Oasis but at its northeastern limit, however, it seems that Senusret I built a palace in the region (Quirke 2005, 8). The dyke and the system of artificial canalisation for extending the agricultural land were begun under the reign of Senusret II and concluded under Amenemhat III.

Lahun was chosen as the site to erect the funerary monuments of Senusret II, which include an enclosure with a mud-brick pyramid, several mastaba-tombs that were likely for the female members of his family, and a satellite pyramid. East of the pyramid was the temple for the king's funerary cult, which is very poorly preserved. The temple was near the settlement, which housed the personnel of the temple as well as the officials and craftsmanship who worked on the pyramid's construction (David 1986, 93). A similar situation can be identified at Abydos South, where a village was found in conjunction with the funerary monument of Senusret III (Quirke 2005, 45).

The settlement was only partially exposed, and only the northern part of its enclosure is known in its full length. It measures around 350 m (260 + 90 after the demarcation wall), while around 290 m of the west wall was exposed. The plan is orthogonal and the rooms are grouped in regular patterns. The settlement was divided in two by a thick demarcation wall, which apparently preserved no gates to connect the two parts. The western part housed the smaller and poorer buildings for the workers (David 1986, 96) or the temple personnel (Quirke 2005, 44). The eastern part, which comprises most of the settlement, housed a large number of residences, from large dwellings similar to palaces, to medium and small houses. The buildings were arranged in blocks separated by quite large streets, which form a regular pattern. The entrance to the city was located at the northeastern corner and it is the only access uncovered to date. The northern section of the settlement housed the largest residential buildings or palaces, while medium and small-barracks houses are located to the south. The largest and highest dwelling was placed in the northwestern corner of the enclosure.

Unfortunately, Petrie failed to record the provenance of the objects, even the most precious, so there is no chance of establishing which type of buildings the textile tools come from. This is even more regrettable because Lahun was a perfect context to understand the social implications of the spinning and weaving activities, and it would have been important to discern if it merely contained domestic production, or if areas of production might have been located near the temple, as in Abydos South.

The town of Lahun was founded during the reign of Senusret II and continued to be used during the reign of his successors, Senusret III and Amenemhat III, according to the textual sources found in the temple (Quirke 2005, 32). During the New Kingdom, the site appears almost entirely abandoned, as a new site flourished to the South of Lahun dyke, namely Gurob. Only scattered evidence that can be dated with certainty to the New Kingdom has been found, and most of this comes from houses reused as tombs. However, the northern part of the western block of houses might have been used as accommodation even in the New Kingdom, since a hank of flax and balls of yarn were also found among objects dated to this period (Quirke 2005, 115). In later periods, the tombs of the inhabitants of Lahun were plundered and reused for most of the 1st millennium BC. Some Ptolemaic burials were located between the settlement and the pyramid, and near the pyramid a tomb with a religious (?) building and a crocodile necropolis were dated to the Roman period (Quirke 2005, 128–9). Furthermore, the Valley Temple of Sesostry II was occupied by a Coptic cemetery, which must be the source for a Coptic assemblage of textiles (Hall 1982, 42).

Lahun has provided an abundant quantity of textile tools and fibres, most belonging to the Late Middle Kingdom, but some of them are later, dated to the New Kingdom and even the medieval. Unfortunately, given the lack of context of the findings, it is not possible to distinguish what belongs to which phase; only in a few instances is it clearly stated.

For this research, it has been decided to study only materials that are in European museums, given the difficulty of locating and gaining access to these type of materials in Egyptian museums. Several museums exhibit objects from Petrie's Lahun excavation, and it was not possible to see them all. Therefore, only the institutions with larger collections have been selected. Most of the items are stored in the Petrie Museum in London, and secondarily in the Manchester Museum. Other items have been studied in the Ashmolean Museum in Oxford, in the British Museum, and in the World Museum in Liverpool.

Unfortunately, a complete catalogue of the objects excavated by Petrie has not been conducted, so it is not possible to understand if the items collected represent only a small percentage of the textile tools from the site or are the majority. However, given their homogeneity, they seem to form a reliable sample study. Hopefully in the future this work might help to create a complete list of the textile implements from Lahun.

For the other sites included in the research, the spindles, spindle whorls, perforated sherds, possible loom weights, spinning bowls, needles, and possible parts of looms were also included. Bone spatulae and pin beaters were also examined to look for signs of wear compatible with their use with soft materials, and to check for possible connections to other textile tools.

5.1.2 Spindles

Lahun has preserved several complete spindles, with spindle whorl on it, as well as single spindle whorls and shaft, which could not be linked to each other (Plate 10). Thirty-three spindles from Lahun have been catalogued, all made of wood. Only a few items in the Manchester Museum were not available for study, and these are therefore marked with a different colour in the catalogue.

A small number of these are preserved in their full length, seven in total: 30.a, 30.b, 30.c.1, UC7306i, UC7306ii, UC59380b, and UC7310a (Table 5.1). Most of the other examples are broken into less than half their length, and some do not preserve either end. The longest spindle measures 38.3 cm and the shortest one 22.9 cm. It is interesting to note that most of the examples have a length very close to 23 cm, while just two examples exceed 30 cm, the already cited example, and another which measures 34.3 cm. Shafts measure 1 cm on average (maximum diameter of the shaft), with most examples between 0.9 and 1.1 cm. The thinnest rod measures 0.77 cm and the thickest 1.46 cm (Fig. 5.1).

The shafts are generally not cylindrical but tend to be thicker in the middle and taper towards a point at one end, while the other is slightly thinner but not so different from the middle. This means that in many cases spindle whorls do not have a cylindrical hole, as it is slightly larger on the lower side than the upper side, with a difference of 1 mm.

As seems clear from this data, two types of spindle were used, although they were both very similar in appearance. A longer shaft, with length over 30 cm and which can reach almost to 40 cm, and a smaller one between 20 and 25 cm. Their weight, however, can vary greatly according to the weight of the whorl, which is the decisive factor. A long and a short spindle can thus both have the same weight.

The upper tip of the spindle can be rounded or flattish, and a groove to attach the fibres for spinning is generally

Table 5.1. Complete spindles from Lahun

Number	*Length (cm)*	*Diameter (cm)*	*Weight (with whorl) (g)*
30.a	38.3	1.13	37
30.b	23.7	1.46	32
30.*c*.1	34.3	0.86	14 + *x*
UC7306i	23.7	1.27	31
UC7306ii	22.9	0.8	28
UC59380b	24.6	1.08	21.5
UC7310a	23.7	0.97	9.34 (without whorl)

present. In Lahun this is generally a long spiral groove, very well shaped, always with an s-direction. The other end of the shaft, when preserved, tends to taper to a point, although not very sharp.

All the preserved examples with the spindle whorl attached to the shaft show that the position of the spindle whorl is immediately below the groove, and therefore these are high-whorl spindles, as represented in tomb paintings, funerary models, and the hieroglyphs themselves (see Table 3.2).

Only three spindles preserve the thread wound around the shaft, and in all cases the thread is under the spindle whorl and already spun (UC7306ii has modern thread wrapped around it). In one case, AN 1889.1198A, different threads are mixed and wound around the same shaft. Very fine thread is present, s-spun and not plied, and a thicker S-plied thread is also visible. Unfortunately, the yarn is very worn on this object. A second spindle, 30.b, shows a thread that has been twisted several times around the shaft. The thread is slightly worn but is s-spun and S-plied. In the third case, 30.a, the thread is inside the hole of the spindle whorl and therefore not clearly visible (Fig. 5.2).

5.1.3 Spindle whorls

Another 71 spindle whorls must be added to the spindle whorls still attached to their spindles (31), a total of 102. Almost all of these are made of wood and are cylindrical in shape. Unfortunately, it is not possible to be certain that the sample examined here is representative of the actual spinning choices in Lahun. In fact, there is currently no

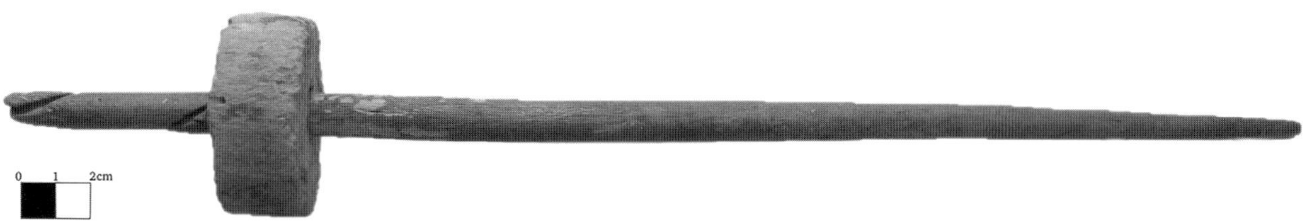

Figure 5.1. Complete spindle from Lahun (courtesy of Manchester Museum, 30.a)

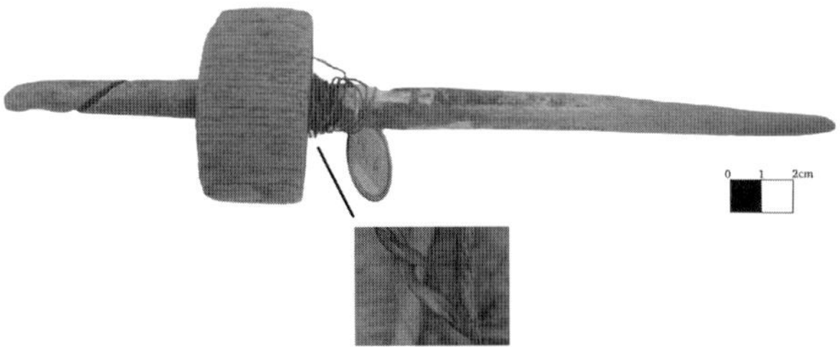

Figure 5.2. Thread around spindle 30.b and its magnification (50×) (courtesy of Manchester Museum)

possibility of knowing how many spindle whorls were collected in total, nor how many were made of materials other than wood. Furthermore, perforated pottery sherds are missing entirely, even if some would have been used, as in other sites such as Amarna. It seems quite probable, however, that the wooden spindle whorls would have largely outnumbered those made of other materials. The choice to use wood rather than the cheaper pottery might have been dictated by the necessity of combining a long rotational movement of the spindle with a light spindle whorl, for which wood is perfectly suited. Furthermore, pottery spindle whorls have the inconvenience of fracturing and breaking if they fall on the ground, which happens quite frequently during the spinning process. Wooden spindle whorls are certainly more resistant but have the inconvenience that their holes tend to warp and enlarge during use, a problem that can easily be solved with the addition of wedges and padding between the spindle shaft and the spindle whorl. It is interesting to note the complete absence of bone spindle whorls, which would perfectly fulfil all these criteria.

The dominant shape of the wooden spindle whorls is cylindrical, which appears the easiest to obtain from a branch or a log. Most of the whorls are worn or covered with substances that do not allow us to understand the dimensions of the log from which they were cut. However, it seems that most of those studied here were cut from small branches, although other examples were cut from medium-large logs, such as UC7309 and UC7310d (Plate 10).

Previous analysis carried out on wooden examples stored in the British Museum has proven that both local and non-local woods were in use. *Ficus sycomorus* is the most used material, but examples were made with wood from the *Abies* species, which is typical of the European region (Cartwright *et al.* 1998, 98).

Other shapes are registered in the catalogue, namely dome and conical, but these are linked to objects that were probably not spindle whorls, such as lids. However, a couple of whorls listed in the catalogue could be considered as conical truncated, as they have a base slightly larger than their top. In this case, the difference in shape compared with the cylindrical whorl is insignificant because the difference in inertia would be negligible (Fig. 5.3).

The diameter of spindle whorls is quite large, as is expected for cylindrical shapes. The minimum value is 3.4 cm, while the maximum is 6.9 cm (excluding the object with 8.3 cm of diameter, because its function is unknown). Most of the items have a diameter spanning between 4.4 cm and 5.4 cm. The average value is 4.7 cm (Fig. 5.4).

The height of the spindle whorl is relevant, since most of the examples studied here are very thick, much more so than the examples from other sites, such as Deir el-Medina. The minimum value is 0.68 cm and the maximum is 3 cm, with an average of 2.3 cm.

The hole where the shaft is inserted seems to be quite large in Lahun. The maximum value is 1.4 cm, while the minimum is 0.38 cm, but most of the objects have a perforation between 1 and 1.2 cm. The values stated refer to the largest part of the hole; as mentioned in the previous paragraph, most of the spindle whorls have a slightly conical hole to better fit the tapering shaft. The difference between the upper and lower parts of the hole generally varies by 1 mm, and this can be in both directions, meaning the largest value can be above the hole or below. In many cases, the holes appear very irregular, given the necessity to insert wedges and padding to fasten the whorl to the shaft, as can be seen from examples in Deir el-Medina.

The weight of the wooden spindle whorls has only been measured for items not attached to spindles, for conservation reasons. Only the general weight (the sum of the spindle and spindle whorl) was available, and thus has been not considered in this chart. Sixty-six weights of wooden spindle whorls have been recorded, with the lightest measuring 5.2 g, and the heaviest 29.6 g. Most of the spindle whorls weigh between 13 and 17 g, and in general are between 10 and 25 g, with very few examples falling outside this range. The average value is 16.6 g. The two objects that are slightly heavier than 5 g may have been something different from spindle whorls, given the very small hole they share. However, a hole of 0.38 cm is not impossible for a spindle whorl, as will be shown in the next section on Gurob.

Several spindle whorls show traces of encrustation, generally more visible on the upper surface of the whorl, but also on the side. In some cases, both sides are encrusted. The nature of this layer is not clear, since no analysis have been conducted on it. A similar phenomenon is present on the whorl from Deir el-Medina, but this seems due to the condition of preservation and it being in contact with the ground. However, David (1986, 234) suggested that it was made of mud or stucco, which was intentionally placed on the whorls as a basis for further painted decoration. Painted decoration seems entirely absent from the objects studied here, but it is certainly present in those from Deir el-Medina, although not over the encrustation layer. Identity marks appear quite frequent and are almost always incised on the side of the whorl. In some cases, it might be possible that the encrustation on the upper or lower side of the

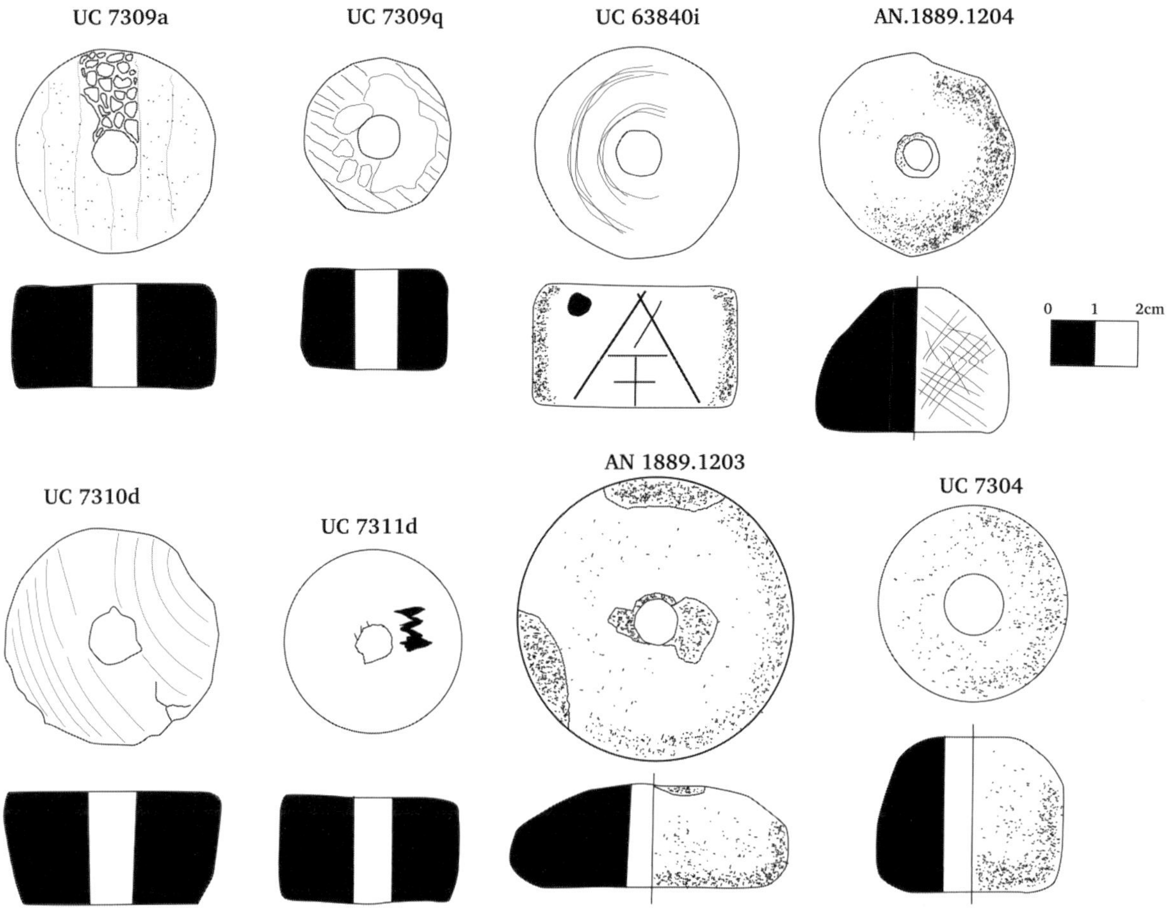

Figure 5.3. Drawing of Lahun spindle whorls

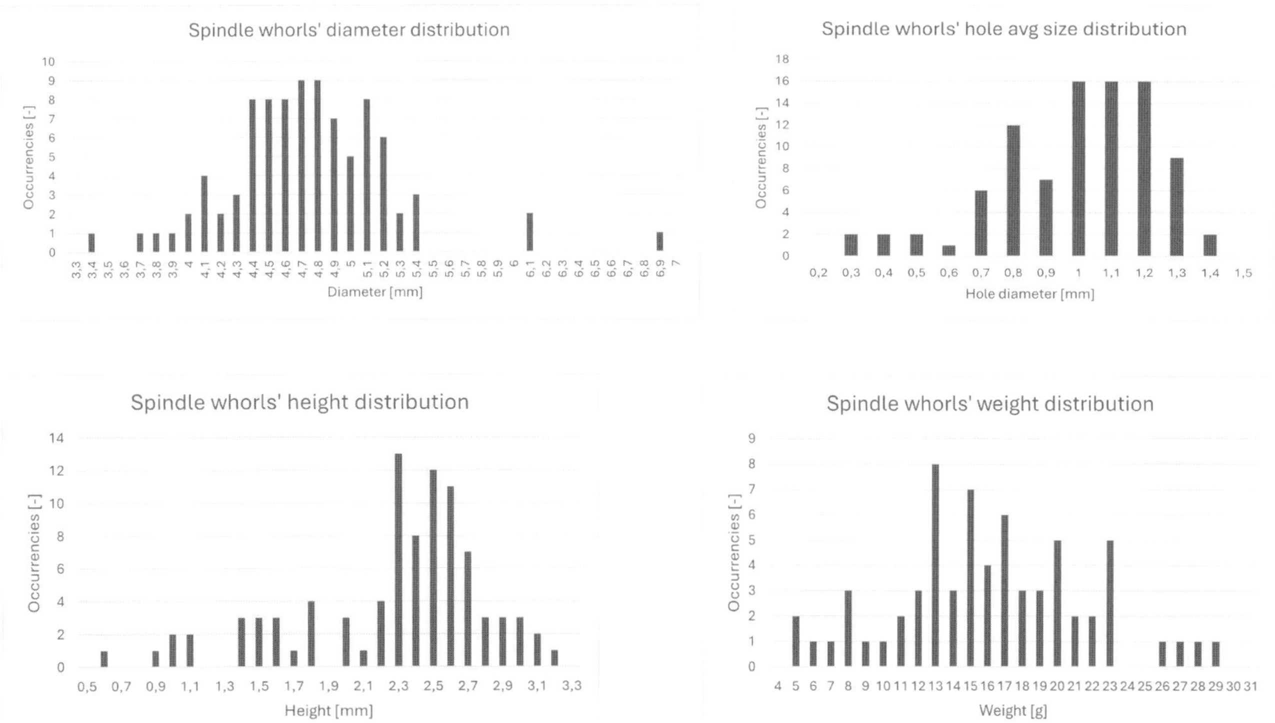

Figure 5.4. Plots of Lahun spindle whorls

whorls covers incisions, which may have been marks. All the signs are geometrical, and no specific hieroglyph can be recognised. The most frequent signs are a combination of crossed lines, and appear quite similar to one another.

Only four spindle whorls made of limestone come from Lahun, and these are quite different from each other (Plate 10). Therefore, these will be treated separately from the homogeneous corpus of wooden spindle whorls. Two are dome-shaped, one is conical, and the last is cylindrical, although one of the bases is slightly smaller. They are very different from each other in terms of dimensions, weight, and surface finish. They have a large diameter, spanning from 4.4 to 6.6 cm, and a height that varies between 2.3 and 3.5 cm. Most of the holes share with the wooden whorls the feature of a slightly conical shape and their dimensions are similar to the wooden examples. The weights are, obviously, much higher than the wooden examples and range between 65 and 137 g. They have a polished surface, except AN.1889.1204, which shows signs of production and was left unpolished. The high weight of UC7304 is quite unrealistic for spinning, but it could have been utilised for plying yarns.

5.1.4 Spinning bowls

During the research, only one spinning bowl from Lahun was traced and studied, n°431 in the Manchester Museum collection. It is made of pottery and should have straight sides (although Petrie's drawings differ for this object), with two loops on the inside, which do not join (Petrie 1890, 25, pl. XIII.58). On the inner part of the loops, which is not visible, grooves left by threads rubbing are perceptible to the touch. Petrie found a large number of these items in his excavation of the site, as its publications demonstrate. He in fact asserts that some crudely cut stone bowls similar to this, with one or two interior loops, were present at the site.[1] Unfortunately, he did not draw these objects, nor give any other information about their quantity or place of discovery.

5.1.5 Weights

Only six objects from Lahun can be identified as weights. Plumb bob weights, lead weights for fishing, and scale weights are not included in the study. Instead, all the items that could be attached to the warp of a loom have been considered. Of these six items, five are made of limestone and one of clay. One of the stone objects has a semi-discoid shape[2] with two through holes near the flat part of the weight. Alongside this flat part, a large groove is incised, which covers the whole length (Fig. 5.5). In Egypt, where the warp-weighted loom appears not to have been used until at least the Late Period, these objects are considered as net weights, and this interpretation is probably correct for two main reasons. The first is the presence of the long, horizontal groove, which could provide a good space for attaching a net, but this does not seem to offer a satisfactory explanation for the warp-weighted loom (Alberti 2011, 29). The second reason is their relative rarity, as they tend to occur in small numbers in each site, with Lisht having the most numerous group. If they were used on a warp-weighted loom, they should have been found in their dozens. Of course, it is possible that the small number of finds depends on the selection of the items made by the excavator, as is the case for spinning bowls. I would therefore consider them as net weights until different, more widespread evidence of their use can be found, as for the Levant (Firth 2015, 167). The other objects are pebbles with superficial grooves that can help to tie a thread or a cord (Plate 11). These can occur with a quite deep groove that runs all around the object on either its longest or shortest side, but also with two or more grooves that cross themselves.

Finally, a clay weight with a single hole and a discoid elliptical shape was recovered. This would be a perfect candidate for a loom weight, but again it is only one object and may have been used for many other purposes than textile production.

5.1.6 Needles

The catalogue of the present study lists 58 copper and bronze needles from the site of Lahun. There is no possibility to ascribe them with certainty to the Middle Kingdom, but their homogeneity seems to indicate a similar chronology for each of them. Their thickness varies between 0.12 cm and 0.3 cm, while the maximum length preserved reaches 11.8 cm. They share a common feature in the technique of their hole production, which has been carved out by punching through the shaft from one side to the other. This action results in a hole that is rounded on one side, while the other has a typical ogival shape (Figs 5.6 and 5.7).

A needle case was also found at the site. It is made of a hollow bone closed in the upper part by various vegetable elements, which are fixed together by a textile, wrapped and knotted around the object. It contains a copper or bronze needle with a thread still inserted into it (Z-plied) and a wooden pin or bodkin (Fig. 5.8).

5.1.7 Spatulae

Only four bone spatulae were traced back to the site of Lahun, to which a wooden beater must be added. Two spatulae are made of thin ribs, and are therefore long and thin. One has a sort of protruding point, while the other has a triangular point, but very rounded. Given their raw material, they are not flat but very arcuate (Fig. 5.7). Another bone spatula is a plane with a triangular point, and the other end is flat. One surface is smooth while the other partially exposes the cancellous bone. It is interesting that it has a different pattern of wear than those of Hazor. The wear is not located at the point, but rather at a lateral-central position. The point is quite smooth with very few traces of trabeculae, and the central part is completely smooth through use. The other, flat end has the cancellous bone totally exposed. The fourth bone

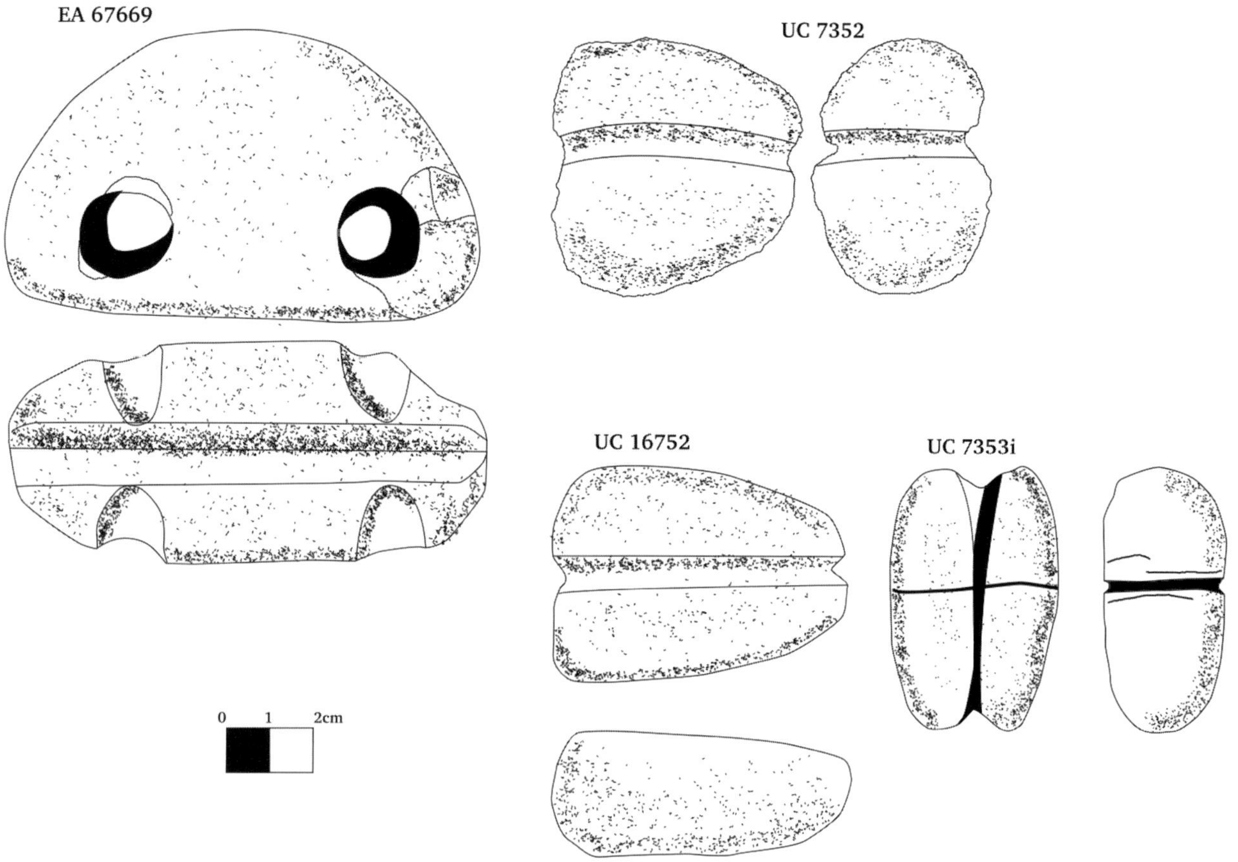

Figure 5.5. Net weights

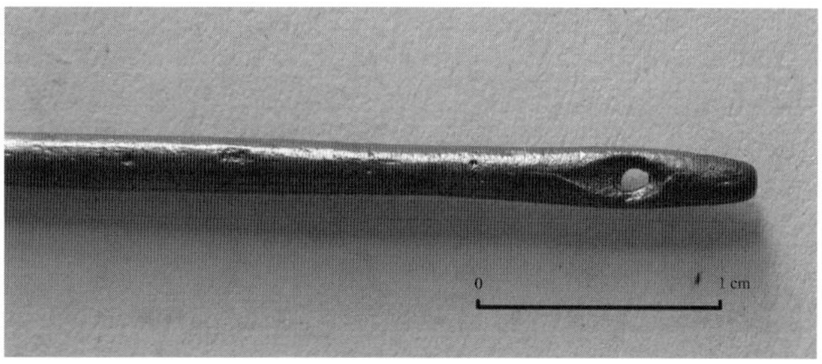

Figure 5.6. Detail of a needle (courtesy of Manchester Museum, 233s)

spatula is broken and only a part of a sharp pen-nib point is preserved. The upper surface is highly polished; the lower part has cancellous bone exposed, except for the final part of the point, where wear traces are clearly visible. Interestingly, it was found inside a ball of thread (695.a). The last object is the so-called weaver's slay, which I prefer to refer as a pin beater. It is a wooden object, slightly arcuate, with one rounded end and the other pointed. It is well carved and no traces of wear are visible. It is quite long, but in line with other spatulae. It is thicker, however, which could suggest that it was used as a beater rather than a spatula.

5.1.8 Heddle jacks

A heddle jack is a small pole with a flat base, a notch, and a 'spoon-shaped' upper part, as described by Winlock (1922, 71) (Plate 11). Their use was discussed in several articles and books (Roth and Crowfoot 1921, 97–101; Barber 1991, 86–8), and very little can be added. The task proposed by Winlock, and derived from an examination of funerary models, was to offer support to the heddle bar during the weaving operation, and it was lowered or removed to open the counter shed. Other scholars were sceptical, as a similar solution is quite complicated and requires large amounts of energy. Another possible explanation was to use these tools to adjust the tension of the warp (Kemp and Vogelsang-Eastwood 2001, 330, fig. 9.17). However, this solution requires the use of cords that should have left wear traces on the rear side of the spoon part, which are not present. Instead, there appears to be extreme amounts of wear on the back of the pole, which may be a result of use, or of reuse as mallet. Whatever their actual use was, there is still an issue: the catalogue lists 11 actual heddle jacks and 7 models. Heddle jacks themselves have a height that ranges between 36.9 cm and 24.7 cm, while models are between 11.9 and 6 cm. These small items were explained by David (1986, 236) as

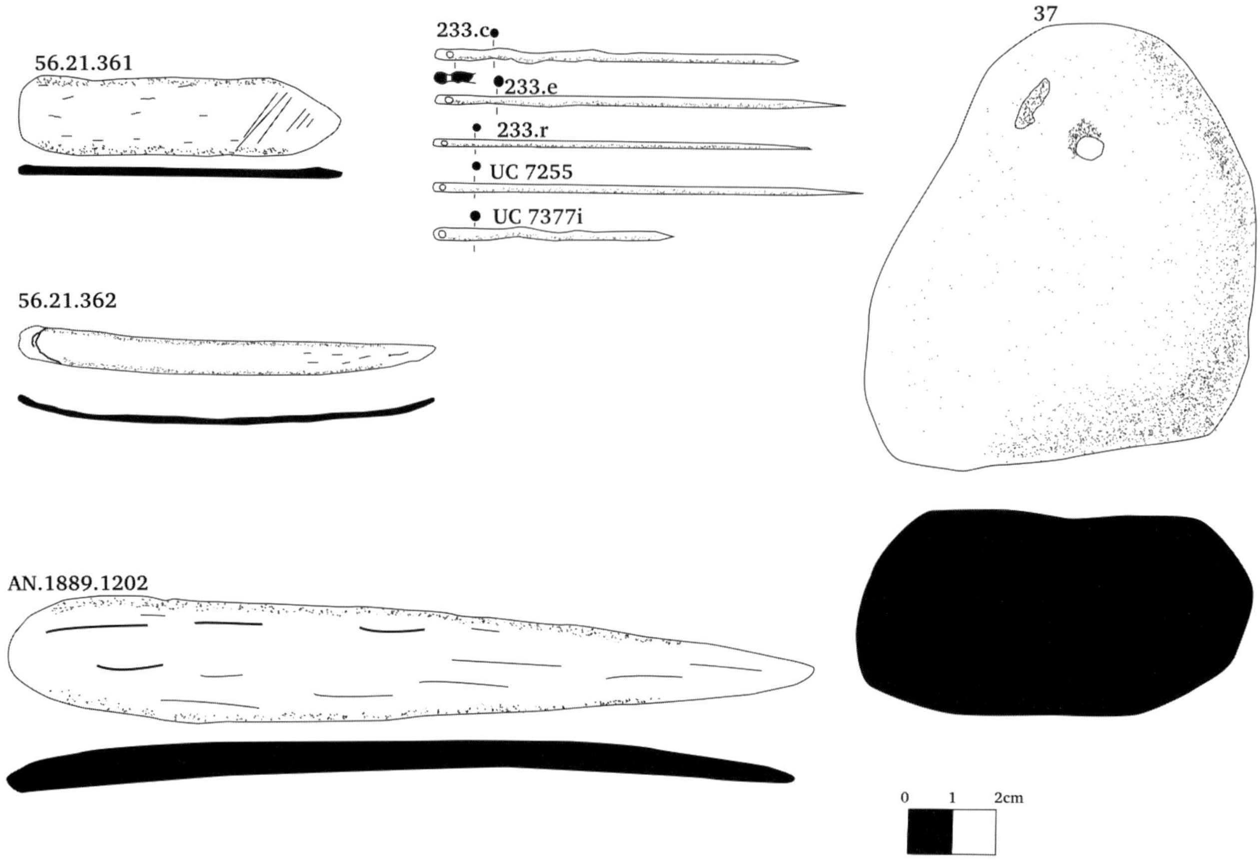

Figure 5.7. Needles, bone spatulae and a weight

toys for children, and I am unable to provide a better explanation. They do not come from funerary contexts and show no traces of use, and one could not be set to stay upright. On one of these model tools (EA 70881) a proto-Canaanite inscription is incised, which is generally interpreted as one of many traces left by foreigners. Two problems arise from this inscription: the first is that it is on the wrong side of use (Cartwright *et al.* 1998, 92), although as previously stated it is possible that this model had no practical use. A more major problem is given by their chronology, since the inscription should be dated to the New Kingdom (Quirke 2005, 95) while their use should be restricted to the Middle Kingdom. This is not entirely true, because even if major settlements of the New Kingdom didn't show the use of heddle jacks, they were also recovered in New Kingdom layers at Lisht (Hayes 1959, 218). Furthermore, there is plenty of evidence that people visited the site during the New Kingdom, so the inscription could be unrelated to the object's use.

5.1.9 Fibres

Textiles are quite rare finds at the settlement of Lahun, and are more likely to have been preserved inside tombs. However, several examples of fibres and threads come from the town, mainly made of flax, but also of wool. Wool from Lahun has long been debated (Barber 1991, 49), but radiocarbon dating has definitively proven that it is medieval and intrusive (Cooke 1993, 15). The problem is that it was found mixed with other remains such as flax, probably due to animal nests. The result is that many materials appear 'contaminated' by wool, even if most of the flax examples should be dated to the Pharaonic period for the presence of splicing.[3]

Furthermore, another chronological issue is given by the lack of a clear indication of provenance for each finding, which could equally be dated to the Middle Kingdom, New Kingdom, or even later (but prior to the splicing demise). The chronology indicated in the catalogue is that used by the institutions that house each object, and which were hopefully able to check all the documents left by Petrie, as well as their connection with other materials.

Several steps of fibre preparation and the spinning process can be identified from these materials. Some bunches of flax were recovered from the site and have been processed to obtain strips of the required thickness. From the material recovered, it seems that no further preparation was required before splicing (*i.e.* like modern combing), as can be seen

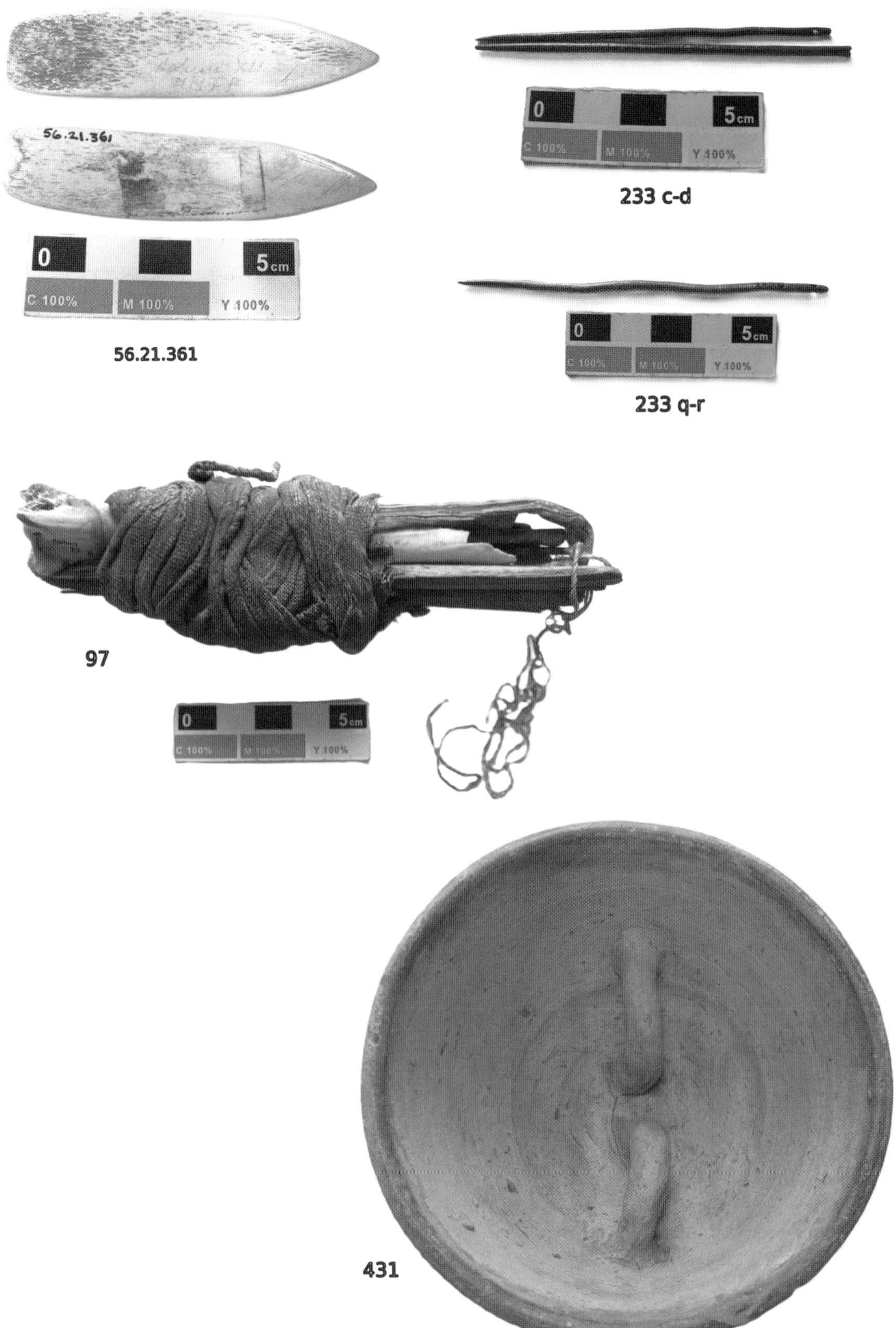

Figure 5.8. Selection of textile tools from Kahun

in 114.i.vii (and especially in 500.a from Gurob). It is a small ball of unspun fibres, with some spliced fibres and plied yarns.[4]

Most of the balls had already been spun, or rather twisted, and show different twist directions, from the normal S, 2S to S, 2z and Z, 2s, as well as examples of cabled threads. The threads and fibres are generally quite degraded, making the analysis more difficult, especially in terms of stating the thread diameter and angle of twist with certainty.

5.1.10 Textual references on textile activities

Some of the texts from Lahun deal with textile production, thus proving that it was a primary activity in the settlement. Two documents appear particularly relevant to understanding the textile industry at this site. The first is UC32203 (Collier and Quirke 2002, 114–17), where the lady of the house, Irer, addresses a man of equal status and reports problems in the weaving production due to her absence for service to the temple, which lasts a month.

Another text, UC32094A (Collier and Quirke 2006, 144–5), lists six women engaged with weaving, some with female relations. Still other texts are accountancy documents which provide evidence of flax fibres, threads, and textiles (Cartwright *et al.* 1998, 93–4). These texts show how textile production was strictly a female role, as only women are listed in connection with weaving. As Quirke stresses (2016, 251), weaving is the only activity entirely carried out by women, as fishing always appears to be connected with men. This is certainly true for Middle Kingdom Lahun. However, the choice to use the term weaving, and not a more general term for textile production, must be highlighted here. In fact, net making requires thread production, which is accomplished using spindles, exactly as threads are required for weaving. In funerary paintings, like the tomb of Khety in Beni Hasan (Newberry 1893, pl. XIII), spinning thread for net making is an activity exclusively carried out by men. This means the men and women used the same tools and shared the same knowledge, even if the two extremely similar activities were performed by different people, likely in different places.

Weaving activity in the Fayum is sometimes linked to the presence of Asiatic peoples. However, as far as Lahun is concerned, there is no proof of their involvement in textile production. In fact, they appear to be employed as servants in the households, as dancers and porters in Senusret II temple, and can also occupy police or military roles. Their role in textile production is suggested by a document concerning a Theban estate, where a large number of Asiatic people are listed in spinning and weaving activities (Papyrus Brooklyn 35.1446; David 1986, 190). The document is dated to the 13th Dynasty and a similar situation may also have been present in Lahun, although there are neither archaeological findings nor textual traces to confirm this.

5.1.11 Conclusions: textile tools in Lahun

Textile tools from Lahun represent an interesting dataset for studying textile production in the Middle Kingdom, and the lack of context for the findings is particularly regrettable considering the importance of the site. Several wooden spindles and spindle whorls have been preserved by the dry climate of the area and have shown a great homogeneity. In fact, spindles are characterised by a cylindrical shape tapering to a point and a spiral groove near the other tip. Two different lengths of shafts can be identified: a longer one, between 30 and 40 cm, and a smaller one between 20 and 25 cm. No further decoration is present. Almost all the spindle whorls studied here are made of wood and have a cylindrical shape. They have quite a large diameter, around 4.7 cm, are fairly thick, with an average height of 2.3 cm, and are quite lightweight, 16.6 g on average, which allows a medium-fine textile production. Their holes are generally warped, probably due to the insertion of padding or wedges to secure the whorl onto the shaft. Some of them show identity marks crudely incised on the surface. No bone or pottery spindle whorls were found in the museums selected for the catalogue, and there would have been little to no evidence of their use. Only four spindle whorls are made of limestone and their dimensions are similar to the wooden examples, although they are much heavier.

Pottery and stone spinning bowls were present at Lahun, but only a single pottery bowl was found. It has rounded sides and a flat base and two loops on the inside, which do not join. Grooves created by thread rubbing are recognisable on the lower side of the loop.

Net weights are present in Lahun in very small quantities and are mainly made of stone. Several shapes are present, from semi-discoid to grooved pebbles, and many fragments of nets have been found at the site, making their usage in connection with nets quite probable. A single clay weight has also been identified, but unfortunately its usage cannot be determined with certainty.

Needles are very homogeneous in terms of materials and typology, with the eye pierced through the shaft. No examples were found of the eye made by bending the upper part of the shaft back on itself, as seen in Megiddo and Beth Shean. Only four bone spatulae and a wooden beater were located, proving this category of object was also used in Lahun (with less certainty for their chronology).

Chronology is a big issue in Lahun, given the absence of safe contexts and the reoccupation of the site in later periods. All the objects under examination might be dated to the New Kingdom, even if this seems quite improbable. This was particularly evident with the wool samples found in the settlement, which could be ascribed to a medieval period only thanks to radiocarbon dating.

Heddle jacks were quite numerous in Lahun, and their connection with textile production appears fairly clear. Much more uncertain is the role of the small models of heddle jacks.

All the textile tools appear to come from the village itself, except in one case. Petrie reports that a tomb of the 20th Dynasty contained: 'a wooden rake of 12 teeth, and a spindle of the Ramesside type' (Petrie 1890, 32). This context is extremely interesting because it proves that, even if only in rare cases, textile tools could be placed among funerary goods.

5.2 Gurob

5.2.1 Introduction

Gurob is situated in Middle Egypt, 25 km west of the Nile, at the entrance to the Fayum Oasis. The Bahr Yusuf flows approximately 3 km east of the site, which in antiquity was connected to the Nile through a great canal, the Mr-Wr, from which the settlement took its ancient name. The Bahr Yusuf ends in the Birket el-Qarun lake, now much smaller than in antiquity. The area saw the flourishing of settlements and funerary monuments, like Lahun, along with palaces and harem for the amusement of the royal court, as well as activities like hunting and fishing.

Petrie excavated Gurob in the same period as Lahun, with two working seasons between 1888 and 1890, and the results were published shortly after (Petrie 1890; 1891). During the second season of work, he was unable to supervise the works by himself and left the leadership to Hughes-Hughes, whose documentation, if it ever existed, was never made available to Petrie and is now permanently lost (Gasperini 2018, 4). He worked at the town site, near the temple, and west of the town at a Ptolemaic and New Kingdom necropolis. After Petrie's excavations, the site was exposed to an intense period of robbery, which compromised our understanding of the area. Brief surveys and excavations were conducted in the following years by E. Chassinat in 1900 and L. Borchardt in 1905 (Thomas 1981, 2–3). C. Currelly and T. Loat conducted more extensive research in 1903–1904, with the necropolis as the main focus. They found the tombs of several infants, a small Proto-dynastic cemetery, Ramesside tombs, and animal burials, including fish, goats, and oxen (Thomas 1981, 2).

Another excavation season was conducted by G. Brunton and R. Engelbach in 1920 and a plan was eventually produced (Brunton and Engelbach 1927, fig. 1). They excavated new tombs, reopened many of the already dug tombs, but by that time the illicit excavations had destroyed many of the monuments.

From the 1930s to 1984, the presence of a military camp prevented further investigations, and archaeological prospections started again in 2005 under the direction of I. Shaw and F. Hagen for the Universities of Liverpool and Copenhagen, lasting until 2012 (Gasperini 2018, 1; Hodgkinson 2018, 189–90). Finally, the works were resumed by the IFAO, and have been under the guidance of M. Yoyotte since 2015.

The area was used as a necropolis for a very long time, from the Predynastic to the Roman Period, although not extensively. The site was particularly exploited during the New Kingdom, from the reign of Thutmosis III to Ramses V (Wachsmann 2013, 95). It is not clear if a settlement was present during the first part of the 18th Dynasty, but it was Thutmosis III who built the royal harem palace and encouraged the flourishing of the site (Thomas 1981, 4; Hodgkinson 2018, 192). The settlement developed as a royal foundation to house the staff linked to the royal harem and provide it with all necessary commodities. The harem palace was first identified by Petrie, who interpreted it as a large temple, and it was subsequently recognised as a palace by Borchardt, and more recently proven by Kemp (1978, 131).

The structure includes two large twin buildings with columns, and is surrounded by a brick enclosure wall. To the north, an area that might have been interpreted as a settlement can be identified (Hodgkinson 2018, 192). The site has also revealed several necropoleis that show signs of social diversity, despite the massive looting activities conducted in modern and ancient times. A 'fort', a mudbrick temple dedicated to Thutmosis III, and an industrial area were also uncovered. This last feature was the subject of the recent excavations by the Liverpool and Copenhagen universities and, interestingly, shows evidence of some textile production (Hodgkinson 2018, 237).[5]

Gurob has provided a large number of textile tools and fibres, most belonging to the New Kingdom. Unfortunately, given the lack of context for the findings, it is not possible to distinguish production areas for many of the objects, nor to set a chronological framework that we can connect to the tools.

For this project, it has been decided to use only materials that are stored in European collections, given the large number of objects collected in past times and the difficulty of locating and gaining access to these types of materials in Egyptian museums. Several museums exhibit objects from the Petrie excavations at Gurob and, similarly for Lahun, it was not possible to see them all. Therefore, only the institutions with larger collections have been selected. Most of the items are stored in the Petrie Museum in London, and secondarily in the Manchester Museum. Other items have been studied in the Ashmolean Museum in Oxford, in the British Museum, and in the World Museum in Liverpool.

Unfortunately, a complete catalogue of the objects excavated by Petrie has not been conducted, so it is not possible to understand if the items collected represent only a small percentage of the textile tools from the site or are the majority. Various types of objects and materials are represented in the catalogue, giving the impression of a much greater diversity than that observed for Lahun.

5.2.2 Foreigners at Gurob and textual sources

Gurob is particularly famous for the long-debated presence of foreigners in the settlement. The first person to hypothesise the presence of a large community of foreigners in Gurob, probably of Aegean origin, was Petrie (1890, 40–5). In his excavations, he found several objects of foreign provenance, as well as a peculiar feature consisting of numerous pits under the floors filled with burnt objects and covered in ash, named 'burnt groups' (Petrie 1891, 16–19). They were located under the floors of buildings he thought to be houses, but which should now be recognised as rooms within the palace.[6] Although the chronology proposed by Petrie has been demonstrated to be wrong, many theories have been proposed to explain the phenomenon.[7]

The burnt groups are not the only evidence (if this can be taken as a piece of evidence) for the presence of foreigners at Gurob. Excluding the evidence presented by Petrie (1890, 39–41) – which was based on bone materials and blonde hair and is nowadays not considered as reliable – some other clues point to the presence of non-Egyptian people in the settlement. This is not the place to discuss all the possible foreign materials found at Gurob, from the Mycenaean pottery (Gasperini 2014) to burial equipment, the names of people or cooking pots,[8] but two objects are relevant to this study: the first is a spindle, the second a papyrus.

The spindle was found in tomb 11 (Brunton and Engelbach 1927, fig. XIII.8) and is now housed in the Museum of Archaeology and Anthropology of Cambridge.[9] It has a wooden shaft and a limestone spindle whorl decorated with patterns in a 'y' form. The peculiarity of this spindle (Barber 1991, 64–6) is that its top preserves the groove where the thread was inserted, yet the spindle whorl is not placed immediately after the groove, but rather is near the opposite point, which means it is a low-whorl spindle. This is contrary to all the Egyptian evidence investigated so far. Two other limestone spindle whorls were found in tombs 217 and 600. Another peculiar feature of this object is that the groove is not cut in an s-direction, as are all the other Egyptian spindles, but instead shows a z-direction. After careful examination of the object, the spiral is definitely oriented in z-direction. However, this is not a decisive factor for this research. In fact, Barber connects the presence of the z-direction groove and the low-whorl to the presence of Aegean spinners. It is true that the z-groove appears different to other spindles from the Egyptian tradition, which generally have an s-directed groove. However, Egyptian textiles are not always s-spun and s-plied, but can be s-spun and Z-plied, or even z-spun and Z-plied. The groove direction is therefore not a clear indication of a foreign spinner. The spindle whorl is very loose on the shaft, and the wooden shaft clearly shows that it was mounted in the wrong position after being found. In fact, an area that is lighter than the rest of the wood is placed directly beneath the groove, as in all the other Egyptian spindles. The hypothesis of a foreign spinner could not, therefore, be supported by this spindle. The fact that the spindle was placed in a tomb is quite remarkable, although this has also been observed in Lahun.

Finally, the textual source Papyrus Gurob III.1 (Wente 1990, 36, n. 34) preserves a letter from a lady of the harem to the king, which probably refers to some foreigners sent to her to learn spinning and weaving.[10] She states that this has happened at another time in the past, so it was not an isolated episode, but probably a consolidated tradition. The document is dated to year two of Seti II, and the first training happened during the reign of Ramesses II.

The letter contains another clue that is extremely interesting. Foreign spinners and weavers who were employed in the royal harem were not chosen because they were skilled at foreign crafts (*e.g.* Syrian women able to produce renowned Syrian textiles), as it is clearly stated that they have to learn to work in the Egyptian way. This means that the final products that were expected from the Gurob palace were completely Egyptian.

There are no indications that exotic textiles were produced in the harem palace, although they may have been present in the settlement if they were traded or produced for foreigners by other workshops, or directly within their households. It is highly probable that exotic textiles were present in Gurob and used by foreigners living in Gurob, as was the case in Amarna. In the stela of *Trr*, the husband is portrayed as wearing a Syro-Canaanite dress, while his wife, who also has a Semitic name, is dressed as an Egyptian woman (Wachsmann 2013, 164, fig. 4.1).

Other documents pertaining to textile production were found in Gurob, and this activity clearly must have had a certain importance to the economy of the town.

One of these documents is a papyrus found in Gurob (UC32795) with a list of dresses for the Hittite spouse of Ramses II, Maat-hor-neferura, some of which were probably produced in Gurob (Gardiner 1948, 45; Wachsmann 2013, 197–8).

An ebony statuette, inscribed with the name of the lady Teye, was found in a tomb near Gurob. This lady bore the title 'chief of weavers' during the reign of Amenhotep III (Thomas 1981, 9, 16). A headrest with the name of Hwy bears the title of 'chief of spinners', giving the idea of a large, well organised textile industry (Thomas 1981, 16).

5.2.3 Spindles

Gurob preserved several complete spindles, with both spindle and spindle whorl preserved, as well as individual spindle whorls and shafts that could not be linked to each other. The catalogue lists 30 spindles from Gurob, all made of wood (Fig. 5.9).

A small number of these are preserved in their full length, 5 in total: UC7812c, UC7809, UC27873iiie, 526l, 526o. Most of the other examples are broken into more than half, and some do not preserve either end. The longest spindle

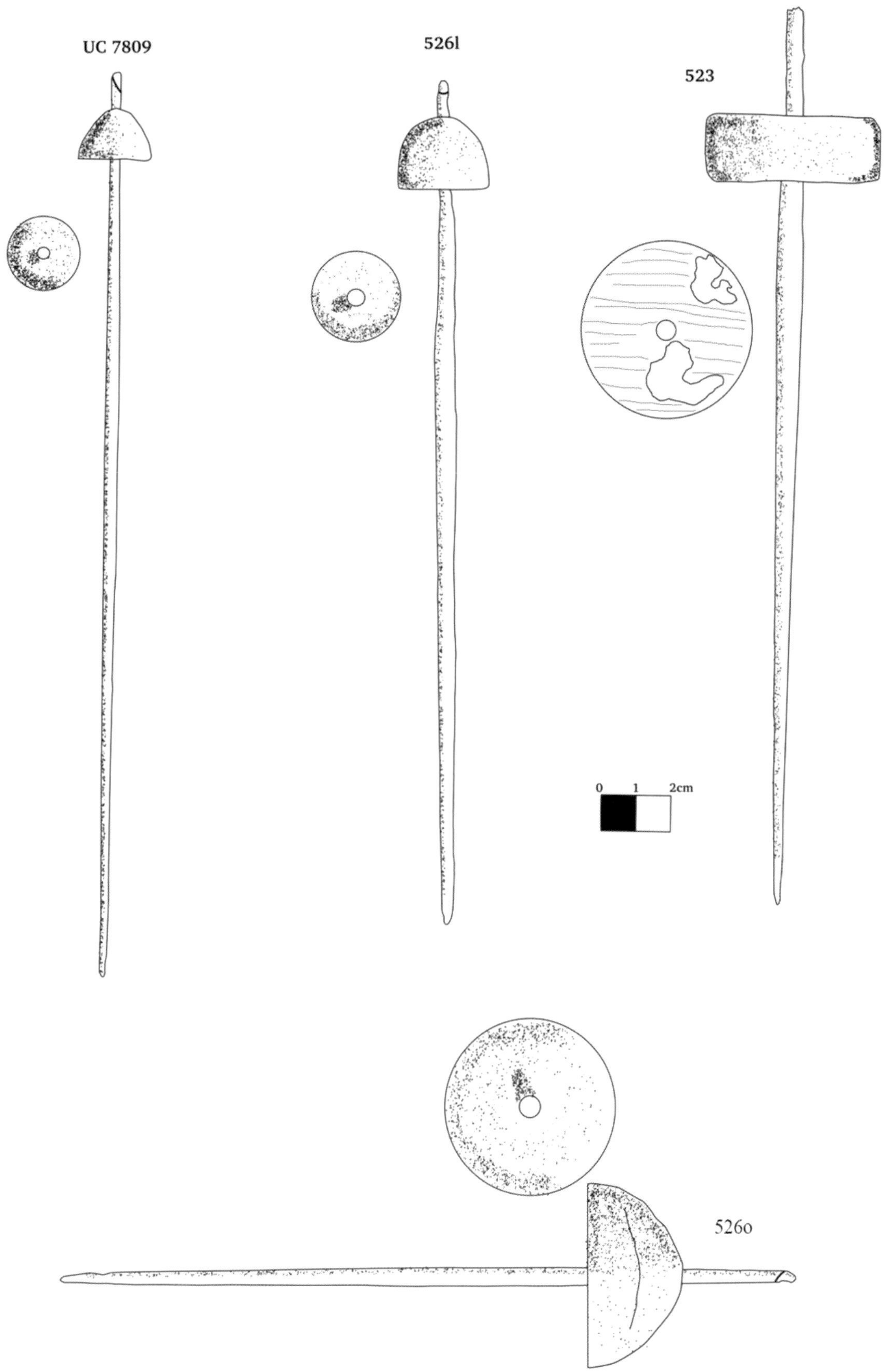

Figure 5.9. Spindles from Gurob

measures 24.5 cm and the shortest 21 cm, but within the broken objects there is a spindle that measures 33.4 cm (UC526m). Most of the objects examined, however, must have had a length between 20 and 25 cm. The picture therefore seems very similar to Lahun and Deir el-Medina, with most of the shaft measuring less than 25 cm, but with few exceeding 30 cm. Shaft diameters measure 0.7 cm on average (the maximum diameter of the shaft), with most of the items ranging between 0.5 and 0.9 cm. The thinnest rod measures 0.4 cm and the thickest 1.04 cm, with values generally lower than those seen in Lahun and Deir el-Medina (Table 5.2).

As in Lahun, the shafts are generally not cylindrical but tend to thicken in the middle and taper towards a point, while the other end is slightly thinner, yet not so different from the middle. In many cases, therefore, spindle whorls have a slightly conical hole which is slightly larger on the lower side than the upper, with a difference of 1 mm.

The upper tip of the spindle can be rounded or flattish and generally has a spiral groove or notch to attach the fibres for spinning. The other end of the shaft, when preserved, tends to taper to a point, although not very sharp. All the preserved examples with the spindle whorl attached to the shaft show that the position of the spindle whorl is immediately below the groove (Plate 12).

Only three spindles preserve fibres wound around the shaft – two objects contain threads mixed into unspun fibres, while one object simply has unspun fibres preserved under a thick layer of encrustation (UC 7812a). 527 preserves an s-plied thread wound around the shaft and placed under the spindle whorl, partially embedded in a layer of encrustation. 526.a has a large quantity of thread wound around the shaft under the spindle whorl, most of it unspun (Plate 12). A thick yarn is Z-cabled and another thread, near the end of the shaft and highly worn, is z-spun or plied.

5.2.4 Spindle whorls

Twenty-two spindle whorls in the corpus are preserved attached to their original shaft, while 75 lack their spindle. The total is 97 spindle whorls, which is a similar number to that of Lahun.[11] Almost all the spindle whorls are made of wood, while only six are made of limestone. No bone spindle whorls, so common in the LBA levels in the Levant, are present, and reworked sherds are also entirely absent. However, the absence of perforated pottery sherds might depend on the choices made by the excavator, as is the case for Lahun and Deir el-Medina. In any case, wood seems to become the preferred material, indeed almost the only one.

Table 5.2. Complete spindles from Gurob

Number	*Length (cm)*	*Diameter (cm)*	*Weight (g)*
UC7812c	23.8	0.46	2.24 (no whorl)
UC7809	24.5	0.41	5.04 (with whorl)
526l	23.3	0.54	8 (with whorl)
526o	21	0.57	22 (with whorl)
UC27873iii e	23.2	0.87	5.5 (no whorl)

In the catalogue, four shapes of spindle whorls are listed: dome, conical, conical truncated, and cylindrical. However, it is not always possible to clearly distinguish between each form, especially in the case of dome and conical objects, which should probably be considered as variants rather than different categories. The conical/dome shape is the dominant form of spindle whorls known from Lahun, with 52 examples listed in the catalogue. The cylindrical shape, which is dominant at all other sites, is well represented at Gurob, with 34 objects, but is far from the most common type (Plate 12). A few spindle whorls have a conical truncated shape, only 5 out of 91 (Fig. 5.10).

No wooden analysis has so far been carried out on Gurob spinning tools, and it was not possible to conduct tests for this thesis. However, it seems that spindle whorls made of soft wood, probably Ficus sycomorus, were present, although other, much more resistant species of wood were certainly also employed. As in the case of Lahun, small branches and larger logs were used to cut the spindle whorls, as can be seen in UC7814ii j and UC7814ii l.

The diameter of the spindle whorls can vary a great deal, given the different types employed at this site. Many of the dome-shaped examples, in fact, have a small base and are quite tall, with an entirely different ratio than the cylindrical whorls, as well as a different inertia. The minimum value is 2.06 cm, while the maximum measures 5.6 cm. The average value is 3.9 cm (Fig. 5.11).

By contrast, the height does not vary much, due to the fact that both cylindrical and conical/dome shape spindle whorls have a similar size. The minimum value is 1.19 cm and the maximum is 2.73 cm, with an average value of 1.9 cm. Cylindrical spindle whorls are, in general, more similar to those from Deir el-Medina rather than Lahun, which are much thicker than those of Gurob.

There is a huge difference in hole diameters, as in Lahun, since the smallest value measures just 0.3 cm and the largest is 1.37 cm. The average value, however, is quite low, just 0.66 cm, while in Lahun it is 1 cm. The value given here is from the largest part of the hole, since many of the holes are slightly conical to allow the shaft to better adapt to the spindle, with an average variation of 1 mm. In at least one case, a wedge is preserved inside the hole of the spindle whorl.

Some of the spindle whorls are still attached to their shaft, and in these cases, their weight is not considered in the charts, since it is the total weight of shaft and whorl. Only the whorls which were no longer attached to the shaft are considered here. 66 weights of wooden spindle whorls have been measured, the lightest 1.4 g and the heaviest 32.1 g. The average value is 10.1 g, which is certainly a light weight.

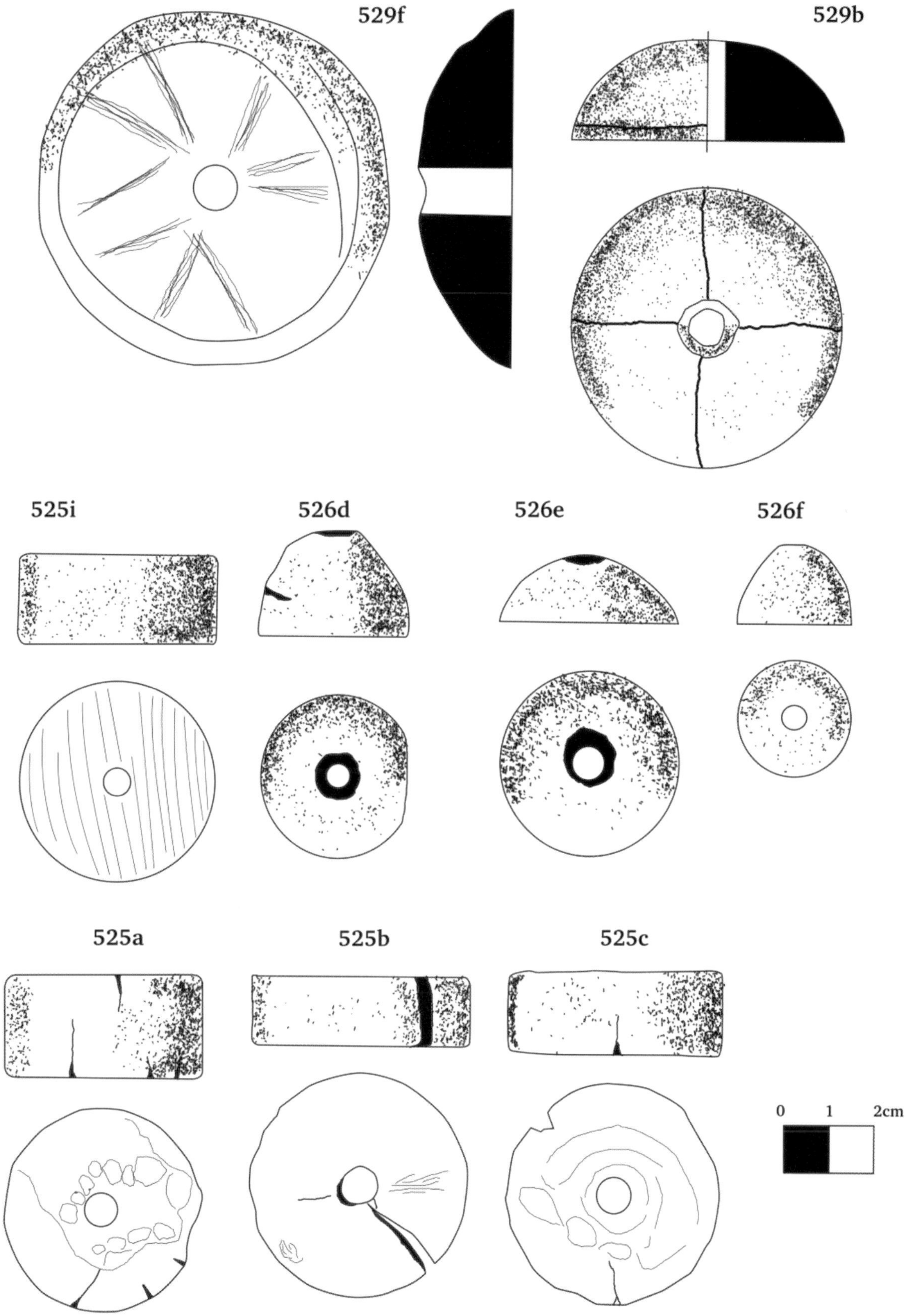

Figure 5.10. Spindle whorls from Gurob

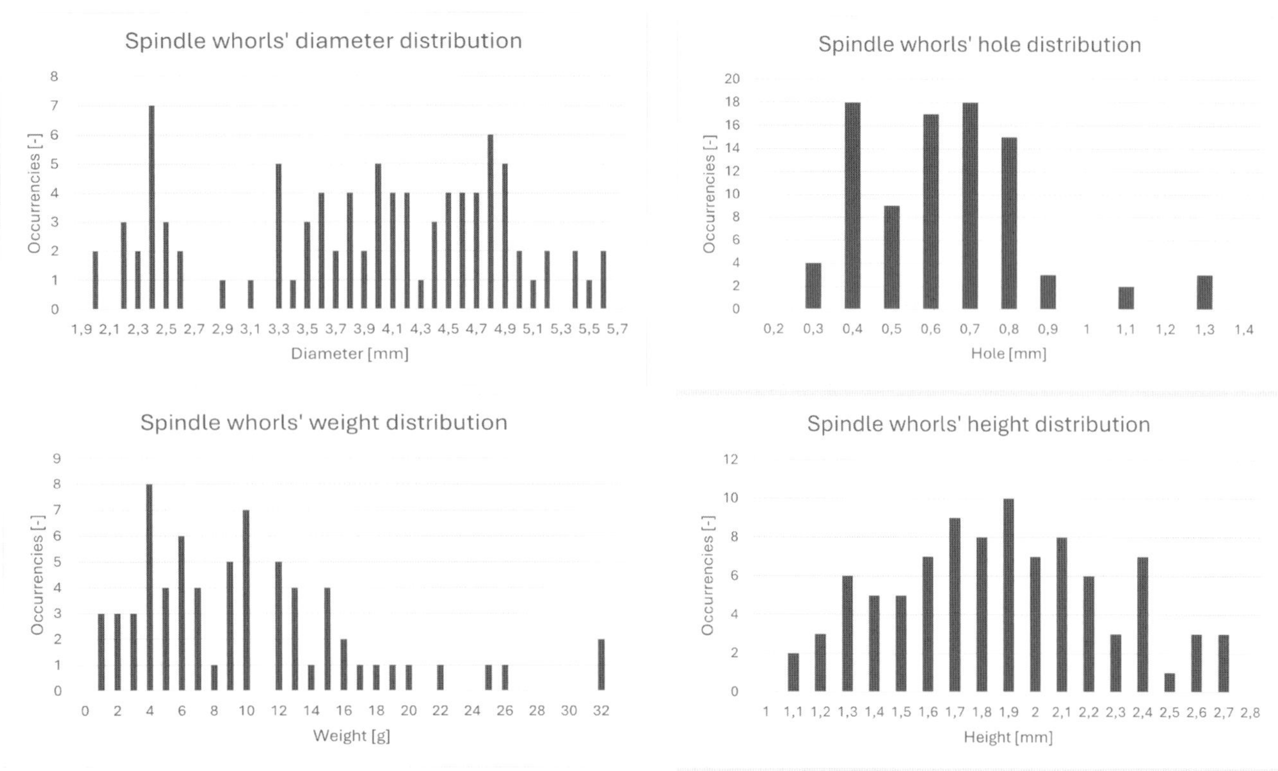

Figure 5.11. Plots of Gurob spindle whorls

Some of the cylindrical and dome-shaped spindle whorls show traces of a patina or encrustation on one or both flat surfaces. As seen for Lahun, this might depend on the condition of preservation of the tools, as it does not seem to follow any precise pattern. Generally, it appears on one side of the whorl, but sometimes on all sides, and can be concentrated in a few spots or cover the entire surface of the object. Fibres, when preserved, are always beneath the encrustation, which suggests a post-depositional phenomenon. However, it seems peculiar that they appear so consistently at all the sites under consideration.

No decoration is apparent on the wooden spindle whorls, and marks seem to be quite rare at the site.

Only six limestone spindle whorls are listed in the catalogue, but a few others must certainly have been present at the site, as was the case for the previously cited example in Cambridge. They are very different to the wooden ones, and thus are treated separately. Two of them have a dome shape, the other four a conical shape. They are quite different from each other in terms of dimensions and weight, but they have in common a large diameter as well as a medium to heavy or very heavy weight. The diameters range between 4.51 to 7.63 cm with a height between 2 and 3.78 cm. As in the case of Lahun, most of the holes are slightly conical, with the largest value at the base and ranging between 0.79 and 1.2 cm. The weights are very close to those of Lahun, ranging between 57.7 g and 133.2 g. Limestone whorls are quite crude in their appearance, with their surfaces barely polished and shapes slightly irregular. Most, however, are decorated on the surface with radial and circular incisions, even though crudely cut. As in the case of Lahun, they appear particularly worn near the 'upper' hole, meaning the hole near the smallest part of the spindle whorl.

Considering all these data, the scale of the textile industry in Gurob appears very similar to that of Lahun, but texts suggest a very different situation, with a large, industrial-scale weaving activity. The number of objects (which is very small) are very similar for the two sites, but this might depend on several factors, from different conditions of preservation at the site to the deliberate choices of the excavators. There is, however, one element which clearly points to a completely different client for the Gurob production. Some of the spindles and spindle whorls are in fact much smaller and lighter than those found in Lahun, Deir el-Medina, and most of those from Amarna. Furthermore, they also have a different shape. The shafts are long and extremely thin, measuring 0.3–0.5 cm in diameter, which appears quite fragile when compared to the other types of spindles. Spindle whorls can be a dome/conical shape, and in this case even very small and light, but some examples of thin shafts and larger spindle whorls are also known. UC7809 is the lightest example, which is complete and weighs just 5 g, considering both shaft and whorl. A similar item, 526 l, weighs 8 g considering both shaft and whorl. Other broken examples are also known.

This means that the yarn produced by these items is different from that produced by other spindles, and must have been much finer and more valuable. Considering that the site was focused on a royal harem, where textiles for queens and the royal court were produced, it seems very reasonable to consider these thin spindles as tools for luxury production.

5.2.5 Spinning bowls

Textual sources provide a picture of an industrial-scale textile production at Gurob, but the archaeological data contradict this view for spindles. Spinning bowls were not recorded from the Petrie excavations, while he did report them at Lahun. Some have been found from I. Shaw's excavations, but in limited numbers (Shaw 2012, 352). Spinning bowls are generally considered a reliable indicator of spinning activities and are well known and widespread throughout Egypt, with many examples from Amarna, Deir el-Medina, Lahun, South Abydos, etc. If a royal textile workshop was present in Gurob, one would have expected to find these in larger quantities.

5.2.6 Weights

Gurob has provided a few net sinkers, but those listed in the catalogue are just a small percentage, since they were clearly not of interest to this study. In fact, they are very small objects made of lead, and the one I measured weighs just 5.7 g. They are definitely net weights, and there is no risk of confusing them with loom weights.

Only one limestone weight was recorded in the museum collections chosen for this research and, in some way, can be considered similar to the weights of Lahun. It is a rounded pebble with a deep groove, which crosses the surface of the object on its shortest side.

If Gurob had housed an Aegean community with foreign spinners and weavers who were free to work for themselves, we should have found some evidence of the use of loom weights of the Aegean type, but none is present. If the communities were Levantine, there would be no chance of seeing this from the weights, since they were rarely attested in the LBA in the Levant.

5.2.7 Needles

Many bronze needles were found in Gurob by Petrie, which are now preserved between the Petrie Museum and the Ashmolean. Of the 73 needles listed in the catalogue, only some of them preserve an eye, and can thus be defined with certainty as needles. This is, in any case, a much greater number than those found for the other sites under study (Fig. 5.12).

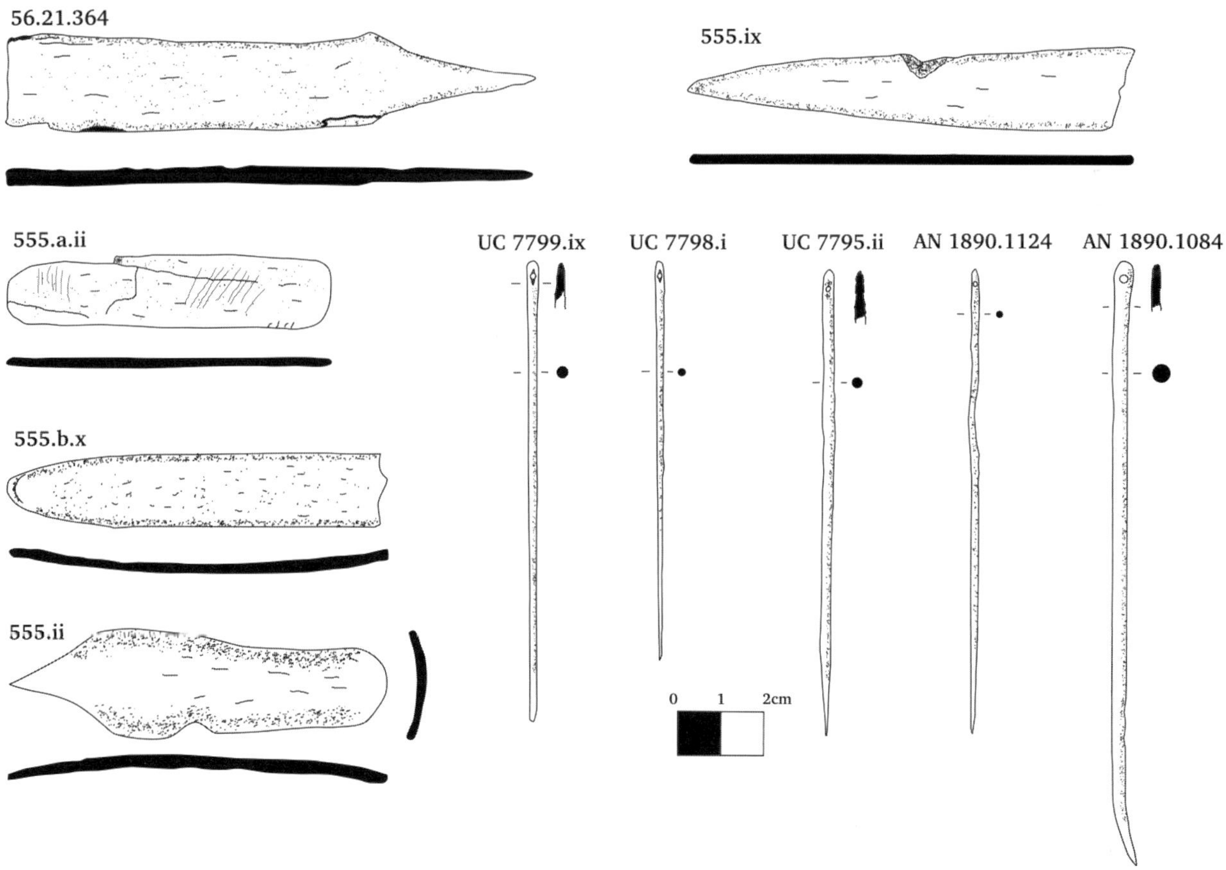

Figure 5.12. Selection of bronze needles and bone spatulae

Needles can be quite thick, with a maximum diameter of 0.3 cm, but most examples have a diameter that ranges between 0.15 and 0.25 cm. They are thicker and longer than the needles used nowadays, but usable for sewing textiles.

They were probably found spread throughout the settlement, but in some cases Petrie reports the finding location, and we can therefore clearly state that they could also be associated with the burnt groups (Petrie 1891, 17–18, pl. XVIII). Interestingly, all the needles under study were made in the same way, with the hole pierced through one end of the shaft. Not a single example with the upper part of the shaft bent back on itself is present, which is a typology widespread in the Levant since the MBA.

5.2.8 Spatulae

Bone spatulae are fairly common in Gurob, with 95 examples listed in the catalogue. They vary a great deal in terms of shape, length, and width, and therefore their usage might vary between one object and the other (Plate 13). Besides the classical shape with a triangular point, pen-nib examples are also quite common. Furthermore, tools with double flat and rounded points are present. Wear traces also vary a lot, with objects only slightly used near the point and the cancellous bone completely exposed and coarse; other examples, meanwhile, show the entire surface under the spatula as smooth. Typically, wear traces are mostly localised near the point, and slowly disappear going towards the other end, similar to those seen in Hazor.

However, some spatulae show a different pattern of wear that is typical of Gurob. In some cases, spatulae were used more intensively on the central or the rear part, probably due to their curved shape, which influenced the zones where the objects had more contact. This means that not only was the point inserted in the fabric (assuming that they were used for weaving), but most of the surface of the object also came into contact with the yarn. A clear example is 555.xi from the Manchester collection.

Entirely different from any other spatula is 555.xiv, which was used on its short side, always in the same direction, and has one edge that is extremely well used and sharp, while the other still shows traces of cancellous bone and is much thicker.

5.2.9 Fibres

Very few textiles were recovered in Gurob, most from tombs, like the famous pair of sleeves for a child's dress (Thomas 1981, 11) and the textiles examined by J. Picton (Picton *et al.* 2016). Much more consistent is the collection of balls of yarn and bundles of threads. The catalogue lists 33 items, including fibres prepared for spinning, spun fibres (actual balls of yarn), textiles with fringes and nets, and mixed materials. All of these are very likely to be made of flax, as appears to be the case examining them by eye or with light magnification. Coarse, thick fibres made of several plied yarns are present, as well as extremely fine yarns, perfect for use in high quality textiles. This is not surprising given the presence of the royal palace, which certainly required luxury textiles. One item appears to bear traces of a blue pigment, while in all other cases colour is not visible. Most of the objects are worn, but some are better preserved, even better than the examples from Lahun.

One of the most interesting objects is 500.a. This is a ball of unspun fibres, which is very well prepared and is in the stage of production that comes immediately before spinning. In fact, it is possible to clearly see that the fibres are attached together by splicing and plying, as is perfectly explained by H. Granger-Taylor (Cartwright *et al.* 1998, 103–4), but not yet spun.

5.2.10 Other tools connected with textile production

Other objects found at Gurob might be linked to textile production. In the Manchester collection, a flax stripper or weaving comb is present. Although this appears similar to other examples from the Roman and Byzantine periods, it may belong to the New Kingdom and be an antecedent of the much more common objects of a later date.

One netting needle is stored in the Petrie Museum. Even if it is not directly connected to the production of textiles, it is worth recalling that net production shared many tools and techniques with textile production.

Two warp spacers (one in Manchester, the other in the Petrie Museum collection) listed in the catalogue certainly belong to looms, although there should be five in total (Kemp and Vogelsang-Eastwood 2001, 339–41). They were used to keep the warp in tension and the yarns parallel, as shown in the newly discovered tomb by the Djehuty project (Rodríguez Frade 2019).

Two weaver's slays or beaters from Gurob are stored in the Petrie Museum (UC 7808 and UC 7824). They were probably inserted between the warp threads to beat the weft. One is broken into three pieces and preserves traces of wear due to rubbing by threads. The other is only partially preserved, and may have had a similar function.

Vertical looms were probably used in Gurob, as was the case for Amarna. In fact, a squared support for anchoring the heddle to the wall, very similar to those from Amarna (Kemp and Vogelsang-Eastwood 2001, 348–51) was also found. However, no limestone supports are known.

5.2.11 Conclusions: textile tools in Gurob

Gurob is a key site to study textile production in Ancient Egypt, and no longer having the chance to study the primary contexts of where the tools were found is a great loss. In fact, it prevents a full understanding of the *chaîne opératoire* of the textile activity. Were spinning and weaving performed in the same places, as seen in Middle Kingdom funerary models, or were homespun threads brought to weaving workshops? Which types of tools were used by the palace, in the industrial area, and in the houses of the common people? Were they at all different? Unfortunately, we will never be able to answer these questions for the items excavated by Petrie, although new excavations may shed light on some of these aspects.

Spindles from Gurob share some aspects with similar items from Lahun, Deir el-Medina, and Amarna, but at the same time they diverge significantly. As in Lahun, two lengths of spindles were probably in use, one measuring almost 25 cm, the other longer than 30 cm. Most of the items show a groove or a short notch at the end where fibres were secured, and the other end is generally pointed. The shafts are not decorated (while the pins are) and, differently from Lahun, can vary between a maximum diameter of 1 cm to a very thin shaft measuring only 0.4 cm in diameter. A similar picture can be seen also for spindle whorls. Most of the whorls are similar to those of Lahun, Amarna, and Deir el-Medina, namely cylindrical with a base larger than the height, but some are completely different. These have a conical/dome shape, are small and very light. The combination of small whorls with thin shafts creates extremely light spindles that would have been used to produce very fine and expensive threads, as is visible in the balls of yarns found at the site. Very few wooden spindle whorls show a mark incised on the surface, and they are not decorated. On the contrary, the few limestone spindle whorls show incised decoration on the surfaces, even if crudely made. All the whorls among the preserved examples are placed in the upper part of the spindle, near the groove.

Few spinning bowls, so far, are known from Gurob, which is certainly unexpected. At a site where texts indicate a strong textile production, we should expect to find dozens of spinning bowls, even if fragmentary. This might be dependent on problems of identification in older excavations (since the second season was led by Hughes-Hughes and not by Petrie), or it is even possible that textile production was practised at very high levels but not at an industrial scale (which would explain the small quantity of tools in general). Given the peculiar modern history of the site, and the heavy damage due to plundering, the military bunker, and erosion, a problem with the archaeological documentation is probably the most likely hypothesis.

Several nets were recovered from the site, and many net weights have been recognised. Since they are very small and light, lead weights are not considered of interest for this research.

As for Lahun, all the needles are made by piercing the shaft from one side to the other, and no examples of needles with the eye bent back on itself are known from the site.

Bone spatulae are quite numerous at Gurob and show different measurements, shapes, and traces of wear due to usage. The large sample of materials allows us to discern various different ways of using these simple tools, by exploiting only the point or by using the entire surface of the tool.

The general picture, which arises from this overview of tools, is quite contradictory. Spinning implements are not very numerous by comparison with other sites such as Deir el-Medina. We should remember, however, that this might depend on the choices of the excavator and the collections selected for this thesis. However, given the large quantity of fibres, balls of thread, bone spatulae, needles, and parts of looms found at the site, it appears that its vocation was more concerned with weaving and finishing textiles than preparing fibres and spinning. These two tasks were certainly performed on the site, as 500.a proves, but apparently were not well attested. This situation appears entirely opposite to the next site, Deir el-Medina.

5.3 Deir el-Medina

5.3.1 Introduction

The village of Deir el-Medina is located on the west bank opposite the modern town of Luxor, in a small desert valley behind the Qurnet Murai slope (Toivari-Viitala 2011, 1). The modern, Arabic, name means 'Monastery of the Town' due to the religious institutions that were located in the ruins of the Ptolemaic temple of Hathor. The village was established to house the workers (and their families) responsible for constructing the royal and princely tombs in the Valley of the Kings and, that of the Queens. It was probably founded by Thutmosis I at the beginning of the 18th Dynasty. The village is surrounded by an enclosure wall, which was first built by Thutmosis I, since his cartouche is stamped on the bricks of the wall. The village was rather small in this period, and only during the reign of Horemheb does it reach approximately 40 houses. Subsequently, more houses were added and a total of 68 houses could be found inside the enclosure, with more outside it, reaching its peak during the Ramesside period.

The Ramesside period is the best known as the great majority of materials and texts belong to the 19th and 20th Dynasties. It was abandoned during the reign of Ramses IX (1099–1069 BC), when the inhabitants sheltered in Medinet Habu and never reoccupied their houses.

Tombs of the inhabitants are located on both sides of the village, the western and eastern cemetery, while the northern part is occupied mainly by votive chapels and temples, and subsequently by the Hathor temple in the Ptolemaic period. Northeast of the temple enclosure is the so called 'Great Pit', a 52 m deep structure of uncertain function, which was used as a rubbish dump in two different phases of the village occupation.

Some remains of the village of Deir el-Medina have been known since the 18th century AD, but only at the beginning of the 19th century do objects collected from the village begin to form consistent collections, especially those of Bernardino Drovetti and Henri Salt (Toivari-Viitala 2011, 10).

The first systematic excavations were led by Ernesto Schiaparelli in 1905 and 1906, and continued briefly in 1909 and 1920, followed by short missions led by Émile Baraize and Georg Möller. The work was resumed by the French Archaeological Institute in Cairo in 1917, and from 1922 to 1951 excavations were directed by Bernard Bruyère (Toivari-Viitala 2011, 10). Works continued in the following years, but most work is now focused on study and conservation projects, under the IFAO direction.

The objects studied from Deir el-Medina come from the collection kept in the Museo Egizio in Turin, and are therefore related to Schiaparelli's excavations.[12] A few items from Georg Möller's excavations can be found at the Neues Museum. All the other items belong to B. Bruỳere excavations, located mostly on site, but also at the IFAO in Cairo and at the Louvre Museum.

Before discussing the objects, it seems useful to briefly introduce the textile tools exposed by Bruyère's excavations, as well as to mention the publications and excavation diaries, as for once these provide information on the contexts of the findings.

5.3.2 Tools from Bruyère's publications

Several tools linked to textile production were excavated by Bernard Bruyère, and in one of his cahiers,[13] he listed textile tools among the works he aimed to publish. Unfortunately, this work never saw the light of day. In his excavation report, textile tools occur rather seldom, despite the large quantity that seems to have been recovered (translated from French by the author):

Pit 1109, 18th Dynasty

> A wooden disc, 0.05 m in diameter and 0.012 m thick, with a round hole in the centre of 0.01 m in diameter. One side of this disc is engraved with a mark, and the other side is coated with mud. This object appears to have been used as part of a tool, possibly a plumb line, by a scribe or a mason (Bruyère 1928, 98).

Excavations in the south-west part of the village

WOODEN OBJECTS

> Bird traps, spindle whorls, shuttles, counterweights for weaving; tool handles for chisels, bronze blades, punches; spatulae and spoons for mixing colours; pegs, box buttons, locks, and latches (Bruyère 1933, 6).

STONE OBJECTS

> Weights, small buckets, plumb lines, spindle whorls and spinning counterweights, marbles, and flint nodules marked with a point (Bruyère 1933, 7).

Work organisation in the village

> The female population, in addition to household chores, also engaged in the spinning and weaving of linen, as evidenced by the fragments of looms, moistening tools (spinning bowls?), spindle whorls, tension counterweights, carding combs, anchoring stakes, bronze needles, and spools of thread that we have found in large quantities. Most of these tools and instruments bear engraved marks that are signs of ownership (Bruyère 1939, 7).

Objects found in the village

> For weaving and spinning, tasks carried out by women, numerous spindle whorls have been found, with half-spherical heads made of limestone or ivory, or cylindrical flat shapes made of wood. Many of these are marked. Wooden shuttles, stone or terracotta tension weights shaped like dates or olives, pierced lengthwise by a hole through which the thread is passed; carding or weaving combs, terracotta spinning cups with handles (ranging from one to four) where the thread is attached, are also found in great numbers, along with black ceramic disc-shaped spools, weaving counterweights, and skeins of linen and palm fibres (Bruyère 1939, 214–15).

> House N.E.V: Wooden spindle whorls, hank of flax (Bruyère 1939, 250).

> In 1922 excavations, in the area of the last five houses of the northwest quarter and of the first three houses of the southeast quarter, several objects were found. Among these items some spinning bowls with two or three loops attached to the bottom were excavated (Bruyère 1939, 262).

> House S.E.IX: several objects among which are spindle whorls (Bruyère 1939, 278).

Tools found in the dumps around the village

> The considerable number of spindle whorls reveals a highly developed spinning and weaving industry among the women. The most common type of spindle whorl is composed of: 1) a cylindrical disc of soft wood (rarely truncated conical, sometimes flattened hemispherical), cut from a round tree branch, with a diameter of 0.04 m to 0.06 m; a thickness of 0.01 m to 0.02 m; the upper surface of this disc is coated with a layer of mud, and the lower surface is sometimes engraved with a mark of ownership (many of these marks are also found on pottery and tools); 2) a rod of soft, light wood, 0.30 m to 0.35 m long, round and 0.07 m to 0.13 m in diameter, tapered to a point at the lower end, rounded and carved with a helical groove for the passage of the thread at the upper end, which extends 0.02 m to 0.04 m above the disc. The groove makes a complete spiral turn in a clockwise direction from bottom to top; it starts at the disc and ends at the centre of the upper end. Often, a fine linen thread is wrapped around the rod against the underside of the disc to prevent it from slipping; another binding, tightened with a small twig, is sometimes placed above the disc. Some hemispherical discs made of hard wood and stone are decorated with flower petals. (Bruyère 1939, 345).

Excavations 1946–1947, findings: two wooden discs of spindle whorl and a wooden shuttle (Bruyere 1952, 69).

Excavations of the 'Great Pit': among the findings are wooden spindle whorls, weaving shuttles and other objects (Bruyère 1953, 66).

Objects found on the hill of dump

Bronze: two sewing needles. Length: 0.10 m.

Spinning and weaving: numerous wooden spindle whorls, shuttles, spools of linen thread and skeins of linen, conical limestone counterweights with grooves for attaching the thread, black earthenware discs of varying diameters (0.01 m to 0.04 m) and 0.15 m thick with grooves, likely used for spinning. Terracotta tensioners (Bruyère 1953, 83).

Objects found north of the chapel of the Amon Ra temple: a cylindrical, wooden spindle whorl with a mark, diameter 5.5 cm; weaving shuttles (Bruyère 1953, 88–9).

Bruyère thus found a very large quantity of textile tools, most of them spindles and spindle whorls made of wood, but also bone and stone examples. Furthermore, he found several spinning bowls, providing another interesting component to our knowledge of textile production in the village. Other objects are more difficult to understand, such as weaving shuttles, and are therefore excluded from this study. Another very interesting feature is that spinning and weaving tools (except needles) never occur in tombs, whether in the eastern cemetery (which is less rich) or the northern or western parts (Bruyère and Jourdain 1937a, 59).

Finally, he found several objects linked to textile production pertaining to the Coptic period of occupation of the site (Bruyère 1948, 48, 92, 118). Therefore, it should always be kept in mind that tools without a secure context of findings need to be more securely dated than what has been done so far, which is based on typological developments.

5.3.3 Tools from the Schiaparelli excavations

Several textile tools are stored in the collection of the Museo Egizio, Turin, and these belong to Schiaparelli's excavations in Deir el-Medina.[14] Unfortunately, Schiaparelli did not record the precise location of each finding. He certainly found them in his excavations of 1905, 1906, and 1920, but the only information available in the Manuscript Inventory is 'one spindle case', without further indication. However, in the inventory, spindles and whorls appear in the list of objects from the *kom*, a sort of rubbish hill on the southern outskirts of the village where he worked in 1906 (Del Vesco and Poole 2018, 108). Probably the only spindles that came from the houses of the village are those listed as S. 9978, found by Schiaparelli in 1909, which is when he continued the excavation of the village.

A further problem with these materials is the lack of a reliable chronology. The Deir el-Medina Worker Village was occupied for a very long period, since it was built under Pharaoh Amenhotep I or Thutmose I and was abandoned during the 20th Dynasty. Moreover, it was once again inhabited during the Ptolemaic age, when Ptolemy IV built a temple there, and was reused during the Coptic Period. Some of the objects under study could, therefore, belong to periods later than the New Kingdom. The typologies of spindles and spindle whorls point to a production in the Pharaonic period, although changes in shapes and materials over time are not reliable parameters of chronology. Three objects were sampled, and ^{14}C analysis was carried out. These tests were made on spindles and spindle whorls from different seasons of the Schiaparelli excavations at Deir el-Medina, in order to arrive at a more certain date for these objects.

The results have provided a wide chronological range, spanning from the New Kingdom and the beginning of the Third Intermediate Period (1400–1000 BC), confirming the initial theory.[15]

5.3.4 Spindles

Schiaparelli brought to Turin from the Deir el-Medina excavations 147 spindles with spindle whorls attached to the shaft, and two spindles without whorls. Only a few objects were complete, five out of the total (S. 07526/074, 07526/108, 09978/7, 09978/3bis, 09978/5bis) and two are nearly complete (S. 07526/027 and 07526/047). To these, another 158 spindles (82 without whorl) from B. Bruyére are still on site, while three are in the Louvre Museum, and 12 are at the IFAO in Cairo. Of these, only one in the Louvre collection is complete. Another complete example was excavated by G. Möller, giving a total of 321 spindles (Fig. 5.13).

Most of the spindles have one or both ends broken, and several have preserved only a few centimetres inside the spindle whorl hole. Complete and nearly complete examples show that these measure between 20 and 30 cm, but can occasionally reach up to 40 cm. The diameters can vary between 0.5 and 1.2 cm, but most of the rods have a diameter between 0.8 and 1 cm, with an average value of 0.9 cm. The shape of the rod is not cylindrical, but tends to taper towards the lower end.

As seen for Lahun and Gurob, two types of spindles must have existed: a longer type, which measured between 30 and 40 cm, and a shorter one, which measured between 20 and 25 cm. The weight and length differences certainly affected the final product and enabled them to produce different qualities of thread (Table 5.3).

Generally, spindles have a flat or rounded top, with an incision to fasten the thread. Both types with a spiral groove or a simple notch are represented (S. 07526/74 and S.

Figure 5.13. Complete spindles from Deir el-Medina (S. 9978-4 bis and S. 07526-74) (courtesy of Museo Egizio)

Table 5.3. Complete spindles from Deir el-Medina

Number	*Length (cm)*	*Diameter (cm)*	*Weight (g)*
ME S. 07526/74	22	1	18 (spindle + whorl)
ME S. 07526/108	21.1	1.1	19 (spindle + whorl)
ME S. 09978/7	35.8	1.2	27 (spindle + whorl)
ME S. 09978/3 bis	32.4	1.1	37 (spindle + 2 whorls)
ME S. 09978/5 bis	37.2	1.1	31 (spindle + 2 whorls)
Louvre E 16541	34.4	0.9	22 (spindle + whorl)
ÄM 23904	36	1.1	28 (spindle + whorl)

07526/97), but the spiral notch is certainly the most common on site. Almost all the preserved items taper towards the other end, except for one example, S. 07526/23, which has a broad, rounded point (Fig. 5.16).

When a spindle whorl is present, it is always placed immediately below the groove, proving that only high-whorl spinning was performed.

In some cases, thread is still attached to the shaft and it is possible to observe the method of fastening (Plate 14). A first coil of thread is wound around the top of the shaft, and a small wooden peg is placed on it. Then, the thread is passed over the peg and the shaft and around the peg to throttle the binding. After this process is completed, spinning can begin.

Other spindles preserve coils of thread without the peg and traces of fibres, where it is not possible to distinguish individual threads. In some cases only partial imprints of fibres have been preserved. In the following list, some remarks on spindles with recognisable threads are given:

- S. 07526/001 – At least two different threads preserved, one s-twisted and the other z-twisted.
- S. 07526/027 – One thread preserved in the spindle whorl hole, S-plied.
- S. 07526/032 – The spun yarn is preserved under the spindle whorl wrapped around the spindle shaft, it is S-plied, while the single twist is not visible. There are also some unspun fibres.
- S. 07526/033 – On the upper part of the shaft a thread that attaches a wooden rod is preserved; the threads present are probably plied but this is not certain. It has a final Z-twist and its single twist is not visible.
- S. 07526/034 – On the upper part of the shaft, under the spindle whorl, a doubled thread with an s-twist is preserved; the single twist is not visible.
- S. 07526/035 – The upper edge of the spindle is broken, although this was likely also the case in ancient times because the fibres are wrapped around the broken part; a thread that attaches a wooden rod is preserved. The fibres are characterised by an S-plied yarn, but the single twist is not visible. The thread itself is rather encrusted and is partially inserted into the spindle whorl hole.
- S. 07526/039 – A couple coils of yarn are preserved under the spindle whorl, but the fibres do not appear to have been twisted or spun.
- S. 07526/099 – Threads inserted into the spindle whorl hole and preserved on the spindle shaft. The thread appears S-plied.
- S. 09978/1 – S-plied threads are attached under the wedge rod which fixes the spindle whorl.
- DeM_2024_M23_0312 – Thread wound around the shaft on the lower side of the spindle whorl. It is S, 2*i.
- DeM_2024_M23_0314 – Unspun fibres attached to the top of the spindle, partially covered by the encrustation that also covers the spindle whorl.
- DeM_2024_M23_0325 – Thread wound around the upper part of the shaft, quite loose. It is tightly twisted in S-direction.

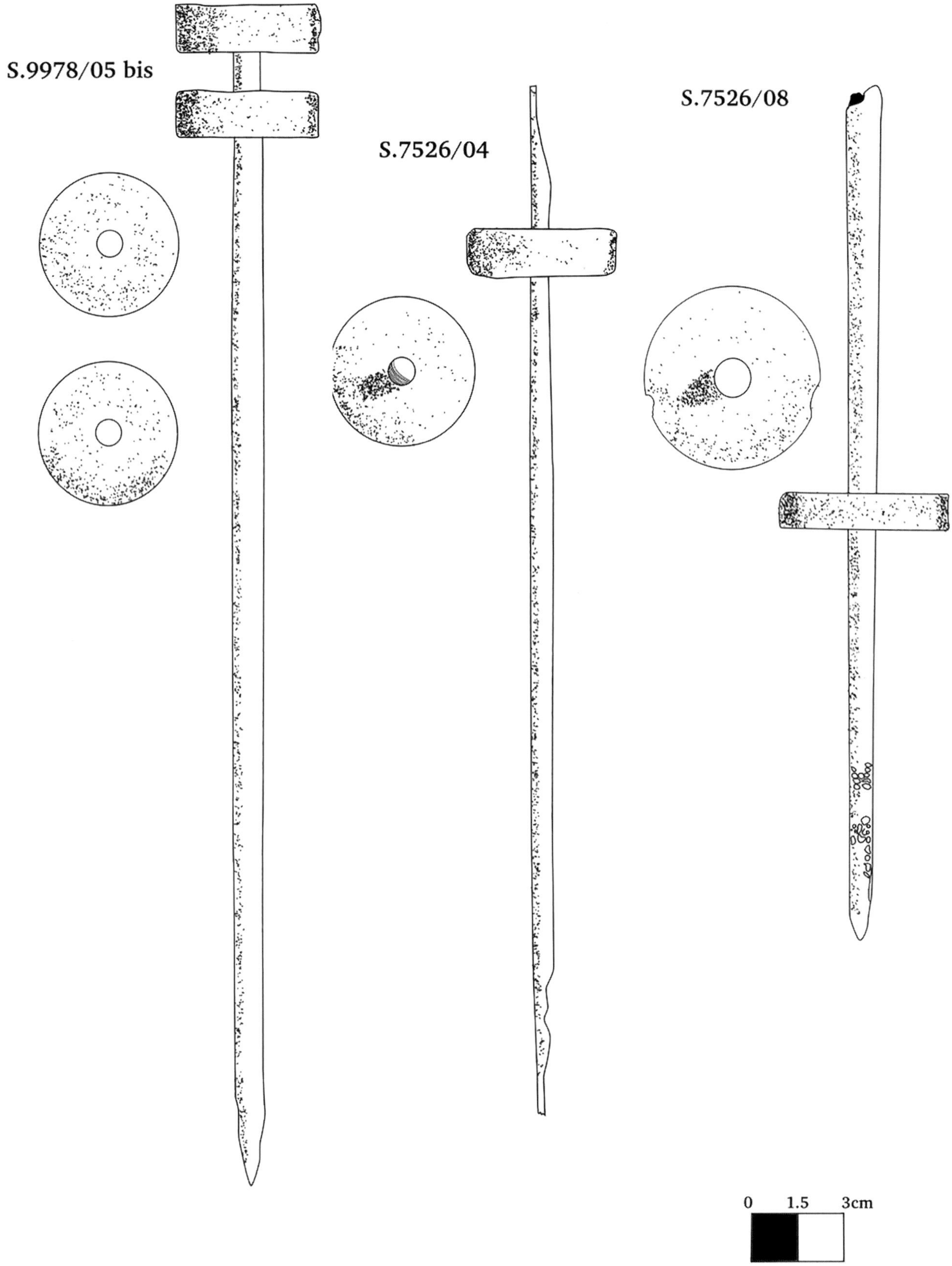

Figure 5.14. Deir el-Medina spindles

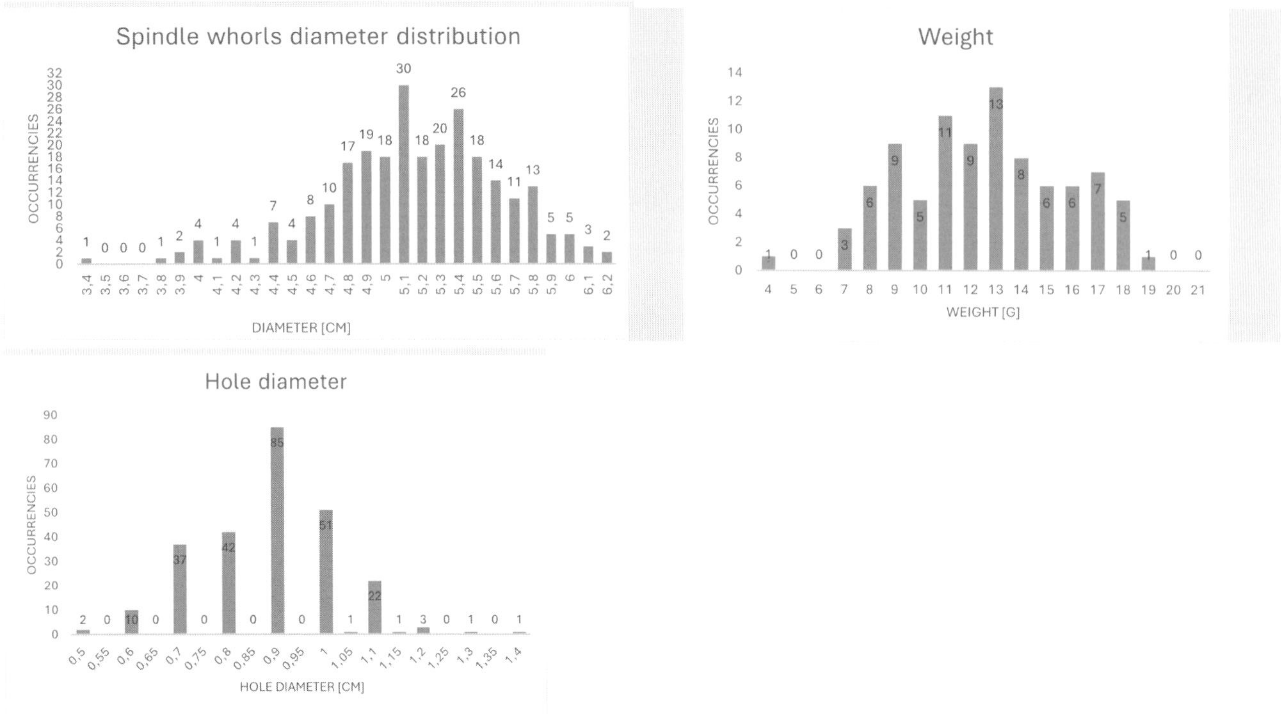

Figure 5.15. Plots of Deir el-Medina spindle whorls

- DeM_2024_M23_0327 – Unspun fibres attached to the top of the spindle, used for fastening a small peg.
- DeM_2024_M23_0328 – Unspun fibres attached to the top of the spindle, used for fastening a small peg. In the middle a loosely plied yarn is also visible, it seems S, 2z. Splicing can only be hypothesised, as it is not visible.
- DeM_2024_M23_0329 - Unspun fibres attached to the top of the spindle, over the spiral groove.
- DeM_2024_M23_0365 – Spliced (?) fibres in s-direction, embedded in a thick layer of encrustation.
- DeM_2024_M23_0385 – Thick yarn in the middle of a shaft. S-twisted.
- DeM_2024_M23_0463 – Thread wound around the upper part of the shaft, and knotted around a wooden peg. Tightly twisted in s-direction and covered with encrustation.
- DeM_2024_M23_0467 – Thread wound around the shaft. Tightly plied in S-direction.
- DeM_2024_M23_0470 – Thread wound around the shaft, partially inside the hole of the spindle whorl. Highly degraded.
- DeM_2024_M23_1103 – Unspun fibres attached to the top of the spindle, over the spiral groove.
- DeM_2024_M23_1148 – Unspun fibres attached to the top of the spindle, used for fastening a small peg.
- DeM_2024_M23_1159 – Unspun fibres attached to the top of the spindle, used for fastening a small peg.
- DeM_2024_M23_1165 – Mix of unspun and twisted fibres in s-direction attached on top of the spindle and on the lower part of the spindle whorl.
- DeM_2024_M23_1220 – Unspun fibres attached to the top of the spindle, used for fastening a small peg.

In most cases, it is difficult to distinguish whether the thread has one or more plied yarns. In some cases, it is clearly evident that the thread is doubled and S-twisted, but in at least two cases a final Z-twist can be seen.

5.3.5 Spindle whorls

The spindle whorls at Deir el-Medina are quite homogenous in terms of their materials, shapes, and dimensions. All the spindle whorls in the Museo Egizio collection are made of wood. Bruyère's excavations, however, seem to have recovered examples of bone, ceramic, and stone spindle whorls, mostly with a dome shape (Bruyère 1939, 214–15). In any case, wood is certainly the primary source for producing whorls, as seen for the other Egyptian contexts. This choice is certain to be due to the availability of wood in the village, largely present in delivery records, and to technical reasons. Although wood is less durable than other materials, the possibility of creating relatively large whorls with a light weight makes it perfect for spinning flax.

In total, I was able to trace 1053 spindle whorls from Deir el-Medina, which should be connected to the New

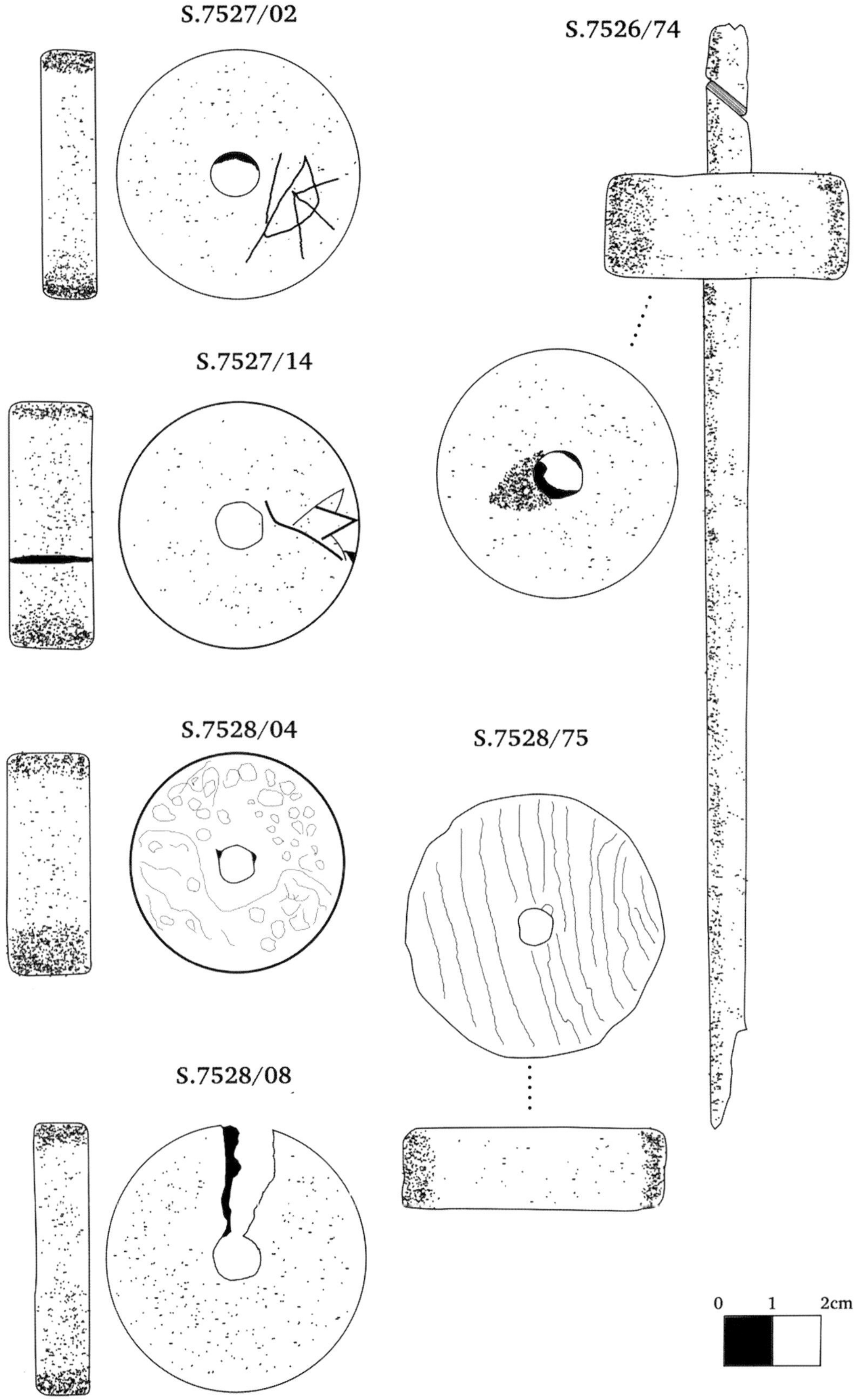

Figure 5.16. Deir el-Medina spindles and whorls

Figure 5.17. Complete spindle from Deir el-Medina (courtesy of the Louvre Museum, E.16542)

Kingdom village. This is by far the largest assemblage of spinning tools I am aware of. Not even Megiddo, a large mound with a millenary occupation, has provided a similar number of spindle whorls (Fig. 5.17).

Eight hundred and thirteen spindle whorls have a cylindrical shape, 12 are discoid, 85 are dome-shaped, four are lenticular, and 12 are perforated sherds. It is worth noting that a strict selection process was carried out, due to the limited period in which I have had access to the materials. Approximately 100 small, roughly rounded stone objects have been discarded, even though some of these may have been used for spinning. All the other objects were clearly well made and easily recognisable, while these stone discs varied a lot in terms of their diameter and characteristics.

Most of the dome-shaped whorls are made of stone, the typical local limestone. These are very large spindle whorls, similar to those found in Kahun and Gurob, and form a distinct category. Fifteen items were made of wood, and in one case a small whorl (1130) is similar to the smallest from Gurob. This is remarkable, as this typology was about one third of the total number of whorls from Gurob, while in Deir el-Medina the ratio is 15/1000.

5.3.5.1 Wooden spindle whorls

Unfortunately, it was not possible to record the entire dataset of spindle whorls, due to the limited access to the on-site storage rooms. The data here provided, are therefore calculated on the basis of those recorded. The spindle whorls have been counted, so the total number is correct. Those looking different from the bulk have been fully registered as well, so it is only part of the cylindrical wooden whorls that is lacking full measurements. The external diameters of the wooden spindle whorls can vary from a minimum of 3.9 cm to a maximum of 6.1 cm, with the majority between 4.9 cm and 5.6 cm in size.

The hole diameters vary between 0.3 and 1.4 cm, with the majority of the diameters ranging between 0.8 and 0.9 cm, as seen in the diagram. Most of the spindle whorls have wider hole diameters at their top and smaller at their bottom to better fit onto the shaft. This expedient does not seem to have been enough to ensure a tight fit, however, as in certain examples vegetable fibres and small pegs have been used as wedges between the whorl and the spindle, and are still present.

Similarly to the other sites, only the weight of complete spindle whorls is included, without the spindle shaft, although a weight is provided in the catalogue for all objects. Weights vary between 4 g and 19 g, with the average between 11 g and 14 g.

Some repairs and ancient restoration activities have been executed on certain spindle whorls, including S. 07527/07, in which a small wooden rod has been inserted to fill a lateral hole and DeM_2024_M23_1185 (Fig. 5.18). Some spindle whorls (S. 07528/066 and DeM_2024_M23_1108) were never completed and are without a central hole (Fig. 5.18). The surface has been polished, however, and some signs of preparation for the hole are visible.

A few spindle whorls are decorated by simple lines drawn with pinkish or black paint, such as S. 07526/109, while others present incised marks, similar to identity marks known from pottery and tools in the village (*e.g.* S. 07526/110, 111, 112, DeM_2024_M23_1100, 1211).[16] Generally, these marks are considered to be linked to the owner of the tool (Vogelsang-Eastwood 2000, 285), but they are known only for male activities and individuals. It would be interesting, in the future, to see if these marks might also have been used by the women of the village.

The painted decorations and incised marks are usually placed on one side, or on the edge of the spindle whorl. It is perhaps notable that these decorations are not placed on the upper side of the spindle whorl, where they would have been visible to the spinner, but rather on the lower side where the thread is wrapped. Whatever their function was, it seems that aesthetic value was not one of the main concerns.

Another typical feature of these whorls, also seen for Lahun materials, is the presence of a thick layer of encrustation on the spindle whorls, which seems absent from other objects from Deir el-Medina.

The encrustation is generally located on the upper part of the spindle rod and the upper surface of the spindle whorl, leaving the other face clean or covered by only a slight patina. In some cases, a very thin layer of a whitish

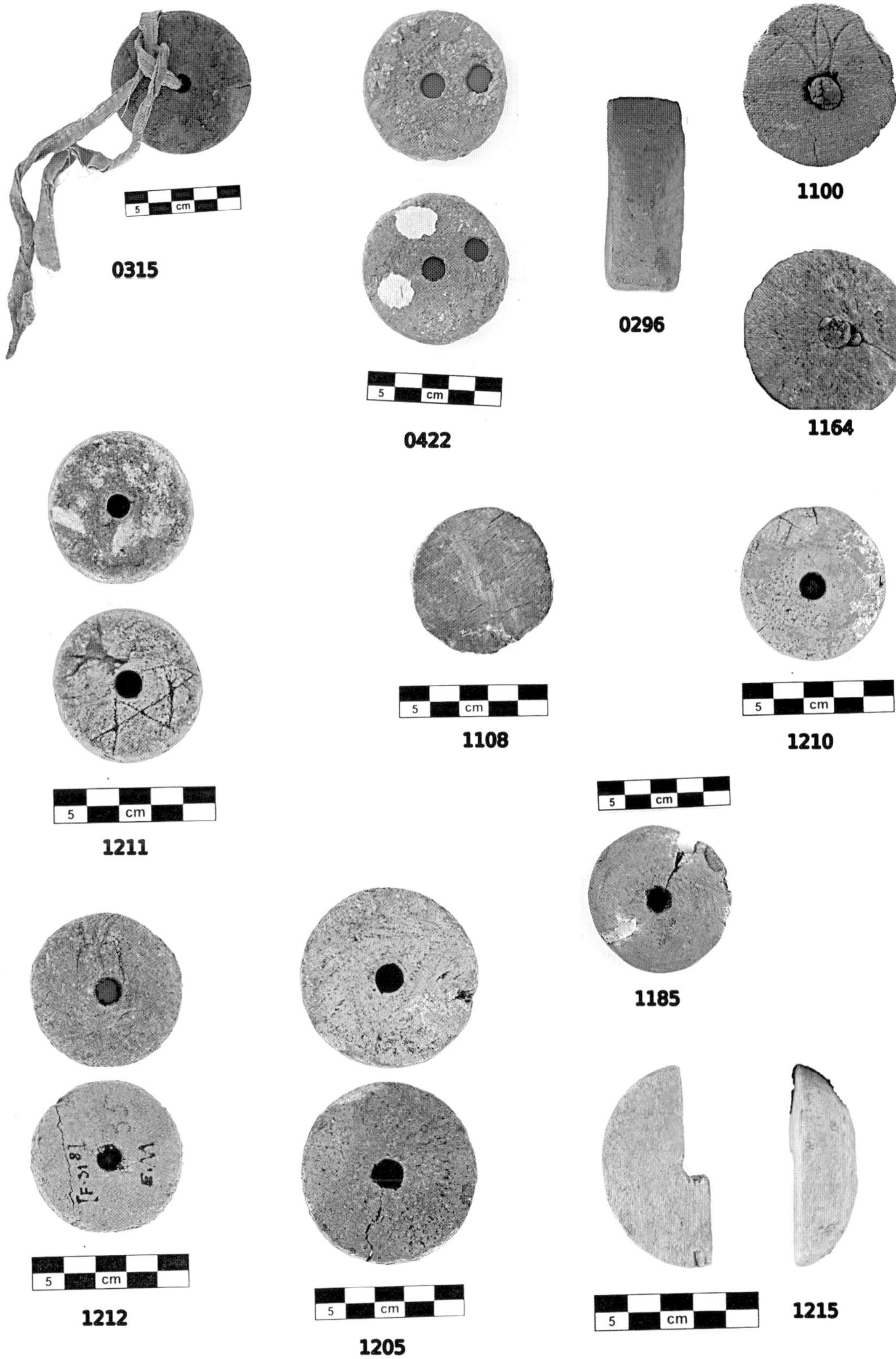

Figure 5.18. Wooden spindle whorls from Deir el-Medina (courtesy of IFAO)

substance is present on this encrustation, which does not seem to be paint or plaster. In one case, a small fragment of fabric is still attached to a spindle whorl (S. 07526/108), perhaps due to the long contact between the two items in the archaeological layer. The fragment measures 1.72 cm × 1.91 cm and is a tabby weave with a sett of 13 × 10 threads per cm^2 (a low quality fabric), with the thread S-twisted in both warp and weft.

Several whorls were left unfinished, with no perforation at all. They look similar to those that are perforated in terms of their measurements, choice of wood, and method of craftmanship and therefore can be considered as spindle whorls. Their presence is interesting, as it is a clear indication that at least part of the process of producing the whorls was done directly on site.

Another interesting feature is that some whorls have been reused for different purposes, and at times they present a double perforation. In one case a cylindrical notch was made along the base of the whorl, which could have accommodated a small peg. In another case, a whorl has been reused and a strip of fabric is fastened to it (probably part of a loincloth).

Finally, a unique spindle (DeM_2024_M23_1160) deserves special mention, as it presents a double spindle whorl, one made of wood and the other from basketry.

5.3.5.2 Stone and ceramic spindle whorls

Of the 1053 spindle whorls from Deir el-Medina, only 79 are made of stone. They have a dome shape, but 10 examples with a discoid shape are present as well (Plate 15). Their dimensions are quite big, with diameters that vary between 2.9 and 7.1 cm, while height can vary between 0.9 and 4.5 cm. Weight can vary between 5.6 to 145 g. As can be inferred already by these measures, there is a large variety of objects included in this category. However, the big dome-shaped whorls are by far the majority. Interestingly, most of them are not complete, with a quite important number broken in half (the second half was not found and could not be recomposed). They are considerably more damaged than the wooden or ceramic spindle whorls. One possible explanation might be that at least some of them have been reused as counterweights, as one case with a string still attached seems to indicate (DeM_2024_M23_0303).

Considering their weight, it is highly probable that most of these whorls were not employed to prepare yarns for weaving, but rather to ply yarns for fishing nets and strings. It will be interesting in the future to test all these typologies of spindle whorls and compare them with the preserved yarns.

These are made of local limestone, and are quite well polished. A few examples exhibit an incised decoration with a floral pattern. Identity marks are also present, and it would be interesting to compare them with those from the more common wooden spindle whorls, to see if there is some kind of specialisation among the workers or some chronological differences. In most cases, the stone whorls are broken, and this allows us to see the production marks inside the hole. The hole generally tapers towards the large base. Similarly to the other sites examined here, the wear traces are mostly around the upper part of the hole. The holes are slightly conical and their diameter varies, allowing the insertion of shaft similar to those attested for the wooden whorls. It is important to note that not a single shaft has been found in connection with the stone whorls.

Finally, a small group of ceramic spindle whorls and perforated sherds is also attested. There are only nine ceramic spindle whorls in total, and their shapes are in general quite flat, varying between discoid, cylindrical, and lenticular. Their dimensions and weights can vary considerably, as the smallest weighs only 12 g and the largest 88 g, and they approximately cover the entire range in between. They were certainly not made for a specific type of product. Perforated sherds, instead, count only 12 examples with a range between 8 and 49 g in weight, though are mostly clustered around light (8–10 g) or quite light (20–26 g) weights. Their rarity is remarkable, but there is a high possibility that this is due to the selection made by the excavator. Furthermore, naturally perforated pebbles are very common on site, and many of the non-documented tools might have acted as a local variation of perforated sherds.

Considering the other sites, it seems relevant to highlight the complete absence of bone spindle whorls during the New Kingdom, which saw the peak of bone use in the Levant as well as the military presence of Egyptians in the area. As seen before, Bruyère mentions them in his reports, but none of them was found in museums or on-site.

Needles

As seen for other sites, the category of needles includes both actual needles and bodkins. Some needles are stored in the Museo Egizio collection, and three in the Louvre Museum, but only some of these can certainly be attributed to Deir el-Medina. In total, 13 needles can be safely ascribed to the excavations at the site, but six of these come from the tomb of Kha. Ten needles are made of bronze, and three are made of wood.

There is no possibility to ascribe them with certainty to the New Kingdom, though it seems quite reasonable that most of them would belong to this phase. The thickness of the bronze needles can vary between 0.2 cm and 0.3 cm, while the maximum length preserved is 12 cm. Unfortunately, needles preserved in the two needle cases cannot be extracted and measured individually. They share a common feature of the technique of hole production, which has been carved out by punching the shaft from one side to the other. This action results in a hole that is rounded on one side, while the other has a typical ogival shape.

Two needle cases come from the tomb of Kha, with several bronze needles still inserted inside. One has two needles and a small razor, and one of the needles has a thread still preserved inside the hole. The thread is quite thick, closed by a knot and Z-cabled. A thread also closes the case, but is different from that of the needle, since it is s-spun, Z-cabled and finally S-plied. The second needle case has four needles inserted, all made of bronze and quite thin.

Three wooden bodkins are also part of the Deir el-Medina findings. All of them are thick, only partially polished and with a large, rounded hole carved into the large head. Two of them are not straight, but form an angle toward the middle of the shaft. One is straight and preserves a thread in the hole. The thread is very thick, s-spun, Z-cabled and finally S-plied.

Bone spatulae have not, so far, been identified on site.

5.3.6 Spinning bowls

Spinning bowls from Deir el-Medina are known from publications and 39 fragments were also found in a storage rooms during the last season of work on site. They will be studied in the future, as it was not possible to include them in this study.

5.3.7 Fibres

Similarly to the other Egyptian contexts, textiles are quite rare finds in the settlement of Deir el-Medina, but are more likely to have been preserved inside tombs. However, several examples of flax fibres and threads do come from the town. Several hanks of flax, skeins and balls of yarn are stored in the Museo Egizio collection, but only some of them can be ascribed with certainty to the Deir el-Medina excavations. The other objects are very likely to have been found at the site, but unfortunately some belong to the Drovetti collection, while for others the provenance has been lost, and therefore a provisional number have been assigned. In the catalogue, only items that were certainly found in Deir el-Medina are listed, and only these will be considered in the present study. Their belonging to the New Kingdom is far from certain, since they could easily have been produced in the Ptolemaic or Coptic period (given the presence of Coptic looms). For some of them, splicing can be detected, and they can therefore be assigned to a date preceding 600 BC.[17]

No unprocessed or partially processed hanks of flax belong to the materials ascribable to Deir el-Medina. Three skeins and five balls of threads of spun linen are listed in the catalogue.

In most of these cases the thread, single or plied, is S-twisted, but within one hank a thick thread has been found, perhaps not originally belonging to that hank, which shows a close Z-twist, which tends to coil in on itself. The threads range in diameter from 0.03 cm at their thinnest to 0.11 cm for the thickest (the Z twist thread just described). The twist angle, when preserved, has an average angle of 45°. A similar situation can be found for the balls of yarn, which are all well preserved, but vary in terms of their constitution. First, it must be noted that there is only one real ball of yarn (S. 7791) according to our modern standard, which is still perfectly preserved. It is not possible to distinguish the material it was wrapped around because of the large quantity of thread. The thread is strictly Z-twisted and splicing is evident. Some large knots are also present at the end of the thread, as well as some other knots inside the ball of yarn. The thread diameter is about 0.04 cm and its twist is between 35° and 40°. It is highly uniform and homogeneous and might be considered as a final product, even if it was only a medium quality thread, certainly not used for weaving fine clothes. The Z-twist might indicate that it would not have been used for weaving, but more likely for sewing, darning other textiles, or producing nets.

Another of the balls of yarn (S. 7788) is an interesting object, being a tow core, around which a small number of different threads have been wrapped. The threads are all S-twisted and the ply is rather evident (S, 2s). Some threads have a very close twist, while in others it is difficult to see it at all, probably because of the state of preservation. The other balls of yarn in the museum's collection present similar situations, with different threads wrapped around an object that seem to be, unlike the first two yarn balls discussed, a kind of makeshift solution, albeit one that is frequently used. The threads are, in fact, wrapped around a ceramic rim fragment (S. 7789), under which some rough fibres are positioned to avoid the thread becoming ruined by rubbing against the core, or around some stones (S. 7790, 7793). In all of these last three cases, the thread is Z twisted, with two or four cables; in one case it is possible to distinguish the Z-ply and an s-twist, and in at least one other case it is possible to distinguish the splicing point.

Lastly, a set of yarns have been wrapped around a circular stone (S. 7794), which was likely previously used as a stopper. The threads look different from each other, with two or three plies, with single s-spun and Z-plied yarns. Their diameter varies from 0.03 to 0.06 cm with small oscillations inside the same yarn, which can be followed only for small segments. The twist angle is varied and depends on the thread preservation conditions; it is attested as between 35° and 40° but also reaches 50° in this example, which is a very wide twist.

5.3.8 Textual references on textile activities

Deir el-Medina is a special context of study for Egyptologists, not only for the rich archaeological evidence of daily life, but mostly because of the impressive quantity of texts and documents that have been preserved. A large collection of papyri, ostraca and graffiti constitute an astonishing corpus to identify the social organisation of the village, the relationship with the state, and many other aspects of daily life. However, some features are not entirely clear, and textile production is certainly one of them.

A massive quantity of documents, mainly ostraca, deal with textiles, from lists of goods received as workers' wages (Grandet 2003, 44, n°866), to a list of personal goods (Grandet 2010, 111), a laundry list (Grandet 2017, 48), and transactions involving textiles (Grandet 2006, 73–5, n° 10071, 94, n°10091). From this type of text, it has been possible to understand the terminology of various types of textiles as well as their price, which is remarkable.[18]

However, who produced these textiles, when, where, for whom, and what the relationship was with those who received them as wages is less clear. Some texts can help to shed light on these aspects, even if not directly.

- The first is an ostracon (O. Cairo CG 25725 + O. IFAO 00137 + O. Louvre E 03259) dated to the end of the 19th and the beginning of the 20th Dynasty, where a father complains in front of the court about his daughter. He sent her a dress when she was ill and she never returned it. Instead, she sent him some vegetable plants, which he worked upon and then wove before giving them back to her.
- A second text (O. Nash 6 = O BM 65936) is a list of the items brought by a man to a woman to marry her, but he was refused twice. He complains that 'she did not even make a garment for his backside'. This must surely be understood in a metaphorical sense, but it is suggestive (Allam 1973, 222–3).
- Another text (O. DM 117) sees a woman asking her sister to send her a garment and prepare some plants (Wente 1990, 156 no. 228).
- A similar text (O. DM 132) sees a woman asking her sister to weave a garment for her (Allam 1973, 99–100).
- Another text (O. Brussels E 6311) features a man receiving yarn for weaving a garment, and with a second delivery of yarn he weaves seven garments (Allam 1973, 53–4).
- Another text (O. DM 131) concerns a list of items given to a man and the objects given in return. Among these, the second man has woven and prepared some textiles (Allam 1973, 99).
- A legal dispute (O. Leipzig 03) before the court for the production and payment of some textiles. Here, textiles are produced by women, and this seems to occur within a weaving shop (Allam 1973, 200).
- Finally, the famous papyrus of Paneb misconduct must be recalled, since he forced the wives of some workmen to weave clothes for him (Černý 1929; Allam 1973, 281–7).

5.3.9 Conclusions: textile tools in Deir el-Medina

Textile tools from Deir el-Medina represent an interesting corpus for studying textile production in the New Kingdom, and the lack of precise context for the findings is particularly regrettable considering the importance of the site. Several wooden spindles and spindle whorls have been preserved by the dry climate of the area, which show a great homogeneity. In fact, the spindles are characterised by a cylindrical shape tapering to one point and a spiral groove near the other tip. Two different lengths of shafts can be identified: a longer one, between 30 and 40 cm, and a smaller one between 20 and 25 cm. No further decoration is present. Almost all the spindle whorls studied here are made of wood and have a cylindrical shape. They have quite a large diameter, mostly between 4.9 and 5.6 cm in size, with an average weight between 11 and 14 g, which allows a fine to medium textile production. The holes are generally warped by the insertion of wooden wedges, as seen on some examples still preserved. Some of these show incised marks on the surface. No bone or stone spindle whorls were found in the Museo Egizio, but they have been recorded from Bruyère's excavations. Needles are very homogeneous in terms of their materials and typology, with the eye pierced through the shaft. No examples of an eye made by bending the upper part of the shaft back on itself, as known in the Levant, were present, although an example is stored in the museum (of unknown provenance). Fibres found by Schiaparelli are all of plant origin, although some texts also preserve a (rare) indication of the presence of wool (Janssen 1975, 292, 443). Interestingly, these appear to be quite rough in quality, suitable for making nets and coarse darning but not for weaving. It must therefore be considered that some of the tools studied here might have been used to produce nets rather than actual textiles, and making nets appears to have been an exclusively male activity.

All the textile tools seem to come from the village, except for the bronze needles, which were found in the tombs.

The tools found by Bruyère seem to confirm the picture that emerges from the analysis of the tools found by Schiaparelli. The spindles are generally long shafts with a groove for the yarn, have a cylindrical spindle whorl, although bone and stone dome-shaped whorls are also known. However, Schiaparelli did not find – or failed to collect – the spinning bowls, which were instead found by Bruyère.

As seen above, three examples of spindles have undergone radiocarbon dating, and the results confirm a New Kingdom date for the sample from the village (S. 9978 from Schiaparelli's Inventory). A slightly later date was provided for the two other samples from the kôm (S. 07528 from Schiaparelli's Inventory). These two contexts were certainly not contemporary, as the results do not show any possible overlap. This means that the spinning activities in evidence at Deir el-Medina were spread over most of the period when the site was in use. However, the number of spindles and spindle whorls recovered, 1362, is astonishing even considering the length of time during which they were produced (especially if compared with Lahun and Gurob). It seems from this data that spinning was a prevalent activity in the village; such a large number of spinning tools would usually be expected from workshops or other areas devoted to thread production, rather than villages. Furthermore, they show a very high degree of homogeneity, both in shapes and in measurements, which seems to point to a certain standardisation of the tools, and thus of the final product. Finally, the presence of unfinished spindle whorls suggests that they were produced in the village, probably by the woodcutters known from the textual sources, given the quality of their manufacture. Wood was locally available in great quantity, even the precious cedar, thanks to frequent deliveries, and obtaining small tools such as spindles and spindle whorls from leftover pieces was probably not an issue.

If we consider the textual evidence from Deir el-Medina, it becomes clear that workers were compensated with textiles and clothing (but not raw fibres), meaning they did not need to produce all the textiles themselves. Additionally, the few texts that discuss textile production suggest it was primarily a domestic activity, generally carried out by women, though some men were also involved. However, the textual sources do not align with the archaeological evidence. The frequent discovery of spinning tools, their high quality and homogeneity all suggest large-scale production by skilled 'craftspeople' who required standardised tools.

One possible explanation for this discrepancy is the widespread use of textiles as a form of payment. Textiles were in high demand, and those included in wages were likely insufficient to meet the needs of the village population. As a result, many, if not all the families processed fibres and produced yarns, which could be used for weaving textiles or making nets. It remains unclear, however, whether weaving was a common activity or if only some families owned looms. In at least one instance, a text refers to a specific place where textiles were woven.

In any case, the surplus yarn and textiles that families were able to produce could provide significant income, in addition to the wages earned from working on the royal tombs. Given the number of tools found at the site, it is plausible that some families participated in a cottage industry, producing yarn for large production centres like temples or palaces, at least during certain phases of the New Kingdom, even though this is not documented in the texts.

Moreover, the textual sources entirely omit any mention of transactions for acquiring textile tools, from spindles to looms or their parts, as well as raw fibres. While the texts from Deir el-Medina offer valuable insights into the organisation of the village, they do not provide clear information about the organisation, scope, or scale of textile production. In this case, archaeological evidence is crucial for understanding the significance of textile (or yarn) production at the site.

5.4 Case studies and the Egyptian development of textile tools

5.4.1 Spindles

Spindles in Ancient Egypt were almost exclusively made of wood, and for this reason they have almost always been preserved in worker villages. Despite the peculiar nature of these worker settlements, which only partially reflect the organisation of the actual Egyptian town, they nonetheless offer some interesting clues as to how spindles were made, enabling us to see certain elements of continuity, as well as some quite distinctive elements.

One exception is represented by the Old Kingdom settlement of Elephantine, where a spindle whorl with a fragment of the shaft still present has been preserved. Interestingly, the shaft is made from a different wood than the whorl (Kopp 2018, 73). Another shaft, without a whorl but with a notch at the top, was probably also a spindle (Kopp 2018, 99, abb. 42).

All the preserved examples of spindle shafts are made of wood – ivory, bone, and metal rods do not seem to have been used for spinning. Almost all the shafts are slender with one end pointed, the other flat or rounded but slightly thicker; the widest point is around one third of the entire length. In some cases, this thickening is not present, and this influences the shape of the spindle whorls' hole. At the top of the spindle, a groove for fastening fibres was cut. Not all examples show it, but the great majority shows its broad usage. Two types of groove are known: one short, simple notch near the broadest end of the spindle; and a long, deep, spiral groove, which covers a large portion of the upper part of the shaft. In some cases, this groove can make a complete turn around the shaft and can measure 4–5 cm. In other cases, only a quarter or half of a round is incised, with a length of 2 cm.

Spindle shafts can differ a great deal in their length and thickness, even for objects from the same site. The longest complete spindle from Lahun measures 38.3 cm, from Deir el-Medina 37.2 cm, and from Gurob 33.4 cm. Several examples, of identical shape, measure between 20 and 25 cm (Fig. 5.17). Three different types of shaft are therefore distinguishable: the first has a fairly large diameter and a length between 20 and 25 cm; the second has the same diameter as the first but is much longer, from 30 to 40 cm; the third is entirely different and is characterised by a very thin shaft and, generally, a small notch incised rather than the cylindrical groove. Shafts are on the short side, generally from 20 to 25 cm, but a couple of (almost complete) examples measure only 16 cm.

The diameters can vary a great deal, from 0.77 to 1.4 cm in Lahun (measuring the thickest point of the shaft), 0.4 to

1 cm in Gurob, and 0.5 to 1.2 cm in Deir el-Medina. The third type of shaft is known only in Gurob, and the thinnest shafts have an average diameter of 3 mm; only at some points do they reach 4 mm, in stark contrast to the other two types.

Gurob presents the largest variability of shafts, with all three types present, while the other sites have only the first and second. Shafts are generally preserved with the spindle whorl still attached (and it was not possible to remove it), so it is not possible to provide their exact weight.

Few examples of spindles are known from Lisht North, mostly from the New Kingdom settlement. They have not been published with their measurements, and the only available data are those present in the Metropolitan Museum online catalogue. Similar to examples from Lahun, Amarna, and Deir el-Medina, they present a wooden shaft tapering towards one end and a groove for fastening fibres to the other. The extremely thin shaft seen in Gurob appears not to be present.

Spindles have almost never been found in Ancient Egyptian tombs. In fact, Egyptians brought with them large sets of objects pertaining to daily life, from food to textiles and writing sets, but spindles are not among them. A couple of exceptions can be found in Lahun (Quirke 2005, 115) and Gurob (Brunton and Engelbach 1927, fig. XIII.8), where a number of spindles were placed inside graves. In the case of Gurob, the example is quite famous due to the fact that it was interpreted as evidence of the presence of foreigners (Barber 1991, 64). In Deir el-Medina, meanwhile, despite the impressive number of textile tools recovered, none are from tombs. Even those of the eastern necropolis (Bruyère and Jourdain 1937b, 63), which belonged to people less wealthy than the western necropolis and where a large number of women were interred, did not contain any spindle or whorl. This fact is very interesting since it seems that spindles never gained a symbolic meaning, whether for the afterlife or to represent the female sphere, in contrast to other cultures. In the Greek and Roman world, in fact, women are frequently represented while spinning and weaving, and spindles become symbols of femininity and of their domestic role (Cottica 2007). A similar situation is also known for the Hittite and Syro-Hittite area, where spindles appear in rituals as symbols of femininity (Haas 1994, 364–5) as well as in funerary monuments (Cecchini 1992, 12; Bonatz 2000, C33, C51, C60–62, C68). In Egypt, however, both women and men are represented while spinning and weaving, suggesting why they were not just associated with the feminine. Spindles can appear in funerary paintings and models but only in the context of representations of daily life activities, likely performed by servants rather than the lady of the house. An Egyptian Penelope, represented in literature and art while working on textiles, would have been inconceivable. There is one Egyptian representation that shows a lady with a spindle: Dirpu, Chantress of Amun during the 21st Dynasty, is represented in a funerary papyrus while holding a spindle in her hand (Bruyère 1939, 230, fig. 120). However, the spindle may be represented here due to its significance in repelling evil forces, as is shown in the hieroglyphic writing; it should thus be interpreted for its phonetic rather than ideographic value.

5.4.2 Spindle whorls

Spindle whorls are known in Egypt from at least the Neolithic period, with a spherical limestone spindle whorl known from the excavations of the Fayyum (Caton-Thompson and Gardner 1934, 40, pl. XII:5). It is interesting to note that in early periods, wooden spindle whorls are rarely used or preserved. In fact, despite some whorls being found in graves (where they had a better chance of being preserved), very few examples of this wooden implement have been found. Stone spindle whorls are, instead, very common. The predominant material seems to be limestone, and spherical shapes are preferred. However, a large number of perforated pottery sherds are also present (see the next section). Unfortunately, the objects that have been studied for this book were fragmentary and no weights can be ascertained. However, their large diameter and quite considerable thickness point to heavy tools to produce thick yarns (which would be perfectly in line with textile fragments known from this period) (Jones 2008, 107).

Early whorls

The Badarian and Predynastic periods cover more than a millennium of history, and it would be very interesting to investigate how spindle whorls changed over this extremely long period, especially considering the impressive changes evident in the textile remains. Unfortunately, very few spindle whorls have been published; when they are, it is very rare that information about measurements and shapes is provided. It is not possible, therefore, to pinpoint specific trends of development over time, or even differences from Upper and Lower Egypt at the same time. Hopefully, if future publications begin to eventually publish mundane materials, a clearer pattern of development will be available.

Maadi represents a virtuous exception, since a great deal of useful information is present in the publications (Hartung *et al.* 2003, 189, abb. 19; Bajeot 2017, 317). An extremely large number of stone spindle whorls were identified in the settlement, although no specimens were found in tombs (Rizkana and Seeher 1988, 52). Three hundred and fourteen objects are outlined in the publication, 299 made of limestone and 15 of basalt, although this last category is very likely to be the so-called 'basalt rings' and will be investigated separately. Several whorls are described as having part of the wooden shaft (burnt or unburnt) still placed in the hole (Rizkana and Seeher 1988, 52, pl. 96). One of these shafts still had plant fibres wound around it, which were used as padding to improve the cohesion of the shaft in the hole

(Rizkana and Seeher 1988, 108). Limestone whorls present a quite rough surface with parallel traces of scratching, likely indications of the manufacture and polishing of the surface. The perforation is hourglass, started from both sides and leaving the hole slightly irregular, with the striation of the drilling still visible in many examples. The diameter of the perforation varies between 0.5 to 1 cm, and weights can vary between 30 to 70 g, pointing to a medium-low quality of yarn production. Different shapes of whorls are present, from discoid or cylindrical examples to dome-shaped and spherical. Conical whorls seem not to be very common, since only eight objects are known (Rizkana and Seeher 1988, 52). Finally, surface decorations might appear in the form of painted rows of dots (although distinct to those of the mace-head models) and incised lines.

In Hammamiah, spindle whorls are very rare in Badarian contexts, but they start to appear more frequently in Predynastic contexts (Brunton and Caton-Thompson 1928, 97–101, 103–4, 106–7, 109–11, pl. LXX, LXXII), although a breccia spindle whorl from grave 5152 should be highlighted. For Maadi, they are made of limestone and have dome or spherical shapes, although cylindrical objects are also known. Even in this case, they come from settlements, not from tombs. Those available for study and listed in the catalogue generally have a diameter of 3.5 cm and a height of 2.5 cm, on average. Most of the items were only partially preserved, but those that are complete have a fairly light weight, from 21.9 g to 31 g. An exception is represented by a completely different object, a ball of unbaked or roughly baked clay with a very warped hole (7623). It is slightly larger and heavier than the whorls.

Few spindle whorls are known from Naqada, whether from graves or settlements. In this case, they are also described as rounded and made of white limestone, though one spindle whorl from a grave was made of pink and white limestone (Petrie *et al.* 1896, 26, 54). Those available for study show several examples of spherical, conical, and dome-shaped whorls, but there is much more variety in their materials. Although limestone is the prevalent material for whorls, it is not the only one. Some examples of chalk whorls are present, as well as one bone, one pottery, and one wooden whorl. The spherical shape is not the most common, but dome spindle whorls are much more frequent. A few examples of conical whorls are also present. The dimensions are very similar to those of Hammamiah, with an average diameter of 3.6 cm and a height of 2.7 cm, but are slightly heavier, from 28 g to 50 g. The bone whorl has a much lighter weight, at 9.5 g. One of the objects (4543) has a hole that is not straight, and at a certain point forms an angle, which prevents using it as a spindle whorl.

Predynastic spindle whorls were also found in the Ballas settlement (Petrie *et al.* 1896, 2, 14) and in graves (Podzorski 1994, 441). All the specimens listed in the catalogue are made of limestone and have similar shapes to those of other Predynastic sites: spherical, cylindrical, and domed. The dimensions are slightly more varied, since the diameters range between 2.7 and 3.8 cm, and height from 1.6 to 3.3 cm. Clearly, the weights are also more varied, since the heaviest weight is 51 g and the lightest 11.9 g. One of the objects (4540) has an incised 'X' mark on the surface. Podzorski (1994, 441) reports that discoid stone spindle whorls are also known from the site.

The site of Abydos has probably preserved a large number of spindle whorls, but it is very difficult to understand this from the publications. In fact, many objects are defined as model mace heads (Naville *et al.* 1914, 15), and very little information is provided. Petrie (1902, 25–6, pl. LII) recorded a very large number of spindle whorls of uncertain date, since they were mostly found in rubbish pits. However, they appear quite similar in shape (almost all dome) and material to those from the Predynastic period. Those listed in the catalogue are all made of limestone and dome or slightly spherical in shape. Their diameters measure 3.3 cm on average, height 2.5 cm and weights range between 23.8 and 40 g.

Other sites have preserved evidence of stone spindle whorls, which are generally spherical or dome-shaped as in the other sites here listed, for example Adaima (Buchez and Midant-Reynes 2002, 448–9, pl. 4.13), Armant (Mond and Myers 1937, 165, 188) and Elephantine (Kopp 2018, 82, pl. 36).

A special section should be dedicated to Hierakonpolis, due to the earlier chronology of the materials (most of them belong to the Early Dynastic period), but also the exceptional nature of the site. Despite the impressive quantity of publications devoted to this key site, spindle whorls have generally received little or no consideration at all. The first mention of whorls at the site is provided by Quibell (Quibell and Green 1902, 2, 10, 17, 22 pl. LXIII–LXIV), though few details are provided. However, these whorls are made of limestone, and from plates they appear mostly dome-shaped or spherical; many have marks incised on the surface, some even hieroglyphic signs (Plate 16). They mainly come from the settlement, but some are also known from graves. Those listed in the catalogue belong to these excavations. In Fairservis' publication (1986) the same, dome-shaped limestone objects are named mace heads in the field registry, loom weights and spindle whorls in the text (1986, 20, pl. 15:9, 15:10, 17:63, 90, 20:7, 23:202). All of these have a dome shape, are fairly tall and have a reasonably large diameter. In fact, the diameters are around 4.4 cm, and heights range between 2.8 and 3.4 cm, and therefore are slightly larger than those discussed so far. However, one of the objects has an incised mark on the side (1986, fig. 23:202), similar to those found by Quibell. Other whorls (partially matching the same materials illustrated by Quibell and Green) are illustrated by B. Adams (1995, 161–3), all of them made of limestone and dome-shaped. Some of these are decorated with radial incisions, and others have marks incised. They are stored in Liverpool, between the Garstang and World Museum, and are therefore included in the catalogue. Almost all the spindle whorls listed in the catalogue are made of limestone and have a dome shape. A peculiar object made of pottery, broken in two pieces, is conical, with the top completely abrased and a hollow base. Its usage is uncertain. Excluding this object, all the other specimens are made of stone and are quite large and heavy. One object exceeds 150 g and should certainly be excluded from being a whorl. The diameters range between 2.9 and 4.6 cm, with an average value of 3.9 cm. Heights vary between 1 and 3.7 cm, with an average value of 2.8 cm. Finally, the weights range between 28.7 and 88.3 g, with an average value of 53 g. Hierakonpolis limestone whorls are therefore slightly larger and heavier than those from other sites, like Maadi. If these are to be considered as actual spindle whorls, the yarns produced with these tools would have been rather thick. It would thus be interesting to compare these with textiles found at the site.

One of the biggest problems of Predynastic spindle whorls is the difficulty in recognising a stone whorl from a stone mace head in the reports. Mace heads are generally larger and heavier than whorls, and produced from more precious stone than simple limestone. However, limestone mace heads can be found, as well as whorls made from other types of stone. Their dimensions should help in recognising the categories of objects, but unfortunately the Ancient Egyptians produced a large number of models of mace heads to be placed in tombs. This second category is much more difficult to distinguish from spindle whorls, especially when they are published without full descriptions (including measurements and use traces), drawings or pictures. For example, at el-Mahasna some models of mace heads are made of pottery and even appear in female tombs (Thomas 2004), as in el-Amrah (Hill and Herbich 2011, 131). In this case, it is very difficult to understand if all these items were in fact mace heads, or if some of them could have been whorls. Even if in this case it is highly probable that they were in fact models of mace heads, since other publications (Ayrton and Loat 1911; Eyckerman and Hendrickx 2011) report objects that can be interpreted as mace heads beyond a doubt, in many other cases the doubt remains. Among mace head models one can find stone objects very similar to the larger implements, as well as pottery and clay objects, at times painted to resemble stone mace heads. However, these objects have three major differences from spindle whorls:

1. Spindle whorls can occur in settlements and sometimes even in tombs, while models of mace heads are generally found in funerary contexts.
2. Models of mace heads 'copy' actual mace heads, not only in materials but especially in shapes. Piriform and conical with convex sides, mace heads are very frequent and therefore these typologies are often represented in models. On the contrary, the dome shape is not usually employed for mace heads, so dome-shaped objects are very likely to be spindle whorls.
3. A model is an object made for display and not for use. Some objects are easily recognised as models since their hole is not made to allow the insertion of a shaft. This does not mean that it is incomplete, but that some obstacles (an angle or a constriction) prevent its true use. Furthermore, wear traces can be interesting, since they should not be present on models, but are very likely to be present on spindle whorls.

Wear traces are frequently present on spindle whorls from the earliest periods. These are small chips near the upper hole, which are not present on the part of the hole on the base (in case of dome or conical whorls). Sometimes, they are much more pronounced and can involve a quite extended part of the dome. Furthermore, they can be found on the external edge, again as small chips, or more substantial breakages. Similar traces were discussed during the 'Tool Workshop' held at the Centre for Textile Research in Copenhagen on 17 December 2014. During the workshop, several spindle whorls that had been used by spinners for years were analysed to understand what type of traces can be left on different materials. The traces visible on some of the materials presented here are compatible with repeated falls on the ground during the spinning process. However, the spinning process that left these traces involves a low-whorl spindle, while Ancient Egypt is known for using high-whorl spindles over its entire dynastic history. This is only partially true, however; the position of the spindle whorl on the spindle is culturally determined, but recent analyses are providing evidence of the use of high-whorl spindles in contexts where the presence of low-whorl spindles should be certain. Generally, this is explained as a technical choice: low-whorl spindles would be used for spinning, while high-whorl spindles would be used for plying. In the Egyptian context, it should be the contrary, with high-whorl spindles used for spinning and low-whorl spindles used for plying. However, during experimental tests, trained spinners have indicated a preference for plying with high-whorl rather than low-whorl spindles. The temptation to connect the presence of low-whorl spindles with other materials, such as wool, or with the z-direction of spinning is very strong. Nevertheless, Egyptian archaeological findings prevent these explanations. In fact, during the Predynastic period, a shift from z- and s-twist, to exclusively s- (for textiles) occurred, while with a low-whorl drop spindle for spinning it would be more common to find z-spun threads. Furthermore, the few woollen textiles from Amarna present the same s-twist as those made of linen and cannot be linked to production with a low-whorl spindle. Finally, evidence from Deir el-Medina shows that z-spinning and plying were made with the same identical spindles that were used for s-spinning, since it is possible to find threads representing both techniques on the same spindle. This evidence, even if not pertaining to the Predynastic period, shows how difficult it is to find a general rule to help explain peculiar features.

Given all these considerations, it seems that the traces on Predynastic spindle whorls (and of later periods) cannot be linked to a specific position on a spindle; only a specifically designed project to analyse wear traces using recreated spindle whorls could shed light on this question.

Old Kingdom

If traces of the textile industry are difficult to find for early periods, they appear positively evanescent in the Old Kingdom. Few settlements of this period have been extensively excavated, and they lack information about how spinning and weaving activity was conducted. One exception is represented by Heit el-Ghurab, on the Giza plateau. This village is famous for its relationship with the Giza pyramids (Lehner 2016), but some textile tools have also been published, albeit without details. Unfortunately, the site did not preserve organic materials, and wooden implements have disappeared. One pottery spindle whorl is all that remains of the spinning industry of the village (Tavares 2004, 10). A few more of stone and ivory have been excavated more recently, together with several perforated sherds and bone spatulae (Hitchens 2018). Another spindle whorl is recorded in dwellings in the area of the Valley Temple of Queen Khent-Kawes. This is made of limestone, with a large diameter measuring 6 cm and a height of 3 cm (Hassan 1943, 62).

A small group of spindle whorls is known from Elephantine and is dated between the 2nd and 6th Dynasty. All the whorls are made of wood, but have slightly different shapes. The oldest has a conical-truncated shape, with evident traces of manufacture and no attempt made to polish the surface. A second whorl has a flat, dome shape. The other whorls, dated to the 5th and 6th Dynasty, have the cylindrical shape that was so common in later periods (Kopp 2018, 73, abb. 42).

Other information can be obtained from iconography. In fact, a fragment of a relief from Saqqara shows a man spinning with a high-whorl spindle, and the spindle whorl is conical. As is the case with all other representations of the spinning process from later periods, the whorl is always placed on top, whether the yarn is produced for nets or for cloth. No spinning bowl appears in this image, but it may not have been present at all. This could mean these bowls were not used in the Old Kingdom, since no example is known from this period, or simply that they were less common while preparing yarn for netting, as depicted by the first male spinner from the left in the tomb of Baqt (see Table 3.2).

Middle Kingdom

Contrary to the Old Kingdom, a large quantity of textile tools were recovered for the Middle Kingdom. The site that has provided the largest collection is certainly Lahun, as presented before. Unfortunately, Petrie's excavations are very likely to have collected only specific materials, leaving aside other types of whorls, as was also the case for Schiaparelli's excavations in Deir el-Medina. The 102 spindle whorls listed in the catalogue are made of wood and have a cylindrical shape. Having a greater diameter than height is a good requisite for spinning flax, although it is possible to use many other shapes of whorls. Furthermore, a cylindrical object is the easiest to obtain when cutting a branch to produce a whorl. The average diameter of spindle whorls from Lahun is 4.7 cm, their height is 2.3 cm, and their weight is 16.6 g. As can be expected, these whorls are generally larger than Predynastic and Early Dynastic whorls, are slightly flatter and certainly lighter. The weight of the whorl is not extremely light, which enables the creation of a wide variety of qualities of thread. In general, a medium-fine quality would probably be expected from these tools. Several whorls feature identity marks. Only four limestone spindle whorls are known from the site, and these are quite similar to those from earlier periods. They are much heavier than wooden whorls, ranging between 65 and 137 g. Their weight is perfectly suited for producing thick yarn as well as for plying and cabling. As for earlier whorls, the upper part of the hole is the most worn area.

Another site where spindle whorls dated to the Middle Kingdom were found is Harageh (Engelbach and Gunn 1923, 10, pl. 11E). Five whorls are listed in the catalogue: four are made of wood and have a cylindrical shape, while one is made of bone and is dome-shaped (Fig. 5.19). The cylindrical wooden whorls are very similar to those of Lahun, and have diameters ranging between 3.1 and 4.9 cm, heights between 2.2 and 2.7 cm, and weights between 13 and 21 g. One shows an incised mark on the side. The bone spindle whorl is entirely different from the wooden examples. In fact, it has a very wide diameter (7.8 cm) and is made of a very thick and dense bone, making it a very heavy object at 114 g.

A limestone spindle whorl is known from the Middle Kingdom settlement of Ezbet Ruschdi (Czerny 2015, 376, abb. T137). It is dome-shaped and measures 4 cm in diameter and is 1.6 cm tall. The hole measures 0.7 cm, which is perfectly suited for spinning.

Figure 5.19. Spindle whorl from Buhen (Petrie Museum UC 21289)

New Kingdom

The largest quantity of spindle whorls is certainly known from the New Kingdom settlements. In fact, several worker villages and settlements are known from this period and organic materials have been preserved.

Deir el-Medina preserved a very impressive collection of spindle and spindle whorls excavated by the Italian Archaeological Mission in Egypt, led by Ernesto Schiaparelli, and by IFAO excavations led by Bernard Bruyère (see section 5.11). Two hundred and fifty-four spindle whorls are stored in the Museo Egizio in Turin, all of which are cylindrical and made of wood. Another 800 are located between the site storage room, the IFAO, and the Louvre Museum. Most of them are made of wood, only a small percentage of this impressive number are made of stone and only a tiny part is made of pottery or reworked sherds. The wooden spindle whorls listed in the catalogue have an average diameter of 5.1 cm, a height of 1.5 cm, and an average weight of 13 g. They are, therefore, slightly larger than in Lahun, thinner, and somewhat lighter. The difference, however, is so small that they can be considered as the same tools seen in Lahun. This means that there is no change in spinning tools and techniques from the Middle Kingdom to the New Kingdom. Only 79 spindle whorls are made of stone. The most common shape is the dome one, but 10 examples with a discoid shape are present as well. Their dimensions are quite big, with diameters that vary between 2.9 and 7.1 cm, while height can vary between 0.9 and 4.5 cm. Weight can vary between 5.6 g to 145 g.

Gurob presents the most interesting material of the entire corpus, since it is partially similar to the other Egyptian contexts, but also shows a completely different set of textile tools. The reason for this difference might be found in the different final consumers of the products, which could be identified as the Royal Harem, very likely within a workshop, but less likely with the presence of foreigners at the site, as was asserted after Petrie's excavations. In total, 97 spindle whorls were collected for this study, 91 made of wood and six made of stone. Cylindrical spindle whorls are not the most common type at this site, but those found in Gurob very much resemble those analysed from Deir el-Medina. Fifty-two spindle whorls have a dome/conical shape, which is almost unknown in other sites, with very few examples known in Deir el-Medina. All measurements of diameter and height are present for this type of shape, even if they are generally smaller and lighter than cylindrical whorls. Some of these dome-shaped whorls are remarkable for their extremely small dimensions and light weight. In fact, their weight can reach 0.4 g, and in general is less than 10 g. The heaviest whorl weighs 15.6 g and the average value is 6.2 g. Even compared to the very thin shafts discussed in the previous section and in section 5.10.3, they are extremely light and delicate objects. Considering that experimental sessions with very small whorls have proven to be highly difficult, requiring a very high degree of concentration (Andersson Strand 2010, 13) and very high quality, well-prepared raw fibres, it seems reasonable to assume that these tools belonged to a royal workshop to produce extra-fine linen threads. In fact, it seems difficult to imagine working with these tools at home, while watching over children or attending other domestic tasks.

Six limestone whorls are listed in the catalogue, all of which are very similar to those examined at Lahun and Deir el-Medina. Their diameters range from 4.51 cm to 7.63 cm, and their heights vary between 2 cm and 3.78 cm. The weights are comparable to those from Lahun, ranging from 57.7 g to 133.2 g, making them suitable for spinning low-quality threads and plying. As with the whorls from Lahun and those from earlier periods, signs of wear near the upper hole suggest a continuity in both the types and methods of use for these objects.

Tell el-Amarna was not selected to be inserted into the corpus since it was fully published (Kemp and Vogelsang-Eastwood 2001). Excavations carried out at the beginning of the century do not provide information about their measurements, but some have been located in museums and studied again. In the worker village, almost all the spindle whorls are made of wood, with just one made of limestone. On the contrary, in the main city wood has rarely been preserved but many stone whorls have been found. In total, 218 spindle whorls are included in the publication, comprising wooden whorls (158), stone whorls (61), and pottery whorls (9). Some perforated discs have also been found (Kemp and Vogelsang-Eastwood 2001, 289). Interestingly, a large number of whorls are dome-shaped, some even made of wood. However, these are not as small as those from Gurob (Kemp and Vogelsang-Eastwood 2001, fig. 8.4, tab. 8.3). Many of the whorls present incised marks. Some are similar to the identity marks seen at the other sites, while others are figurative patterns such as palm leaves, rosettes, and a fish (Kemp and Vogelsang-Eastwood 2001, 289, fig. 8.10). Interestingly, the whorl distribution is not even, whether between houses in the village or between the village and the main city.

Other New Kingdom sites have provided some evidence of spindle whorls, but in very low quantities. One example is Matmar, where several spindle whorls were found in the general rubbish and the granaries near the temple area (Brunton 1948, 67). At least three wooden spindle whorls of cylindrical shape and four of limestone are listed in the text (Brunton 1948, 67, 71). One of the limestone whorls is conical and has a decoration made from a pink lotus pattern. Three of the wooden spindle whorls still have their shaft present, even if only partially preserved. A complete shaft with a groove is represented near the whorls, and is very likely to be the shaft of a spindle (Brunton 1948, fig. LII).

It is highly likely that a large quantity of spindle whorls were found in Lisht North, but very little is known from the publications (Mace 1921, 11; Arnold 1996, 19; Moeller 2016, 360–1). More information can be inferred by the Metropolitan Museum online catalogue (Fig. 5.20). First, wooden spindle whorls very similar to those known from Lahun, Amarna, and Deir el-Medina are well represented, with cylindrical and conical truncated examples. Even a specimen with a double whorl is known. To these, some stone whorls must be added. One (15.3.691) shows radial incised decorations. Of those with pictures available, two are dome-shaped and two have a conical shape, and are very large; one has the wooden shaft still attached, but unfortunately only a small part has been preserved.

Many other sites have provided only single specimens of spindle whorls (see catalogue), such as Tell el-Retaba, where a dome limestone whorl was found (Rzepka *et al.* 2012, 268, figs 36–37), or such implements are simply indicated as being present, with no other information given.

Post-Ramesside period

Very few textile tools are known from periods later than the New Kingdom and the beginning of the Third Intermediate Period. Even when these materials are present, they are rarely published. For example, several spindle whorls (and a few spinning bowls and net weights) were present in Medinet Habu, but no further information is given (Hölscher 1954, 16, 74).

5.4.3 Perforated sherds

As discussed in Chapter 2, perforated sherds are pottery fragments that were reworked to obtain a roughly circular object with a hole either in the middle or slightly off-centre. It is very difficult to understand which of these were actually spindle whorls from the publications, since they rarely report information on the characteristics of the hole – the key element in understanding how they were used. However, it seems probable that these simple tools were quite ubiquitous, even at sites where they are not mentioned.

The earliest perforated sherds are known from the Fayyum A period (Caton-Thompson and Gardner 1934, 33). A couple of these sherds are listed in the catalogue, and it is possible to see that they are completely different from one another (Fig. 5.21). In fact, one has the hole pierced centrally, which was made by perforating from both sides, although it has been somewhat regularised; the other has the hole off-centre and made from one side. Some of these

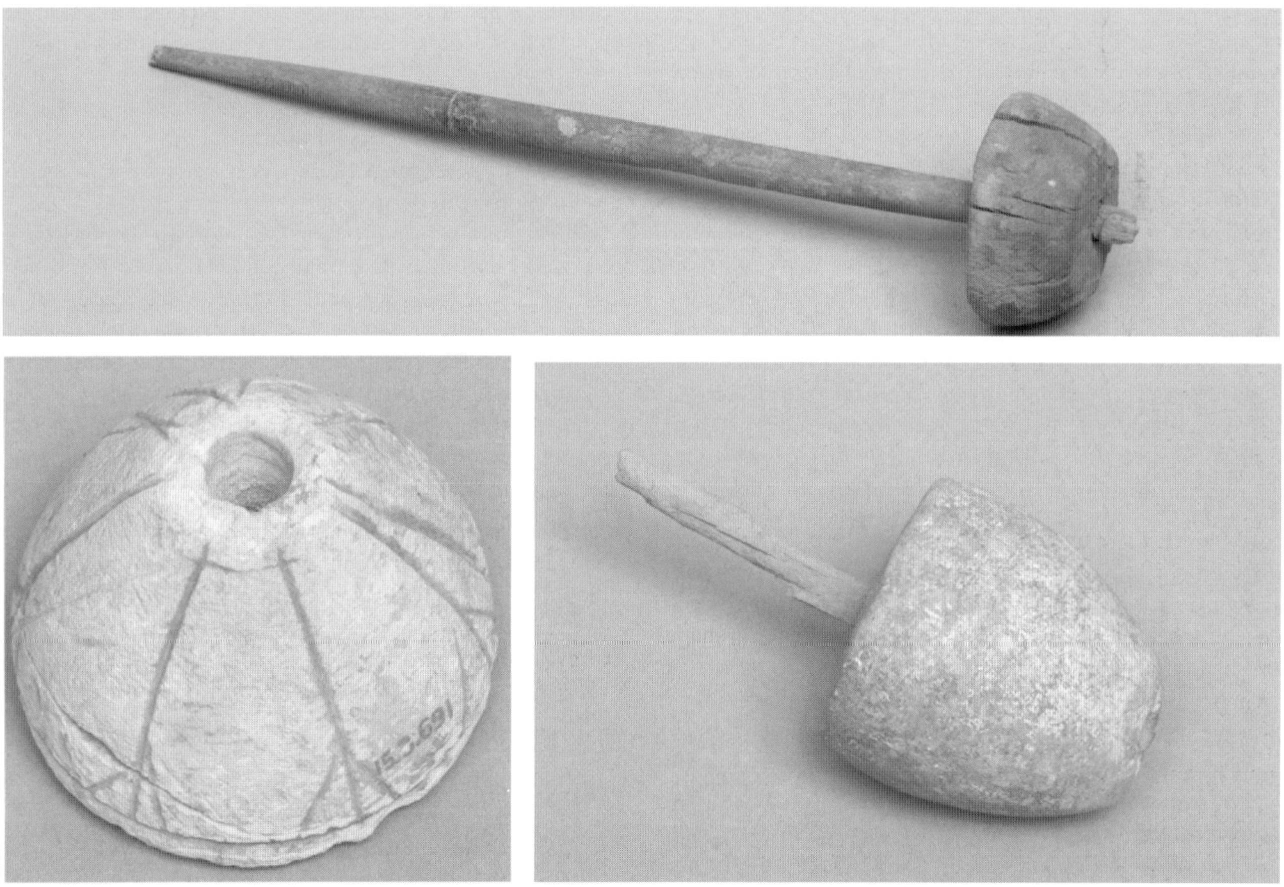

Figure 5.20. Spindles and spindle whorls from Lisht 11.651.681, 15.3.687, 15.3.691 (courtesy of the Metropolitan Museum)

Figure 5.21. Neolithic whorl from Fayyum (courtesy of the Petrie Museum, UC2932)

rounded sherds with perforations are also known from Merimde-Benisalame (Eiwanger 1982, 80).

Badarian settlements have been proven to use these tools as well, and some are present in the catalogue (Brunton and Caton-Thompson 1928, 5, 8, 34, pl. XXVII). In Badari, they are generally found in villages, but at least one specimen comes from a tomb.

A fairly large corpus is known from Maadi, where they are found at all levels of the settlements, (Rizkana and Seeher 1987; Rizkana *et al.* 1989). One hundred and four discs are recorded, although some do not have a perforation (Rizkana *et al.* 1989, 12, pl. 2), therefore can be ruled out from spinning activities. The perforation is made by drilling the object from both sides and has an hourglass shape. The diameters vary a great deal, from 3 to 14 cm; two thirds of the discs have a diameter less than 8 cm, and may have been used as whorls; the others with larger diameters are too big for the category of objects under consideration. A very interesting feature of Maadi is that a large number of unpierced sherds were found *in situ*, which were used as lids for jars, while pierced discs are not used as lids (Rizkana *et al.* 1989, 12). The proposed exclusion of their usage as spindle whorls at the site, given the presence of many limestone spindle whorls, has to be totally rejected. In fact, reworked sherds are much lighter than large stone whorls and could have been used for spinning thinner threads. Other perforated sherds from Maadi are recorded by Hartung (Hartung *et al.* 2003, 187, abb. 19) and Bajeot (2017, 161).

Several Predynastic sites have preserved perforated sherds, but they have not always been recognised as such. For example, in Tell el-Farkha they are considered to be tokens (Kołodziejczyk 2015, 36). Clearly, some of them are too small to have been used as whorls, especially because the hole is too small. However, some of the 'clay circles' are not perforated sherds but purposely made objects, and are thus probably spindle whorls. Measurements would have helped to better understand these objects. Tell el-Farkha did not provide many spindle whorls, but does have a large collection of spinning bowls. However, it is possible that the number of whorls might increase if we take into considerations some of the 'tokens'.

The site of Hammamiya has preserved some perforated sherds from Predynastic levels (Brunton and Caton-Thompson 1928, 103, 107, 114, pl. LXVI, LXX, LXXI, LXXIV). Some of these are included in the catalogue and have diameters ranging between 3.3 and 6.6 cm, with weights between 8.4 and 66.3 g. Almost all of them have an hourglass perforation, except for one example which has a conical perforation. Two objects have the perforation unfinished.

Many perforated sherds come from the site of Adaima (Buchez and Midant-Reynes 2002, 443–5). Sixty-three objects are recorded in the publication, almost all perforated, and most of them come from the settlement. Their diameters range from 5 to 10 cm, with an average value of 4 cm; only one object has a diameter larger than 6.5 cm. The hole diameter ranges between 0.3 and 0.8 cm, which is suitable for inserting a shaft.

Hierakonpolis provides another large set of perforated sherds, which have recently been recognised (Drewsen 2016, 13). One hundred and fifty perforated sherds were stored at the site but not yet studied; from a brief study of the drawings, they seem very similar to those from other sites, and are present in the catalogue.

It is also interesting to highlight that the great majority of these tools come from settlements, but that a small number also come from tombs, as is the case for the sherd from Ballas (Podzorski 1994, 441, pl. 59).

Perforated sherds also appear in later dynastic periods in Egypt, but they are much more difficult to find. In fact, publications rarely mention mundane objects and if it is difficult to find spindle whorls, while perforated sherds are almost impossible to locate. A couple are known for the Old Kingdom settlement of Elephantine (Kopp 2018, 93), while others have been published by S. Hitchens (2018).

Some pottery perforated sherds are mentioned in the mastaba of Ptahshepses Abusir (Charvát 1981), and four were found in the pr-Sna in Abydos South (although two of these appear to be very small) in a context where textile production seems quite probable (Smith 2010, 254).

No perforated sherds come from Lahun, Gurob, and only a very small number from Deir el-Medina, but this is certainly not due to their absence, but rather to choices made when recording and collecting materials. Even the complete publication of Tell el-Amarna excludes perforated sherds from the list. Only two of them are considered as possible spindle whorls, but we are at least able to understand that they were a quite common find at the site (Kemp and Vogelsang-Eastwood 2001, 277, fig. 8.6).

A very interesting context is provided by Deir el-Ballas, where a domestic textile workshop was identified by Lacovara (1990, 7, 23). It was located in Room 5a of house E, situated in an area to the west of the North Palace enclosure. Together with perforated sherds, several other objects were found, such as a spinning bowl, fragments of spun woollen thread, raw wool, and possibly part of a loom.

5.4.4 Spinning bowls

A spinning bowl is a bowl with a loop or an element to hold the prepared yarn during spinning and plying to control the supply of yarn. In Egypt, spinning bowls have been found at a great number of sites, both in Upper and Lower Egypt.

They have been recognised from iconographical representations and the first known examples were, until recently, dated to the Middle Kingdom. Spinning bowls are also known from the Aegean world and the oldest known example comes from Myrtos in Crete, dated to the Early Minoan II (which corresponds to the last part of the Old Kingdom). This predates the Egyptian examples and has challenged the theory of an Egyptian origin for the artefact. Furthermore, as seen in Chapter 4, Ghassulian spinning bowls were possibly present in the Beersheba region and constitute the oldest specimens known so far.

A closer look at Predynastic materials from Egypt shows that some bowls that could have been used in relation to spinning are present at the site of Tell el-Farkha, in the eastern Nile Delta. They were dated to the first part of the Naqada III period (EB Ib). These bowls were found in various trenches from Eastern, Western, and Central Koms. The excavators were not sure about their function because of various factors: first, the early chronology makes these spinning bowls the earliest examples in Egypt and, excluding the Levantine specimens, in the Mediterranean area. Second, their appearance, with a diaphragm instead of loops inside, is quite different from all other known specimens. Third, only 30 fragments of spinning bowls were found, too small a quantity for the entire settlement over 200 years. Finally, no textile tools were excavated except for a very limited number of spindle whorls. The first two elements of doubts are of no concern, since spinning bowls vary a great deal in morphology and scholars have only indicated their invention in the Middle Kingdom because there was no other evidence for preceding periods. There were no technical changes in weaving setts nor in textiles at the beginning of the Middle Kingdom that could justify their invention at that moment in time. The small number found (which is not the case for Farkha) in fact seems normal for these findings (*e.g.* in Deir el-Medina only 39 pottery spinning bowls have been retrieved in the storerooms). The only problem could be the scarcity of other textile tools at the site, but these might simply not have been preserved or, as seen in the preceding section, been differently labelled.

Another Predynastic spinning bowl might be recognised in one (S. 4087) of the two bowls from Heliopolis and stored in the Museo Egizio, Turin (Spinazzi-Lucchesi 2018, 116–18). It is very similar to examples from Farkha, since it has a central diaphragm with four holes instead of loops, and does not show signs of a potter's wheel. This bowl comes from Ernesto Schiaparelli's excavations of the site of Heliopolis, 20 km northeast of Cairo. The site was a very important religious centre and was occupied from the Predynastic Period until the Late Period.

Not a single example of a spinning bowl is known, however, from Old Kingdom settlements. This might not seem surprising, given the difficulties in finding textile tools in publications for this period (as already seen for spindle whorls and perforated sherds), but in fact it does pose a problem. Spindles and spindle whorls may have been made of wood and therefore not preserved, but spinning bowls are very likely to have been preserved and their total absence from settlements such as Giza and Elephantine, or domestic and priestly contexts in Abusir, is suspicious. It might be caused by the difference in appearance from later examples and, as was the case for Farkha and Heliopolis, they were not recognised as spinning bowls until very recent years. However, they could not have been used in the Old Kingdom, and other tools or techniques might have been employed, as suggested by the already mentioned Saqqara relief.

With the beginning of the Middle Kingdom, evidence of spinning bowls becomes very frequent and widespread throughout Egypt. In iconography (see Table 3.2), they appear in wooden funerary models and in tomb scenes inside weaving workshops, and on models they are carved with two loops inside (for example UC 6665i).

Several archaeological contexts have preserved spinning bowls, and probably the most famous is Lahun. Petrie reports having found a large number of these bowls made of pottery or limestone, but he published just one bowl, and only one was available for study. In this case, the bowls were probably found inside houses, as is the case for Amarna and Deir el-Medina.

A very interesting context is Abydos South. The funerary temple of Senwsret III contained some refuse pits, in which large quantities of pottery, mud jar-stoppers, leftover basketry, matting, cordage, and linen textiles were found. In a refuse pit in the east block, a spinning bowl was also found (Wegner *et al.* 2000, 108, fig. 16). Furthermore, a small number of fragments were found in temple deposits

(Wegner 2007, 245–7, fig. 103:58). Over a dozen fragments were found in pr-Sna, on the northeastern side of the temple (Smith 2010, 256), together with four perforated sherds, four net sinkers, and nine copper needles. Unfortunately, wood has not been preserved in this area. Not far from the temple and the Shena, a worker village was present, but materials from this village have not yet been published. The presence of spinning bowls in the temple and the production area suggests that textile production occurred in the temple and for the temple itself, as is known for the temple of Karnak and the Ramesseum.

Spinning bowls appear quite frequently in Tell el-Dab'a from the Middle Kingdom and Second Intermediate Period contexts, contrary to other textile tools (Bader 2001, 99, abb. 21a; Aston and Bietak 2004, 166, 243, fig. 110, pl. 177, 293; Czerny 2012, 59, fig. 7). At least 17 fragments of spinning bowls are recorded (Czerny *et al.* 1999, 59, 104–6, 199, pl. XIX), with a typology featuring a flat base and almost straight sides. It is similar to the object published for Lahun, but very different from that listed in the catalogue. They have two loops on the inside, and a possible example with a single loop is also present. All of these come from houses, with just one example from a street. Other Middle Kingdom contexts are represented by Abu Ghalib (Larsen 1941, fig. 14), Karnak North (Allen 1997, 33), and Memphis (Bourriau and Gallorini 2016, 190, fig. 102).

Spinning bowls continued to be produced during the New Kingdom and the largest assemblages are those of Tell el-Amarna and Deir el-Medina. Amarna preserved both stone and pottery bowls (Kemp and Vogelsang-Eastwood 2001, 291, fig. 8.15), generally made of marl clay, but silt was sometimes employed. All the specimens have two loops on the bottom of the bowl, except one example which has two loops added to the inside rim (Kemp and Vogelsang-Eastwood 2001, 293, fig. 8.16).

In Deir el-Medina, several spinning bowls were recognised and have been published by Nagel (1938, 183–6, figs 152–8); these can have two or three loops at the bottom of the bowl. In this case, as in Amarna, grooves caused by the friction of thread are clearly visible. A fragment of a limestone spinning bowl is also mentioned.

Although they were not mentioned in Petrie's reports of excavations at Gurob, they were found in the new excavations conducted by I. Shaw and F. Hagen (Shaw 2012, 352).

An interesting context is the already cited textile workshop from Deir el-Ballas (Lacovara 1990, 7, 23) where a spinning bowl was found in the same context as some perforated sherds and wool. Wool does not need to be spun with the aid of a spinning bowl, since the fibres are too short to produce roves through splicing. This finding might suggest that they were used for plying rather than spinning, as posited by Vogelsang-Eastwood (1987, 85–7). Other New Kingdom contexts are Tell el-Retaba (Rzepka *et al.* 2017, 39), Pi-Ramses (Laemmel 2008, 178), and Tell el-Hebua (Allen 1997, 33). A couple of spinning bowls are known from Medinet Habu, which belong to the New Kingdom strata (Hölscher *et al.* 1939, 84, pl. 57) and to the Post-Ramesside layers (22nd Dynasty) (Hölscher 1954, 74).

Their production continued in the Third Intermediate Period and the Late Period, but they seem to disappear following the Macedonian conquest. Examples of sites where these late bowls were found are Lisht North (Hayes 1959, 412; Allen 1997, 35), the already cited examples of Medinet Habu, Abu Imram, and Mendes (Allen 1997, 36).

5.4.5 Bone spatulae and beaters

As seen earlier, pin beaters are a wide and miscellaneous category of objects, some of which may have been used in textile production for beating threads and keeping warp in place. It is very difficult to understand which of these could have been used in weaving when handling them, and is practically impossible to see it from the publications. In this chapter, the principal evidence for these beaters will be introduced with the hope that in the future, many more studies will be dedicated to this very difficult category.

Several objects that may have been used as beaters were found in the Neolithic Fayyum Kom W and K. Some of these show a very sharp point that would not have been suitable for the purpose intended here, but others resemble specimens such as those at Far'ah and the Peruvian bone (Caton-Thompson and Gardner 1934, 34, XII:8–9). One bone spatula with a rounded point is also listed in the catalogue.

Some possible pin beaters were also known from excavations in Merimde-Benisalame, where they appear to have been longitudinally cut to obtain a long, thin point (Junker 1929, 237, abb. 12; 1930, taf. 11). To these, some fragments of bone spatulae with rounded or triangular points can be added (Junker 1929, 237, pl. XIIb). One of the spatulae with a rounded point is almost complete. Another specimen is very short and has a long, thin pen-nib point, while the other end is perfectly rounded (Junker 1930, taf. XI).

Some possible beaters could have been found in Badarian contexts. Three come from male graves in Badari, but little information can be extracted from the publication (Brunton and Caton-Thompson 1928, 14, 16, pls XXVII:4, XX:16).

Predynastic contexts have preserved some of these tools, for example from the settlement of Badari (Brunton and Caton-Thompson 1928, 44, pl. LVIII), Maadi (Bajeot 2017, 158), and Abydos (Naville *et al.* 1914, 4, pl. IIIa).

In Adaima, several pin beaters were found, all made from tibia or metapodial bones from Ovis capra. Some preserve points that are very thin and sharpened and cannot have been used as the Peruvian examples, but could still have been used for beating parts of weft threads, although a usage as borers cannot be ruled out. However, others have stronger and more rounded points that would be perfect for keeping warp threads in order (Buchez and Midant-Reynes 2002, 436–7, pls 4.4–6).

For the Old Kingdom, seven bone points (spatulae) were found in Giza, which are described as having a pen-nib point and fine striation on the surface, possibly due to the process of manufacture. However, from the only available picture, it seems that a rounded point is present, and that another object could be part of a pin beater (Tavares 2004, 11). Some fragments of bone rods and bone points might also have been pin beaters (Hitchens 2018, 14).

From Kafr Ammar, three bone spatulae dated to the Old Kingdom are listed in the catalogue. One of these (UC 37337) is very well shaped and preserved, with a pen-nib point and a rounded end. The other two examples are very similar to this one in shape, but one is thinner than the others. Several points and broken objects were also found at the site, and among these, pin beaters may have been present (Fig. 5.22).

Four bone spatulae are known from Lahun, all from reworked ribs. One of the objects was found inside a ball of thread, which is a very interesting link to its usage in connection with textile production. To these objects a wooden beater can be added, which is entirely different from the examples examined here. In fact, its shape resembles that of bone spatulae, but it is much larger and thicker. No bone pin beaters have been found. Traces of wear are very visible on some of the bone spatulae, showing that they were not used for their point, but rather in the middle of the spatula.

New Kingdom evidence of bone spatulae is abundant. Gurob has preserved a very large collection of bone spatulae, with 95 examples present in the catalogue. Both triangular and pen-nib points are present, as well as rounded ends. These are made from ribs and many examples have convex profiles, which influence the traces of wear. In fact, in many cases the traces of wear are not localised near the point, but rather in the middle of the spatula.

The objects called pin beaters in Amarna are here labelled as bone spatulae, to distinguish them from the metapodial bones cut to obtain a point. They have pen-nib points as well as triangular and rounded points, as in Gurob. Traces of wear have been analysed with a microscope, together with some specimens from Gurob, and the results show that the fine striation present on the surface is due to the process of polishing and manufacture rather than the rubbing of threads (Kemp and Vogelsang-Eastwood 2001, 368–70). This is certainly true, at least for part of them, and the article by Cheval and Radi (2013) makes a good point in this sense. However, wear traces are easily recognisable in the Gurob and Lahun specimens, since entire areas of the spatulae have been polished and cancellous bone is no longer visible due to contact with soft materials, presumably fibres.

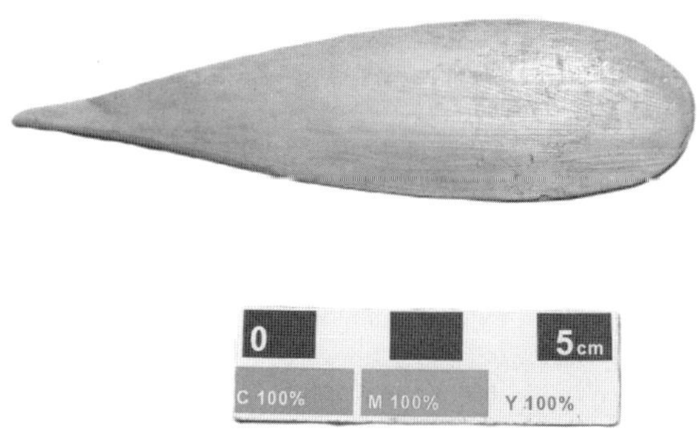

Figure 5.22. Bone spatula from Kafr Ammar (courtesy of the Petrie Museum, UC 37337)

Actual pin beaters are not known from these two sites, but have instead been found in Deir el-Ballas, in the already cited textile workshop. Two are complete tools, while two are partially preserved (Lacovara 1990, 7, fig. 2.3). A pin beater and fragments of other specimens are also known from Abydos, where they are labelled as 'netting needles' (Ayrton *et al.* 1904, pl. LVII:25–27).

From levels II and III of Kom Rabi'a, 20 bone spatulae were found. They are dated to the Late 18th Dynasty–Early Ramesside period. They were cut from bovine ribs, characterised by a large, flat, and slightly concave shape. Evidence of manufacture is no longer visible, since the edges have been smoothed by wear. On the concave side, cancellous bone is sometimes visible (Giddy 1999, 162, pl. 35). All the complete specimens present a long triangular point and a rounded end, except one which only has a rounded end. No pen-nib examples are known from the site.

From this brief survey of Egyptian materials, it seems fairly clear that bone spatulae and pin beaters were known and used since the Neolithic period, and continued to be utilised for almost all the Pharaonic period, with very few changes in their shape or material.

5.4.6 Basalt rings

Basalt rings have been widely discussed for the Levant (see Chapter 4) and these considerations will not be repeated here. It is also a category of objects that seems almost absent from Egypt for the EBA, but also for later periods. However, a few examples of basalt rings are known in one Egyptian site. Some basalt rings, considered as spindle whorls, have been published for Maadi (Rizkana and Seeher 1988, 53, pl. 95:17–22). Fifteen examples made of vesicular basalt are known from the site and their distribution is quite uneven. Analysis carried out on these tools has proven that they were not produced in Egypt, but were imported from Palestine (Porat and Seeher 1988).

5.4.7 Loom weights and net weights

The category of net weights includes a very broad typology of objects, presenting features that are suitable for attaching a thread, such as grooves or holes. Given the long-standing debate about what is a loom weight and what is a net weight, all objects that can belong to one of the two categories will be considered. The aim is to understand which objects may have been used as loom weights (but may have had other purposes), and which objects certainly cannot have been loom weights. This part of the work has been conducted while trying to avoid prejudice concerning the presence or absence of the warp-weighted loom in Egypt during certain periods. For this reason, all the objects are labelled simply as 'weights', without associating a preconceived function. The comparison with Levantine loom weights has been crucial during the study to better understand objects from Ancient Egypt.

The first weights are known from the Neolithic Fayyum K, where some stones, roughly rounded or ovoid, present a concavity in the middle which runs around the entire diameter (Caton-Thompson and Gardner 1934, pl. XXIX:7–9). This type of section is suitable for winding a thread.

Stone weights are known from Merimde, where they are defined as net weights and placed in relation to the large collection of fishing tools, such as the harpoons, fishhooks, and nets that are present at the site (Eiwanger 1982, 80).

Similar to the stone weights from the Fayyum and Merimde are the weights from Omari. At this site, 19 specimens were collected, most made of limestone (Debono and Mortensen 1992, 59, 152, pl. 32). They were not grouped together but found scattered around the site, and none of them was found in context with the net that was also discovered at the site.

Three limestone objects found in Maadi are very likely to have been weights (Rizkana and Seeher 1988, 50, 106, pl. 92: 8, 9, 10). One has an ovoid shape, while the other two are smaller and almost spherical. All of them have a groove along the middle that goes around its diameter, and surface and groove are roughly worked.

Some Early Dynastic weights are recorded in Hierakonpolis (Adams 1995, 166–9). These have a different shape from those of earlier periods, since they are almost cylindrical and do not have a single central groove, but rather two or three grooves. For the examples with two, the grooves are located almost at the end of the side. Furthermore, a longitudinal groove is present on the base. One example presents two holes. They are made not of stone but of Nile silt pottery.

Weights of similar shape to those from Hierakonpolis are also known from Old Kingdom contexts, as is the case for Abusir and Kom el-Hisn (Wenke *et al.* 2016, 333, fig. 11.6), proving the continuity of their use.

Some objects that might be interpreted as weights have been found in the Middle Kingdom funerary temple of Senwosret III. According to Wegner (2007, 269), some loom weights were found in the deposits outside the temple, together with baskets and cords, but no spindle whorls were found in that context. The work of Smith (2010, 258, fig. 110) concerning the productive area outside the temple describes four loom weights. One is made of limestone, with several grooves carved upon it, and it may possibly resemble the objects seen at Hierakonpolis. Three other objects are made of baked pottery and have a lunate shape, with two through holes.

The largest batch of weights known so far in Egypt comes from the Middle Kingdom levels of the fortress of Buhen (Emery *et al.* 1979, 112–15, pls 40–41). Seventy of these weights are listed in the catalogue. They can be made of stone (limestone, sandstone, and even serpentinite), baked clay, and even of mud and unbaked clay. Their shape and measurements vary a great deal. Within the group of baked clay objects, which represents the majority, one can find a singular item, such as UC 21365, which is quite flattish, oval, and with a hole at each end. Similar to more ancient types is UC 21263, which has an almost rectangular shape, with two grooves at the end. An example of a discoid elliptical weight is UC 21286 but, in contrast to those studied by the CTR, it has a groove along its base. The most common category is represented by the lunate weights, similar to Abydos. These have two holes, one near each corner, and a groove along the base.

Those made of stone are mostly carved in sandstone, but limestone is also quite common. Several shapes can be distinguished – one common form (*e.g.* UC 21265, 21266) is a sort of trapezoidal object with a groove running along the centre, the length of the longest side. Similarly, another type has grooves crossing through its surface, as in the example from Lahun, as well as in UC 21278, and UC 21281. Finally, a discoid elliptical weight (UC 21282) is made of sandstone. Three objects are made of clay and mud and certainly cannot be considered as net sinkers (UC 21287, 21366, 21367). Two of these have a discoid elliptical shape, while one, fragmentary, has a semi-discoid shape.

Weights found in Lahun, albeit in very small quantities, are similar. Tell el-Dab'a has also provided evidence for weights, but in this case the shapes are reminiscent of the more ancient examples from Hierakonpolis. In fact, they are mostly ovoid, made of stone with a groove at each end (Czerny *et al.* 1999, 114, abb. 52), but an example of a semi-discoid pottery weight is also present (Czerny 2015, 377, taf. 137, 208).

Weights are quite common findings in the New Kingdom sites, with examples at: Abydos (pottery, semi-discoid, and ovoid with lateral grooves) (Ayrton *et al.* 1904, 37, LVII); Elephantine, where several weights have been interpreted as net-weights given the total absence of other evidence for textile production (Arnold 2015, 154); Matmar (Brunton 1948, LII, LXV), although these are probably from the Third Intermediate Period (Aston and Bader 1998); Amarna (Kemp and Vogelsang-Eastwood 2001, 394); and Kom Rabi'a (Giddy 1999, 195–7, pls 39–41).

Several weights are known from Tell el-Retaba, Wadi Tumilat, and are predominantly made of limestone, although some are also crafted from clay (Jarmuzek 2010; Rzepka *et al.* 2017). These weights are perforated and can be described as discoid, which sets them apart from other types of weights previously described. This is the only instance in which several objects may be interpreted as loom weights for the period under consideration. While this uniqueness warrants caution in interpretation, the possibility that a warp-weighted loom (or more than one) was known and used in Tell el-Retaba remains a distinct possibility.

As seen in this brief presentation of the main evidence for 'weights' from Egypt, several types of objects are included in this broad category. A few examples are listed in the catalogue to give an idea of the different measurements and weights from the objects under consideration. Starting from stone examples, it is very likely that they were used as net weights. In fact, stone resists water better than pottery, and it would thus be natural to employ it. Furthermore, many of the types discussed here are represented in funerary paintings (Brewer and Friedman 1989) and wooden models (such as the Meketra fishing model) attached to nets. Finally, due to their enduring presence from the Neolithic down to the Pharaonic period, during times when it is very difficult to imagine the existence of a warp-weighted loom in Egypt, it is highly probable that these were used as net sinkers.

Much more difficult to understand is the purpose of pottery weights. For those that are similar to the stone examples, it is more probable that they would have been used in the same way as their stone counterparts. The semi-discoid typology is more complicated; first, examples of these weights have been found in contexts where textile production is very likely, such as Abydos South, making their use as loom weights quite probable. However, the groove on the base of these objects means that they had to be attached to something longitudinally, meaning for their entire length, rather than with their shortest side near the next weight. This implies that each weight occupied a large space and thus, on a warp weighted loom, warps attached to these weights would be very loose. While it is possible to use them in this way, it is very unlikely – it would have made much more sense to attach them to an object that has no problems with limited space or the packing of threads, such as a net. In conclusion, it seems, from the evidence here collected, that no warp-weighted loom ever existed in Egypt before the Third Intermediate Period and almost all the objects studied here should be interpreted as net weights. This would not be an issue even in the context of Abydos South, since spinning implements were used for producing textiles as well as nets. The very few examples made of unbaked clay should be considered as counterweights, which could have been used for many purposes.

5.4.8 Needles

Needles, contrary to the other textile tools, are frequently found in excavations and are quite well published, so they seem to be present in almost every Egyptian context.

Several needles are known from Badarian sites. In Badari, one rounded bone needle is from the settlement (Area 5400), but the vast majority come from graves (5112, 5390, 5705, 5739, 5745, 5747) (Brunton and Caton-Thompson 1928, 5, 7, 11, 16, pl. XX, XXIII, XXIV, XXVII). All are made of bone or ivory, have a rounded perforation, and can be straight as well as bent or rounded. The measurements can vary greatly, from 6 to 11 cm in length and 0.3 to 0.5 cm in thickness. They are very thick, very different to modern needles, and could have been used to sew rough textiles, join pieces of leather, or as bodkins and netting needles. There is no correlation between sex or age of the tomb owners and the presence of needles. Three needles come from the same grave.

Some needles are known from the Badarian levels at Mostagedda, from both the settlement and graves (Brunton 1937, 19, 21, 22, 46, 54, pl. XXII, XXV, XXXII).

Only one needle is known from Predynastic graves in Badari, while two were recovered from the village, one made of bone and one of copper, still attached to a textile (Brunton and Caton-Thompson 1928, 46). Only one bone needle comes from Hammamiyah (Brunton and Caton-Thompson 1928, 103, pl. LXXIIa:29), and five from Mostagedda, from both the settlement and graves (Brunton 1937, 88–9, pl. XXV). A few needles are also known from the settlement of Maadi, but no further information is given, except that they are made of bone (Hartung *et al.* 2003, 187). Two of the Predynastic graves of el-Amrah contained a needle, in both cases made of copper. Both are male graves, and it also interesting to note that in this period fishing implements were placed inside female graves (Randall-MacIver *et al.* 1902, 16, 17, 19).

The catalogue lists some Predynastic needles from Naqada, Tarkan, and Koptos. These are all made of copper, except one specimen from Naqada, which is made of silver. It is extremely small and thin, similar to our modern sewing needles (Petrie *et al.* 1896, 53, pl. LXV). Most of the copper needles come from graves, and in one case three were found in a single tomb (Petrie *et al.* 1896, 24, tomb 3). Measurements can vary a great deal, from 8.5 to 5.5 cm (except the one made of silver).

One of the most surprising findings is that needles were placed in the royal tombs of the first dynasties. Petrie found a fairly large collection of needles inside Early Dynastic tombs in Abydos and Giza, and some of them are listed in the catalogue. The two most impressive specimens are made of gold, and the hole is made by piercing the shaft (Petrie and Griffith 1901, 6, pl. IV). They are very small and thin and are now wrapped in a coarse textile that probably has nothing to do with them. However, not only precious examples are found in these tombs, but also long, thick examples made of copper (see AN 1896–1908 E.1236) and bone/ivory bodkins (AN 1896–1908 E.1337). Several needles are also reported in Dreyer's reports on Umm el-Qaab (Dreyer *et al.* 1996;

1998; 2000; 2003) and Helwan (Saad 1947, 27, pl. XVIIa; 1951, 39, pl. LIIIa). Some bone needles were also found in tombs at Minshat Abu Omar (van der Brink 1992, 135).

The presence of needles in tombs continues in the following periods. Petrie reported the finding of 11 or more bronze needles and three thicker ones from a mastaba in Maidum, which should be dated to the 4th Dynasty (Petrie 1892, 18–19, pl. XXIX). Needles were found in seven female Old Kingdom graves (Odler 2015, 49). A couple of examples of this long-lasting tradition may be found in Tell el-Dab'a, where they were found in graves dated to the Second Intermediate Period (Habachi *et al.* 2001, 175) and Qantir (Habachi *et al.* 2001, 179), as well as from the tomb of Kha in Deir el-Medina, where two needle cases were located.

Needles continue to also be common in settlements and several examples are known from Lahun, Gurob, and Deir el-Medina. All the metal examples share the same identical methodology of fabrication, the hole of which was made by simply perforating the shaft from one side to the other. This technique also spread to the Levant. However, from the MBA onwards in that region another type of needle is common, with the eye obtained by bending the upper part of the shaft back on itself. This typology of needles is not common in Egypt, and is represented by only a few examples, which may well be considered an import from the Levantine region. One is known from Tell el-Dab'a (Philip 2006, 126, fig. 56; Czerny 2015, 390), one from Lisht (MET 22.1.984), and the other from Kom Rabi'a (Giddy 1999, 1355, pl. 38).

From this brief presentation of sewing tools from Egypt, three features can be noted. The first is the production of bone and metal needles from the earliest periods, alongside bodkins. To these, wooden implements should certainly be added, as can be seen in the findings from Deir el-Medina. Second, the manufacture of metal needles remains unchanged over time, with the holes continuing to be produced simply by perforating the shaft from one side to the other. Finally, needles can be part of the funerary equipment for both rich and poor individuals, even kings. The significance of needles in tombs is worth considering: what practical or symbolic meaning they might have is unclear. Certainly, rulers and wealthy individuals did not engage in sewing textiles, and some of these objects are too thin and small to be used for fastening garments. Additionally, needles are the only objects connected to textile production to be found in tombs after the Predynastic period. The presence of needles in tombs is frequently associated with embalming, but this is obviously possible only from fully dynastic periods. It is impossible to be certain if the reason for needles being placed in Predynastic graves remains the same throughout Egyptian history, or if there were other reasons for this funerary practice. Certainly, sewing mummies was not an option in the 1st and 2nd Dynasties, and other explanations should be found. Furthermore, large sets of needles were found in the tombs of Kha and Merit, yet neither of them has been eviscerated (Bianucci *et al.* 2015). Whatever the significance of displaying needles in tombs was in the various periods, it does not seem to be strongly connected with embalming rituals.

5.4.9 Conclusions about Egyptian textile tools

The textile industry has left many traces in the archaeological contexts of Ancient Egypt, even if they are not evenly distributed over time and space. Many items linked to spinning and weaving are known from Neolithic and Predynastic settlements, but far fewer have been found for the Dynastic period. Leaving aside the workers village of Lahun, Amarna, Gurob, and Deir el-Medina, very few items are known from other contexts. Unfortunately, Ancient Egyptian people did not use textile tools as funerary goods (although some exceptions exist), and this has precluded us from finding many of these items.

Spindles are almost exclusively known from worker villages. All the known examples of spindle shafts are made of wood, while ivory, bone and metal rods seem not to have been employed for spinning. Three types of wooden shafts were in use: a short, thick shaft between 20 and 25 cm; a long, thick shaft, ranging between 30 and 40 cm; and a third type, with a short but very thin shaft, which is so far known only from Gurob. Almost all the shafts tend to taper towards a pointed end, while the other end may be rounded or flat. At the top of the spindle, a groove for fastening fibres is incised, which can be a simple notch or a long, deep, spiral groove.

The first spindle whorls seem to appear in the Neolithic period, with the Fayyum finding of a limestone spindle whorl. In the Predynastic period, limestone spindle whorls appear to have dominated, generally with spherical or dome shapes, but other stones might be used as well. These tools were found both in graves and in settlements. It is noteworthy that only a single example of a wooden whorl has been preserved from this period. It is therefore possible that they were not frequently used. Early Dynastic whorls from Hierakonpolis show a great continuity with earlier periods, since almost all of them are made of limestone and are dome-shaped. They present incisions on the surface that could be early examples of identity marks. Predynastic and Early Dynastic spindle whorls present some difficulties in recognising them, since they are quite large and heavy and could be confused with light mace heads, or indeed models of mace heads. The context of the findings (settlement or burial), as well as their traces of wear (which would certainly not be expected in models) can help to distinguish between the two categories.

Very few spindle whorls have been found in Old Kingdom contexts, while the Middle Kingdom is much better documented. Many wooden spindle whorls are known from

Lahun, all of which are cylindrical in shape, except four limestone whorls, which have a dome shape, as in earlier periods. Other sites show a similar situation to that of Lahun, and this would thus probably have been common. New Kingdom spindle whorls show no differences from Middle Kingdom ones regarding their shape and measurements. Almost all are cylindrical and made of wood, with rare examples of dome-shaped limestone whorls. One exception is Amarna, where stone and wooden whorls are present in almost equal quantity, while in Deir el-Medina stone and ceramic spindle whorls represent just a small percentage. Gurob stands apart, since a large number of its spindles and whorls are entirely different from those known at the other sites. Those in Gurob are dome-shaped, extremely small and light, and were certainly used to produce extra-fine, luxury yarns. Very few whorls are known for the 1st millennium (contrary to the Levantine context), but they appear to continue the typologies known from the New Kingdom.

For spindle whorls, it is very probable that we must add at least some of the perforated sherds found in Egypt. The earliest examples are again known from the Fayyum A period, which continued to be produced in the Badarian and Predynastic periods. It is very likely that they were used to produce quite thin threads, while limestone whorls were used to produce thicker yarn, or for plying. Although very few examples have been published for the Pharaonic period, their sporadic occurrence in archaeological contexts prove that they continued to be used. Furthermore, two contexts that are very likely to have been textile workshops (templar and domestic) have preserved evidence of the usage of perforated sherds.

Another tool for spinning, the spinning bowl, is known in Egypt from at least the final phase of the Predynastic period and continued to be used until the Late period or even later. However, not a single fragment is known from the Old Kingdom layers. This might depend on several factors, from a general lack of evidence of textile activities in this period, to a different shape of bowl which excavators did not recognise. Finally, their abandonment in the Old Kingdom, although unlikely, cannot be ruled out. A very large number of spinning bowls are known from the Middle Kingdom and New Kingdom layers, and all sites considered here have provided examples of them.

Pin beaters appear for the first time in the Fayyum culture, while bone spatulae are attested from excavations in Merimde. These simple tools, which can be used for many different purposes, can present smooth surfaces as a result of constant contact and rubbing with soft materials, possibly yarn. Similar objects continue to be found later in the Predynastic and Dynastic periods, with very few changes in their shapes and measurements.

Net weights/loom weights have been a matter of discussion since Mace's publication of the Lisht material in 1922 (Mace 1922). Their simple shape is suitable for both weaving and fishing. So far, no comprehensive study has been published on these objects. Within this work, the most important findings of weights have been discussed and an attempt has been made to cover the broadest period possible. It has revealed the presence of these very simple tools from Neolithic and Predynastic periods onwards, with very few changes in terms of shape or material. They have been found in contexts where other textile tools are known, but also where very little is known about spinning and weaving. They can be very small or quite large and heavy, and the lightest objects were certainly not used for weaving. However, the presence of recognisable depictions of some of these tools, as well as the length and shapes of others, seem to point to their being used for fishing rather than weaving.

Bone needles are known from at least the Badarian period, with copper needles appearing slightly later. They are ubiquitous in settlements throughout all periods of Egyptian history and also occur in tombs – a remarkable fact, given that textile tools were generally excluded from graves after the Predynastic era. Notably, needles (and bodkins) are found not only in the burials of poorer and middle-class individuals but also in royal tombs. Their distribution shows no apparent gender distinction, as they appear in both male and female graves.

Interestingly, these needles do not seem to have been used for fastening cloth or in the embalming process. They were crafted from a variety of materials, including bone, copper, bronze, silver, and gold, suggesting that material choice was not a primary consideration. Their widespread presence and diversity might imply a symbolic or religious significance, though its precise meaning remains unclear.

Archaeological evidence of textile tools from Ancient Egypt predominantly indicates domestic production, widespread throughout the country, with minimal changes in tools during the entire pre-classic period. A notable exception is the introduction of the wooden spindle whorl, which did not replace stone whorls but complemented them in producing finer yarns. Perforated sherds continued to be made and likely served the same purpose as wooden whorls. Spinning bowls underwent slight modifications in shape yet remained in use from the Predynastic to the Late Period. Needles, beaters, and spatulae showed no significant change throughout the period under consideration; variations in shape and size – particularly for needles and bodkins – were probably related to differing functions.

Net weights exhibit considerable typological variety, reflecting both changes from Prehistoric to Pharaonic times and elements of continuity. Despite this extensive archaeological record, little is known about large-scale textile workshops from material remains. Iconographic and textual sources, however, frequently reference them, with available texts indicating that most large workshops were attached to temples and palaces. Domestic textile production remains largely undocumented in texts, even at Deir el-Medina, where written sources are otherwise abundant. In contrast, the archaeological record points to an intensive production of textiles or yarn, suggesting the possible existence of a broader, cottage-industry-scale production.

Sites such as Abydos South and Gurob offer insights into the archaeological contexts of textile workshops, although they differ markedly. At Abydos South, no wooden tools have survived, and spindle whorls are scarce, but dozens of spinning bowl fragments were discovered in the same context. In contrast, Gurob has yielded preserved wooden implements, including spindles and spindle whorls – though fewer than might be expected. Knowledge of the palace-associated workshop at Gurob is derived mainly from textual evidence. The exceptional lightness of some tools strongly suggests the production of fine textiles, likely the royal linen mentioned in texts.

Continuity emerges as the defining characteristic of Egyptian textile tools, though this does not preclude significant innovations – such as the introduction of the vertical two-beam loom. Interestingly, no changes in spinning tools coincide with this innovation, and the transition from the Middle Kingdom to the New Kingdom brought no transformations in spinning equipment. This continuity is remarkable, given the major technological and social developments of the New Kingdom, including the advent of tapestry weaving, the employment of male weavers, and the replacement of the horizontal ground loom with the vertical two-beam loom. Furthermore, the iconographic evidence seems to point to a shift from the drop spinning to the grasped spindle spinning, with threads passing through a hook or a circle in the New Kingdom. Yet, spindles do not seem to change. The only documented innovation in material culture related to weaving is the appearance of warp spacers for the vertical loom.

An important point to note is the clear cultural shift regarding the inclusion of textile tools in funerary contexts. During the Predynastic period, placing such tools in graves was a common practice. However, this tradition becomes exceedingly rare in the Dynastic period, indicating a significant change in the symbolic or practical associations of these objects with the afterlife. Unfortunately, the transition from the Predynastic to the Old Kingdom remains poorly understood regarding textile production. Future research focusing on these seemingly mundane tools could significantly enhance our understanding of Egyptian textile manufacture across periods.

Notes

1 'The dishes with two loops in the bottom which are like large class of roughly cut stone objects, which have similarly two loops (or occasionally only one) in the bottom' (Petrie 1890, 25).

2 Semi-discoid is a different shape from the crescent shape of loom-weights that can be found in Anatolia. See Wisti Lassen 2015, 127, fig. 4.4.1.

3 A technique that was no longer in use in Egypt after 600 BC (Cartwright *et al.* 1998, 106).

4 For an in-depth analysis of this technique on the materials from Lahun see Cartwright *et al.* 1998, 104, fig. 1.

5 Another interesting element is the scarcity of textile tools found by I. Shaw's recent excavations (Hodgkinson 2018, 203).

6 For a detailed and updated discussion of these assemblages, see Gasperini 2018.

7 For the Urnfield culture see Wachsmann 2013, 178–99; for a Hittite tradition see Politi 2001, 107–11; for a reassessment see Gasperini 2018. More circumstantial is the hypothesis by Gasperini (2018, 301), who considers them to be secondary depositions after robberies occurred in the 21st Dynasty.

8 For a detailed discussion see Thomas 1981, 5–6; Wachsmann 2013, 178–99; Gasperini 2018.

9 1921.587 A. Weight given in the museum database is 103.9 g, while Barber reported 150 g (Barber 1991, 64).

10 Although weaving is not clearly stated, it seems a likely interpretation.

11 See the consideration on the reliability of the sample for Lahun.

12 These are fully discussed and catalogued in Spinazzi-Lucchesi 2018.

13 Cahier 3, 1934–35, 20: 'utensiles de ménage. Balais, fusaïoles, navettes, poids' https://www.ifao.egnet.net/bases/archives/bruyere/?sujet=Kom+sud+-+Village&os=35.

14 The study of the materials at the Museo Egizio began during a thesis for the Scuola Interateneo di Specializzazione in Beni Archeologici of Universities of Trieste, Udine and Venice. After the thesis, the materials were re-examined, and some were sampled by an archaeobotanist, Mauro Rottoli, who also conducted the wood identification.

15 For a more detailed discussion see Spinazzi-Lucchesi 2018.

16 These marks have been recorded and will be part of the comprehensive study on Deir el-Medina's identity marks by B. Haring and K. Van der Moezel.

17 See the similar issue for Lahun.

18 See the publications by Janssen (1975; 2008), mainly focused on terminology.

6

Conclusions: Tools in contact

Egypt and the Southern Levant show evidence of a close relationship since the early periods, although this was subject to change over time. To what extent did political and commercial contacts influence textile production and tools? Certainly, textiles and textile tools were used as diplomatic gifts, which proves that royal courts had knowledge of both categories. In fact, among the cloth in Tutankhamun's tomb, a tunic with non-Egyptian motifs was found, which could have been produced somewhere in the Levant, possibly linked to the Mitanni kingdom (Vogelsang-Eastwood 1999, 80–6). Spinning tools also formed part of the diplomatic gifts between the Mitannian court of Tushratta and the Egyptian king Amenhotep III, since in a letter from Amarna, precious spindles made of gold and valuable stones such as lapis lazuli are listed among the goods (Adler 1976, 196–7, 346, Kn25; Wisti Lassen 2010, 276). However, no traces of these precious gifts have been identified archaeologically, and the tunic of Tutankhamun has no comparison in any extant textile. Several texts report the presence of Asiatic peoples in Egyptian textile workshops (Cartwright *et al.* 1998, 92–4; Kemp and Vogelsang-Eastwood 2001, 433–4), as seen at Gurob, but also in the tomb of Rekhmira in Thebes. Should we thus expect to see some differences in the textiles, tools, or techniques employed? From the evidence presented here, the answer is no.

When considering spindles, it is notable that all examples found in Egypt throughout the entire period under study are made of wood. Despite textual references to metal spindles – and their attestation in numerous Near Eastern contexts during the 3rd millennium BC – none have been discovered in Egypt. In the Levant, a new type of bone and ivory spindle emerges, distinguished by characteristic incised lattice and band decorations. However, no examples of this typology have been found in Egypt. At Gurob, some wooden shafts bearing similar decorative patterns were recovered (Thomas 1981, 61–2, pl. 18), yet they lack the grooves necessary for attaching thread, suggesting they should be identified as pins rather than spindles. While there is no evidence of Levantine influence on Egyptian spindle forms, establishing potential Egyptian influence in the Levant is even more challenging. The exclusive use of wooden spindles in Egypt contrasts with the poor preservation of wood in Levantine contexts, making it virtually impossible to determine whether Egyptian styles or techniques were ever adopted there.

A similar pattern emerges when examining spindle whorls. In the early stages of the Egyptian textile industry, perforated sherds and dome-shaped whorls – primarily made of limestone, though occasionally of other stones – were widely used. In contrast, Levantine sites exhibit a preference for discoid stone spindle whorls and biconical pottery whorls, a typology entirely absent from Egypt. Although Egypt's spinning industry developed relatively late compared to the Levant (a conclusion drawn from the limited Neolithic settlement evidence), it appears to have employed a distinct set of tools for yarn production.

When it comes to fibres, however, there are considerably more similarities between the two regions in terms of processing techniques and spinning directions (Jones 2008, 114). Yet, these parallels may not indicate direct knowledge transfer but rather independent responses to a shared natural phenomenon – flax naturally favours an S-twist direction.

For later periods, particularly the Egyptian Old Kingdom, the evidence is sparse. Few textile-related artefacts are known from this era, making any firm conclusions impossible. In contrast, Middle and New Kingdom settlements yield extensive collections of spindle whorls, predominantly wooden, though stone and bone examples are also present. Meanwhile, in the Levant, the MBA marks the introduction of dome-shaped bone spindle whorls, which become widespread during the LBA. This type of whorls, which could function as a mark of technological transfer, seems entirely absent from Egypt. In fact, very few bone spindle whorls are known from Egyptian contexts, mostly from Tell el-Amarna, and they seem not to share the same measurements or decoration that are known from the Levant. Even more surprising is their absence from Deir el-Medina, where they seem not to have been used. It is a pity that so few sites in Egypt have preserved evidence of textile production in the 1st millennium BC, which corresponds to the period of maximum production (to our knowledge) of textile tools in the Levant. During this period, the Southern Levant sees a flourishing of stone spindle whorls, which are quite small and light, usually made of steatite or limestone, but occasionally from harder stones. Again, this type of whorls is apparently absent from Egypt, where spindle whorls appear quite similar to those of earlier periods. For spindles, it is very complicated to trace Egyptian materials in the Levant, since the vast majority of whorls are made of wood. The few Egyptian stone whorls generally have a dome shape and are heavy; the dome shape is also very common in the Levant, and has been found in many different weights, but they are generally lighter than their Egyptian parallels.

Perforated sherds is a category common to both areas but, unfortunately, they appear to also be used in many other areas of the world without connection to those investigated here. In both areas, they appear quite common in early periods, becoming much rarer in later periods, when other materials and typology of whorls become predominant. However, Egyptian documentation becomes much more elusive concerning the presence of these mundane objects, and their usage and presence can thus only be speculated from a few hints present in publications. In the future, we hope that excavation reports from Egyptian sites will start to give more information about these tools.

Basalt rings appear in the Levant during the Chalcolithic period and are fairly widespread during the EBA and, to a lesser extent, the MBA and the Iron Age. There are potentially two categories present inside this group, with the smallest and most refined objects used as spindle whorls, while no definitive interpretation has been found for the second group. The large area in which they have been found is impressive, certainly originating in the Southern Levant, but also reaching some northern Levantine sites and Egypt. An analysis of the basalt has proven that they could have been produced quite far from the site where they were excavated, and examples found in Egypt (from Maadi and possibly Tell el-Farkha; Mączyńska 2008), were certainly Levantine imports. There are relatively few of them (although possibly in the future they will be recognised at other Egyptian sites), and they are apparently located only in the Nile Delta and in Predynastic contexts. Whatever their function may have been, they never appear to have gained popularity in Egypt. Spinning bowls warrant separate consideration. They first appear in Levantine Chalcolithic contexts, predating the earliest Egyptian examples, which are not attested before the Late Predynastic period. In both regions, these tools seem to vanish for an extended period before reappearing in Egypt during the Middle Kingdom – albeit in entirely different shapes. In the Levant, they re-emerge in the LBA and Iron Age I, only to nearly disappear in subsequent layers.

Despite their recurring presence, spinning bowls are generally found in very small quantities, even at sites with well-documented textile production. Their distribution appears somewhat random: they are present at sites under direct Egyptian control, at locations with minimal Egyptian influence, and sometimes absent from strongly Egyptian-controlled settlements. However, their relative scarcity, coupled with a clear association with the Egyptian garrison at Beth Shean, suggests that they may have been produced specifically for Egyptian families residing in the Levant. Notably, they seem never to have achieved widespread popularity – except at Beth Shean – indicating usage confined to a limited group. While spinning bowls have been discovered at sites containing only Levantine textile tools, it is important to consider the material bias in the archaeological record: Egyptian spindles and spindle whorls were typically made of wood, which rarely survives. Therefore, the absence of certain artefacts may reflect preservation issues rather than cultural preferences. Another plausible explanation for their overall rarity – yet concentrated presence in the Beth Shean region – is their potential use in flax preparation.

This hypothesis assumes that flax fibres were first spliced and then spun – a process well documented in ancient Egypt but far less certain for the inhabitants of the Southern Levant. Shamir (2015) explicitly states that splicing was abandoned in the region at the end of the MBA, and Vogelsang-Eastwood (1987) suggests that spinning bowls were instead used for plying threads. If so, these tools could have been employed for processing both flax and wool, thereby weakening their direct association with the flax fields of the Beth Shean Valley.

However, the reintroduction of spinning bowls into the Levant appears closely tied to Egyptian rule. By this time, Levantine communities no longer practised flax splicing, making it highly likely that these tools were used primarily by Egyptian spinners stationed in the region. Their presence is thus not merely a reflection of local textile traditions but an active expression of Egyptian technological influence. Far from being incidental, the use of spinning bowls under Egyptian control underscores the persistence of Egyptian fibre-processing methods abroad, reinforcing the cultural and economic integration of local production into the Egyptian imperial system.

Loom weights and net sinkers form another widely debated category, particularly regarding their implications for the adoption of the vertical two-beam loom and the warp-weighted loom. It is highly likely that both Egypt and the Southern Levant extensively used the horizontal ground loom during their early phases, with its use probably continuing in parallel with other loom types in later periods. Conical loom weights begin to appear in the Southern Levant during the MBA, providing clear evidence for the adoption of the warp-weighted loom. However, their limited number suggests that another type of loom – likely the horizontal ground loom used in earlier periods – remained in use alongside this innovation. Significantly, the high-quality craftsmanship of these weights, their association with sealing practices, and their discovery at elite sites such as Tel Kabri strongly indicate their connection to high-status textile production.

Notably, these distinctive and easily recognisable loom weights are absent from contemporary Egyptian sites. This absence, reinforced by iconographic evidence, suggests that the warp-weighted loom was unknown or unused in Egypt during this period. The contrast highlights differing technological choices between the two regions, with the Southern Levant embracing the warp-weighted loom for elite production while Egypt maintained other established weaving methods.

At a certain point, a new type of loom – the vertical two-beam loom – was developed. While its exact time and place of origin remain uncertain, many scholars propose a Southern Levantine origin. This hypothesis is based on the loom's design, which combines elements of two loom types: one horizontal with two beams and one vertical, both known in the Levant, while Egypt had only the horizontal version. The vertical two-beam loom first appears in New Kingdom Egyptian iconography, marking a shift in Egyptian weaving technology. Meanwhile, in the Levant, the number of loom weights diminishes during the LBA, suggesting that both regions might have shared the same weaving technology during this period.

Though loom weights did not entirely disappear from the Levant, their scarcity indicates that warp-weighted looms were becoming increasingly obsolete. It's important to clarify that the potential use of the vertical two-beam loom in the Levant, though not yet proven, should not be directly attributed to Egyptian rule. As seen with spinning bowls, weaving and spinning traditions were difficult to alter, and Egyptian domination was unlikely to have been so absolute as to impose changes in these deeply ingrained practices at every social level.

Instead, the spread and adoption of the vertical two-beam loom were probably driven by practical considerations: it could be used in smaller spaces than the horizontal loom and may have offered technical advantages. Additionally, changing fashion in the LBA may have required specific types of textiles, such as dense tabby fabrics, which were difficult to produce with a warp-weighted loom. The vertical two-beam loom, with its different technical characteristics, may have been better suited to these needs.

It is also crucial to recognise that the adoption of the new loom was likely not uniform across all social contexts. Home production would have continued using older looms – whether horizontal ground looms or warp-weighted looms – particularly in less elite contexts where the newer loom was not as accessible or necessary.

A significant revolution occurred in the Levant during the 1st millennium BC, marked by the widespread discovery of thousands of poorly shaped clay loom weights. This suggests the broad adoption of the warp-weighted loom across all levels of society, from textile workshops linked to temples to domestic production, as indicated by the ubiquitous presence of loom weights. Similarly, the shift to the two-beam loom in the Levant was likely driven not by the end of Egyptian control over Canaan but by evolving textile demands that the warp-weighted loom was better suited to produce.

In contrast, in Egypt, such a revolution did not take place until the Greek and Roman periods, when loom weights began to appear in large quantities (*e.g.* Plinthine: Pesenti and Saleh 2018; Nelson Island: Gallo 2009). This delayed shift reflects a different trajectory in Egyptian textile practices, where the transition to newer loom technologies occurred much later than in the Levant. Several Egyptian sites, however, have shown the presence of objects that are sometimes defined as loom weights, and sometimes as net sinkers. By examining the contexts of these findings, as well as their chronology (which saw their appearance in Prehistoric phases), the specific shape of the pottery types, and their representations in grave paintings and reliefs, it seems possible to postulate a usage as net weights for the vast majority of these tools. The few objects made of mud and clay, which certainly could not be used in water, should be considered as counterweights, with many possible usages.

Bone spatulae and pin beaters are common in both areas since the Neolithic periods, and although not all of them should be linked with textile production, it is very likely that a substantial number of them were employed for beating weft and keeping the warp in order. They are especially common in the New Kingdom Egyptian and Iron Age Levantine contexts, but so far it has not been possible to link their use to specific looms or textiles. Furthermore, similar tools appear widespread in many regions of the world, similar to perforated sherds. This was probably a very reasonable, cheap solution for working with looms. We should also remember that wooden spatulae and beaters were certainly known and used, as in modern textile production, since some wooden objects found in Egyptian contexts were very likely to have been used in this way.

Needles are the last category to be examined. They seem to share some parallels between the two areas, since bone needles with large heads are quite widespread in early periods, and are subsequently replaced by metal needles. However, this could largely depend on the diffusion and availability of metals and metal objects in general. In the MBA, the Levantine region saw the introduction of a new typology of needle, with an eye realised by bending the upper part of the shaft back on itself, a typology that would never be introduced in Egypt. In fact, Egypt would continue to produce its needles by punching the shafts from one side to the other throughout its history.

From the documentation examined here, it seems clear that Egypt and the Southern Levant, although geographically – and in many periods commercially and politically – close, did not permit a transfer of textile tools between the two areas, nor is it likely that technologies were shared. This is not surprising, since textile production is a very deeply culturally rooted craft, which has undergone slow changes over time.

The lack of permeability to foreign traditions and techniques is particularly evident in Egypt, where almost no Levantine tools can be identified. Despite textual references suggesting that a significant number of Asiatic peoples were employed in Egyptian weaving workshops, these foreign workers were not valued for their specific skills or expertise. Instead, they were trained to adopt Egyptian methods, as highlighted by a papyrus from Gurob. This implies that the Egyptians had little interest in incorporating foreign textile practices, preferring instead to maintain their own established techniques.

While many foreigners lived in Egypt, and some even wore their traditional attire, there is little evidence to suggest that these people retained their own customs and practices in any significant way. In many instances, they appear to have fully adopted Egyptian clothing and cultural norms. This is especially evident in funerary stelae, which, while likely idealised, still reflect a striking absence of foreign elements in everyday Egyptian life. Archaeological evidence is equally sparse when it comes to foreign objects or traditions, further reinforcing the idea that Egypt's textile production was heavily focused on local styles. Exotic garments and textiles, though perhaps available for trade, were rarely produced within Egypt itself. This suggests that Egypt was far more inward-looking in terms of its textile production, choosing to focus on its own established methods and styles, while incorporating foreign goods only when they were imported or traded.

To conclude, while both Egypt and the Levant underwent significant changes in textile production during the periods under consideration, the similarities between their developments are minimal. The evidence points less to direct cultural or political influence and more to the influence of practical, technological needs that were unique to each region. The shifts in tools and techniques appear to be driven by the specific demands of each society, rather than by a cross-cultural exchange of knowledge. The lack of direct influence between the two areas underscores the independence of their textile industries and highlights the distinctive paths they followed in their technological evolution.

Bibliography

Adams, B. 1995. *Ancient Nekhen: Garstang in the City of Hierakonpolis*. New Malden.

Adler, H.-P. 1976. *Das Akkadische des Königs Tusratta von Mitanni*. Kevelaer.

Adovasio, J.M. 1975. 'The Textile and Basketry Impressions from Jarmo'. *Paléorient* 3: 223–30.

Adovasio, J.M., O. Soffer, D.C. Hyland, B. Klima and J.A. Svoboda. 2001. 'Perishable industries from Dolni Vestonice I: New insights into the nature and origin of the Gravettian'. *Archaeology Ethnology and Anthropology of Eurasia* 2(6): 48–65.

Alberti, M.E. 2011. 'Textile Industry Indicators in Minoan Work Areas: Problems of Typology and Interpretation'. In *Purpureae Vestes I. Textiles y Tintes Del Mediterráneo En Época Romana*, edited by C. Alfaro, J.P. Wild and B. Costa, 25–36. Valénsia.

Albright, W.F. 1938. *The Excavation of Tell Beit Mirsim in Palestina*. New Haven.

Allam, S. 1973. *Hieratische Ostraka und Papyri aus der Ramessidenzeit.* Tübingen.

Allen, S.J. 1997. 'Spinning Bowls: Representation and Reality'. In *Ancient Egypt, the Aegean, and the Near East: Studies in Honour of Martha Rhoads Bell*, edited by J. Phillips, 17–38. San Antonio.

Andersson, E. 1999. *The Common Thread, Textile Production during the Late Iron Age–Viking Age*. Lund.

Andersson, E. 2003. *Tools for Textile Production – from Birka and Hedeby*. Vol. 8. Stockholm.

Andersson Strand, E. 2010. 'The Basics of Textile Tools and Textile Technology'. In *Textile Terminologies in the Ancient Near East and Mediterranean from the Third to the First Millennia BC*, edited by M.-L. Nosch and C. Michel, 10–22. Oxford.

Andersson Strand, E. 2015. 'The Basics of Textile Tools and Textile Technology – from Fibre to Fabric'. In *Tools, Textiles and Contexts: Investigating Textile Production in the Aegean and Eastern Mediterranean Bronze Age*, edited by E. Andersson Strand and M.-L. Nosch, 75–100. Oxford.

Andersson Strand, E. 2018. 'Early Loom Types in Ancient Societies'. In *First Textiles: The Beginnings of Textile Manufacture in Europe and the Mediterranean*, edited by M. Siennicka, L. Rahmstorf and A. Ulanowska, 17–30. Oxford.

Andersson Strand, E. and M.-L. Nosch. 2015. *Tools, Textiles and Contexts: Investigating Textile Production in the Aegean and Eastern Mediterranean Bronze Age*. Oxford.

Ariel, D.T. 1990. *Excavations at the City of David 1978–1985. 2. Imported Stamped Amphora Handles, Coins, Worked Bone and Ivory, and Glass*. Qedem 30. Jerusalem.

Arnold, D. 1981. *Der Tempel Des Königs Mentuhotep von Deir El-Bahari: 3. Die Königlichen Beigaben*. Mainz am Rhein.

Arnold, F. 1996. 'Settlement Remains at Lisht-North'. In *Haus und Palast im alten Ägypten*, edited by M. Bietak, 13–21. Wien.

Arnold, F. 2015. 'Clean and Unclean Space: Domestic Waste Management at Elephantine'. In *Household Studies in Complex Societies: (Micro) Archaeological and Textual Approaches: Papers from the Oriental Institute Seminar Household Studies in Complex Societies, Held at the Oriental Institute of the University of Chicago, 15–16 March 2013*, edited by M. Müller, 151–68. Chicago.

Ashton, S.-A. 2011. 'Egyptian Hair Combs in the Fitzwilliam Museum'. In *Under the Potter's Tree: Studies on Ancient Egypt Presented to Janine Bourriau on the Occasion of Her 70th Birthday*, edited by D. Aston, B. Bader, C. Gallorini, P. Nicholson, S. Buckingham and J. Bourriau, 19–44. Leuven.

Aston, D.A. and B. Bader. 1998. 'Einige Bemerkungen zum späten Neuen Reich in Matmar'. *Mitteilungen des Deutschen Archäologischen Instituts Abteilung Kairo* 54: 19–48.

Aston, D.A. and M. Bietak. 2004. *Tell El-Dab'a XII. A Corpus of Late Middle Kingdom and Second Intermediate Period Pottery*. Wien.

Ayrton, E. and W.L.S. Loat. 1911. *Pre-Dynastic Cemetery of El Mahasna*. London.

Ayrton, E., C.T. Currelly and A.E.P. Weigall. 1904. *Abydos III*. London.

Bader, B. 2001. *Tell el-Dab'a XIII: Typologie und Chronologie der Mergel C-Ton Keramik: Materialien zum Binnenhandel des Mittleren Reiches und der Zweiten Zwischenzeit*. Wien.

Bader, N.O. 1993. *Tell Maghzaliyah: An Early Neolithic Site in Northern Iraq*. Tucson.

Baines, P. 1989. *Linen: Handspinning and Weaving*. London.

Bajeot, J. 2017. *Predynastic Maadi in Context: The Research of the Italian Expedition Revisited (1977–1986)*. Studi di Preistoria Orientale 4. Roma.

Balfanz, K. 1995. 'Bronzezeitliche Spinnwirtel Aus Troia'. *Studia Troica* 5 (11): 7–44.

Banning, E.B. 2012. 'The Southern Levant'. In *A Companion to the Archaeology of the Ancient Near East*, edited by D.T. Potts, 396–414. https://doi.org/10.1002/9781444360790.ch21.

Banning, E.B., R. Dods, J. Field, I. Kuijt, J. Mccorriston, J. Siggers, H. Taani and J. Triggs. 1992. 'Tabaqat Al-Bûma. 1990. Excavations at a Kebaran and Late Neolithic Site in Wadi Ziqlab'. *Annual of the Department of Antiquities of Jordan* 36: 43–69.

Bar-Adon, P. 1980. *The Cave of the Treasure: The Finds from the Caves in Naḥal Mishmar*. Jerusalem.

Barber, E.W. 1991. *Prehistoric Textiles: The Development of Cloth in the Neolithic and Bronze Ages with Special Reference to the Aegean*. Princeton, N.J.; Chichester.

Bard, K.A. 2003. 'The Emergence of the Egyptian State (3200–2686 BC)'. In *The Oxford History of Ancient Egypt*, edited by I. Shaw, 61–88. Oxford.

Bar-Oz, G. and R. Yeshurun. 2014. 'The Bone Tools from the Cave of the Treasure at Nahal Mishmar'. *Journal of the Israel Prehistoric Society* 44: 240–7.

Bar-Yosef, O. and D. Alon. 1988. 'Nahal Hemar Cave'. *Atiqot* 18: 50–8.

Bechar, S. 2017. 'The Middle and Late Bronze Age Pottery'. In *Hazor VII*, edited by A. Ben-Tor, S. Zuckerman, S. Bechar and D. Sandhaus, 190–470. Jerusalem.

Bellinger, L. 1959. 'Craft Habits. Part II, Spinning and Fibers in Warp Yarns'. *Textile Museum Workshop Notes* 20: 1–4.

Ben-Arieh, S. and G. Edelstein. 1977. 'Tombs near the Persian Garden'. *Atiqot* 12: 1–88.

Bender Jørgensen, L. 1992. *North European Textiles until AD 1000*. Aarhus.

Bender Jørgensen, L. and A. Rast-Eicher. 2018. 'Fibres for Bronze Age Textiles'. In *Creativity in the Bronze Age: Understanding Innovation in Pottery, Textile, and Metalwork Production*, edited by L. Bender Jørgensen, J.R. Sofaer and M.L. Stig Sørensen, 25–36. Cambridge. https://doi.org/10.1017/9781108344357.

Bender Jørgensen, L., A. Rast-Eicher and W. Wendrich. 2023. 'Earliest Evidence for Textile Technologies'. *Paléorient. Revue Pluridisciplinaire de Préhistoire et de Protohistoire de l'Asie Du Sud-Ouest et de l'Asie Centrale* 49–1 (June): 213–28. https://doi.org/10.4000/paleorient.2479.

Ben-Dov, R. 1999. 'Loom Weights.' In *Tel 'Ira: A Stronghold in the Biblical Negev*, edited by I. Beit-Arieh, 445–51. Tel Aviv.

Ben-Dov, R. and L. Gershuny. 2011. *Dan III: Avraham Biran Excavations 1966–1999: The Late Bronze Age*. Jerusalem.

Ben-Shlomo, D. 2010. *Philistine Iconography a Wealth of Style and Symbolism*. Orbis Biblicus et Orientalis 241. Fribourg, Göttingen.

Ben-Tor, A. 2012. 'Tools and Weapons'. In *Hazor VI: The 1990-2009 Excavations: The Iron Age*, edited by A. Ben-Tor, D. Ben-Ami, D. Sandhaus, S. Bechar and T. Kuper-Blau, 530–41. Jersualem.

Ben-Tor, A. 2016. *Hazor: Canaanite Metropolis, Israelite City*. Jerusalem.

Ben-Tor, D. 2007. *Scarabs, Chronology, and Interconnections: Egypt and Palestine in the Second Intermediate Period*. Fribourg.

Ben-Yosef, E., O.A. Shamir and J.E. Levy. 2017. 'On Early Metallurgy and Textile-Production Technologies in the Southern Levant: A Response to Langgut et al. (2016)'. *Antiquity* 91: 765–76.

Bergfjord, C., S. Karg, A. Rast-Eicher, M.-L. Nosch, U. Mannering, R.G. Allaby, B.M. Murphy and B. Holst. 2010. 'Comment on "30,000-Year-Old Wild Flax Fibers"'. *Science* 328 (5986): 1634. https://doi.org/10.1126/science.1186345.

Bergfjord, C., U. Mannering, K.M. Frei, M. Gleba, A.B. Scharff, I. Skals, J. Heinemeier, M.-L. Nosch and B. Holst. 2012. 'Nettle as a Distinct Bronze Age Textile Plant'. *Scientific Reports* 2 (1): 664. https://doi.org/10.1038/srep00664.

Betts, A., K. van der Borg, A. de Jong, C. McClintock and M. van Strydonck. 1994. 'Early Cotton in North Arabia'. *Journal of Archaeological Science* 21 (4): 489–99. https://doi.org/10.1006/jasc.1994.1049.

Bianucci, R., M.E. Habicht, S. Buckley, J. Fletcher, R. Seiler, L.M. Öhrström, E. Vassilika, T. Böni and F.J. Rühli. 2015. 'Shedding New Light on the 18th Dynasty Mummies of the Royal Architect Kha and His Spouse Merit'. *PloS One* 10 (7): e0131916.

Biran, A., R. Ben-Dov and B. Arensburg. 2002. *Dan II: A Chronicle of the Excavations and the Late Bronze Age 'Mycenaean' Tomb*. Jerusalem.

Boertien, J.H. 2013. *Unravelling the Fabric: Textile Production in Iron Age Transjordan*. Ph.D. dissertation, University of Groningen.

Bonatz, D. 2000. *Das syro-hethitische Grabdenkmal: Untersuchungen zur Entstehung einer neuen Bildgattung in der Eisenzeit im nordsyrisch-südostanatolischen Raum*. Mainz.

Bonn, A.G., H. Moyer and M.R. Notis. 1993. 'The Typology and Archaeometallurgy of the Copper-Base Artifacts'. In *The Late Bronze Egyptian Garrison at Beth Shan: A Study of Levels VII and VIII*, edited by F.W. James and P.E. McGovern, 1: 203–20. Philadelphia.

Borgna, E. 2003. 'Attrezzi per filare nella tarda età del bronzo italiana: connessioni con l'Egeo e con Cipro'. *Rivista di Scienze Preistoriche*, 519–48.

Borla, M. and C. Oliva. 2014. 'Il riscontro inventariale dei reperti tessili conservati nei depositi del Museo Antichità Egizie di Torino. Note circa l'esame di un lotto di tessuti faraonici provenienti dalla «cachette» di Deir el-Bahari (DB 320)'. In *Antichità egizie e Italia. Prospettive di ricerca e indagini sul campo. Atti del III Convegno Nazionale Veneto di Egittologia Ricerche sull'antico Egitto in Italia*, edited by E. Marcello Ciampini and P. Zanovello, 85–92. Antichistica 6. Venezia. https://edizionicafoscari.unive.it/it/edizioni4/libri/978-88-97735-97-7/.

Borla, M. and C. Oliva. 2017. 'The Mummies of the "Three Sisters" in the Museo Egizio: A Case Study. Conservation and Studies of Textiles and Bandages'. In *Proceedings of the XI International Congress of Egyptologists: Florence, Italy 23–30 August 2015*, edited by M.C. Guidotti and G. Rosati, 462–67. Oxford.

Bourriau, J. and C. Gallorini. 2016. *The Survey of Memphis VIII Kom Rabia: The Middle Kingdom and Second Intermediate Period Pottery*. London.

Brandl, B. 2009. 'Scarabs, Seals, Sealings and Seal Impressions'. In *Excavations at Tel Beth-Shean 1989-1996. Vol. III. The 13th-11th Century BCE Strata in Areas N and S*, edited by N. Panitz-Cohen and A. Mazar, 636–84. Jerusalem.

Braun, E. 2004. *Early Beth Shan (Strata XIX–XIII): G.M. Fitzgerald's Deep Cut on the Tell.* University Museum Monograph 121. Philadelphia.

Braun, E., D. Ilan, O. Marder, S. Shalev and Y. Braun. 2013. *Early Megiddo on the East Slope (the 'Megiddo Stages'): A Report on the Early Occupation of the East Slope of Megiddo; Results of the Oriental Institute's Excavations, 1925–1933.* Chicago.

Breasted, J.H. 1976. *Egyptian Servant Statues.* New York.

Breniquet, C. 2008. *Essai sur le tissage en Mésopotamie: des premières communautés sédentaires au milieu du IIIe millénaire avant J.-C.* Paris.

Breniquet, C. 2010. 'Weaving in Mesopotamia during the Bronze Age'. In *Textile Terminologies in the Ancient Near East and the Mediterranean from the 3rd to the 1st Millennia BC*, edited by C. Michel and M.-L. Nosch, 52–67. Oxford.

Breniquet, C. 2020. 'Early Wool of Mesopotamia, *c.* 7000–3000 BC. Between Prestige and Economy'. In *The Competition of Fibres: Early Textile Production in Western Asia, South-East and Central Europe (10,000–500 BCE)*, edited by W. Schier and S. Pollock, 17–26. Oxford; Philadelphia.

Breniquet, C. and C. Michel. 2014. *Wool Economy in the Ancient Near East.* Oxford.

Brewer, D.J. and R. Friedman. 1989. *Fish and Fishing in Ancient Egypt.* Warminster.

Briend, J., J.-B. Humbert and É. Puech. 1980. *Tell Keisan: 1971–1976, Une Cité Phénicienne En Galilée.* Fribourg; Göttingen; Paris.

Brunton, G. 1937. *Mostagedda and the Tasian Culture: British Museum Expedition to Middle Egypt, Years 1/2.* London.

Brunton, G. 1948. *Matmar.* London.

Brunton, G. and G. Caton-Thompson. 1928. *The Badarian Civilisation and Predynastic Remains near Badari.* London.

Brunton, G. and R. Engelbach. 1927. *Gurob.* London.

Bruyère, B. 1928. *Rapport Sur Les Fouilles de Deir El Médineh (V; 1927).* Fouilles de l'Institut Français d'Archéologie Orientale Du Caire 5,2. Le Caire.

Bruyère, B. 1933. *Rapport sur les fouilles de Deir el Médineh (V; 1930).* Fouilles de l'Institut Français d'Archéologie Orientale du Caire 8,3. Le Caire.

Bruyère, B. 1939. *Rapport sur les fouilles de Deir el Médineh 1934–1935, Le village, les décharges publiques, la station de repos du col de la vallée des rois.* Fouilles de l'Institute français d'archéologie orientale du Caire 16. Le Caire.

Bruyère, B. 1948. *Les fouilles et les découvertes de constructions (1935–1940).* Vol. 1. Fouilles de l'Institut Français d'Archéologie Orientale du Caire 20. Le Caire.

Bruyère, B. 1952. *Rapport sur les fouilles de Deir el Médineh (annees 1945–1946 et 1946–1947).* Fouilles de l'Institut Français d'Archéologie Orientale du Caire 21. Le Caire.

Bruyère, B. 1953. *Rapport sur les fouilles de Deir el Médineh (années 1948 à 1951).* Fouilles de l'Institut Français d'Archéologie Orientale du Caire 26. Le Caire.

Bruyère, B. and G. Jourdain. 1937a. *Rapport Sur Les Fouilles de Deir El Médineh (1933–1934). Première Partie: La Nécropole de l'Ouest. Vol. 1.* Le Caire.

Bruyère, B. and G. Jourdain. 1937b. *Rapport sur les fouilles de Deir el Médineh (annees 1934–35) deuxième partie: La nécropole de l'est.* Le Caire.

Buchez, N. and B. Midant-Reynes. 2002. *Adaïma 1.* Le Caire.

Bunimovitz, S. and Z. Lederman. 2015. 'Migration, Hybridization, and Resistance: Identity Dynamics in the Early Iron Age Southern Levant'. In *The Cambridge Prehistory of the Bronze and Iron Age Mediterranean*, edited by A.B. Knapp and P. van Dommelen, 252–65. Cambridge. https://doi.org/10.1017/CHO9781139028387.019.

Bunimovitz, S. and Z. Lederman. 2016. 'Iron Age Artifacts'. In *Tel Beth-Shemesh: A Border Community in Judah. Renewed Excavations 1990–2000: The Iron Age*, edited by S. Bunimovitz and Z. Lederman, 560–602. Tel Aviv; Winona Lake, IN.

Burnham, H.B. 1965. 'Çatal Hüyük – The Textiles and Twined Fabrics'. *Anatolian Studies* 15: 169–74.

Cahill, J.M. 2006. 'The Excavations at Tell El-Hammah: A Prelude to Amihai Mazar's Beth-Shean Valley Regional Project'. In *'I Will Speak the Riddles of Ancient Times': Archaeological and Historical Studies in Honor of Amihai Mazar on the Occasion of His Sixtieth Birthday*, edited by A.M. Maeir, P.R. de Miroschedji and A. Mazar, 429–59. Winona Lake, IN.

Capel, A.K., G. Markoe and B.M. Bryan. 1996. *Mistress of the House, Mistress of Heaven: Women in Ancient Egypt.* Easthampton, MA.

Carington Smith, J. 1976. *Spinning, Weaving and Textile Manufacture in Prehistoric Greece: From the Beginning of the Neolithic to the End of the Mycenaean Ages; with Particular Reference to the Evidence Found on Archaeological Excavations.* Thesis University of Tasmania.

Cartwright, C., H. Granger-Taylor and S. Quirke. 1998. 'Lahun Textile Evidence in London'. In *Lahun Studies*, edited by S. Quirke, 92–111. Reigate.

Cassuto, D. 2008. 'Bringing Home the Artifacts: A Social Interpretation of Loom Weights in Context.' In *The World of Women in the Ancient and Classical Near East*, edited by B. Alpert Nakhai, 63–77. Newcastle-upon-Tyne.

Cassuto, D. 2012. 'Weaving Implements'. In *Tell es-Safi/Gath I: The 1996–2005 Seasons*, edited by A.M. Maeir, 467–84. Wiesbaden.

Cassuto, D. 2017. 'Modes of Textile Production in Cultic Contexts in the Iron Age Southern Levant: The Finds from Tell Es-Safi/Gath'. In *Textiles and Cult in the Ancient Mediterranean*, edited by C. Brøns and M.-L. Nosch, 189–98. Oxford.

Cassuto, D. 2018. 'Textile Production at Iron Age Tell Eṣ-Ṣâfi/Gath'. *Near Eastern Archaeology* 81 (1): 55–58.

Caton-Thompson, G. and E.W. Gardner. 1934. *The Desert Fayum.* London.

Cecchini, S.M. 1992. 'Gli Avori e Gli Ossi. Appunti Sull'attività Tessile in Siria Del Nord Durante l'Età Del Ferro'. *Tell Afis e l'età Del Ferro,* edited by S. Mazzoni, 3–27. Pisa.

Cecchini, S.M. 2000. 'The Textile Industry in Northern Syria during the Iron Age According to the Evidence of the Tell Afis Excavations'. In *Essays on Syria in the Iron Age. Ancient Near Eastern Studies Supplements 7*, edited by G. Bunnens, 211–33. Leuven.

Cecchini, S.M. 2011. 'Loomweights and the Textile Industry in North Syria in the Early Iron Age'. In *On Cooking Pots, Drinking Cups, Loomweights and Ethnicity in Bronze Age Cyprus and Neighbouring Regions. An International Archaeological Symposium Held in Nicosia, November 6th–7th 2010*, edited by V. Karageorghis and O. Kouka, 195–202. Nicosia.

Černý, J. 1929. 'Papyrus Salt 124 (Brit. Mus. 10055)'. *The Journal of Egyptian Archaeology* 15 (1): 243–58.

Chambon, A. 1984. *Tell El-Far'ah I: L'age du Fer.* Paris.
Chambon, A. 1993. 'Far'ah, Tell El- (North)'. In *The New Encyclopedia of Archaeological Excavations in the Holy Land*, edited by E. Stern, 2: 439–40. Jerusalem.
Charloux, G. 2006. *Artisanat et Urbanisation de La Palestine à l'âge Du Bronze Ancien: Apport de l'étude Des Céramiques à La Structure Sociale.* Unpublished dissertation. Université Panthéon-Sorbonne - Paris I.
Charvát, P. 1981. *The Pottery: The Mastaba of Ptahshepses*. Praha.
Cheval, C. and G. Radi. 2013. 'Les Lames de Tissage, Critères de Détermination et Perspectives de Recherche'. In *Regards Croisés Sur Les Outils Liés Au Travail Des Végétaux: Actes Des Rencontres 23–25 octobre 2012: XXXIII Rencontres Internationales d'Archéologie et d'Histoire d'Antibes = An Interdisciplinary Focus on Plant-Working Tool*, edited by P.C. Anderson, C. Cheval and A. Durand, 323–40. Antibes.
Çilingirŏglu, Ç. 2009. 'Of Stamps, Loom Weights and Spindle Whorls: Contextual Evidence on the Function(s) of Neolithic Stamps from Ulucak, Izmir, Turkey'. *Journal of Mediterranean Archaeology* 22 (1): 3–27.
Cimadevilla, M. 2012. 'Loom Weights and Spindle Whorls'. In *Hazor VI: The 1990–2009 Excavations: The Iron Age*, edited by A. Ben-Tor, D. Ben-Ami, D. Sandhaus, S. Bechar and T. Kuper-Blau, 559–63. Jerusalem.
Collier, M. and S. Quirke. 2002. *The UCL Lahun Papyri: Letters*. Oxford.
Collier, M. and S. Quirke. 2006. *The UCL Lahun Papyri: Accounts*. Oxford.
Cooke, W.D. 1993. 'W.F. Petrie and the Weavers Waste'. *Archaeological Textile Newsletter* 17: 14–15.
Cooke, W.D., M. El-Gamal and A. Brennan. 1991. 'The Hand-Spinning of Ultra-Fine Yarns, Part 2. The Spinning of Flax'. *Bulletin de La Centre International d'Etude des Textiles Anciens* 69: 17–23.
Cortes, E. 2011. 'An Early Weaving Scene'. In *Dawn of Egyptian Art. Catalogue of Exhibition (Metropolitan Museum of Art, New York, April 10 - August 5, 2012)*, edited by D. Craig Patch, 94–5. New York.
Cottica, D. 2007. 'Spinning in the Roman World: From Everyday Craft to Metaphor of Destiny'. In *Ancient Textiles, Production, Craft and Society, Proceedings of the First International Conference on Ancient Textiles, Held at Lund, Sweden, and Copenhagen, Denmark, on March 19–23, 2003*, edited by C. Gillis and M.-L. Nosch, 220–8. Oxford.
Crewe, L. 1998. *Spindle Whorls: A Study of Form, Function and Decoration in Prehistoric Bronze Age Cyprus*. Studies in Mediterranean Archaeology and Literature 149. Jonsered.
Cristiani, E. 2008. 'Notes on Bone Tools for Textile Production'. *In Tell Abu Al-Kharaz in the Jordan Valley 1. The Early Bronze Age*, by P.M. Fischer, 401–3. Wien.
Crowfoot, G.M. 1921. 'Spinning and Weaving in the Sudan'. *Sudan Notes and Records* 4 (1): 20–38.
Crowfoot, G.M. 1931. *Methods of Hand Spinning in Egypt and Sudan*. Halifax.
Crowfoot, G.M. 1937. 'Of the Warp-Weighted Loom'. *Annual of the British School at Athens* 37: 36–47.
Crowfoot, G.M. 1960. 'Textiles and Matting'. In *Excavations at Jericho: The Tombs Excavated in 1952–4*, K.M. Kenyon, 518–26. Jerusalem.
Czerny, E. 2012. 'F/1, Str.e: An Early Middle Kingdom Settlement Site'. In *Handbook of the Pottery of the Egyptian Middle Kingdom, vol. II: The Regional Volume*, edited by R. Schiestl and A. Seiler. Wien.
Czerny, E. 2015. *Tell el-Dab'a XXII; 'Der Mund der beiden Wege': die Siedlung und der Tempelbezirk des Mittleren Reiches von Ezbet Ruschdi*. Wien.
Czerny, E., J. Boessneck and A. von den Driesch. 1999. *Tell el-Dab'a IX: eine Plansiedlung des frühen Mittleren Reiches*. Wien.
Dagan, A. and D.R. Cassuto. 2016. 'Horvat Shimon: A Small-Scale 8th Century BCE Workshop for Textiles in the Southern Coastal Plain'. *Israel Exploration Journal* 66: 34–54.
Daviau, M. 2002. *Excavations at Tall Jawa, Jordan, vol. 2, The Iron Age Artefacts*. Culture and History of the Ancient Near East 11/2. Leiden; Boston; Köln.
David, A.R. 1986. *The Pyramid Builders of Ancient Egypt: A Modern Investigation of Pharaoh's Workforce*. London; New York.
Davidovich, U. 2013. 'The Chalcolithic – Early Bronze Age Transition: A View from the Judean Desert Caves, Southern Levant'. *Paléorient* 39, no. 1 (2013): 125–38. https://doi.org/10.3406/paleo.2013.5491.
Davies, G.I. 1986. *Megiddo. Cities of the Biblical World*. Cambridge.
de Contenson, H. 1995. *Aswad et Ghoraifé: sites néolithiques en Damascène (Syrie) aux IXème et VIIIème millénaires avant l'ère chrétienne*. Beyrouth.
de Contenson, H. 2000. *Ramad: Site néolithique VIIe et VIIe millénaires avant l'ère chrétienne*. Beyrouth.
de Garis Davies, N. 1913. *Five Theban Tombs (Being Those of Mentuherkhepeshef, User, Daga, Nehemaway and Tati)*. London.
de Garis Davies, N. 1929. 'The Town House in Ancient Egypt'. *Metropolitan Museum Studies* 1, no. 2: 233–55.
de Garis Davies, N. 1948. *Seven Private Tombs at Kurnah*. London.
de Garis Davies, N. and N. de Garis Davies. 1933. *The Tomb of Nefer-Hotep at Thebes*. New York.
de Marco, A.G. and G. Eschenbrenner-Diemer. forthcoming. *Cosmetic Objects from Deir El-Medina. A Comprehensive Study*. Fouilles de l'Institut Français d'Archéologie Orientale du Caire. Cairo.
de Marco, A.G. and P. Marini. 2023. 'Manufatti lignei dimenticati: lo studio dell'artigianato del legno a Deir el-Medina'. *Quaderni Del Museo Del Papiro* 19, 239–56.
de Miroschedji, P. 1988. *Rapport sur les trois premières campagnes de fouilles à Tel Yarmouth (Israël): (1980–1982)*. Paris.
de Miroschedji, P. 1993. 'Far'ah, Tell El- (North)'. In *The New Encyclopedia of Archaeological Excavations in the Holy Land*, edited by E. Stern, 2:433–38. Jerusalem.
de Vaux, R. 1947a. 'La Premiére Campagne De Fouilles A Tell el-Far'ah, Près Naplouse'. *Revue Biblique* 54 (3): 394–433.
de Vaux, R. 1947b. 'La Première Campagne de Fouilles à Tell el-Far'ah, Près Naplouse: Rapport Préliminaire (Suite)'. *Revue Biblique* 54 (4): 573–89.
de Vaux, R. 1948. 'La Seconde Campagne de Fouilles a Tell el-Far'ah, Près Naplouse'. *Revue Biblique* 55 (4): 544–80.
de Vaux, R. 1951. 'La Troisième Campagne De Fouilles A Tell el-Far'ah Près Naplouse: Rapport Préliminaire (Suite)'. *Revue Biblique* 58 (4): 566–90.

de Vaux, R. 1952. 'La Quatrieme Campagne de Fouilles a Tell El-Far'ah, Pres Naplouse'. *Revue Biblique*, 59 (4): 551–83.

de Vaux, R. 1955. 'Les Fouilles de Tell el-Far'ah, Près Naplouse'. *Revue Biblique* 62 (4): 541–89.

de Vaux, R. 1957. 'Les Fouilles de Tell el-Far'ah Près Naplouse: Sixieme Campagne'. *Revue Biblique*, 64 (4): 552–80.

de Vaux, R. 1961. 'Les Fouilles De Tell el-Far'ah: Rapport Préliminaire sur ses 7e, 8e, 9e Campagnes, 1958–1960'. *Revue Biblique* 68 (4): 557–92.

de Vaux, R. 1962. 'Les Fouilles de Tell el-Far'ah: Rapport Préliminaire Sur Les 7e, 8e, 9e Campagnes, 1958–1960 (Suite)', *Revue Biblique* 69: 212–53.

Debono, F. and B. Mortensen. 1992. *El Omari: A Neolithic Settlement and Other Sites in the Vicinity of Wadi Hof, Helwan.* Mainz am Rhein.

Del Vesco, P. and F. Poole. 2018. 'Deir El-Medina in the Egyptian Museum of Turin. An Overview, and the Way Forward'. In *Out of the Box. Selected Papers from the Conference 'Deir El-Medina and the Theban Necropolis in Contact' (Liège, 27–29 October 2014)*, edited by A. Dorn and S. Polis, 97–130. Liège.

Demichelis, S., E. Fiore Marocchetti and M. Borla. 2024. 'Il telo funerario dello scriba reale Butehamon (Provv. 8500 + Provv. 569/172)'. *Aegyptus* 1, 143–81. https://doi.org/10.26350/001217_000134.

Desrosiers, S. 2010. 'Textile Terminologies and Classifications: Some Methodological and Chronological Aspects'. In *Textile Terminologies in the Ancient Near East and Mediterranean from the Third to the First Millennia BC*, edited by M.-L. Nosch and C. Michel, 23–51. Oxford.

Dothan, T. 1963. 'Spinning-Bowls'. *Israel Exploration Journal* 13 (2): 97–112.

Dothan, M. 1971. *Ashdod II–III: The Second and Third Seasons of Excavations, 1963, 1965, Soundings in 1967*. Jerusalem.

Dothan, T. 1998. 'Initial Philistine Settlement: From Migration to Coexistence'. In *Mediterranean People in Transition: Thirteenth to Early Tenth Centuries B.C.E.,* edited by S. Gitin, A. Mazar and E. Stern, 148–61. Jerusalem.

Doyen, J.-M. 1986. 'L'outillage en Os des Sites de Tell Abou Danné et d'Oumm el-Marra (Campagnes 1975–1983): Quelques Aspects de l'artisanat en Syrie du Nord du III au I Millénaire'. *Akkadica*, no. 47: 30–74.

Drewsen, A. 2016. 'Twirling the Whorl'. *Nekhen News* 28: 13–14.

Dreyer, G., E.-M. Engel, U. Hartung, T. Hikade, E.C. Köhler, F. Pumpenmeier, A. Von den Driesch and J. Peters. 1996. 'Umm El-Qaab. Nachuntersuchungen Im Frühzeitlichen Königsfriedhof 7./8. Vorbericht'. *Mitteilungen Des Deutschen Archäologischen Instituts. Abteilung Kairo* 52: 11–81.

Dreyer, G., R. Hartmann, U. Hartung, T. Hikade, H. Köpp, C. Lacher, V. Müller, A. Nerlich and A. Zink. 2003. 'Umm El-Qaab. Nachuntersuchungen Im Frühzeitlichen Königsfriedhof: 13./14./15. Vorbericht'. *Mitteilungen Des Deutschen Archäologischen Instituts. Abteilung Kairo* 59: 67–138.

Dreyer, G., U. Hartung, T. Hikade, E.C. Köhler, V. Müller and F. Pumpenmeier. 1998. 'Umm El-Qaab. Nachuntersuchungen Im Frühzeitlichen Königsfriedhof-9./10. Vorbericht'. *Mitteilungen Des Deutschen Archäologischen Instituts. Abteilung Kairo* 54: 77–167.

Dreyer, G., A. von den Driesch, E.-M. Engel, R. Hartmann, U. Hartung, T. Hikade, V. Müller and J. Peters. 2000. 'Umm El-Qaab. Nachuntersuchungen Im Frühzeitlichen Königsfriedhof 11./12. Vorbericht'. *Mitteilungen Des Deutschen Archäologischen Instituts. Abteilung Kairo* 56: 44–129.

Ebeling, J. 2012. 'Ground Stone Artifacts'. In *Hazor VI: The 1990-2009 Excavations: The Iron Age*, edited by A. Ben-Tor, D. Ben-Ami, D. Sandhaus, S. Bechar and T. Kuper-Blau, 542–58. Jerusalem.

Eiwanger, J. 1982. 'Die neolithische Siedlung von Merimde-Benisalâme: vierter Bericht'. *Mitteilungen des Deutschen Archäologischen Instituts, Abteilung Kairo* 38: 67–82.

Emery, W.B., H.S. Smith and A. Millard. 1979. *The Fortress of Buhen: The Archaeological Report*. London.

Engelbach, R. and B.G. Gunn. 1923. *Harageh*. London.

Eyckerman, M. and S. Hendrickx. 2011. 'The Naqada I Tombs H17 and H41 at El-Mahasna, a Visual Reconstruction'. In *Egypt at its Origins 3: Proceedings of the Third International Conference 'Origin of the State: Predynastic and Early Dynastic Egypt', London, 27th July–1st August 2008*, edited by R.F. Friedman and P.N. Fiske, 379–429. Leuven.

Fairservis, W.A. 1986. *The Hierakonpolis Project Season January to May 1981: Excavation on the Kom el-Gemuwia*. Poughkeepsie, NY.

Finkelstein, I. 1986. *'Izbet Sartah: An Early Iron Age Site near Rosh Ha'ayin, Israel*. Oxford.

Finkelstein, I. 2012. 'Tell El-Far'ah (Tirzah) and the Early Days of the Northern Kingdom'. *Revue Biblique*, 331–46.

Finkelstein I., E. Arie, M.A.S. Martin and E. Piasetzky. 2017. 'New Evidence on the Late Bronze/Iron I Transition at Megiddo: Implications for the End of the Egyptian Rule and the Appearance of Philistine Pottery'. *Ägypten und Levante* 27: 261–80.

Finkelstein, I., D. Ussishkin and B. Halpern. 2000. 'Introduction: The Megiddo Expedition'. In *Megiddo III: The 1992–1996 Seasons*, edited by I. Finkelstein, D. Ussishkin and B. Halpern, 1–13. Tel Aviv.

Finkelstein, I., D. Ussishkin and E.C. Cline. 2013. 'The 2004–2008 Seasons'. *In Megiddo V: The 2004–2008 Seasons*, edited by I. Finkelstein, D. Ussishkin and E.C. Cline, 3–19. Tel Aviv.

Firth, C.M. and B.G. Gunn. 1926. *Excavations at Saqqara: Teti Pyramid Cemeteries*. Le Caire.

Firth, R. 2015. 'Mathematical Analysis of the Spindle Whorl and Loom Weight Data in the CTR Database'. In *Tools, Textiles and Contexts: Investigating Textile Production in the Aegean and Eastern Mediterranean Bronze Age*, edited by E. Andersson Strand and M.-L. Nosch, 153–95. Oxford.

Fischer, P.M. 2008. *Tell Abu Al-Kharaz in the Jordan Valley 1. The Early Bronze Age*. Wien.

Fischer, P.M. 2009. 'Textile Production at Tell'Abū Al-Kharāz, Jordan Valley'. In *A Timeless Vale: Archaeological and Related Essays on the Jordan Valley in Honour of Gerrit van Der Kooij on the Occasion of His Sixty-Fifth Birthday, Archaeological Studies Leiden University*, edited by E. Kaptijn, L.P. Petit and G. van der Kooij, 19: 109–17. Leiden.

Fischer, P.M. 2014. *Tell Abu Al-Kharaz in the Jordan Valley 3 The Iron Age*. Wien.

Fitzgerald, G.M. 1930. *The Four Canaanite Temples of Beth-Shan: Part II. The Pottery*. Philadelphia.

Fitzgerald, G.M. and C. Bache. 1935. *Beth-Shan: Earliest Pottery / Tell Billa: First Assyrian Level*. Philadelphia.

Fluck, C., A. De Moor and P. Linscheid, eds. 2015. *Textiles, Tools and Techniques of the 1st Millenium AD from Egypt and*

Neighbouring Countries: Proceedings of the 8th Conference of the Research Group 'Textiles from the Nile Valley' Antwerp, 4–6 October 2013. Tielt.

Forbes, R. 1956. *Studies in Ancient Technology, Fibres and Fabrics of Antiquity*, vol. 4. Leiden.

Fuller, D., A. Bogaard, M. Charles and D. Filipovic. 2014. 'Macro- and Micro-Botanical Remains from the 2013 and 2014 Seasons'. In *Çatalhöyük 2014 Archive Report*, edited by S. Haddow, 118. https://www.catalhoyuk.com/sites/default/files/media/pdf/Archive_Report_2014.pdf.

Fuller, D., L. Champion, C. Cobo Castillo and A. den Hollander. 2024. 'Cotton and Post-Neolithic Investment Agriculture in Tropical Asia and Africa, with Two Routes to West Africa'. *Journal of Archaeological Science: Reports* 57: 104649. https://doi.org/10.1016/j.jasrep.2024.104649.

Gachet-Bizollon, J. 2007. *Les Ivoires d'Ougarit et l'art Des Ivoiriers Du Levant Au Bronze Récent*, vol. 16. Paris.

Gal, Z., A. Yardenna, U. Baruch, Y. Goren, M. Kislev, R. Kletter, L. Kolska Horwitz, *et al.* 2000. *Horbat Rosh Zayit: An Iron Age Storage Fort and Village. Vol. 8*. Jerusalem. https://doi.org/10.2307/j.ctt1fzhfg1.

Gallo, P. 2009. 'Isola di Nelson III. L'insediamento greco (Fine IV-Inizi III sec.a.C.). Campagne 2005'. In *Ricerche Italiane e Scavi in Egitto*, vol. III, edited by R. Pirelli, 109–16. Il Cairo.

Gardiner, A.H. 1948. *The Wilbour Papyrus: 2: Commentary*. London.

Garfinkel, Y. 1999. *The Yarmukians: Neolithic Art from Sha'ar Hagolan*. Jerusalem.

Garstang, J. 1907. *The Burial Customs of Ancient Egypt as Illustrated by Tombs of the Middle Kingdom: Being a Report of Excavations Made in the Necropolis of Beni Hassan during 1902-3-4*. London.

Gaspa, S. 2017. 'Textiles in Assyrian and Babylonian Temples from the 1st Millennium BCE'. In *Textiles and Cult in the Ancient Mediterranean*, edited by C. Brøns and M.-L. Nosch, 145–73. Oxford.

Gasperini, V. 2014. 'Mycenaean and Cypriot Pottery from Gurob in the Manchester Museum Collection: A Test of Trade Network Theories for the New Kingdom Fayum'. *Journal of Ancient Egyptian Interconnections* 6 (2): 10–22.

Gasperini, V. 2018. *Tomb Robberies at the End of the New Kingdom: The Fayum Case – The Gurob Burnt Groups Reinterpreted*. Oxford.

Getsov, N. and O. Bazilai. 2009. 'Nahal Betzet II and Ard El Samra: Two Late Prehistoric Sites and Settlement Patterns in the Akko Plain'. *Journal of The Israel Prehistoric Society*, 81–158.

Gibbs, K.T. 2008. 'Pierced clay disks and Late Neolithic textile production'. In *Proceedings of the 5th International Congress on the Archaeology of the Ancient Near East: Madrid, April 3–8 2006. Vol. 3 Vol. 3*, edited by J. Córdoba, M. Molist, C. Peréz, I. Rubio, S. Martínez, 89–96. Madrid.

Giddy, L.L. 1999. *Kom Rabi'a: The New Kingdom and Post-New Kingdom Objects: The Survey of Memphis II*. London.

Gilligan, I., F. d'Errico, L. Doyon, W. Wang and Y.V. Kuzmin. 2024. 'Paleolithic Eyed Needles and the Evolution of Dress'. *Science Advances* 10 (26). https://doi.org/10.1126/sciadv.adp2887.

Gleba, M. 2008. *Textile Production in Pre-Roman Italy*. Oxford.

Gleba, M. 2012. 'From Textiles to Sheep: Investigating Wool Fibre Development in Pre-Roman Italy Using Scanning Electron Microscopy (SEM)'. *Journal of Archaeological Science* 39 (12): 3643–61. https://doi.org/10.1016/j.jas.2012.06.021.

Gleba, M. and S. Harris. 2019. 'The First Plant Bast Fibre Technology: Identifying Splicing in Archaeological Textiles'. *Archaeological and Anthropological Sciences*, 2329–46.

Gleser, R. 2016. 'Beginnings Revisited Again: About the Inversion of the Sequence of Manufacturing, the Origins of Early Weaving and the Vertical Warp-Weighted Loom'. In *Southeast Europe and Anatolia in Prehistory Essays in Honor of Vassil Nikolov on His 65th Anniversary*, edited by K. Bacvarov and R. Gleser, 79–91. Bonn.

Golani, A., E. van den Brink, A. Boas, Y. Goren, O. Shamir, L. Horwitz, O. Marder, D. Mayer and Y.M. Rowan. 1999. 'Salvage Excavations at the Early Bronze Age IA Settlement of Azor'. *Atiqot* 38: 1–49.

Good, I. 1999. *The Ecology of Exchange: Textiles from Shahr -i Sokhta, Eastern Iran*. Unpublished PhD, University of Pennsylvania.

Gopher, A. and E. Eisenberg. 2001. 'Groundstone Artifacts and Small Finds'. In *Tel Te'o: A Neolithic, Chalcolithic and Early Bronze Age Site in the Hula Valley*, edited by E. Eisenberg, A. Gopher, R. Greenberg, Y. Goren, N. Halperin, G. Kahila Bar-Gal, L. Kolska Horwitz, A. Miller Rosen, S.A. Rosen, S. Sadeh and P. Smith, 139–50. Jerusalem.

Goshen, N., A. Yasur-Landau and E.C. Cline. 2013. 'Textile Production in Palatial and Non-Palatial Contexts: The Case of Tel Kabri'. In *Textile Production and Consumption in the Ancient Near East: Archaeology, Epigraphy, Iconography*, edited by M.-L. Nosch, H. Koefoed and E. Andersson Strand, 45–53. Oxford.

Götze, A. 1902. 'Die Kleingeräte Aus Metall, Stein, Thon Und Ähnliche Stoffen'. In *Troia Und Ilion: Ergebnisse Der Ausgrabungen in Den Vorhistorischen Und Historischen Schichten von Ilion*, edited by W. Dörpfeld, 320–423. Athens.

Grandet, P. 2003. *Catalogue des ostraca hiératiques non littéraires de Deîr el-Médîn'eh, Vol. IX, Nos. 831–1000*. Le Caire.

Grandet, P. 2006. *Catalogue des ostraca hiératiques non littéraires de Deîr el-Médînéh, Vol. X, Nos 10001–10123*. Le Caire.

Grandet, P. 2010. *Catalogue des ostraca hiératiques non-littéraires de Deir el-Médînéh, vol. XI, Nos 10124–10275*. Le Caire.

Grandet, P. 2017. *Catalogue des ostraca hiératiques non littéraires de Deîr el-Médînéh, Vol. XII, Nos. Nos 10276–10405*. Le Caire.

Grant, E. 1932. *Ain Shems Excavations: (1928-1929-1930-1931)*. Haverford.

Greiss, E.A.M. 1957. *Anatomical Identification of Some Ancient Egyptian Plant Materials*. Le Caire.

Guy, P.L.O. and R.M. Engberg. 1938. *Megiddo Tombs*. Chicago, Ill.

Haas, V. 1994. *Geschichte der hethitischen Religion*. Leiden.

Habachi, L., E.-M. Engel, P. Jánosi, C. Mlinar and E. Czerny. 2001. *Tell El-Dab'a. I*. Wien.

Hald, M. 1946. 'Ancient Textile Techniques in Egypt and Scandinavia'. *Acta Archaeologica* 17: 49–99.

Hall, R.M. 1982. 'Garments in the Petrie Museum of Egyptian Archaeology'. *Textile History* 13 (1): 27–45. doi:10.1179/004049682793690922.

Hall, R.M. 1986. *Egyptian Textiles*. Aylesbury.

Hallmann, A. 2016. 'Textiles from Tomb II in Deir El-Bahari: Preliminary Report from Season 2012/2013'. *Polish Archaeology in the Mediterranean* XXIV (February): 247–56. https://doi.org/10.5604/01.3001.0009.9910.

Hallmann, A. 2017a. 'Clothing (Non-Royal), Pharaonic Egypt'. In *The Encyclopedia of Ancient History*, 1–9. DeKalb.

Hallmann, A. 2017b. 'Tissu En Lin Peint de Sennefer'. In *À l'œuvre on Connaît l'artisan... de Pharaon ! Un Siècle de Recherches Françaises à Deir El-Medina (1917–2017)*, 92–4. Milano.

Hallmann, A. 2018. 'Unwrapping Ancient Egyptian Fashion'. *The Oriental Institute News and Notes* 239: 6–15.

Hallmann, A. 2023. *Ancient Egyptian Clothing: Studies in Late Period Private Representations*. Harvard Egyptological Studies 20. Leiden.

Harlow, M., C. Michel and M.-L. Nosch, eds. 2014. *Prehistoric, Ancient Near Eastern & Aegean Textiles and Dress*. Oxford. https://doi.org/10.2307/j.ctvh1drkt.

Harris, S. 2010. 'Smooth and Cool, or Warm and Soft: Investigating the Properties of Cloth in Prehistory'. In *North European Symposium for Archaeological Textiles X: NESAT X*, edited by E. Andersson Strand, M. Gleba, U. Mannering, C. Munkholt and M. Ringgaard, 104–12. Oxford.

Harrison, T.P. 2004. *Megiddo 3: Final Report on the Stratum VI Excavations*. Chicago.

Harrison, T.P. 2012. 'The Southern Levant'. In *A Companion to the Archaeology of the Ancient Near East*, edited by D.T. Potts, 629–46. Ann Arbor. https://doi.org/10.1002/9781444360790.ch33.

Hartung, U., M. Abd el-Gelil, A. von den Driesch, G. Fares, R. Hartmann, T. Hikade and C. Ihde. 2003. 'Vorbericht uber neue Untersuchungen in der pradynastischen Siedlung von Maadi'. *Mitteilungen des Deutschen Archäologischen Instituts Abteilung Kairo* 59: 149–98.

Hassan, S. 1943. *Excavations at Gîza 4*. Cairo.

Hayes, W. 1953. *The Scepter of Egypt 1: A Background for the Study of the Egyptian Antiquities in The Metropolitan Museum of Art: From the Earliest Times to the End of the Middle Kingdom*. Cambridge, MA.

Hayes, W. 1959. *The Scepter of Egypt 2: A Background for the Study of the Egyptian Antiquities in the Metropolitan Museum of Art*. Cambridge, MA.

Helbæk, H. 1963. 'Textiles from Çatal Höyük'. *Archaeology* 16: 39–46.

Hikade, T. 2012. 'Egypt and the Near East'. In *A Companion to the Archaeology of the Ancient Near East*, edited by D.T. Potts, 833–49. Ann Arbor. https://doi.org/10.1002/9781444360790.ch33.

Hill, J.A. and T. Herbich. 2011. 'Life in the Cemetery: Late Predynastic Settlement at El-Amra'. In *Egypt at Its Origins 3: Proceedings of the Third International Conference 'Origin of the State: Predynastic and Early Dynastic Egypt', London, 27th July–1st August 2008*, edited by R. Friedman and P.N. Fiske, 109–35. Leuven.

Hitchens, S. 2018. 'Dressing the Pyramids in Cloth and Cordage: Spinning and Weaving at the Pyramids.' *AERAGRAM Newsletter of Ancient Egypt Research Associates* 19 (1), 12–15.

Hodgkinson, A.K. 2018. *Technology and Urbanism in Late Bronze Age Egypt*. Oxford.

Hoffmann, M. 1964. *The Warp-Weighted Loom: Studies in the History and Technology of an Ancient Implement*. Kragero.

Hölscher, U. 1954. *The Excavations of Medinet Habu, V*. Chicago.

Hölscher, U., R. Anthes and K.C. Seele. 1939. *The Excavations of Medinet Habu II. The Temples of the Eighteenth Dynasty*. Chicago.

Hornung, E., R. Krauss and D.A. Warburton, eds. 2006. *Ancient Egyptian Chronology*. Leiden.

James, F.W. 1966. *The Iron Age at Beth Shan: A Study of Levels VI–IV*. Philadelphia: University of Pennsylvania Museum of Archaeology and Anthropology.

James, F.W. and P.E. McGovern. 1993. *The Late Bronze Egyptian Garrison at Beth Shan: A Study of Levels VII and VIII*. Philadelphia.

Janssen, J.J. 1975. *Commodity Prices from the Ramessid Period: An Economic Study of the Village of Necropolis Workmen at Thebes*. Leiden.

Janssen, J.J. 2008. *Daily Dress at Deir El-Medîna: Words for Clothing*. London.

Janssen, J.J. and R. Janssen. 1990. 'Candlewick Coverlets'. *Discussions in Egyptology* 16: 53–61.

Janssen, R. 1996. 'The linens of Idu'. In *Untersuchungen zu Idu II, Giza: ein interdisziplinäres Projekt*, edited by R. Germer and B. Schmitz, 47–56. Hildesheim.

Janssen, R. 2020. 'The Pleated Dress of Nywty.' *PalArch's Journal of Archaeology of Egypt/Egyptology* 17 (1).

Jarmuzek, L. 2010. 'Loom-Weights or Net-Weights?' *Göttinger Miszellen: Beiträge Zur Ägyptologischen Diskussion* 226: 17–24.

Johl, C.H. 1924. *Altägyptische Webestühle und Brettchenweberei in Altägypten*. Leipzig.

Jones, J. and R. Oldfield. 2007. 'Egypt's Earliest Linen'. *Egyptian Archaeology* 29: 33–5.

Jones, J. 2002. 'The Textiles at Abydos: New Evidence'. *Mitteilungen Des Deutschen Archäologischen Instituts, Abteilung Kairo* 58: 323–40.

Jones, J. 2008. 'Pre-and Early Dynastic Textiles: Technology, Specialisation and Administration during the Process of State Formation'. In *Egypt at its Origin 2. Proceedings of the International Conference 'Origin of the State. Predynastic and Early Dynastic Egypt', Toulouse (France), 5th–8th September 2005*, edited by B. Midant-Reynes, Y. Tristant, J. Rowland and S. Hendrickx, 99–132. Leuven.

Jones, J. 2014. 'The Enigma of the Pleated Dress: New Insights from Early Dynastic Helwan Reliefs'. *The Journal of Egyptian Archaeology* 100 (1): 209–31.

Junker, H. 1929. 'Vorläufiger Bericht über die Grabung der Akademie der Wissenschaften in Wien auf der neolithischen Siedelung von Merimde-Benisalame (Westdelta): vom 1. bis 30. März 1929.' *Anzeiger der Akademie der Wissenschaften in Wien* 16–18: 156–248.

Junker, H. 1930. 'Vorläufiger Bericht über die zweite Grabung der Akademie der Wissenschaften in Wien auf der vorgeschichtlichen Siedlung Merimde-Benisalâme: vom 7. Februar bis 8. April 1930'. *Anzeiger der Akademie der Wissenschaften in Wien* 5–13: 21–82.

Kaplan, J. 1958. 'Excavations at Wadi Rabah'. *Israel Exploration Journal* 8: 149–60.

Kaplan, J. 1969. 'Ein El Jerba'. *Bulletin of the American Schools of Oriental Research* 194: 2–39.

Karg, S. 2020. 'Neolithic Flax Production in the Pre-Alpine Region: Knowledge Increase since the 19th Century'. In *The Competition of Fibres: Early Textile Production in Western Asia, South-East and Central Europe (10,000–500 BCE)*, edited by W. Schier and S. Pollock, 141–52. Oxford.

Karg, S., C. Spinazzi-Lucchesi and A. Diederichsen. 2023. 'Flax for Seed or Fibre Use? Flax Capsules from Ancient Egyptian Sites (3rd Millennium BC to Second Century

AD) Compared with Modern Flax Genebank Accessions'. *Genetic Resources and Plant Evolution*, 2485–96. https://doi.org/10.1007/s10722-023-01753-y.

Kemp, B.J. 1978. 'The Harim-Palace at Medinet El-Ghurab'. *Zeitschrift Für Ägyptische Sprache Und Altertumskunde* 105 (1): 122–33.

Kemp, B.J. and G.M. Vogelsang-Eastwood. 2001. *The Ancient Textile Industry at Amarna*. London.

Kenyon, K.M. 1960. *Excavations at Jericho: The Tombs Excavated in 1952–4*. Jerusalem.

Kenyon, K.M. and T.A. Holland. 1965. *Excavations at Jericho: The Tombs Excavated in 1955–6*. Jerusalem.

Kołodziejczyk, P. 2015. 'Egyptian Predynastic Tokens: Traces of Magic or Economic Activity?: The Beginnings of Abstract Writing and Calculating System or a Relic of Early Magical Practices'. In *The Wisdom of Thot: Magical Texts in Ancient Mediterranean Civilisations*, edited by G. Bąkowska-Czerner, A. Roccati and A. Świerzowska, 27–42. Oxford.

Kopp, P. 2018. *Funde Und Befunde Aus Der Umgebung Des Satettempels: Grabungen von 2006–2009*. Elephantine 24. Wiesbaden.

Kvavadze, E., O. Bar-Yosef, A. Belfer-Cohen, E. Boaretto, N. Jakeli, Z. Matskevich and T. Meshveliani. 2009. '30,000-Year-Old Wild Flax Fibers'. *Science* 325: 1359. https://doi.org/10.1126/science.1175404.

Lacovara, P. 1990. *Deir El-Ballas: Preliminary Report on the Deir El-Ballas Expedition, 1980–1986*. Winona Lake, IN.

Laemmel, S. 2008. 'Preliminary Report on the Pottery from Area Q IV at Qantir/Pi-Ramesse: Excavations of the Roemer-Pelizaeus Museum, Hildesheim'. *Ägypten Und Levante / Egypt and the Levant* 18: 173–202.

Lamon, R.S. and G.M. Shipton. 1939. *Megiddo I. Seasons of 1925–34. Strata I–V*. Chicago.

Langgut, D., N. Yahalom-Mack, S. Lev-Yadun, E. Kremer, M. Ullman and U. Davidovich. 2016. 'The Earliest Near Eastern Wooden Spinning Implements'. *Antiquity* 90 (352): 973–90.

Larsen, H. 1941. *Vorbericht über die schwedischen Grabungen in Abu Ghâlib, 1936/37*. Augsburg.

Larsson, M. 2013. 'Cultivation and Processing of Linum Usitatissimum and Camelina Sativa in Southern Scandinavia during the Roman Iron Age'. *Vegetation History and Archaeobotany* 22 (6): 509–20.

Laurito, R. 2013. 'Textile Production: Notes on Spinning and Weaving Tools'. In *Arslantepe. Late Bronze Age. Hittite Influence and Local Traditions in an Eastern Anatolian Community*, edited by F. Manuelli, 224–33. Arslantepe IX. Roma.

Laurito, R., C. Lemorini and A. Perilli. 2014. 'Making Textiles at Arslantepe, Turkey, in the 4th and 3rd Millennia BC. Archaeological Data and Experimental Archaeology'. In *Wool Economy in the Ancient Near East and the Aegean: From the Beginnings of Sheep Husbandry to Institutional Textile Industry*, edited by C. Breniquet and C. Michel, 151–68. Oxford.

Lehner, M. 2016. 'The Name and Nature of the Heit El-Ghurab Old Kingdom Site: Workers Town, Pyramid Town, and the Port Hypothesis'. In *The Pyramids: Between Life and Death: Proceedings of the Workshop Held at Uppsala University, Uppsala, May 31st to June 1st, 2012*, edited by I. Hein, N. Billing and E. Meyer-Dietrich, 99–162. Uppsala.

Lernau, O. 2006. 'Fish Remains'. In *Megiddo IV: The 1998–2002 Seasons*, edited by I. Finkelstein, D. Ussishkin and B. Halpern, 474–97. Tel Aviv.

Levy, J. 2019. 'Clothes Maketh (Hu)Man: Textile Production in the Southern Levant in the Chalcolithic Period'. In *Studies in Archaeology and Ancient Cultures in Honor of Isaac Gilead*, edited by H. Goldfus, M.I. Gruber, S. Yonah and P. Fabian, 172–202. Oxford.

Levy, J. 2020. *The Genesis of the Textile Industry from Adorned Nudity to Ritual Regalia: The Changing Role of Fibre Crafts and Their Evolving Techniques of Manufacture in the Ancient Near East from the Natufian to the Ghassulian*. Oxford. https://doi.org/10.2307/j.ctv10qqz8b.

Levy, J. and I. Gilead. 2012. 'Spinning in the 5th Millennium in the Southern Levant: Aspects of the Textile Economy'. *Paléorient*, 127–39.

Levy, J. and I. Gilead. 2013. 'The Emergence of the Ghassulian Textile Industry in the Southern Levant Chalcolithic Period (*c.* 4,500–4,000 BCE)'. In *Textile Production and Consumption in the Ancient Near East*, edited by M.-L. Nosch, H. Koefoed and E. Andersson Strand, 26–44. Oxford.

Liu, R.K. 1978. 'Spindle Whorls. Part I: Some Comments and Speculations'. *The Bead Journal* 3: 87–103.

Liverani, M. 1988. *Antico Oriente: storia, società, economia*. Roma.

Liverani, M. 2008. 'The Late Bronze Age. Materials and Mechanisms of Trade and Cultural Exchange'. In *Beyond Babylon: Art, Trade, and Diplomacy in the Second Millennium B.C.*, edited by J. Aruz, K. Benzel and J.M. Evans, 161–8. New York.

Lloyd, A.B. 2000. 'The Late Period (664–332 BC)'. In *The Oxford History of Ancient Egypt*, edited by I. Shaw, 369–94. Oxford. https://doi.org/10.1093/oso/9780198150343.003.0012.

Loud, G. 1948. *Megiddo II Seasons of 1935–39*. Oriental Institute Publications 52. Chicago.

Lucas, A. and J. Harris. 1962. *Ancient Egyptian Materials and Industries*. London.

Lumb, D.R.A. 2014. 'Textile Traditions of Northwest Syria during the Early Iron Age'. In *Textile Trade and Distribution in Antiquity*, edited by K. Dross-Krüpe, 141–50. Wiesbaden.

Macalister, R.A.S. 1912. *The Excavation of Gezer: 1902–1905 and 1907–1909*. London.

MacCorriston, J. 1997. 'The Fiber Revolution: Textile Extensification, Alienation and Social Stratification in Ancient Mesopotamia'. *Current Anthropology: A World Journal of the Sciences of Man* 38(4), 517–35.

Mace, A.C. 1921. 'The Egyptian Expedition 1920–1921: I. Excavations at Lisht'. *The Metropolitan Museum of Art Bulletin* 16. 11: 5–19. https://doi.org/10.2307/3254484.

Mace, A.C. 1922. 'Loom Weights in Egypt'. *Ancient Egypt* 23, 75–76.

Mączyńska, A. 2008. 'Some Remarks on Egyptian-Southern Levantine Interrelations in the First Half of the 4th Millennium BC'. In *Egypt at Its Origin 2. Proceedings of the International Conference 'Origin of the State. Predynastic and Early Dynastic Egypt', Toulouse (France), 5th–8th September 2005*, edited by B. Midant-Reynes, Y. Tristant, J. Rowland and S. Hendrickx, 763–81. Orientalia Lovaniensia Analecta 172. Leuven.

Maeir, A.M. and N. Panitz-Cohen. 2004. *Bronze and Iron Age Tombs at Tel Gezer, Israel: Finds from Raymond-Charles Weill's Excavations in 1914 and 1921*. Oxford.

Malek, J. 2003. 'The Old Kingdom (c. 2686–2160 BC)'. In *The Oxford History of Ancient Egypt*, edited by I. Shaw, 89–117. Oxford.

Mallet, J. 1988. *Tell el-Far'ah 2. Stratigraphie des vestiges du bronze moyen*. Paris.

Mårtensson, L., E. Andersson, M.-L. Nosch and A. Batzer. 2006. *Technical Report Experimental Archaeology, Part 2:2 Whorl or Bead? 2006: Tools and Textiles – Texts and Contexts Research Program*. Copenhagen. https://ctr.hum.ku.dk/research-programmes-and-projects/previous-programmes-and-projects/tools/technical_report_2-2__experimental_arcaheology.pdf

Mårtensson, L., M.-L. Nosch and E. Andersson Strand. 2009. 'Shape of Things: Understanding a Loom Weight'. *Oxford Journal of Archaeology* 28 (4): 373–98.

Martin, M.A.S. 2009. 'The Egyptian Assemblage'. In *Excavations at Tel Beth-Shean 1989–1996. Vol. III. The 13th–11th Century BCE Strata in Areas N and S*, edited by N. Panitz-Cohen and A. Mazar, 434–77. Beth-Shean Valley Archaeological Project. Jerusalem.

Martin, M.A.S. 2016. 'Egyptian-Type Pottery'. In *Pharaoh in Canaan: The Untold Story*, edited by D. Ben-Tor, 69–70. Jerusalem.

Mazar, A. 2003. 'Beth Shean in the Second Millenium BCE: From Canaanite Town to Egyptian Stronghold'. In *The Synchronisation of Civilisations in the Eastern Mediterranean in the Second Millennium B.C. II: Proceedings of the SCIEM 2000 – EuroConference Haindorf, 2nd of May–7th of May 2001*, edited by M. Bietak and E. Czerny, 323–39. Contributions to the Chronology of the Eastern Mediterranean 4, Bd. 29. Wien.

Mazar, A. 2006. 'Beth Shean from the Late Bronze Age IIB to the Medieval Period: A Summary'. In *Excavations at Tel Beth-Shean, 1989–1996, vol. I., From the Late Bronze Age IIB to the Medieval Period*, edited by A. Mazar, 26–47. Jerusalem.

Mazar, A. 2007. *Excavations at Tel Beth-Shean: 1989–1996, Vol. II., The Middle and Late Bronze Age Strata in Area R. Beth-Shean Valley Archaological Project*. Jerusalem.

Mazar, A. 2009. 'Introduction'. In *Excavations at Tel Beth-Shean 1989–1996, vol. III., The 13th–11th Century BCE Strata in Areas N and S*, edited by N. Panitz-Cohen and A. Mazar, 1–32. Jerusalem.

Mazar, A. 2010. 'Tel Beth-Shean: History and Archaeology'. In *One God, One Cult, One Nation: Archaeological and Biblical Perspectives*. Beihefte zur Zeitschrift für die Alttestamentliche Wissenschaft 405, edited by R. Gregor Kratz, B. Corzilius, H. Spieckermann and T. Pilger, 239–72. Berlin.

Mazar, A. 2012. 'Area R (EB III–IBA): The Stratigraphy and Architecture'. In *Excavations at Tel Beth-Shean: 1989–1996. Vol. IV. The 4th and 3rd Millennia BCE*, edited by A. Mazar, 86–122. Jerusalem.

Mazar, A. 2019. 'Weaving in Iron Age Tel Rehov and the Jordan Valley'. *Journal of Eastern Mediterranean Archaeology & Heritage Studies Journal of Eastern Mediterranean Archaeology & Heritage Studies* 7 (1): 119–38.

Mazar, A. and R.A. Mullins. 2006. 'Introduction'. In *Excavations at Tel Beth-Shean, 1989–1996, vol. I., From the Late Bronze Age IIB to the Medieval Period*, edited by A. Mazar, 3–25. Jerusalem.

Mazar, A. and N. Panitz-Cohen. 2001. *Timnah (Tel Batash) II: The Finds from the First Millennium BCE*. Jerusalem.

Mazar, A. and N. Panitz-Cohen. 2006. 'Area S: The Stratigraphy and Architecture of the Iron Age IIA and Later Structures'. In *Excavations at Tel Beth-Shean, 1989–1996, vol. I, From the Late Bronze Age IIB to the Medieval Period*, edited by A. Mazar, 173–201. Jerusalem.

Mazar, A. and Y. Rotem. 2012. 'The Small Finds from the Early Bronze and Intermediate Bronze Ages'. In *Excavations at Tel Beth-Shean: 1989–1996. Vol. IV. The 4th and 3rd Millennia BCE*, edited by A. Mazar, 350–99. Jerusalem.

Mazar, A. and A. Sumaka'i Fink. 2006. 'Area P: Stratigraphy and Architecture'. In *Excavations at Tel Beth-Shean, 1989–1996, vol. I, From the Late Bronze Age IIB to the Medieval Period*, edited by A. Mazar, 202–69. Jerusalem.

Mellink, M.J. 1969. 'Excavations at Karataş-Semayük in Lycia, 1968'. *American Journal of Archaeology* 73 (3): 319–31. https://doi.org/10.2307/503513.

Midant Reynes, B. 2014. 'Prehistoric Regional Cultures'. In *UCLA Encyclopedia of Egyptology*, edited by W. Grajetzki and W. Wendrich. Los Angeles. https://escholarship.org/uc/item/4zz9t461.

Midant Reynes, B., J. Guilaine and N. Grimal. 2003. *Aux origines de l'Egypte: du néolithique à l'émergence de l'état*. Paris.

Moeller, N. 2016. *The Archaeology of Urbanism in Ancient Egypt: From the Predynastic Period to the End of the Middle Kingdom*. Cambridge.

Molist Montaña, M., C. Barrachina and M. Gangonells. 1996. 'Mobiliario Diverso'. In *Tell Halula (Siria). Un Yacimiento Neolítico del Valle Medio del Eufrates. Campañas de 1991 y 1992*, edited by M. Molist Montaña, 125–33. Madrid.

Mond, R.L. and O.H. Myers. 1937. *Cemeteries of Armant I*. London.

Moore, A.M.T., G.C. Hillman and A.J. Legge. 2000. *Village on the Euphrates. From Foraging to Farming at Abu Hureyra*. Oxford.

Moorey, P.R.S. 1980. *Cemeteries of the First Millennium BC at Deve Hüyük, Near Carchemish: Salvaged by TE Lawrence and CL Woolley in 1913*. Oxford.

Moulhérat, C. and G. Spantidaki. 2009. 'Cloth from Kastelli, Chania'. *Arachne. Occasional Publication for the History of Costume and Textiles in the Aegean and Eastern Mediterranean* 3: 8–15.

Müller, H.W. 1940. *Die Felsengräber der Fürsten von Elephantine: aus der Zeit d. mittleren Reiches*. Glückstadt.

Murphy, T.M., N. Ben-Yehuda, R.E. Taylor and J.R. Southon. 2011. 'Hemp in Ancient Rope and Fabric from the Christmas Cave in Israel: Talmudic Background and DNA Sequence Identification'. *Journal of Archaeological Science* 38, no. 10: 2579–88.

Nadel, D., A. Danin, E. Werker, T. Schick, M.E. Kislev and K. Stewart. 1994. '19,000-Year-Old Twisted Fibers From Ohalo II'. *Current Anthropology* 35 (4). 451–8.

Nagel, G. 1938. *La céramique du Nouvel Empire à Deir el Médineh*. Le Caire.

Naville, E., T.E. Peet, H.R. Hall and K. Haddon. 1914. *The Cemeteries of Abydos: Pt. 1: 1909–1910. The Mixed Cemetery and Umm el-Ga'ab*. London.

Negahban, E.O. 1996. *Marlik: The Complete Excavation Report*. Philadelphia.

Newberry, P.E. 1893. *Beni Hasan* 2. London.

Newberry, P.E. and F.L. Griffith. 1893. *Beni Hasan*. London.

Nodet, É. 1980. 'Fusaïoles et Pesons'. In *Tell Keisan: 1971–1976, Une Cité Phénicienne En Galilée*, edited by J. Briend, J.-B. Humbert and É. Puech, 316–21. Fribourg; Göttingen; Paris.

Nosch, M.-L. and C. Gillis, eds. 2007. *Ancient Textiles. Production, Craft and Society*. Oxford.

Nosch, M.-L. and C. Michel, eds. 2010. *Textile Terminologies in the Ancient Near East and Mediterranean from the Third to the First Millennia BC*. Oxford.

Odler, M. 2015. 'Copper Model Tools in Old Kingdom Female Burials'. In *Current Research in Egyptology 2014: Proceedings of the Fifteenth Annual Symposium, University College, London, 2014*, edited by M.S. Pinarello, 39–58. Oxford.

Olofsson, L., E. Andersson Strand and M.-L. Nosch. 2015. 'Experimental Testing of Bronze Age Textile Tools'. In *Tools, Textiles and Contexts: Investigating Textile Production in the Aegean and Eastern Mediterranean Bronze Age*, edited by E. Andersson Strand and M.-L. Nosch, 75–100. Oxford.

Oren, E.D. 1973. *The Northern Cemetery of Beth Shan*. Leiden.

Oren, R. 2002. 'Loom Weights and Spindle Whorls'. In *Tel Kabri: The 1986–1993 Excavation Season*, edited by A. Kempinski, 363–72. Tel Aviv.

Orrelle, E., R. Eyal and A. Gopher. 2012. 'Spindle Whorls and Their Blanks'. In *Village Communities of the Pottery Neolithic Period in the Menashe Hills, Israel: Archaeological Invesigations at The Sites of Nahal Zehora. 2*, edited by R. Barkai and A. Gopher, 632–56. Tel Aviv.

Paice, P. 2004. 'Chapter Six: The Small Finds'. In *Megiddo 3: Final Report on the Stratum VI Excavations*, edited by T.P. Harrison, 59–104. Oriental Institute Publications 127. Chicago.

Panitz-Cohen, N. 2012. 'Complementary Material to Tel Beth-Shean Volumes II–III'. In *Excavations at Tel Beth-Shean: 1989–1996. Vol. IV. The 4th and 3rd Millennia BCE*, edited by A. Mazar, 435–7. Jerusalem.

Panitz-Cohen, N. and A. Mazar. 2009. 'Area S: Stratigraphy and Architecture'. In *Excavations at Tel Beth-Shean 1989–1996, vol. III. The 13th–11th Century BCE Strata in Areas N and S*, edited by N. Panitz-Cohen and A. Mazar, 94–194. Jerusalem.

Panitz-Cohen, N. and N. Yahalom-Mack. 2009. 'Textile-Related Objects and a Basket Imprint'. In *Excavations at Tel Beth-Shean 1989–1996. Vol. III. The 13th–11th Century BCE Strata in Areas N and S*, edited by N.Panitz-Cohen and A. Mazar, 737–41. Jerusalem.

Perrot, J. 1966. La troisieme campagne de fouilles a Munhata (1964), *Syria* 43, 49–63.

Perrot, J., N. Zori and Y. Reich. 1967. 'Neve Ur, Un Nouvel Aspect Du Ghassoulien'. *Israel Exploration Journal*, 201–32.

Pesenti, M. and R. Saleh. 2018. 'Le Secteur 8 Du Site Côtier de Plinthine (Maréotide). Un Espace Multifonctionnel d'époque Saïte et Perse?' *Bulletin de Liason de La Céramique Égyptienne* 28, 5–49.

Petrie, W.M.F. 1890. *Kahun, Gurob and Hawara*. London.

Petrie, W.M.F. 1891. *Illahun, Kahun and Gurob, 1889–90*. London.

Petrie, W.M.F. 1892. *Medum*. London.

Petrie, W.M.F. 1902. *Abydos 1*. London: Egypt Exploration Fund.

Petrie, W.M.F. 1928. *Gerar*. London.

Petrie, W.M.F. 1932. *Ancient Gaza II. Tell El Ajjul*. London.

Petrie, W.M.F. and G. Brunton. 1924. *Sedment 1*. London.

Petrie, W.M.F. and F.L. Griffith. 1901. *The Royal Tombs of the Earliest Dynasties. 1901 Part 2*. London.

Petrie, W.M.F., G. Brunton and M.A. Murray. 1923. *Lahun II*. London.

Petrie, W.M.F., M.A. Murray and E.J.H. Mackay. 1931. *Ancient Gaza: Tell el-Ajjūl*. London.

Petrie, W.M.F., J.E. Quibell and F.C.J. Spurrell. 1896. *Naqada and Ballas*. London.

Peyronel, L. 2004. *Gli Strumenti Di Tessitura Dall'età Del Bronzo All'epoca Persiana*. Roma.

Pfälzner, P. 2012. 'Levantine Kingdoms of the Late Bronze Age'. In *A Companion to the Archaeology of the Ancient Near East*, 770–96. Ann Arbor. https://doi.org/10.1002/9781444360790.ch41.

Philip, G. 2006. *Tell El-Dab'a XV: Metalwork and Metalworking Evidence of the Late Middle Kingdom and the Second Intermediate Period*. Wien.

Piankoff, A. 1957. *Mythological Papyri*. New York.

Picton, J., J. Johnston and I. Pridden. 2016. 'Report to the Ministry of Antiquities on a Study Season on the Gurob Textiles'. https://www.gurob.org.uk/reports/JP_Textiles_Report_2016.pdf

Podzorski, P.V. 1994. *The Northern Cemetery at Ballâs, Upper Egypt: A Study of the Middle and Late Predynastic Remains*. Salinas, CA.

Politi, J. 2001. 'The Papyri and the'Burnt Groups'. *Göttinger Miszellen: Beiträge Zur Ägyptologischen Diskussion*, 182: 107–11.

Poppa, R. 1978. *Kamid El-Loz 2*. Bonn.

Porada, E. 1965. *Ancient Iran; the Art of Pre-Islamic Times*. London.

Porat, N. and J. Seeher. 1988. 'Petrographic Analysis of Pottery and Basalt from Predynastic Maadi'. *Mitteilungen des Deutschen Archäologischen Instituts: Abteilung Kairo* 44: 215–28.

Postgate, J.N. and J.A. Moon. 1982. 'Excavations at Abu Salabikh, 1981'. *Iraq* 44 (2): 103–36.

Qadi, N. 2001. The ground stone industry. In *Jebel Abu Thawwab (Er-Rumman), Central Jordan – The Late Neolithic and Early Bronze Age I Occupation*, edited by Z. Kafafi, 155–84. Berlin.

Quibell, J.E. and F.W. Green. 1902. *Hierakonpolis 2*. London.

Quirke, S. 2005. *Lahun: A Town in Egypt 1800 BC, and the History of its Landscape*. London.

Quirke, S. 2016. 'Women of Lahun 1850–1700BC: An Exercise in Historical Archaeology'. In *Archaeology and Women: Ancient and Modern Issues*, edited by S. Hamilton, R. Whitehouse and K.I. Wright, 246–62. Walnut Creek, CA.

Rahmstorf, L. 2003. Clay spools from Tiryns and elsewhere. An indication of foreign influence in LH III C? In *Περιφέρεια του Μυκηναϊκού Κόσμου. Β΄Διεθνές Διεπιστημονικό Συμπόσιο/ The Periphery of the Mycenaean World. 2nd International Interdisciplinary Colloquium. Lamia 26–30.9.1999*, edited by N. Kyparissi-Apostolika and M. Papakonstantinou, 397–415. Lamia.

Rahmstorf, L. 2005. 'Ethnicity and Changes in Weaving Technology in Cyprus and the Eastern Mediterranean during the 12th Cent. BC'. In *Cyprus: Religion and Society from the Late Bronze Age to the End of the Archaic Period: Proceedings of an International Symposium on Cypriote Archaeology, Erlangen, 23–24 July 2004*, edited by V. Karageorghis, H. Matthaus and S. Rogge, 143–69. Mohnesee-Wamel.

Rahmstorf, L. 2011. 'Handmade pots and crumbling loomweights: "Barbarian" elements in the eastern Mediterranean in the last quarter of the 2nd millennium BC'. In *On Cooking Pots, Drinking Cups, Loomweights and Ethnicity in Bronze Age*

Cyprus and Neighbouring Regions, edited by O. Kouka and V. Karageorghis, 315–30. Nikosia.

Rahmstorf, L., M. Siennicka, E. Andersson Strand, M.-L. Nosch and J. Cutler. 2015. 'Textile Tools from Tiryns'. In *Tools, Textiles and Contexts. Investigations of Textile Production in the Bronze Age Eastern Mediterranean*, edited by E. Andersson Strand and M.-L. Nosch, 267–78. Oxford.

Randall-MacIver, D., F.L. Griffith and A.C. Mace. 1902. *El Amrah and Abydos, 1899–1901*. London.

Rast-Eicher, A. 2005. 'Bast before Wool: The First Textiles'. In *Hallstatt Textiles – Technical Analysis, Scientific Investigation and Experiment on Iron Age Textiles*, edited by P. Bichler, K. Grömer, R. Hofmann-de Keijzer, A. Kern and H. Reschreiter, 117–35. Oxford.

Rast-Eicher, A. 2008. *Textilien, Wolle, Schafe der Eisenzeit in der Schweiz*. Basel.

Rast-Eicher, A. 2018. 'In the Beginning Was the Fibre'. In *Considering Creativity: Creativity, Knowledge and Practice in Bronze Age Europe*, edited by J. Sofaer, 117–32. Oxford.

Rast-Eicher, A. and L. Bender Jørgensen. 2013. 'Sheep Wool in Bronze Age and Iron Age Europe'. *Journal of Archaeological Science* 40 (2): 1224–41. https://doi.org/10.1016/j.jas.2012.09.030.

Rast-Eicher, A., S. Karg and L. Bender Jørgensen. 2021. 'The Use of Local Fibres for Textiles at Neolithic Çatalhöyük'. *Antiquity* 95 (383): 1129–44. https://doi.org/10.15184/aqy.2021.89.

Reichert, A. 2020. 'Texile Materials in the Mesolithic and Neolithic and Their Processing'. In *The Competition of Fibres: Early Textile Production in Western Asia, South-East and Central Europe (10,000–500 BCE)*, edited by W. Schier and S. Pollock, 166–79. Oxford.

Rizkana, I. and J. Seeher. 1987. *Maadi 1: The Pottery of the Predynastic Settlement*. Mainz am Rhein.

Rizkana, I. and J. Seeher. 1988. *Maadi 2. The Lithic Industries of the Predynastic Settlement*. Mainz am Rhein.

Rizkana, I., J. Boessneck, E. Pernicka, A. Hauptmann, R. Ziegler, A. von den Driesch-Karpf and J. Seeher. 1989. *Maadi III The Non-Lithic Small Finds and the Structural Remains of the Predynastic Settlement*. Mainz am Rhein.

Rodríguez Frade, P. 2019. 'Escenas De Telares En La Tumba Capilla de Ramose y Su Restauración. Mision Española En Dra Abu El-Naga'. *Boletín de La Asociación Española de Egiptología* 28: 77–94.

Rodríguez Frade, P. 2022. 'Tissus de chanvre trouvés par la mission archéologique espagnole à Dra Abou el-Naga'. *Bulletin de l'Institut français d'archéologie orientale* 122 (July), 493–523. https://doi.org/10.4000/bifao.12494.

Rodríguez Frade, P. 2024. 'The Mummification Deposit in the Courtyard of TT 209: Description of its Fabrics and Questions it Raises'. *Trabajos de Egiptologia*, 1–34. https://doi.org/10.25145/j.

Roodenberg, J.J., T.J. Wilkinson and S. Bayri-Bakan. 1984. 'Surveys and Soundings at Kumartepe. An Interim Report'. *Anatolica* XI: 1–16.

Rooijakkers, T.C. 2012. 'Spinning Animal Fibres at Late Neolithic Tell Sabi Abyad, Syria?' *Paléorient*, 93–109.

Roth, H.L. and G.M. Crowfoot. 1921. 'Models of Egyptian Looms'. *Ancient Egypt* 4: 96–101.

Ruiz de Haro, M. 2018. 'From East to West: The Use of Spinning Bowls from the Chalcolithic Period to the Iron Age.' In *First Textiles: The Beginnings of Textile Manufacture in Europe and the Mediterranean*: Proceedings of the EAA Session Held in Istanbul (2014) and the 'First Textiles' Conference in Copenhagen (2015), edited by M. Siennicka, L. Rahmstorf and A. Ulanowska, 81–90. Oxford.

Ryder, M.L. 1965. 'Report of Textiles from Çatal Hüyük'. *Anatolian Studies* 15: 175–6.

Ryder, M.L. 1983. *Sheep and Man*. London.

Ryder, M.L. and T. Gabra-Sanders. 1987. 'A Microscopic Study of Remains of Textiles Made from Plant Fibres'. *Oxford Journal of Archaeology* 6 (1): 91–108. https://doi.org/10.1111/j.1468-0092.1987.tb00143.x.

Rzepka, S., M.N. El-Din, A. Wodzinska and L. Jarmuzek. 2012. 'Egyptian Mission Rescue Excavations in Tell El-Retaba. Part 1: New Kingdom Remains'. *Ägypten und Levante* 22: 253–87.

Rzepka, S., J. Hudec, L. Jarmuzek, V. Dubcová, L. Hulková, A. Wodzinska, A. Sefcáková and E. Stopková. 2017. 'From Hyksos Tombs to Late Period Tower Houses. Tell el-Retaba Seasons 2015–2016'. *Ägypten und Levante* 27: 19–86.

Saad, Z.Y. 1947. *Royal Excavations at Saqqara and Helwan, 1941–1945*. Le Caire.

Saad, Z.Y. 1951. *Royal Excavations at Saqqara and Helwan, 1945–1947*. Le Caire.

Sass, B. 2000. 'The Small Finds'. In *Megiddo III: The 1992–1996 Seasons*, edited by I. Finkelstein, D. Ussishkin and B. Halpern, 349–423. Tel Aviv.

Sauvage, C. 2013. 'Spinning from Old Threads: The Whorls from Ugarit at the Musée d'Archéologie Nationale (Saint-Germain-En-Laye) and at the Louvre'. In *Textile Production and Consumption in the Ancient Near East: Archaeology, Epigraphy, Iconography*, edited by M.-L. Nosch, H. Koefoed and E. Andersson Strand, 189–214. Oxford.

Sauvage, C. 2014. 'Spindles and Distaffs: Late Bronze and Early Iron Age Eastern Mediterranean Use of Solid and Tapered Ivory/Bone Shafts'. In *Prehistoric, Ancient Near Eastern & Aegean Textiles and Dresses*, edited by M.-L. Nosch, C. Michel and M. Harlow, 184–226. Oxford.

Savage, S. 2011. 'From Maadi to the Plain of Antioch: What Can Basalt Spindle Whorls Tell Us About Overland Trade in the Southern Levant During the Early Bronze Age?' In *Daily Life, Materiality, and Complexity in Early Urban Communities of the Southern Levant: Papers in Honor of Walter E. Rast and R. Thomas Schaub*, edited by M.S. Chesson, W.E. Aufrecht, I. Kuijt, W.E. Rast and R.T. Schaub, 119–38. Winona Lake, Ind.

Scheffer, A. and H. Granger-Taylor. 1994. 'Textiles'. In *Masada: The Yigael Yadin Excavations 1963–1965: Final Reports. 4*, edited by Y. Yadin, 153–227. Masada Reports. Jerusalem.

Schick, T. 1988. 'Nahal Hemar Cave: Cordage, Basketry and Fabrics'. *Atiqot* 18: 31–43.

Schick, T. 1995. 'A 10,000 Year Old Comb from Wadi Murabba'at in the Judean Desert'. *'Atiqot* 27: 199–202.

Schick, T. 2002. 'The Early Basketry and Textiles from Caves in the Northern Judean Desert'. *'Atiqot*: 223–39.

Schmidt, E.F. 1937. *Excavations at Tepe Hissar, Damghan*. Philadelphia.

Schneider, T. 2003. *Ausl ä Nder in Ä Gypten w ä Hrend Des Mittleren Reiches Und Der Hyksoszeit. Teil 2: Die Ausl ä Ndische Bev ö Lkerung*. Mainz.

Schoop, U.-D. 2014. 'Weaving Society in Late Chalcolithic Anatolia: Textile Production and Social Strategies in the 4th Millennium BC'. In *Western Anatolia before Troy. Proto-Urbanisation in the 4th Millennium BC?: Proceedings of the International Symposium Held at the Kunsthistorisches Museum Wien, Vienna, Austria, 21–24 November, 2012*, edited by B. Horejs and M. Mehofer. https://doi.org/10.26530/oapen_625897.

Sebbane, M. 2014. 'The Hoard from the Nahal Mishmar, and the Metal-Working Industry in Israel in the Chalcolithic Period'. In *Masters of Fire: Copper Age Art from Israel*, edited by M. Sebbane, 114–38. Tel Aviv.

Shamir, O. 1996. 'Loomweights and Whorls'. In *Excavations at the City of David: Monographs of the Institute of Archaeology, the Hebrew University of Jerusalem, 4. 1978–1985: Various Reports*, edited by Y. Shiloh, D.T. Ariel and A. de Groot, 1985: 135–70.

Shamir, O. 2003. 'Spindle Whorls from Qiryat Ata in: A. Golani. Salvage Excavations at the Early Bronze Age Site of Qiryat Ata'. *Israel Antiquity Authority Reports* 18: 209–14.

Shamir, O. 2004. 'The Spindle Whorls from Ashqelon, Afridar–Area E. *Atiqot* 45: 97–100.

Shamir, O. 2007a. 'Loomweights and Textile Production at Tel Miqne-Ekron: A Preliminary Report'. *Up to the Gates of Ekron': Essays on the Archaeology and History of the Eastern Mediterranean in Honor of Seymour Gitin,* 43–49. Jerusalem.

Shamir, O. 2007b. 'Textiles, Loom Weights and Spindle Whorls'. In *Excavations at Kadesh Barnea (Tell El-Qudeirat) 1976–1982*, edited by R. Cohen and H. Bernick-Greenberg, 255–68. Jerusalem.

Shamir, O. 2009. 'Appendix: A Linen Textile Fragment'. In *Excavations at Tel Beth-Shean 1989-1996. Vol. III. The 13th–11th Century BCE Strata in Areas N and S*, edited by A. Mazar and N. Panitz-Cohen, 608. Jerusalem.

Shamir, O. 2013. 'Tel 'Amal: Loomweights'. *Hadashot Arkheologiyot Excavations and Surveys in Israel* 125. http://www.hadashot-esi.org.il/images//Tel-Amal-English.pdf.

Shamir, O. 2014. 'Textiles, Basketry and Other Organic Artifacts of the Chalcolithic Period in the Southern Levant'. In *Masters of Fire: Copper Age Art from Israel*, edited by M. Sebbane, 139–52. Tel Aviv.

Shamir, O. 2015. 'Textiles from the Chalcolithic Period, Early and Middle Bronze Age in the Southern Levant'. *Archaeological Textiles Review* 57: 12–25.

Shamir, O. and A. Rast-Eicher. 2020. 'Continuity and Discontinuity in Neolithic and Chalcolithic Linen Textile Production in the Southern Levant'. In *The Competition of Fibres: Early Textile Production in Western Asia, South-East and Central Europe (10,000–500 BCE)*, edited by W. Schier and S. Pollock, 27–38. Oxford.

Sharon, I. 2014. 'Levantine Chronology'. In *The Oxford Handbook of the Archaeology of the Levant: c. 8000–332 BCE*, edited by M. Steiner and A.E. Killebrew, 45–65. Oxford.

Shaw, I. 2003a. 'Egypt and the Outside World'. In *The Oxford History of Ancient Egypt*, edited by I. Shaw, 314–30. Oxford.

Shaw, I. 2003b. *The Oxford History of Ancient Egypt*. Oxford.

Shaw, I. 2012. 'New Fieldwork at the Medinet El-Gurob New Kingdom Settlement: Investigating a Harem Palace Town in the Faiyum (Summary of the 2009–10 Seasons)'. In *Achievements and Problems of Modern Egyptology*, edited by G. Belova, 348–64. Moscow.

Shishlina, N.I., O.V. Orfinskaya and V.P. Golikov. 2003. 'Bronze Age Textiles from the North Caucasus: New Evidence of Fourth Millennium BC Fibres and Fabrics'. *Oxford Journal of Archaeology* 22 (4): 331–44. https://doi.org/10.1046/j.1468-0092.2003.00191.x.

Smith, J.S. 2013. 'Tapestries in the Bronze and Early Iron Ages of the Ancient Near East'. In *Textile Production and Consumption in the Ancient Near East: Archaeology, Epigraphy, Iconography*, edited by M.-L. Nosch, H. Koefoed and E. Andersson Strand, 161–88. Oxford.

Smith, V.E. 2010. *Modeling the Mechanics of Temple Production in the Middle Kingdom an Investigation of the Shena of Divine Offerings Adjacent to the Mortuary Temple of Senwosret III at Abydos, Egypt*. Ann Arbor, Mich.

Spinazzi-Lucchesi, C. 2018. *The Unwound Yarn. Birth and Development of Textile Tools Between Levant and Egypt*. Venezia.

Stevenson, A. 2016. 'The Egyptian Predynastic and State Formation'. *Journal of Archaeological Research* 24 (4): 421–68.

Stordeur, D. and M. Lebreton. 2008. 'Figurines, pierres à rainures, "petits objets divers" et manches de Mureybet'. In *Le Site Neolithique De Tell Mureybet: Syrie Du Nord: En hommage à Jacques Cauvin*, edited by J. Jose Ibañez, 619–43. Oxford.

Svilar, M.M. 2017. 'Searching for late neolithic spinning bowls in the central Balkans'. *Starinar* 67: 21–32.

Tata, G. 1995. *The Development of the Egyptian Textile Industry*. Unpublished PhD. Ann Arbor.

Tavares, A. 2004. 'The Hidden Industry. Weaving at the Workers' Settlement'. *AERAGRAM Newsletter of Ancient Egypt Research Associates* 7(2): 10–11.

Taylor, J. 2003. 'The Third Intermediate Period (1069–664 BCE)'. In *The Oxford History of Ancient Egypt*, edited by I. Shaw, 330–68. Oxford.

Thomas, A.P. 1981. *Gurob: A New Kingdom Town. Introduction and Catalogue of Objects in the Petrie Collection*. Warminster.

Thomas, A.P. 2004. 'Some comments on the Predynastic cemetery at el Mahasna'. In *Egypt at its Origins: Studies in Memory of Barbara Adams: Proceedings of the International Conference 'Origin of the State, Predynastic and Early Dynastic Egypt', Kraków, 28th August–1st September 2002*, edited by S. Hendrickx, R. Friedman, K. Cialowicz and M. Chlodnicki, 1041–54. Leuven.

Toivari-Viitala, J. 2011. 'Deir El-Medina (Development)'. *UCLA Encyclopedia of Egyptology* 1. https://escholarship.org/uc/item/6kt9m29r.

Tufnell, O. 1958. *Lachish IV: The Bronze Age*. Oxford.

Tufnell, O., C.H. Inge and L. Harding. 1940. *Lachish II: The Fosse Temple*. Oxford.

van den Brink, E. and T.E. Levy. 2002. 'Interaction Models, Egypt and the Levantine Periphery'. In *Egypt and the Levant: Interrelations from the 4th through the Early 3rd Millennium BCE*, edited by E. van den Brink and T.E. Levy, 3–38. London.

van der Brink, E.C. 1992. 'Tombs of the Elite in Minshat Abu Omar'. In *The Nile Delta in Transition; 4th–3rd Millenium B.C.: Proceedings of the Seminar Held in Cairo, 21–24 Oct. 1990, at the Netherlands Institute of Archaeology and Arabic Studies*, edited by E.C. van der Brink, 127–50. Tel Aviv.

Van Dijk, J. 2003. 'The Amarna Period and the Later New Kingdom'. In *The Oxford History of Ancient Egypt*, edited by I. Shaw. Oxford.

van 't Hooft, P.P.M., M.J. Raven, E.H.C. van Rooij and G.M. Vogelsang-Eastwood. 1994. *Pharaonic and Early Medieval Egyptian Textiles*. Leiden.

van Zeist, W. and G.J. de Roller. 1991. 'The Plant Husbandry of Aceramic Çayönü, SE Turkey'. *Palaeohistoria* 33/34: 65–96.

Vandier d'Abbadie, J. 1937. *Catalogue Des Ostraca Figurés de Deir El Médineh: Vol. 1 (Fasc. 1–2)*. Le Caire.

Venturi, F. 2020. *Tell Afis: The Excavations of Areas E2–E4, Phases V–I, the End of the Late Bronze, Iron Age I Sequence: Stratigraphy, Pottery and Small Finds*. Firenze.

Vila, E. and D. Helmer. 2014. 'The Expansion of Sheep Herding and the Development of Wool Production in the Ancient Near East: An Archaeozoological and Iconographical Approach'. In *Wool Economy in the Ancient Near East and the Aegean: From the Beginnings of Sheep Husbandry to Institutional Textile Industry*, edited by C. Breniquet and C. Michel, 22–40. Oxford.

Vogelsang-Eastwood, G.M. 1987. 'A Note on the So-Called "Spinning Bowls"'. *Ex Oriente Lux. Jaarbericht van Het Vooraziatisch-Egyptisch Genootschap* 30: 78–88.

Vogelsang-Eastwood, G. 1988. 'A Re-Examination of the Fibres from the Çatal Hüyük Textiles'. *Oriental Carpet and Textile Studies* 3 (1): 15–19.

Vogelsang-Eastwood, G. 1993. *Pharaonic Egyptian Clothing*. Leiden.

Vogelsang-Eastwood, G. 1999. *Tutankhamun's Wardrobe: Garments from the Tomb of Tutankhamun*. Rotterdam.

Vogelsang-Eastwood, G. 2000. '11. Textiles'. In *Ancient Egyptian Materials and Technology*, edited by P.T. Nicholson and I. Shaw, 268–97. Cambridge.

Völling, E. 2008. *Textiltechnik Im Alten Orient: Rohstoffe Und Herstellung*. Würzburg.

Wachsmann, S. 2013. *The Gurob Ship-Cart Model and its Mediterranean Context*. College Station, TX.

Waetzoldt, H. 1972. *Untersuchungen Zur Neusumerischen Textilindustrie*. Centro per le Anctichità e la Storia dell'Arte del Vicino Oriente. Roma.

Walton Rogers, P., A. Rast-Eicher and L. Bender Jørgensen, eds. 2001. *The Roman Textile Industry and its Influence. A Birthday Tribute to John Peter Wild*. Oxford.

Wegner, J. 2007. *The Mortuary Temple of Senwosret III at Abydos*. New Haven, CT; Oxford.

Wegner, J., V. Smith and S. Rossell. 2000. 'The Organization of The Temple Nfr-KA of Senwosret III at Abydos'. *Ägypten und Levante* 10: 83–125.

Wendrich, W. 1999. *The World According to Basketry: An Ethno-Archaeological Interpretation of Basketry Production in Egypt*. Leiden.

Wenke, R.J., R.W. Redding and W. Wetterstrom. 2016. *Kom el-Hisn (ca. 2500–1900 BC). An Ancient Settlement in the Nile Delta*. Bristol.

Wente, E.F. 1990. *Letters from Ancient Egypt*. Edited by E.S Meltzer. Atlanta.

Wheeler, M. 1982. 'Loomweights and Spindle Whorls'. In *Excavations at Jericho IV: The Pottery Type Series and Other Finds*, by K.M. Kenyon and T.A. Holland, 623–37. London.

Wild, J.P. 1970. *Textile Manufacture in the Northern Roman Provinces*. Cambridge.

Winlock, H.E. 1922. 'Heddle-Jacks of Middle Kingdom Looms'. *Ancient Egypt* 22: 71.

Winlock, H.E. 1955. *Models of Daily Life in Ancient Egypt: From the Tomb of Meket-Rē' at Thebes*. New York.

Wisti Lassen, A. 2010. 'Tools, Procedures and Professions: A Review of the Akkadian Textile Terminology'. In *Textile Terminologies in the Ancient Near East and Mediterranean from the Third to the First Millennia BC*, edited by M.-L. Nosch and C. Michel, 272–82. Oxford.

Wisti Lassen, A. 2015. 'Weaving with Crescent Shaped Loom Weights. An Investigation of a Special Kind of Loom Weight'. In *Tools, Textiles and Contexts: Investigating Textile Production in the Aegean and Eastern Mediterranean Bronze Age*, edited by E. Andersson Strand and M.-L. Nosch, 127–35. Oxford.

Yadin, Y., Y. Aharoni, E. Dunayevski, T. Dothan and R. Amiran. 1958. *Hazor I: An account of the first season of excavations, 1955. The James A. de Rothschild Expedition at Hazor.* Jerusalem.

Yadin, Y., Y. Aharoni, R. Amiran, T.K. Dothan, I. Dunayevsky, J. Perrot and M. Dothan. 1989. *Hazor III–IV: An Account of the Third and Fourth Seasons of Excavations, 1957–1958*. Edited by A. Ben-Tor. Jerusalem.

Yahalom-Mack, N. 2007. 'The Textile Industry.' In *Excavations at Tel Beth-Shean: 1989–1996. Vol. II. The Middle and Late Bronze Age Strata in Area R*, edited by A. Mazar, 661–8. Jerusalem.

Yahalom-Mack, N. and A. Mazar. 2006. 'Various Finds Form Iron Age II Strata in Area P and S'. In *Excavations at Tel Beth-Shean, 1989–1996, vol. I. From the Late Bronze Age IIB to the Medieval Period*, edited by A. Mazar, 468–504. Jerusalem.

Yasur-Landau, A. 2010. *The Philistines and Aegean Migration at the End of the Late Bronze Age*. Cambridge.

Yasur-Landau, A. 2012. 'The Role of the Canaanite Population in the Aegean Migration to the Southern Levant in the Late 2nd Millenium BC'. In *Materiality and Social Practice. Transformative Capacities of Intercultural Encounters*, edited by J. Maran and P.W. Stockhammer, 190–7. Oxford.

Yasur-Landau, A., A. Goshen, E. Andersson Strand, M.-L. Nosch and J. Cutler. 2015. 'Textile Tools from Tel Kabri, Israel'. In *Tools, Textiles and Contexts: Investigating Textile Production in the Aegean and Eastern Mediterranean Bronze Age*, edited by E. Andersson Strand and M.-L. Nosch, 346–9. Oxford.

Younker, R.W. 2003. 'The Iron Age in the Southern Levant'. In *Near Eastern Archaeology: A Reader*, edited by S. Richard, 367–82. Winona Lake, Ind. https://doi.org/10.1515/9781575065472-053.

Zohary, D., M. Hopf and E. Weiss. 2012. *Domestication of Plants in the Old World: The Origin and Spread of Domesticated Plants in Southwest Asia, Europe, and the Mediterranean Basin*. Oxford. https://doi.org/10.1093/acprof:osobl/9780199549061.001.0001.

Zuckerman, S. 2013 'Hazor in the Early Bronze Age'. *Near Eastern Archaeology* 76(2): 68–73.

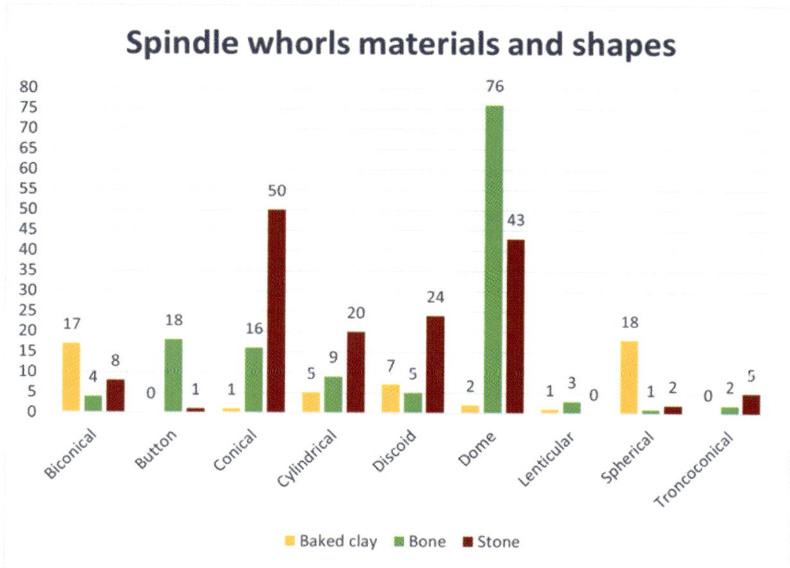

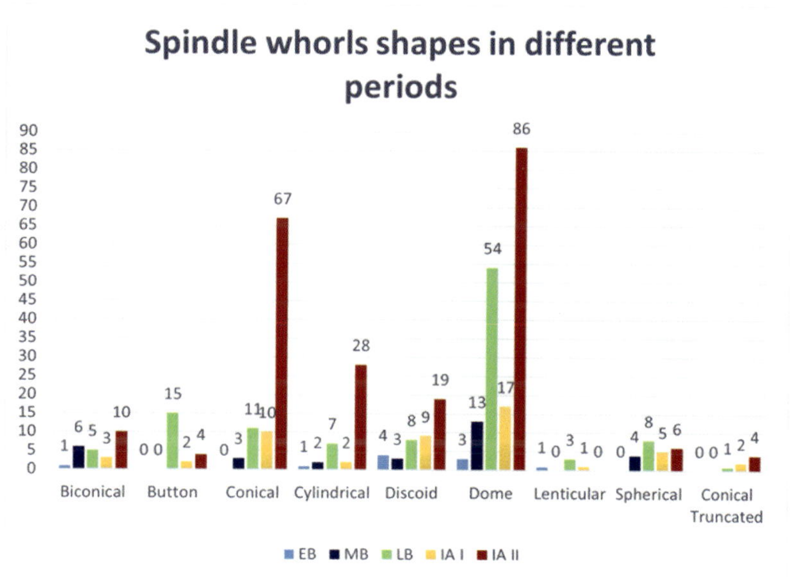

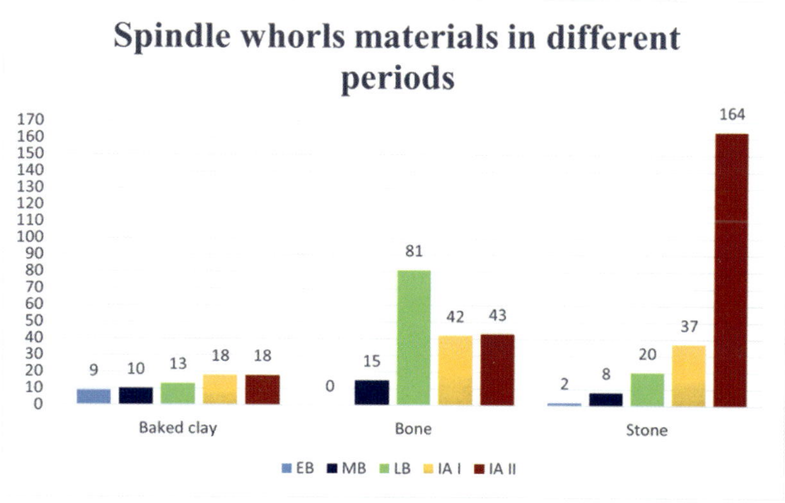

Plate 1. Plots of Megiddo spindle whorls

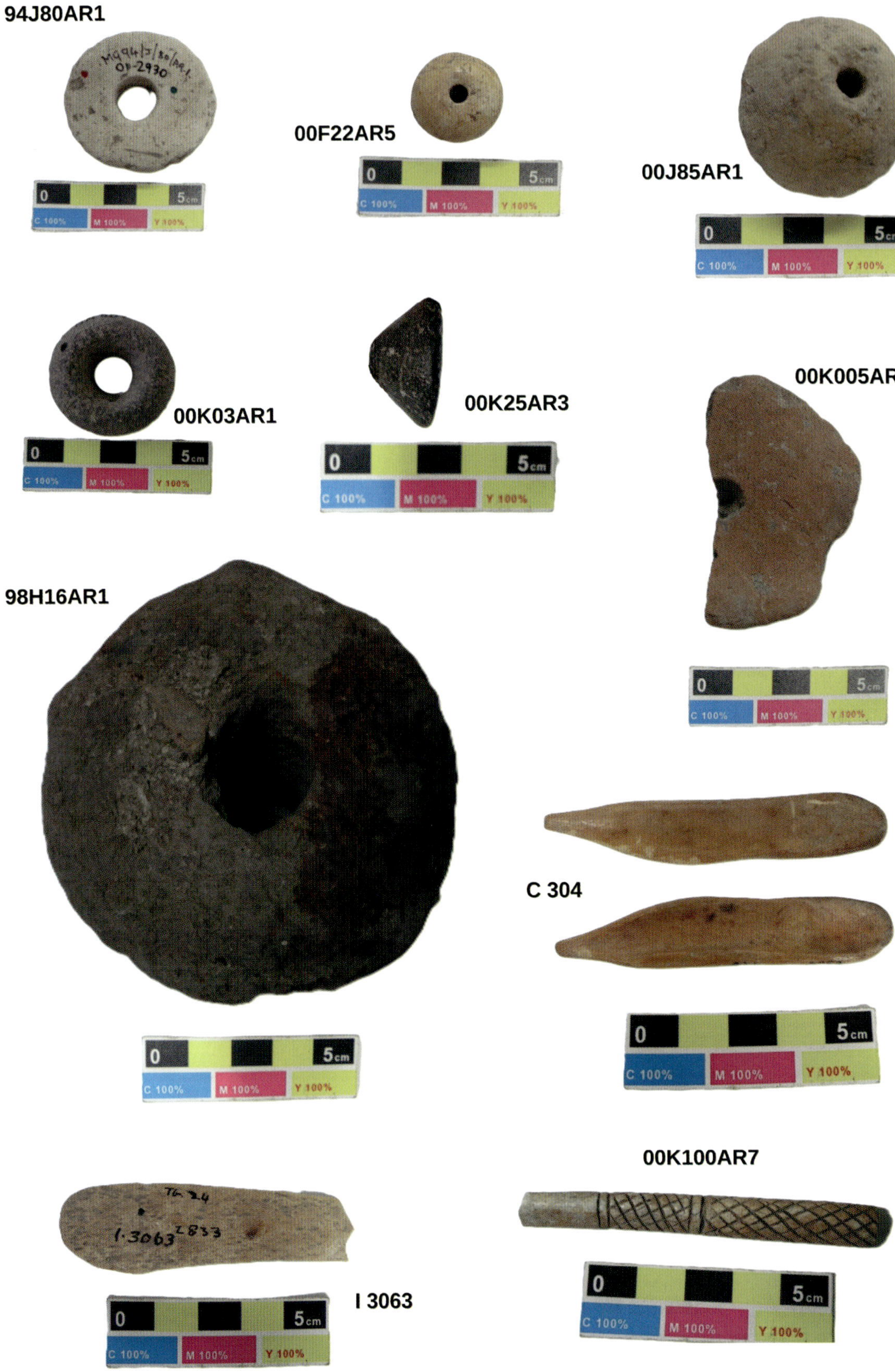

Plate 2. Selection of Megiddo textile tools 94J80AR1, 00F22AR5, 00J85AR1, 00K03AR1, 00K25AR3, 00K005AR3, 98H16AR1, C304, I 3603, 00K100AR7 (courtesy of the Israel Antiquity Authorities)

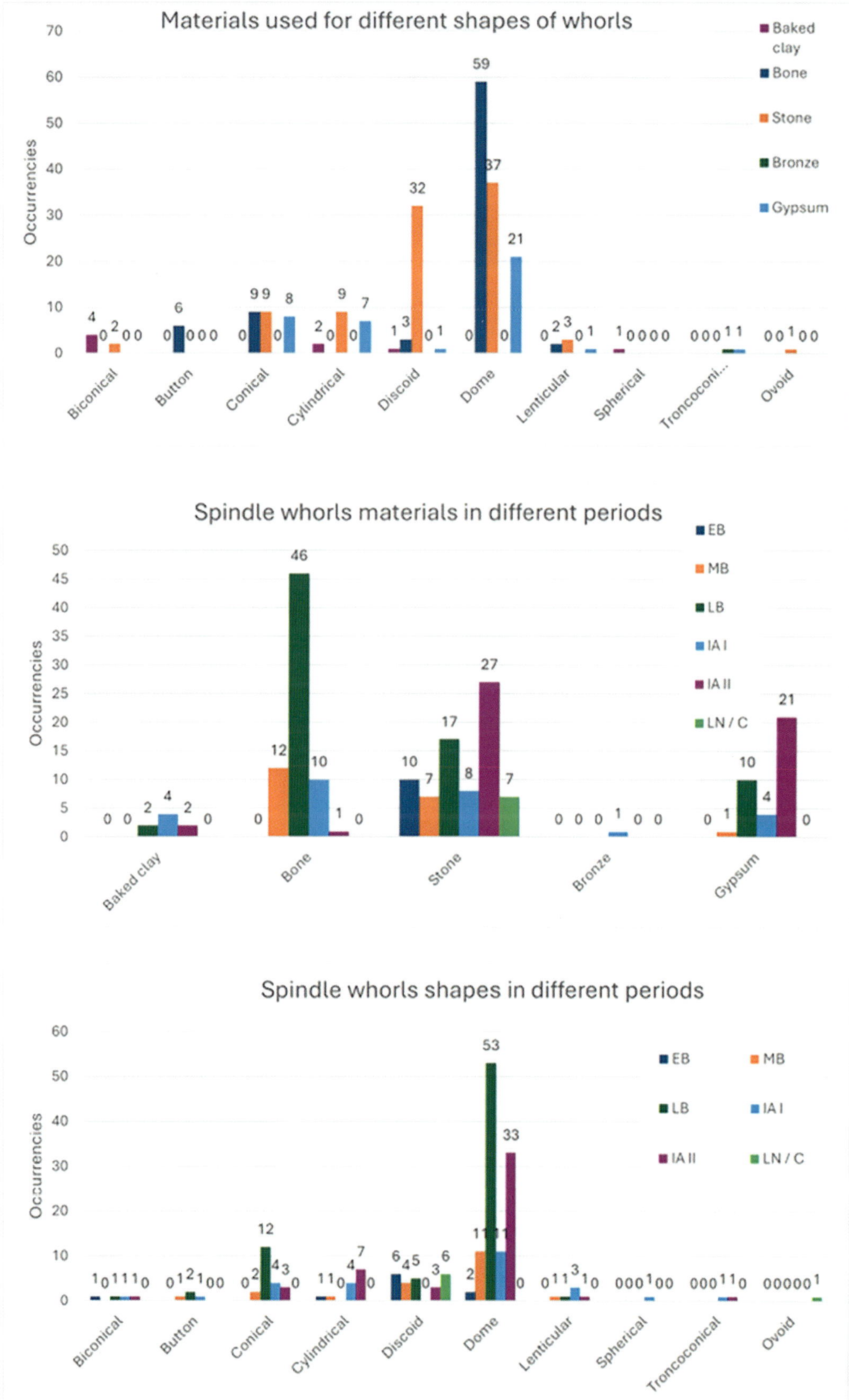

Plate 3. Plots of Beth Shean spindle whorls

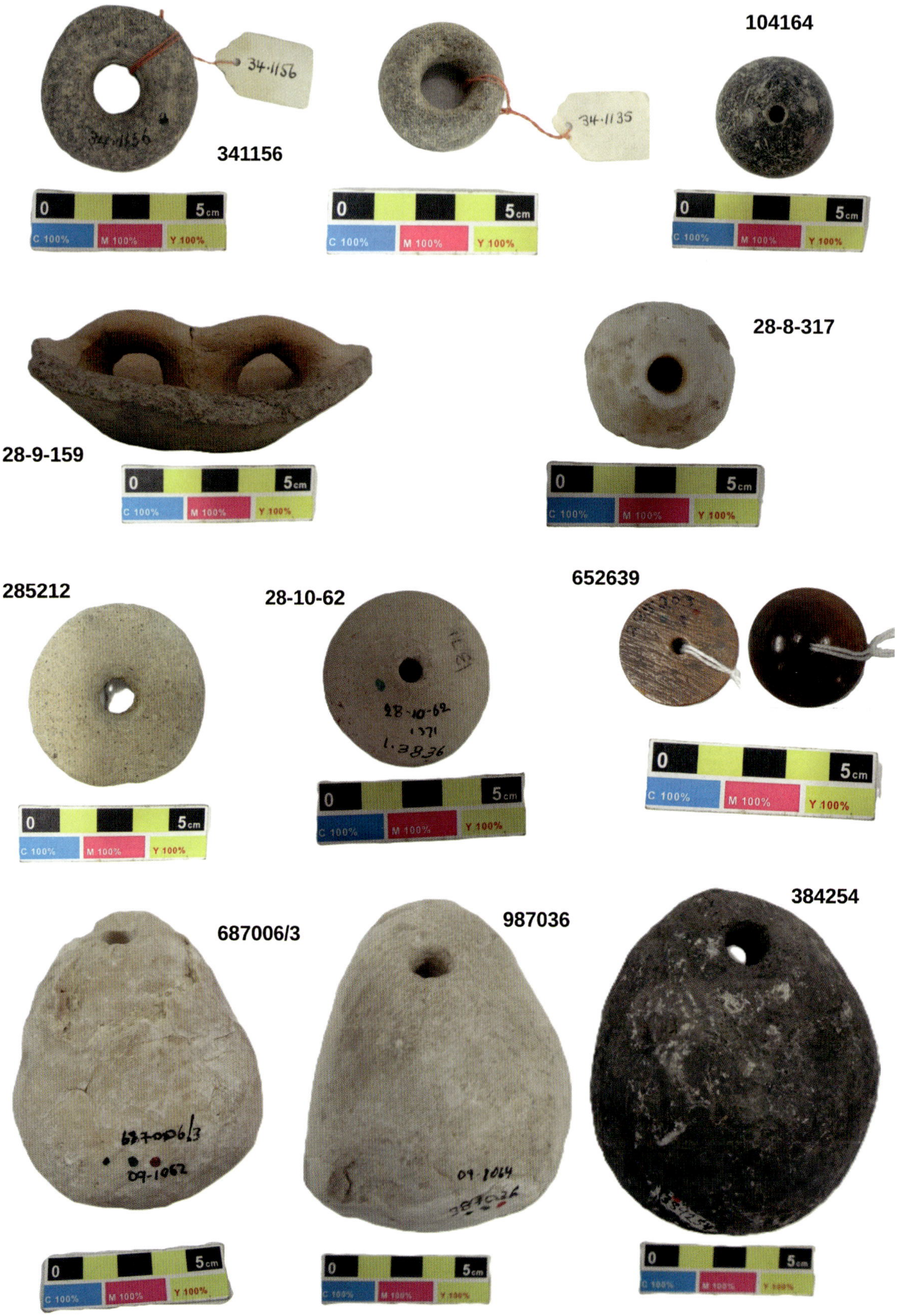

Plate 4. Selection of Beth Shean textile tools 341156, 341135, 104164, 28-9-159, 28-8-317, 285212, 28-10-62, 652639, 687006/3, 987036, 384254 (courtesy of the Israel Antiquity Authorities)

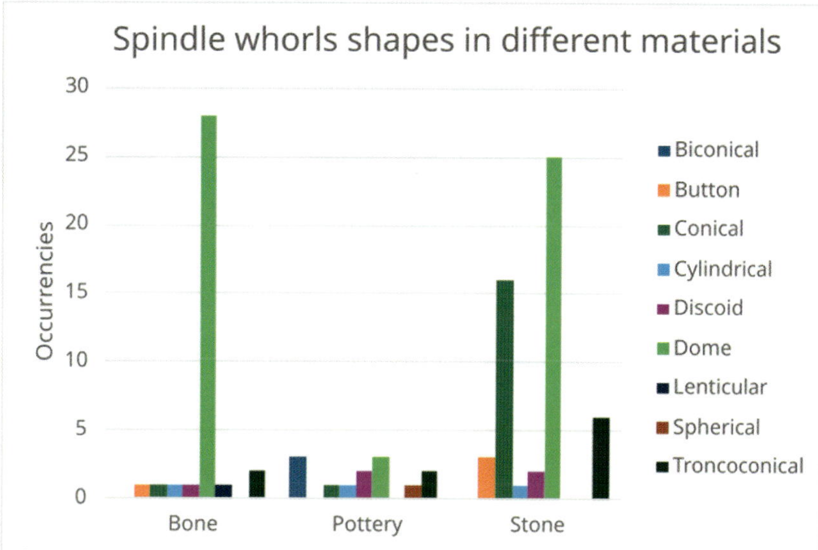

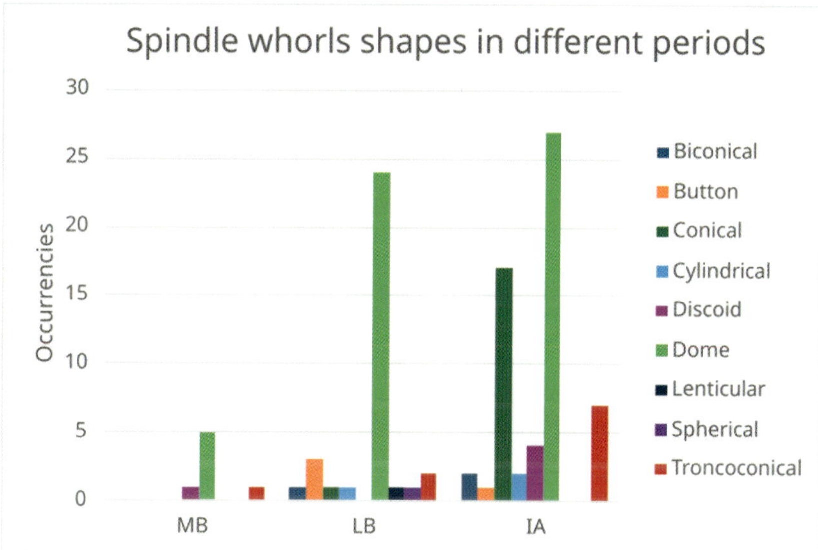

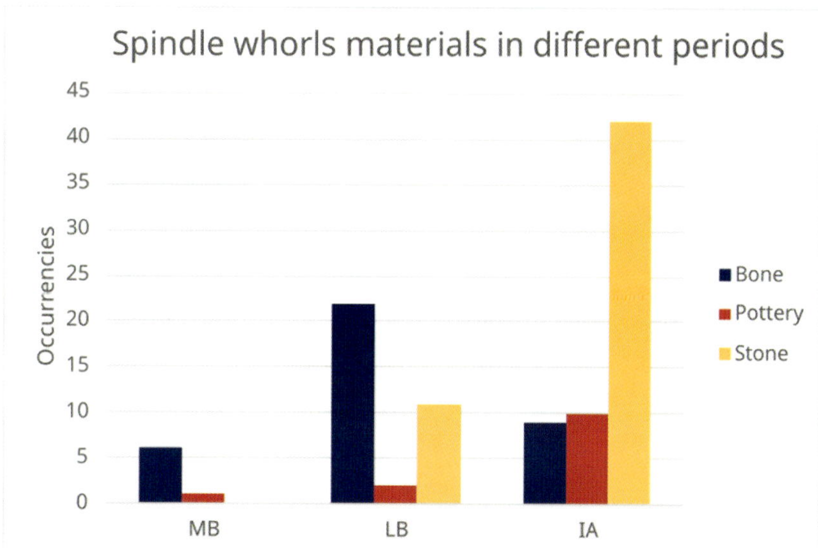

Plate 5. Plots of Hazor spindle whorls

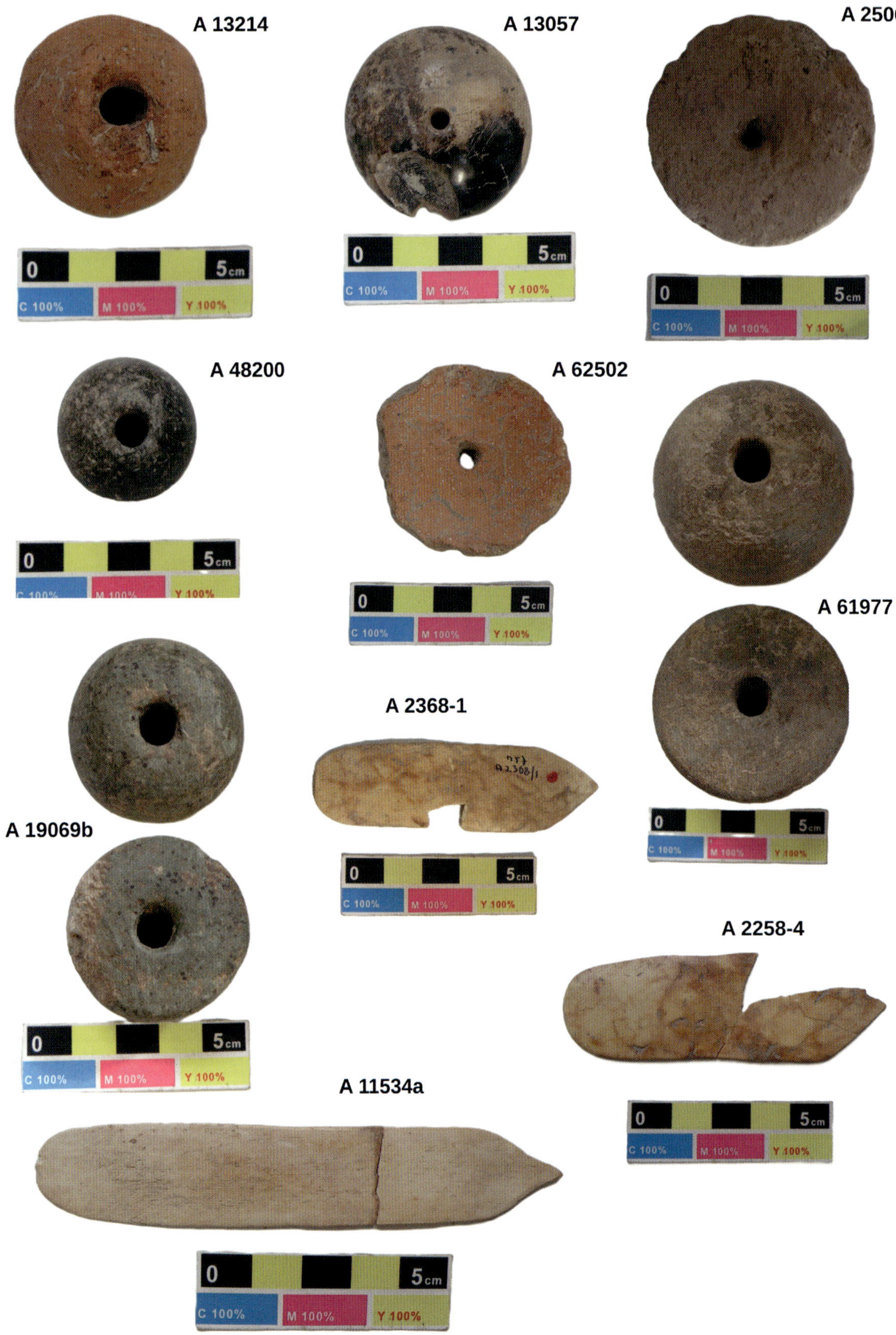

Plate 6. Selection of Hazor textile tools A 13059, A 13214, A 13057, A 25065, A48200, A 62502, A 61977, A 19069b, A 2368-1, A 2258-4, A 11534a (courtesy of the Selz Foundation Hazor Excavations in Memory of Yigael Yadin)

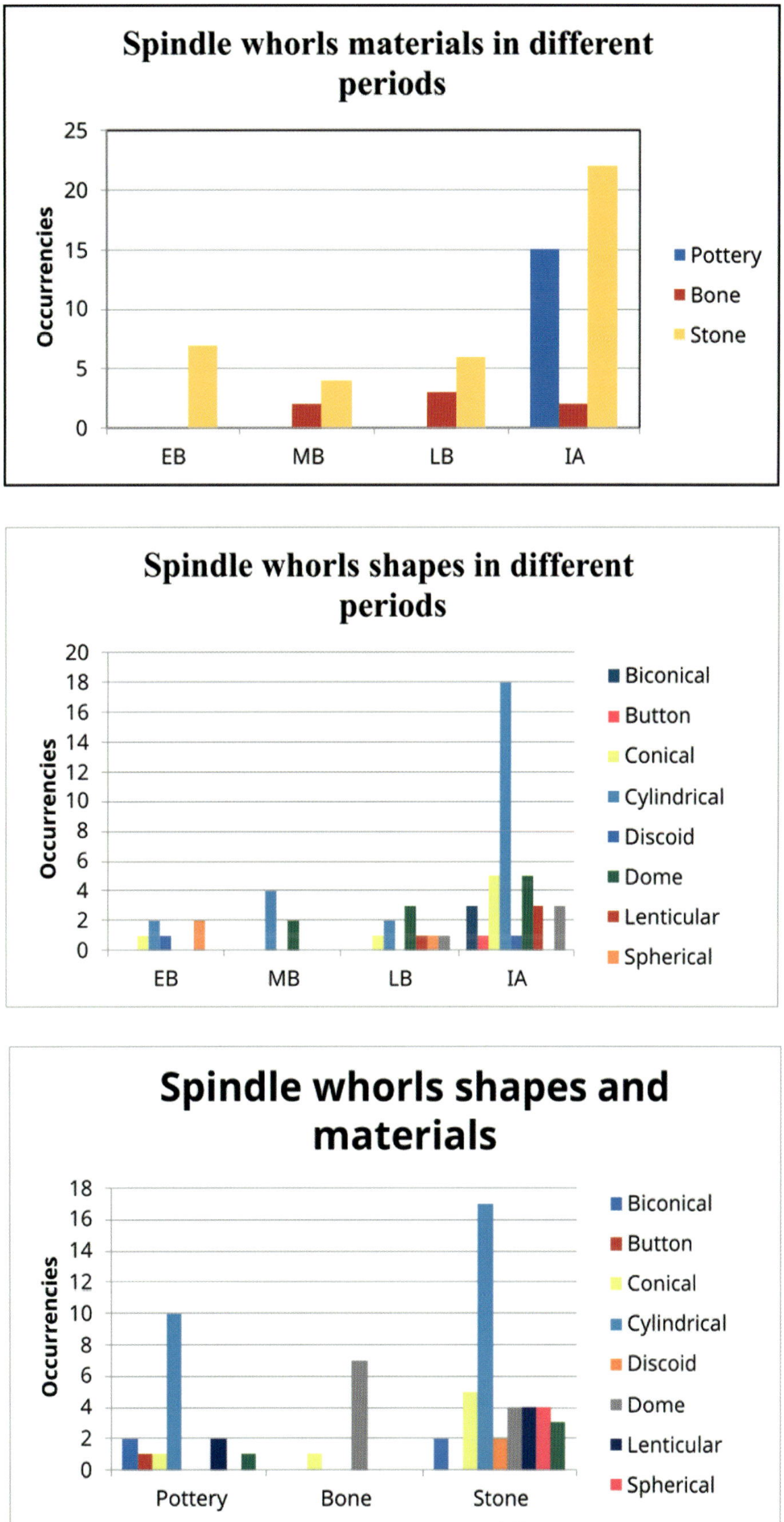

Plate 7. Plots of Tell el-Far'ah (N) whorls

Plate 8. Selection of Tell el-Far'ah (N) textile tools, F. 3468, F. 347, F. 1510-24, F. 1510-30, F. 2936, F. 156, F. 1510-01 (courtesy of the École Biblique)

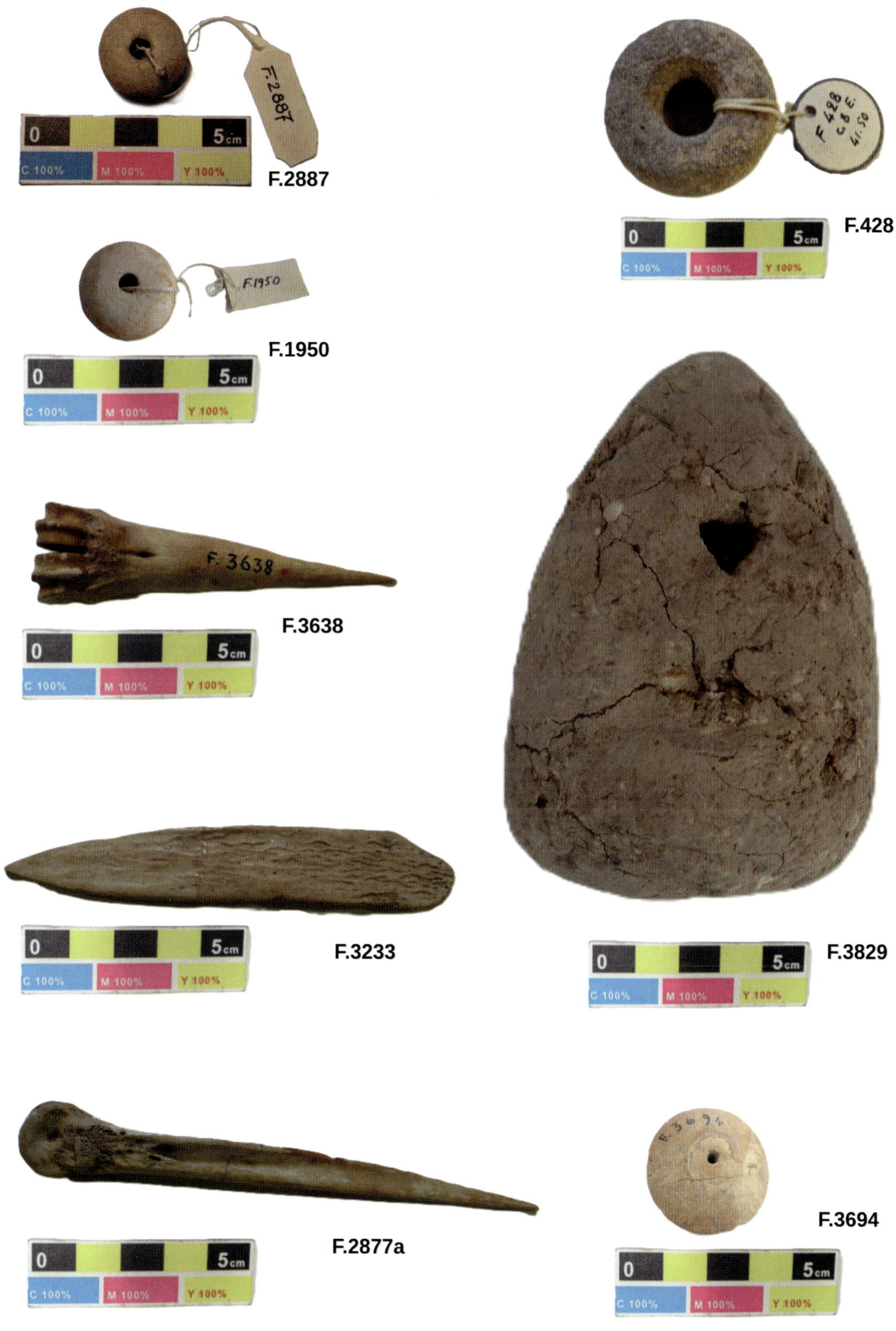

Plate 9. Selection of Tell el-Far'ah (N) textile tools, F. 2887, F. 428, F. 1950, F. 3829, F.3638, F. 3233, F. 2877a, F. 3694 (courtesy of the École Biblique)

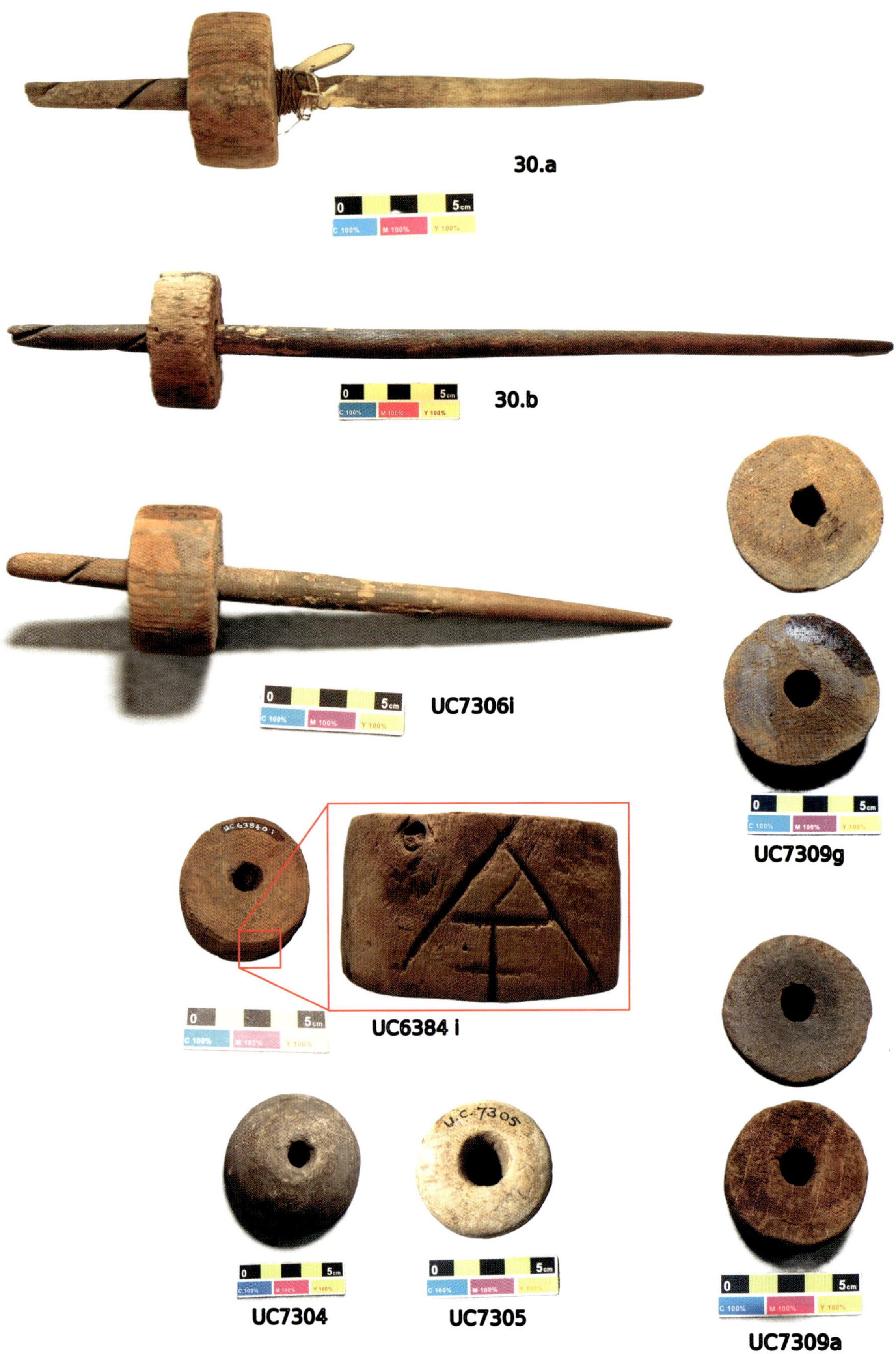

Plate 10. Spindles and whorls from Kahun

50.c

UC7353 i

UC7352

UC21329

UC16752

UC 59021

Plate 11. Selection of textile tools from Kahun

Plate 12. Wooden spindles and whorls from Gurob

Plate 13. Bone spatulae from Gurob (courtesy of Manchester Museum, 555.a.ii, 555.b.x, 555.b.v, 555.i, 555.vii, 555.xviii)

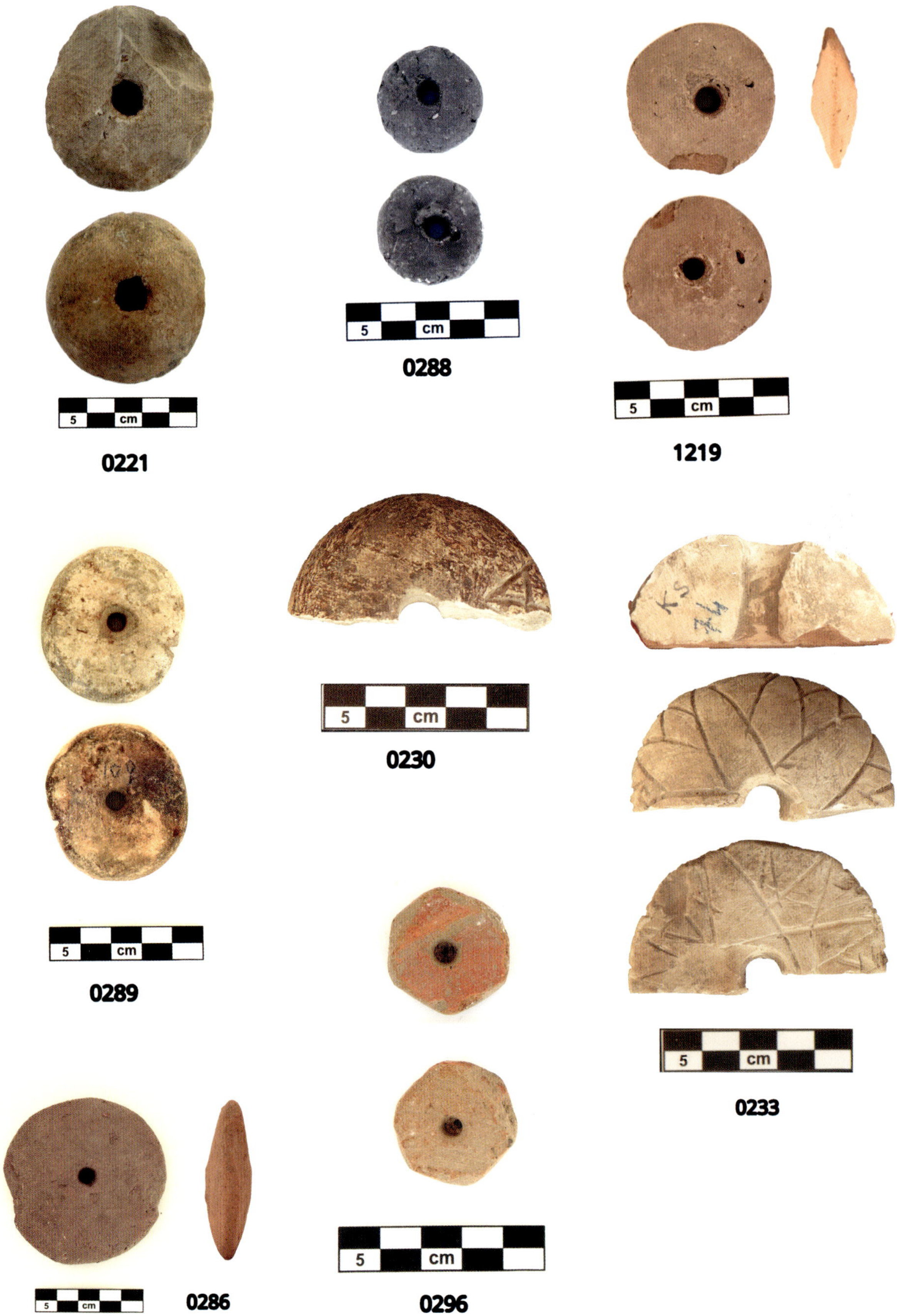

Plate 14. Stone and ceramic spindle whorls from Deir el-Medina (courtesy of IFAO)

Plate 15. Weight, wooden spindles and spinning bowl from Deir el-Medina (courtesy of IFAO)

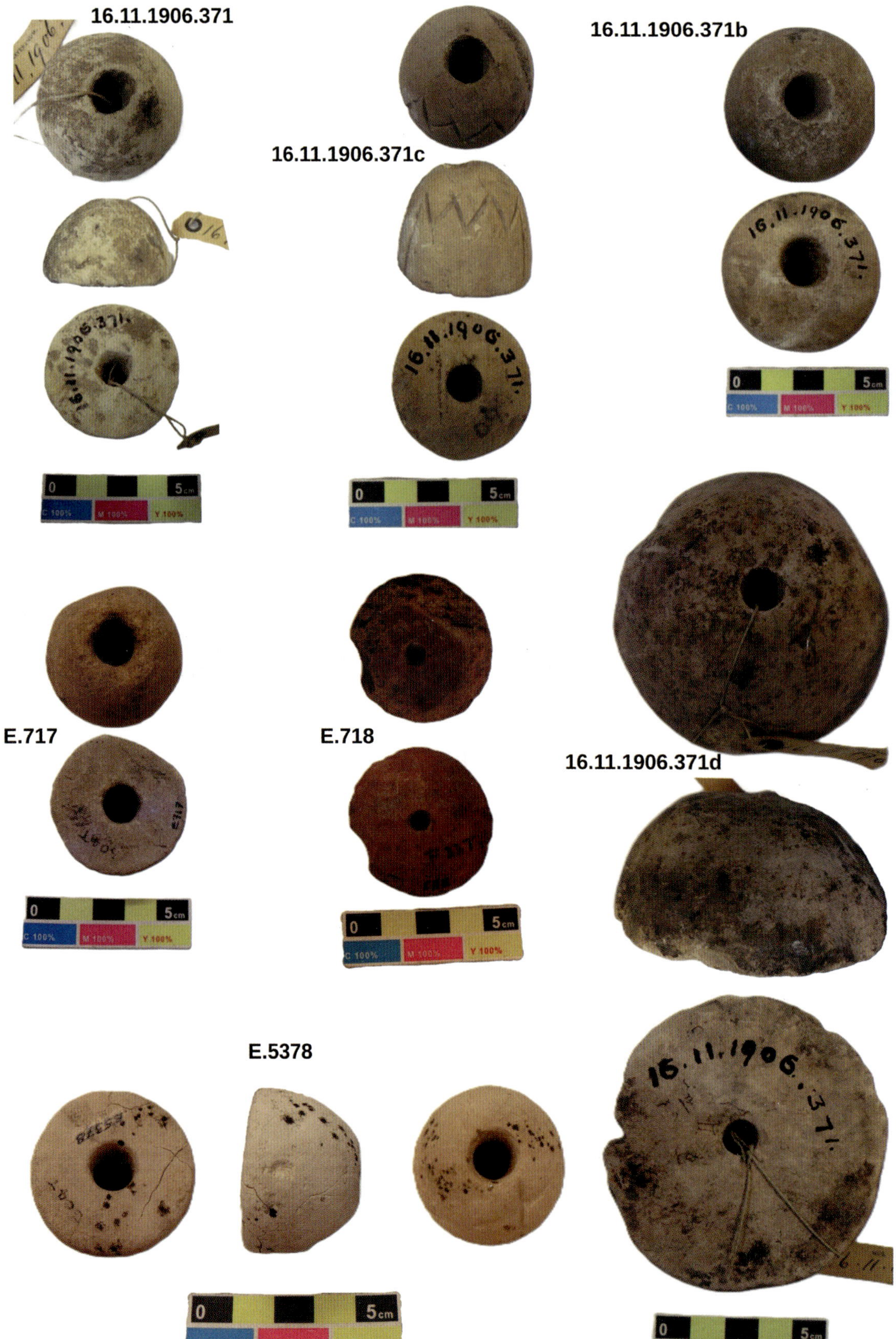

Plate 16. Selection of Hierakonpolis textile tools 16.11.1906.371, 16.11.1906.371b, 16.11.1906.371c, 16.11.1906.371d, Courtesy of the Liverpool World Museum. E.717, E718, E.5378 (courtesy of the Garstang Museum)